Cruise Tourism Management

Cruise Tourism Management

Ravindra Ahuja

RANDOM PUBLICATIONS
NEW DELHI (INDIA)

Cruise Tourism Management

ISBN 978-93-5111-935-7

Published in 2016 in India by

Reprint 2019

RANDOM PUBLICATIONS

4376-A/4B, Gali Murari Lal, Ansari Road
New Delhi-110 002
Phone : +9111-43580356, 011-23289044, 011-43142548
e-mail: sales@randompublications.com,
info@randompublications.com, randomexports@gmail.com

Type Setting by : Friends Media, Delhi-110089
Printed at : Mehra Printers, Delhi-110 092

Preface

Cruise tourism is the fastest growing segment of the travel and tourism industry. With its growth has come concern about the impact of cruise tourism on coastal and marine environments, local economies, and on the socio-cultural nature of port communities. These three areas are key elements in any analysis focused on Caribbean sustainable tourism development, and form a critical base from which to consider strategies to ensure the sustainable development of cruise tourism.

The cruise industry has become one of the fastest growing sectors within tourism over the last decade and can now be classed as a discipline of its own. On the other hand, cruise ships and its passengers can bring both advantages and disadvantages to its visiting destinations. Moreover, it is crucial to recognise that the sector has grown rapidly within the last few decades and it has become one of the most important sectors within the tourism industry. Interestingly, according to Cruise Lines International Association, (2009) the cruise industry carried 12.6 million passengers worldwide in 2009. Radically, there have been some significant discussions around the social and environmental impacts, and the perceived costs and benefits associated with the development of cruise tourism.

Predominantly, cruise tourism can indeed have a negative socio-cultural impact on a destination. The fact that a large capacity of cruise passengers of all nationalities and cultures can arrive at any one time can put pressure on the local communities. The most obvious negative aspect that comes to mind is the fact that the host destinations will have in some way westernised in order to cater for the cruise passengers that visit therefore the traditional cultures of the place have been lost.

The cruise ship industry is the fastest growing segment in the travel industry and has had an annual growth rate of 8.0% since 1980. Just imagine about 339 active cruise ships with well over 10.9 million gross tons and about 296,000 beds. In 2007, the worldwide cruise passengers grew to 12.9 million. According to the Cruise Industry Report 2012 by the Florida Caribbean Cruise Association, the 2011 passenger number was over 16 million, of which 11.2 million originated in North America. The forecasted numbers for 2012 forecast was 17.0 million worldwide, with the preferred destination being the Caribbean. The cruise lines continue to add new ships and exciting options to ensure continued growth.

This book explores the theory, issues, impacts and management considerations surrounding the growing industry of cruise tourism.

– Author

Contents

1

Cruise Tourism

Tourist cruises are a relatively modern activity, originating in the early 1970s in Miami, United States of America for cruises throughout the Caribbean. Their development coincided with a transformation of the transatlantic passenger business resulting from competition with the airline industry. The cruise line industry has been able to create a new market where none existed before. Since that time, North American and subsequently global demand for tourist cruises has been growing at a very strong pace, accounting for robust annual growth of 8 per cent over more than 20 years. The strength of this subsector is reflected in the fact that the largest cruise lines now occupy the highest ranks of the tourism and leisure sector, as measured by shareholder capital and annual profits.

In a market where supply generates demand, supply has grown in parallel with demand, having exceeded 300,000 bed-places by 2006. This is roughly equivalent to half of all hotel capacity in Southeast Asia. It is as if a major destination could somehow become mobile and move from one place to another throughout the year. This makes it a delocalized and global business but with a tremendous impact in terms of rapid establishment, positioning and the image of a country or specific destination in world marketsor at least in regional markets. This sector requires study not only because of its economic impact and growth, but also because of its complexity, since the marketing and organisational techniques applied revalidate its success year after year, in terms of reducing costs, improving service, and attracting new customers at a rate of nearly 30 per cent per year – while also gaining the loyalty of repeat customers. Putting simple ideas into practice can produce enormous benefits. Accordingly, tourist cruises provide a source of lessons that can be meaningfully applied to other segments, such as hotels.

The ability to maintain these rates of growth, without showing signs of fatigue, has been the result of decisive investments by cruise operators in innovation and constant improvement. Every year new ships enter into service, offering innovative activities and facilities, such as ice-skating. Every year brings significant changes in the business structure of this dynamic subsector, and marketing innovations to attract more customers. The continuously dynamic character of the tourist cruise line business has made it necessary for the World Tourism Organization to undertake an updating and in-depth revision of the first edition of its study on cruises, which the Organization published in 2003. Along with these many changes, the activity has also seen a significant expansion in knowledge – particularly with respect to relations and interaction among cruise lines and tourist destinations, the two main protagonists in a cruise line's itinerary. Following the excellent reception enjoyed by the first edition, UNWTO considered it necessary to respond to demand from the various National Tourism Administrations, who have sought greater knowledge about cruise lines as they relate to destinations. The results also include a specific survey designed for destinations, ports and cruise lines. In view of the increase in maritime traffic and security needs, a section has also been included on maritime regulations, prepared by the International Maritime Organization, the United Nations agency specialised in maritime affairs.

In a similar vein, as part of the special attention given to relations between destinations and cruise lines, and given that a tourist cruise liner is in essence a marine resort, reference is made to some concrete cases in that regard, including Mexican public policy on cruises, the promotional activities of Barcelona and comprehensive economic analyses of Malta and Costa Rica. As these cases suggest, destinations and cruise lines need not necessarily be considered incompatible – on the contrary, there are significant areas for cooperation and mutual benefit. Detailed study is needed to identify and act on these appropriately, based on economic impact in affected destinations and rigourous analysis of the relationship between destinations and cruise lines. Examples of the great progress made over the last four years in that direction are provided in this study.

The prospects for the future are excellent: the tourist cruise market has still not reached full maturity and is barely incipient in some regions of the world. It therefore seems safe to say that this growth will continue beyond 2010. The market is developing vigourously in Europe and is expected to do the same in Asia and the Pacific. This study describes the major forces that will shape development of the cruise market over the medium and long term.

CRUISE TOURISM: ECONOMIC, SOCIO-CULTURAL AND ENVIRONMENTAL IMPACTS

Leisure cruising today is completely different from the picture that we have from this activity in the 1970s. In the early days, casinos, shore excursions, port lectures, shopping programmes, spa services were inexistent. The sector has evolved from a very small part of the oceanic passenger industry into a complete and complex vacation business, including all the different sectors of the travel industry. It is well-known that cruise industry has been experiencing an important expansion in the past 20 years. Cruise tourism can be traced back to the beginning of the 1960s coinciding with the decline of transoceanic ship travel and the introduction of the first non-stop air travels between the USA and Europe. The 1970s and 1980s were a period of moderate growth, increasing from half a million passengers in 1970 to 1.4 million passengers in 1980 and 3.8 million passengers in 1990.

In the 1990s this kind of leisure tourism reached Europe, Asia and Oceania and started a period of high growth. Currently, there are more than 30 ships scheduled to join the global fleet over the next four years representing investments over US$ 20 billion. North Americans represent more than 80 per cent of all worldwide market but, according to some experts, European and Asian markets promise great possibilities of growing. The participation of the cruise sector in the international worldwide tourism corresponds to 1.6 per cent of the total tourists and 1.9 per cent of the total number of nights. Revenue of cruise corporations represents the 3 per cent of the total international tourism receipts. Even though, its relative significance in the tourism industry is still rather modest, the cruise sector is the fastest growing segment in the travel industry and has achieved to increase at almost twice the rate of land based tourism. The number of berths on offer (representing the 0.6 per cent of the total supply of beds in hotels and similar accommodations) has increased in more than 500 per cent between 1980 and 2007.

For many destinations, in particular small Caribbean islands, cruises constitute more than 50 per cent of the total of tourism arrivals generating important receipts through the services supplied by the port and expenditures of passengers and crew. It is expected that the cruise industry continues growing regardless of being perceived as a direct contender of sun and stay over tourism.

Cruises are destinations in themselves and, viewed in this way the cruise sector is between the top ten destinations both in number of arrivals and receipts. According to Kester (2002), the average revenue per cruise trip is almost as high as the average receipts per international tourist arrivals. But the distribution of income from cruise industry is not equitable. Most ports obtain small contributions from the use of the port as a cruise destination and cruise tourism provide few real jobs and business opportunities for local residents. Cruise passengers seem to spend less than 30 per cent of the expenditure of a land tourist. Approximately 40 per cent of the bed days sold by the cruise industry are to Caribbean but, according to the World Travel and Tourism Council, 'the economic contribution of cruise tourism to the Caribbean economies is arguably negligible'. From the other hand, most cruise ships are registered in a country offering a 'flag of convenience' like Bahamas, Panama, or Liberia. As foreign corporations, cruise lines avoid taxation, labour laws, environmental standards, etc. Flags of convenience also restrict the rights of workers and are used to pay low wages.

As ship order books and passengers number grow, so do significant impacts at different levels: socio-cultural, economic, politic and environmental. There are few researches concerning the effects of cruising in destinations, particularly those related to cost-benefits analysis of the cruise industry activity. Furthermore, it is uncertain whether major players in the cruise industry (local governments, population, shore operators, etc.) are taking proactive measures to ensure a sustainable future for cruise tourism destinations. Although difficult to quantify, social, cultural, environmental and economic impacts, should be taken into account by decision makers in port states, particularly island ports of call. Management techniques, such as regional collaboration to levy head taxes in order to increase economic benefits and limiting total cruise passengers to reduce social impacts must be coordinated between local governments. There is a common belief that having cruise ships arriving to a destination produces a major economic impact on the local economy. This is the main argument used by policy makers to spend millions of dollars to build a cruise ship dock without knowing how many ships will arrive and its real economic impact. Because of the cruise industry's boom, many policy makers want to take advantage, and possibly this is the main reason why governments, especially in Latin America, provide surveys and data about the cruise passenger's expenditure which are not adequately justified. Ports are quick to claim that each cruise passenger spends more than $100 during a port call, even without any serious argument. From this they simply deduce that a cruise with 4,000 passengers and 2,000 crews generates revenues for $6,000,000.

The belief that cruise passengers expenditures at port are high comes from the prototype of cruise passenger and movies related to cruises in the 1970s. Also the 'Love Boat' television series contributed to create this image of cruises. In the 1920s cruising was the preferred mode of travel for the world's social elites. This believe do not take into account that cruises today are accessible to almost everyone and that some type of cruising must be considered part of the low cost tourism. On average, cruise passengers today have even less income than those who cruised in the 1980s. In any case, between the very few studies on cruise passenger expenditures, a 1994 study commissioned by the Florida-Caribbean Cruise Association found passengers spent on average $89.72 per passenger per port in the Caribbean region. Nevertheless the big fraction of income generated by the cruise activities remains to the cruise companies, ports have still some profits. But at the same time they also obtain costs and problems associated with the arrivals of ships, cruise passengers and crews. This part of the story is even more unknown than the amount of money that a cruise passenger generates as income for a local economy.

The cruise industry presenting some data which permit us to analyse its growth, describe the market of cruises and compare different destinations. The impacts generated by cruise ship activity at different levels: socio-cultural, economic, politic and environmental. We also include a description of taxes and subsidies applied to the cruise industry- and we compare different destinations.

OVERVIEW OF THE CRUISE SECTOR

The Cruise Industry Growth

The cruise ship industry has been the fastest growing segment in the travel industry around the world. The growth of the industry can be measure from different sides. In particular, economists are interested in measuring supply, demand and output of the sector. Cruise passengers number is usually cited as a measure of demand (Bull, 1996).

ECONOMIC EFFECTS

Cruise tourism expenditure has direct, indirect and induced effects on the economy of a destination. The direct effect is on a supplier who sells goods and services directly to cruise vessels, cruise passengers and crew. Expenditures related to cruise vessel include port costs, marine expenses, food and beverages, fuel, water, maintenance. Cruise passengers expenditures include those that are not part of the cruise itself, such as taxis, souvenirs, shore excursions, food and beverages, etc. Crew expenditures include restaurants, retail goods, recreational activities, transport, etc.

Indirect effects result from the purchases of direct suppliers like goods from other companies. Induced effects arise from the expenditures of direct and indirect recipients produced from their increased incomes.

It is not an easy task to measure direct and indirect effects of cruise activity. As described by Braun et al. (2002), one of the main difficulties lies in the fact that many cruise lines sail under flags of convenience and employ worldwide crews coming. Most cruise ships are registered in the Bahamas, Liberia or Panama. Dwyer and Forsyth (1988) develop a framework for assessing the economic impact of cruise tourism for a nation and its sub regions. According to CLIA (2007) the major economic impacts of the US cruise industry during 2006 included the indirect economic impacts, the expenditures of the cruise lines and their crew and passengers was responsible for the generation of $35.7 billion in gross outputs, a 10.2 per cent increase over 2005. This, in turn, generated just under 348,000 jobs throughout the country paying a total of US$ 1.7 billion in wages and salaries. These total economic impacts affected practically every industry in the USA: non-durable goods manufacturing, professional and technical services, travel services, durable goods manufacturing, financial services, airline transportation and wholesale trade.

Economic contribution of the cruise industry depends on the category of the port: homeport or port of call. A home port is a destination from which ships begin and end. While a port of call is just an intermediate stop. Normally, a cruise passenger spends less than ten hours in a port of call.

The cruise business has in a homeport like Miami, Port Canaveral, among others, direct impacts on almost every segment of the travel industry: transport, hotels and resort, restaurants, attractions, etc. A large portion of cruise passengers spend a night or more in the destination while they wait to embark. For instance, In Seattle the average is 1.6 nights spending $63 per passenger per night. The size of the destination influences the intensity of economics effects of the cruise activity. The focusing on the effects of cruise ships on small island nations (McKee, 1988), shows that the economic impacts are destination-specific and that smaller host territories may better served by concentrating upon luxurious vessels. A cruise ship represents all four faces of the tourism industry: transportation, accommodation (including food and beverages), attractions and tour operators. In this sense, cruise ships are also direct competitors of the major land based resorts as Cancun, Cozumel, Orlando, Las Vegas, etc. Seidl et al. (2006) note that the case for Costa Rica, the season peaks of cruise tourism and other form of tourism occurs at the same time putting cruise passengers in direct competition with other tourists for the same touristic goods.

In taking people to various destinations the cruise ships are a substitute for air travel. As floating hotels, they offer accommodation services. More and more, cruise ships features as resorts and it is well known that a substantial minority of cruise ship passengers do not even disembark in the different port destination that are visited. Given the recent boom of the cruise industry activity it is difficult to find data to analyse the economics of cruise tourism. Most works today has been based on observational data. Dwyer et al. (2004) and data collected by cruise lines provide estimates of cruise-related expenditure using data for Cairns in Far North Queensland but they advise that their results must be regarded as tentative because they do not have the required data. Chase and Alon (2002) introduces a Keynesian model to evaluate the impact of cruise tourism and tests it on the economics of Barbados, but using data of tourist expenditures instead of cruise passenger's expenditures.

Cruise data are scarce and not homogenous. The best data bases are from North America, the Caribbean and Oceania. For destinations outside the Americas and Oceania it is, even, very difficult to approximate the number of cruise passengers. This is the reason why most of the empirical studies refer to destinations in those mentioned regions. The paper by Ikeda and Jaswar (2002) present a prediction method of travel demand of cruise ships in Japan. It is one the few empirical studies using data from an Asian destination.

One of the main differences between cruise tourism and traditional tourism is that factors of production of the cruise industry can be acquired from a range of countries. Normally, a tourist destination capital can be sourced internationally but the other factors inputs are obtained from the tourist destination country. No such limitations apply to cruising. Cruise companies can operate as multinational firms where resources do not need to be acquired from a specific country.

The cruise industry has the potential to provide economic benefits to a port state. However, accommodation of large cruise ships into port requires a great deal of initial capital investment in infrastructure as well as maintenance costs. As cruise ships continue to grow larger, further investment may be required. Under these types of tourism scenarios with high infrastructure or environmental costs, rapid growth of tourism may result in a stagnation of or even a decline in GDP. Without significant foreign investment into this infrastructure, it is questionable whether construction of large cruise ship terminals could pass a cost-benefit analysis.

Cruise Lines

Among the reasons that can explain the spectacular growth of the industry, can be mentioned the price of the packages. Recently, cruise lines have designed short duration cruises. Package of two or three nights which people can take a cruise ship from Miami to Bahamas or Barcelona to Palma (Majorca). These kinds of cruises are addressed to an increasing target: younger and more active passengers. The prices of packages that cost less than $100 per day.

Another reason of the growth of the success of cruises is the fact that usually the ship itself is the major tourist attraction. A considerable portion of the cruise passengers do not disembark because they have the enough facilities to entertainment on board. Arguably, cruise lines are the most benefited with the activity. More than 50 per cent of land-based activities are sold on board by themselves. From the value paid by cruisers for on shore activities, the local tour operator receives between a 50 per cent and sometimes 25 per cent of that value. Tourism service providers who want to appear in advertisements delivered on board (videos, brochures, etc.) have to pay for it. There is a high cost of participation in the most important annual industry event. The range goes from $16,500 including registration and booth (Klein, 2005a).

Continuing with the benefits to cruise ship companies, there is a figure designed by them: 'the dream islands'. These territories are private islands property of each cruise line, eight in the Caribbean (Disney Cruises has Causeway Cay, Norwegian Cruise Line owns Great Stirrup Cay and Royal Caribbean owns Coco Cay). This clearly reduces the economic benefit to communities not to disembark at the destination. There are no profits for the chain of local tourism and cruise lines obtain all incomes, from rental of aquatic equipment, food and beverages to souvenirs that are sold to passengers on board. Like any great business, cruise industry, is a strong lobbying group of lawmakers in port destination (homeports and port of calls). The amount of cruise industry spending on lobbying the US Congress. It was also noted that power with the participation of the Carnival Corporation as a partner of the firm Puerto Cancun-Xcaret, SA de CV, whom the Mexican government gave the construction and operation of a terminal for big ships. The fact generated a heated debate.

Wholesaler Receptive Tourism Operator

These companies are able to underbid, then so, they dominate the operation of tours and shore excursions in the port destination. Small local tourism operators and providers not only resign themselves to profit what the cruise line deems fit, but they would have to deal with displeased passengers. These operators prefer not to vie with cruise lines for fear of losing the small part of the business that they share. In addition, one of the risks that they have to take is the fact that passengers buy their excursions two days or even one day before arrival in port, this involves not to get the passengers they were expecting. It could be more or it could be much less. An attraction will therefore not know if they are going to receive 30 or 300 passengers until the day before or even on the morning arrival. A coach company will not know whether one or six coaches.

Hotel Sector

Cruise sector causes apprehension to hotel managers for reasons as the non-payment of taxes compared with those who pay these entrepreneurs. In Aruba, hotels and operators feel that their traditional packages lose ground to ships scheduled. With regard to these disagreements, Manuel Butler Halter (expert from the WTO) states that cruise sector growth and traditional tourism sector are not irreconcilable if they develop diversification and motivation policies in destinations.

It also mentioned the essential benefits for the destinations where cruise ships arrivals, including:

- a Expenditures on destination: form of purchases, excursions and hotel nights in home ports
- b Importance and benefits for the local commerce
- c Desire to at least 50 percent of total passengers arrived to return by other means of transport
- d *In ports:* Expenditures, investments in terminals and basic element in the policies of the city (SECTUR, 2003).

ENVIRONMENTAL EFFECTS

Other critical effects are the environmental impacts. As ship order book and passenger number grow, so do cruise impacts on the environment and local communities. Johnson (2002) exposed the environmental cruise tourism impacts identified by a study of British Airways in Seychelles:

1. Modifications to the natural and built environment to enable destinations to serve as a cruise line destination involve loss of natural habitat, exploitation of local construction.
2. Operational impacts related to the use of energy, water and those such as antifouling and accidental or deliberate physical damage to marine ecosystems.
3. Impacts associated with transferring people to and from departure and destinations points; it increases the use of air travel.
4. The impacts of recreational activities on wildlife such as disturbance and littering, and pressures on endangered species though exploitation for gifts and curios.

The environmental costs of the sector are incalculable due to the cruise industry it is, in general terms, an unregulated activity. Furthermore, it is difficult to gauge widely its impacts, despite enforcing environmental standards for the industry. One US-based civil society group, Bluewater, describes cruise ships, which can carry as much as 5,000 passengers and crew, as 'floating cities' producing large volumes of waste. The different types of waste and damage produced by a typical ship of 3000 passengers. All of them are included in the Protocol 1978 known as MARPOL 73/78 (Copeland, 2008).

These environmental impacts are mainly generated in coastal areas close to the busiest port destinations, including Miami, Nassau, Alaska, Cozumel, among others. Much of the protesting against the cruise industry originates in the USA, the biggest market and where major owners of cruise lines are headquartered. Several environmental groups have been persistent in their attempts to get the industry to act more responsibly. There is little evidence that cruise companies are tackling the effects of cumulative environmental impacts.

Some suggestions have been presented (The Ocean Conservancy, 2002) to regulate cruise activities, including: reducing and regulating cruise ship discharges to improve the water; improving monitoring and inspection; strengthening enforcement mechanisms; training programmes, and so on. Following Johnson (2002), he describes one of the few cases which marine damage was attributable to a cruise line, it was Holland American Line. They developed an ecological project, is the rehabilitation of Cayman coral reef ecosystem by. They carried out a successful restoration that involved salvaging damaged reef fragments, removing rubble, reattaching living corals and monitoring.

Another types of environmental impacts can be mentioned:

a. Degradation of vegetation caused by conduct, choice of landing sites
b. *Its effects:* Erosion, destruction of plants
c. Degradation of historical sites caused by conduct, overuse, collection of artifacts; physical and visual impacts are the main effects

d. Degradation of geological sites caused mainly by conduct producing physical and visual impacts.

In each destination there is an outer space waiting to be affected by the arrival of the millions of cruise passengers around the world: An archaeological heritage, a natural reserve, a barrier reef, a national park. This issue has, of course, its defenders, who are questioning permanently the value of the economic development that can be reached by scarifying these spaces

SOCIAL AND CULTURAL EFFECTS

Cruise ships are between the most preferred types of vacation space. In this sense, it is important to understand what occurs in a vacation space. Specifically, in the space where coincides cruise passengers, stay- over tourists and residents. It has been observed that a highly concentrated tourism generates more negative perceptions from residents towards tourist. Crowds disrupt usual routing and activities associated with cruise tourism can themselves be a problem (Klein, 2005b). This situation is not only for residents but also for stay over tourists who have to spend lot of time in the row to visit a monument or museum, not finding space in the discotheque. And at the end, they feel themselves confused with the horde (Jaramillo, 2001).

There is a large literature concerning the relationship between residents and guests, and how tourism impacts communities. But it is not the same to the segment of cruise ship industry, despite the strong expansion of the sector. Tourism researchers have been based, mainly, on the economic aspects; however, according to Ap (1990), during the past two decades increased attention has been focused on the social and cultural effects of tourism. Communities are constantly creating and reinventing culture in social processes; and similarly, the perception of cultural authenticity by host communities is changing (Olsen, 2002).

Gibson and Bentley (2006) cited that these 'social effects are broad ranging and refer to the ways in which tourism contributes to changes in value systems, family relationships, individual behaviour, safety levels, moral conduct, collective lifestyles, creative expressions, traditional ceremonies, and community organisations'. It has been reported in some Caribbean destinations about the loss of the regional language. Local residents have been adopted habits and patterns from the visitors.

The level of satisfaction in a destination depends on the good experience that a tourist has in it. As Mannell and Kleiber (1997) affirmed, people's behaviour and experience is understood by the influence of the social situation (like the presence and behaviour of other people) and the influence of they bring to the situation. There are series of reactions triggered by the wave of cruise tourism. The competition for a space is highly noticeable in the small island destinations, where the ratio cruise tourists per resident are large. This is the case for Cozumel, a Mexican Island in the Southern Caribbean coast with a population of 73,000. If they had to support, in a day, seven mega ships with twenty thousand passengers, the overcrowding would be imminent and extremely difficult to handle.

Nova Scotia (a Canadian village of 120 inhabitants) experiences scarcity of a public service such as transport. In a day with a high presence of cruise passengers, the village provides 50 buses that bring congestion and pollution, and compete with pedestrian on the villager's roads (Klein, 2005b). In fact, local residents avoid the central business district while cruise ships are in port (Loper, 2005).This situation differs from ports as Miami, Barcelona and other European destinations, where the number of cruise visitors is small compared with tourists or the number of residents. One of the services that is scarce in the competition for a space is transport (taxis and tourism buses) because cruise passengers create an artificial large demand only for some particular days. Other space is fought for the informal salespeople (mobile) who also want to benefit from the presence of the cruise passengers.

In addition to the social impacts mentioned, one special issue is highlighted: the labour issue. One of the advantages for cruise lines which sale under a FAO (Flag of Convenience) is that they do not precise to pay a legal minimum wage. There are several failed attempts brought to the US Congress. Allegations presented by the International Transport Worker's Federation-ITWF- are representative but, normally, cruise companies are treated more favourable. ITWF affirms 'Below docks on many cruise ships is a hidden world of long hours, low pay, insecurity and exploitation'. Some of them, flagged by Panama, lobbied hard to obtain an exemption of the obligation to provide a day of rest per week to workers. The racism and other forms of discrimination, rape, harassment at work, are reported globally. In fact, web sites are dedicated to victims by rape, disappearances, etc.

CRUISE TOURISM: AWAITING BALLAST

Even after numerous discussions and symposiums, India has not progressed far from where it was a few years ago in cashing in on domestic and international cruise tourism. India's legacy ports still fail to look at cruise ships with the same seriousness as they do towards freight ships. The Cruise Tourism Policy which was approved by the Union Cabinet in 2008 has no absolute clarity on what the real benefits are, and if any have been reaped from the policy. The contribution of cruise tourism to the country's tourism exchequer therefore remains hazy. According to estimates from industry sources, not more than one lakh cruise ship passengers disembarked at Indian ports in 2010-2011. Compare this with data released by the European Cruise Council (ECC), which said that the total contribution of the cruise tourism industry to the European economy was GBP 29.66 billion in 2011. In addition, the cruise tourism industry provided employment to 63, 834 people in the UK. In India, cruise tourism is still spoken of as 'having great potential' but going beyond the talk, the real action remains sluggish.

When the world began to talk of a cruise holiday as an alternative to land-based vacation, it was expected to take off in a big way particularly because of its all-inclusive appeal. In many ways, Indians have begun to take to cruising, but there is immense opportunity still to be tapped. Star Cruises provided a taste of what a cruise holiday is when they began operations in India. That coupled with the desire to travel has meant that Indians are experimenting with cruises in other parts of the world, including the Mediterranean region, Alaska and the South East Asian circuit.

But the country has fallen behind in attracting cruise ships to its own ports. A complex tax regime coupled with tedious immigration processes is costing the Indian government precious foreign exchange. According to a report published by the UNWTO, as the cruise business has continued to grow in the past few years, four clear segments have emerged; luxury, premium, budget and contemporary. The fastest growing has been the contemporary segment which has been defined as the 'large-scale consumption' or the most popular segment. But even as cruise ship companies have been increasing capacity to cope with this demand, India has adopted a lukewarm approach in welcoming them to its legacy ports including Mumbai, Goa, Kochi and Mangalore.Gautam Chadha, chief executive, TIRUN Travel Marketing, which represents Royal Caribbean Cruises, Azamara Club Cruises and Celebrity Cruises says, "Since the past 15 years, cruise holidays have been the new holiday opportunity. Earlier it was resorts and spas and then cruise ships came along. We are seeing five-six per cent growth since the past five years, but it is still a challenge marketing them in India."

He points out that the closest ship to India sails from Singapore and this gives people lesser opportunity to opt for a cruise holiday than if an Indian port was used as a turnaround port. Already, UAE is racing ahead in the cruise tourism sector and is expecting a 50 per cent growth in 2012, according to the Sharjah Commerce and Tourism Development Authority. Meanwhile, according to the Dubai Tourism Development Company (DTDC), Dubai welcomed some 420,000 cruise passengers in 2012. The newly developed cruise terminal welcomed some 108 cruise ships last year. Compare this with India's paltry figure and it becomes evident how behind we are.

Looking at it from an inbound perspective, Keki Master, VP, JM Baxi Shipping Corporation, who is passionate about India's potential as a cruise tourism destination says that there is a 10-12 per cent increase year on year in the number of international vessels calling at Indian ports. "If comparing India to Dubai of Singapore, one must remember that we have financial constraints. The various issues are being addressed by the ministry Of Shipping, but it is a long process given the bureaucratic procedures. The political situation in Dubai and Singapore is quite different from the way things are run in India. The various ports have raised their concerns, but they are slow in being implemented."

GRIM REALITY

So why are many of the big international ships giving India a miss? Michael Haidar Ali, Micato Tours, whose guests sail on Royal Caribbean Cruises, Azamara Club Cruises, Silver Sea Cruises, Crystal Cruises, Cunard Cruise Line and Carnival Cruise Lines says, "There are a lot of ships calling in India, but there is too much bureaucracy and it dissuades them from coming back. For example a 3000 passenger capacity ship has to provide four to five passport copies of each passenger at each port."

This is in stark contrast with international air travel. He points out that international air carriers only have to provide the flight manifest to the authorities.In addition, there is the recurring issue of high port charges. It may be remembered that Louis Cruises which ventured into the Indian market two years ago with sailings from Kochi eventually stalled operations. According to representatives of the company, the charges for a single call at Kochi port were US$ 25,000. Compare this with the fee at Maldives - US$ 2,500 for 24 hours or Colombo - US$ 4,000.

Going beyond, when you compare port charges in India with other ports in South East Asia, the fee is quite high. The argument here is that ports make far higher revenue from freight ships and that from the macro perspective, cruise ships hardly contribute to the overall profits of the ports. Chadha contradicts this view. According to him, ports were never meant to operate as commercial enterprises.

The purpose of port trusts was twofold; Firstly, the profits made were to be used to continually upgrade the port infrastructure and secondly, they should contribute to the economic development of the community. "This is the sole purpose why port trusts were set up. It has been forgotten. A mindset change is required. Also, for the first time the legacy ports have realised that they are facing competition from the smaller ports and that they have to re-invent themselves."

GETTING OUR ACT TOGETHER

Haidar Ali adds, "To give you an idea, last season (Between October-April 2011) 45-50 ships called at Mumbai Port and the capacity ranged from 100 to 3000 guests. Most ships end up stopping in India only if they are passing through. In many cases, they use Indian ports as the turnaround port, where passengers disembark and catch a flight back home and a new set of passengers get onboard the ship. We need to develop itineraries which encourage ships to sail for a month or two in India. We are trying hard with several US cruise lines and targeting westerners to go on a cruise in India. Last year, we had a ship in India and it was full. We want them to spend more time here. Earlier Mumbai was a turnaround port, but we lost out to Dubai which developed a very good cruise terminal."The cruise tourism workshop which concluded in Goa recently saw participation from port authorities, the ministry of Shipping, ministry of Tourism and private stakeholders in the industry.

One of the objectives of the workshop was to provide training to immigration and other front-line staff. The workshop also drew up recommendations to develop India as a cruise tourism destination. Speaking to Express TravelWorld about the outcome of the workshop in Goa, Yashveer Singh, director, India Tourism, Government of India said that there was a need for state governments to be more proactive in this regard. "Recommendations were made at the workshop. We recognise that infrastructure is a major impediment, whether for international cruises or domestic. Marketing of port destinations and tourist spots is also extremely important and passenger facilitation, through coaches, taxis, guides and restaurants."According to Chadha, there was also a strong need to standardise procedures at all ports including immigration and customs. After the 26/11 attacks in Mumbai, ports began to operate on heightened security, but Chadha points out that we should not go overboard and turn ships away under the guise of security. "Guest satisfaction determines how a destination will be rated," he says. Haider Ali agrees about standardisation of procedures at all ports. "This meeting in Goa was very important. I don't blame the authorities, we understand that every port has different security procedures, but most countries follow standard procedures at all of their ports. With the world changing, cruise tourism is going to grow. Things slowed down after 9/11 and then again after the terror attacks in Mumbai. But this is slowly changing, ships are coming back with high occupancy," he says. Master says, "The culture and heritage that we have in India is unmatched when compared to Dubai. Each port has something different to offer to a passenger, but unfortunately we have not been able to package it and present it to foreign cruise lines in a composite manner."

Already, revenues are being lost on Indians spending on cruising abroad. AmaWaterways, a company which operates small luxury cruises in Europe, Africa and parts of South East Asia, has appointed a local representative here in India to market the cruises to outbound travellers. Unless the Ministries of Tourism and Shipping in conjunction with the ports, decide to convert the recommendations made into actual deliverables, more international cruise lines will, recognising India's potential as an emerging middle-class market, cash in on the lucrative opportunity. Situational factors should also be looked at closely. Piracy in the Suez Canal has meant that many cruise ships are exploring sailing through other waters. The Indian Ocean is waiting to be tapped. As Chadha aptly pointed out, "Cruise shipping is India's best kept secret," and it's quite certain that if its potential as a revenue generator is not taken seriously, cruise shipping will continue to remain India's best kept secret.

CRUISE TOURISM SCENE IN INDIA

Travelers are seen opting and experimenting with cruise products by adding it into their travel itinerary. It is fast emerging as a new marketable commodity/ product. Growing at the rate of 12 per cent per annum globally, this sector has witnessed some activity in India as well in recent times. However it is still in its infancy in India. Cruise Ships are like moving township studded with state of art facilities and variety of recreational activities. The idea is fast catching, as journey on board cruise liners is not only pleasurable, but also comparatively free from sea travel health hazards. Experience in the Caribbean, Latin American and South-East Asian countries indicate that huge amount of foreign exchange can be earned and employment can be provided on shore by providing the right policy environment and infrastructure for the growth of cruise shipping.

Cruise liners are launching additional new ships to cater to the increasing passenger capacity and maintain its product pricing in order to remain in business. Cruises are no longer considered the privilege of the rich and the elderly and today more and more younger tourists are cruising. This industry annually generates US$ 14 billion world-wide and enjoys a passenger base of over 10 million, which is expected to almost double by 2009. As regards number of cruise ships, projections/forecasts are that the number will increase. By the end of 2011, revenues are projected to increase 13.5 per cent with cruise currently accounting for travel Two to Four percent of market share of the total vacation industry. Thus there remains plenty of room for growth. India tourism planners have noticed the potential in this sector and have accordingly putting greater emphasis for Cruise Tourism. Emphasis is also for its economic benefits which can accrue to country's interst. "There is tremendous scope for cruise tourism in the country given India's strong domestic tourism sector, growing middle class and the country's 7517 km long coast time said Kumari Selja Union Minister for Tourism while launching Louis cruise Operation recently.

The Principal beneficiary of the Cruise Shipping is the economy of the respective maritime nations where the cruise vessels call. Cruise Shipping world over, is seen as employment generating leisure activities. On an average about 1000 passengers travel on a vessel; (medium size). When such vessels arrive at a Port, automatically there is demand for a whole lot of services. Thus a cruise call results in gainful employment to a lot of people, and the earning could be in foreign currency if the tourists are foreigners. Cruise ships also require bunkers, provisions, bonds stores in large quantities agency service, crew etc. All these demands can be met locally. To that extent, there will be contribution to the Indian economy.

In respect of the current status of the cruise industry of India, it has been seen that while the growth rate witnessed globally in cruise shipping sector (in terms of cruise ship fleet and passengers carried) is in the range of 10 per cent to 20 per cent, Indian coastline is not witnessing the same growth pattern. At present, no Indian shipping line owns any luxury cruise liner. As regards the trend in Cruise (foreign lines) passengers landing at Indian ports, it may be seen from the Statement given below that the no. of cruise passengers have been increasing since 2004-2005

Year	Number of Cruise Tourists
2003-04	28000
2004-05	27760
2005-06	152827
2006-07	240307

While on statistics; it is also learnt from other sources that a total number of 106 cruise ships called at Indian ports in 2008-09 as compared to 55 in 2003-04. Similarly the number of passengers increased from 34, 372 in 2003-04 to 2,40,307 in 2006-07. It went down in 2008 due to global economic slowdown.

The number itself shows the possible rate of growth in cruises tourism sector in India. About five to six million people, out of which 60,000 people are from India. India thus holds 5 per cent market share in the world wide cruises business. This was told by Mr. Ankur Bhatia Executive Director Bird group while talking about immense potential India holds while launching Silversea cruises operations recently in Dec, 2009.

The worldwide scenario on cruise tourism as per CRISIL report is as follows:

- In 2004, there were 339 active Ocean Cruise vessel operated by cruise lines around the world, with the global fleet amounting to a total of 10.9 million gross tons.
- Cruises carry 10.3 million passengers, which constituted 1.5 per cent of global travelers who used cruise liners making it a US$15 billion industry and enjoys a passenger base of over 10 million, which is expected to almost double by 2009.
- Globally the cruise industry is a horizontally concentrated market with 4 large players holding more than 81 per cent of the world supply of berths, more than 17 brands and 114 ships. Cruise liners are regularly launching new ships and adding new destinations. Royal Caribbean's have launched new ships recently and added new destinations.
- The cruise tourists represent a rich and demanding category with high expectations regarding comforts aboard the liner, variety of activities on board, a variety of destinations at every port, state of the art conveniences during transit and a seamless travel.
- Cruise liners have equally high requirements from the ports at which they call, principal expectations being proximity of access to major markets, quality and availability of port infrastructure and services, competitive cost of port services, capacity of the port to accommodate and process high volumes of passengers efficiently and the quality of the destination in terms of shore based attractions available.
- International ports have dedicated cruise terminals designed to satisfy the cruise liners and the cruise tourists. Dubai, Singapore, Hongkong are well-known for their state of art Cruise terminals.
- As per research conducted by leading cruise industry associations, Cruise passengers are high spenders with international average working out to $ 94 per cruise tourists per port.
- Sustained product development in line with global demand trends, strategic positioning and marketing backed by consolidated investment in infrastructure and a strong human resource network are sine-quo-non to success in the cruise sector.
- It is a supply driven market because cruise liners are ever in search of new markets, new itineraries and new destinations. If adequate

facilities, services and infrastructure are provided, they will in turn attract more and more cruise operators.

- India's reputation as an enchanting, exotic, historic and beautiful destination would enable the country to make an instant international cruise positioning and move into the cruise destination market. Cruise operators and liners are more than ever searching for new destinations and itineraries.
- India's 7,517 Kms long coastling and strong port positioning imparts a natural advantage to the country to attract international cruise lines.
- India's positioning in South East Asia and its proximity to already popular cruise destinations would enable strong cruise circuits to be created over a period of time.
- India's strong domestic tourism sector would enable the country to achieve a strong domestic cruise sector that could complement the growth and support viability.
- India's impressive growth in the tourism sector would impart an important advantage to its cruise tourism positioning mutually strengthening each other.
- The cruise ports selected for development are also strong tourism states, especially Goa, Chennai, Kochi and Mumbai. This could provide an important platform for cruise tourism to takeoff.
- While takeing about recent developments in India, ohter than the back waters in Kerala and Motor launch services between kolkata (canning) and sunder bans, also there are other river cruise through the country's innumerable water ways and among these, the unique river cruises run by the Assam Bengal Navigation company on the river Brahmaputra in Assam and Bengal is a success story. Assam cruises run by Assam -

Bengal Navigation Company started their first river cruise on the Brahamputra in 2003 and subsequently pioneered the Hooghly cruises in west Bengal from 2006. Cruises operate in Assam from October to April and in Bengal virtually throughout and the year. The sunder ban cruises take tourists into one of the world's last great wildness areas and a vast tract of tribal creeks and mangrove swamps. Infact if properly organized, the cruises can be linked with cruises from the Bangladesh border up to the historic city of Patna. Potential is very much there in eastern India to boost cruise tourism. Madhya Pradesh and Goa are popular cruises destinations now.

17. Silver sea cruises recently joined partnership with Bird Travels to attract high and luxury cruises market in India, Star cruises market in India, which played on important role star cruises now called Genting Hongkong Limited) have worked successfully towards catering to the up market cruises clients for quite some time in India and brought in good volume of tourists,

Among the other leading cruises Liners bringing tourists to India carnival Italy based Costa cruises, part of carnival corporation is soon going to start promoting Asian itineraries in India market by Jan 2010 and proposing to add itineraries to Dubai - Mumbai - Maldives and Egypt - Yemen - Oman - Dubai. The ship will dock in Mumbai over night cruising. These are very positive indication for future growth of cruise tourism in India.

The objectives of the Cruise Shipping Policy is to give proper directives to the growth of this segment - keeping in view the growing popularity of cruise tourism, Government of India has taken an initiative for developing cruise shipping as one of the thrust areas and is working to formulate a Cruise Shipping Policy with the following objectives:

- To develop India both as Source and Destination Market with the state of art infrastructure and appropriate marketing strategy.
- To increase the number of cruise ship calls and passenger arrivals in a sustainable manner.
- To achieve a target of 10 lakh cruise passenger landings per year by the end of 2010.
- To strengthen inter-sectoral linkages, whereby cruise liners source the requisite supplies of goods and services from local Indian suppliers.
- To consolidate existing ports of call, explore other ports and suitable anchoring sites on the Indian coast with a view to making additional cruise ship calls to other areas of the country.
- To operational appropriate promotional programme that would effectively convert cruise passengers to long stay visitors.
- To maximize the benefits from the cruise industry and at the same time protect environment and sustain the natural resources of India.
- To ensure that the cruise shipping industry in India becomes internationally competitive with other destinations and contributes to the economy in terms of generation of foreign exchange, income, employment and business opportunities.
- To attract the right segment of foreign tourists to cruise shipping in India.
- To popularize cruise shipping with Indian tourist.
- To enhance absorptive capacity of the country by developing existing and new visitor attractions, including event attractions in line with India's efforts to improve the tourism product.

Naturally Question arises into mind what steps are being taken by the Ministry of Tourism for development of Cruise Tourism in the country if there is so much potential. Ministry of Tourism is very proactive in this respect and Ministry of Tourism extends financial assistance to the State Government/ UT Administrations for development of tourism infrastructure including cruise tourism under Product/Infrastructure Development for Destinations and Circuits scheme and to Port Trust Authorities under the scheme of Assistance to Central Agencies for Infrastructure Development.

Ministry of Tourism had sanctioned ₹. 1450.00 lakh to Cochin Port Trust, Kochi for development of tourism infrastructure at the Cochin Port under scheme of Assistance to Central Agencies for Infrastructure Development in 2008-09. Also Ministry of Tourism had sanctioned ₹. 52.70 lakh to Poompuhar Shipping Corporation Ltd. Chennai for purchase of ferries in Tamil Nadu in 2008-09. Similarly the Ministry of Tourism has taken several steps to promote India as a Cruise Destination abroad, which include.

- Ministry of Tourism jointly with FICCI organized a Seminar Initiative on furthering Cruise Tourism in India on September 4, 2008 in New Delhi.
- Cruise tourism in India has been specifically promoted at various international platforms such as World Travel Mart, London, ITB Berlin and Arabian Travel Marts.
- Ministry of Tourism through its office at New York participated in the Sea - trade Cruise Shipping Convention, Miami held from 16th to 19th March, 2009.
- M/s Ocean Cruise India P.Ltd., was operating cruise services from Goa to Lakshadweep via Cochin, since January 2007. However they have intimated that they are withdrawing their services on the Indian Coasts in the current year 2009 and may start operations in 2010.
- Leading Port Trusts have been requested to upgrade their cruise terminal infrastructures to world class standards.
- The Proposals for developing cruise terminal infrastructural for New Mormugao Port Trust has been received in the Ministry for providing assistance under the scheme of assistance central agencies for infrastructure development and being processed for financial assistance as given to understand from Ministry's Annual Report.
- Hon'ble Minister of Tourism and Housing and Urban Poverty Alleviation has written letter to the Chief Minister of Goa for creating security arrangement around Mormugao Port and clearing of fishing jetty and slums at Kharewado which is close to Mormugao Port. Clean environment is essential for successful operation.

There are some bottleneck areas in the development and promotion of Cruise tourism in the country and for rapid growth urgent action is needed to streamline the operations. Despite the inherent advantages/economic benefits and tremendous potential of Cruise Shipping sector, the country has not witnessed any worthwhile growth, as compared to the growth withnessed in Latin America and South East Asia in this segment. Cruise Shipping is an international industry and its efficiency judged by the contribution it makes to the country's economy and is governed by the industry structure and policy package in place.

Various relevant components are:

- Focused Policy on Cruise Shipping covering various aspects,
- Well developed port-infrastructure, cruise terminals etc,
- Availability of cruise liners
- Conductive Fiscal regime.
- Hassle free immigration and transit facilities,
- Marketing strategy, focusing cruise lesson with promotional material in various languages and safety norms and trained manpower.
- Connectivity to on-shore destinations by various modes (road, rail, air and inland water transport and support services.
- Duty free bunkering and
- Institutional framework for holistic development of Cruise Shipping.

Similarly there are the fiscal issues/deterrents that have de-motivated the Cruise liners from operating in India. The levy of tax on oil and other taxes act as a disincentive for international cruise wanting to operate in India. For providing a conducive fiscal regime to encourage cruise shipping, the following steps are needed.

Service Tax Levied by the central government on services like massage/ beauty parlors, sauna bath etc, if the cruise ship is on a coastal circuit taking these activities out side the preview of service tax will be a minor concession which will promote cruise shipping.

- Since states are direct beneficiary of cruise passengers consuming a Varity of services, the state government may not levy entertainment tax on the shows/ activities on the board a cruise ship by way of amendment in their respective statute. This is a small concession but good way to boost cruise.
- Duty free shops on board a foreign cruise vessel are required to be sealed when they convert to coastal leg such an act may become an irritant for passengers on board. It would be desirable that the shops are not sealed and duty free goods continue to be provided the passengers.
- The custom duty on bunkering for coastal Cruise ship is presently around 33 per cent. Therefore a foreign flag vessel if not engaged in coastal trade in India and purchase bunker in India the bunkering is 33 per cent cheaper as compare to the purchase of bunker by a vessel having an Indian flag or a foreign flag engaged in coastal trade of India. This makes cruise shipping operations in Indians water economically unviable. In view of this, it is proposed to provide duty free bunkering of cruise ship-Indian or foreign doing coastal runs, which will go long way providing fillip to cruise Tourism.

- In every country, the international jurisdiction for any maritime business is 12 nautical miles. Beyond this is international waters and income earned or accrued outside of those 12 nautical miles will be tax free. The enhancement of EEZ from 12 nautical miles to 200 nautical miles by changing the definition of India's territorial waters act as a deterrent for cruise liners.

There is always consistent effort to solve the taxation issue and Ministry of Tourism is seized with the matter. With regard to taxation issues relating to cruise shipping activities, it is understood that the Ministry of Tourism had already written to the department of Revenue requesting stimulus packages through appropriate budgetary measures for boosting cruise tourism in the country. Similarly there are problems about hassle free, quick immigration clearance for cruise passengers and Cruise Shipping Policy have partially dealt of such issues. This is a continuous process. Based on experience things can be revised from time to time. Ministry of Tourism sanctions Central Financial Assistance to State Government/Union Territories for development of Tourist infrastructure and promotion of tourism including River and Backwater Cruise Tourism Products on the basis of the proposals received from them, subject to availability of funds and inter-se priority. These projects are sanctioned under "Product/Infrastructure Development Destinations and Circuits" Scheme. For promotion of river tourism financial assistance is given to states for procurement of cruise vessels, boats, catamaran, rice boats, houseboats, glass bottom boats, water sports equipment etc.

The following are the main projects sanctioned for development of Cruise Tourism:-

- Development of Brahmaputra River front and Cruise vessels on Brahmaputra in Assam for ₹. 365.52 lakh in 2006-08.
- Development of Circuit on river Godavari and Krishna in Andhra Pradesh for ₹. 425.95 lakh in 2007-08.
- Ministry of Tourism has sanctioned an amount of ₹. 2042.35 lakh and released ₹. 1021.18 lakh for development of Ganga Heritage River Cruise in West Bengal in 2008-09.
- Ministry of Tourism has sanctioned a mega project for integrated development of infrastructure for, Heritage and Hinterland Tourism in Goa including Mandovi and Zuari river with CFA of ₹. 4309.91 lakh to the State Government of Goa in the financial year 2008-09.

In the recent endeavors, we can talk about Volvo Ocean Race. Volvo Ocean Race-India Stopover at Cochin was held from 3rd to 13th December 2008. Volvo Ocean Race is one of the most exciting adventure sporting events in the world, which stopped over in India for the first time in the 35 years history of the race. This spectacular Ocean marathon was in Cochin Port for 10 days from the 3rd to 13th December, 208 making it the first Asian different countries like the US, Ireland, Russia Spain, Sweden etc. the event attracted hundreds of other luxury Yacht and sailing vessel. Five Luxury cruise ships were also present Cochin during the event.

A large contingent of international travel media, sailing enthusiasts, corporates and members of the business community converged in Cochin during the 10 day stopover when Cochin under the international spotlight. The event reached to more than 1.8 million viewers in more than 180 countries which put the Volvo Ocean Race among the worlds top most sports events in terms of Global Media Congress. Cochin port trust developed a state of the art media centre which accommodated about 200 media professionals from the national and international media and also organized a festival during this period.

The event was jointly hosted by the Cochin Port Trust and Department of Tourism, Government of Kerala making it special events including regatta, food festival, open air concerts and cultural events which showcased our country in all its glory and colour, India's people, art and culture. Ministry of tourism is also participated by taking five stalls in the festivals for showcasing rural art, craft and textiles from different rural tourism sites. River cruising in Madhya Pradesh or high sea cruising in Goa are well established very popular.

Future is great provided positive steps are taken. It is essential to restore services which were run earlier by M/s ocean cruises India P. ltd. which was operating cruise services from Goa to Lakshadweep via coachin and star cruise operating Mumbai - Goa etc - they really attracted lot of domestic tourists and tourists enjoyed cruising experience. These cruise operators be requested to restart their operation by giving suitable incentives from the Government In last account over 150,000 domestic tourists utilized the cruise services to their satisfaction. It created good number of jobs for locals.

Good news is that Myanmar based Pandaw River cruises will launch its maiden 15 day vayage sailinge the river Ganges between Kolkata and Varanasi named RVBengalpandaw, plans to operate 10 cruise journeys including upstream and downstream from March, 2010 as is known from various press reports.

Similarly Louis Cruises now comes to Kochi and becomes first company to tap new cruise policy of the Government of India. For cruises operations Louis has chosen Kochi as its home post in India and is offering services on two routes: Kochi - Maldives and Kochi - on both routes, the operator is offering four day itineraries and has deployed a large vassal christened Mr. Aquamarine. The vassal has 525 cabins with a maximum capacity of 1250 passengers, three restaurants, a swimming pool, a discothèque, duty free and travel value shops, and dedicated space for outdoor spots etc. We need more such operations.

DEVELOPMENT OF CRUISE TOURISM IN INDIA

Today India is experiencing success in many spheres of economy and is rapidly gaining the leading positions in the world rates. Among other industries leisure activities are steadily advanced, and touristic business is becoming more and more sustainable. On the one hand, the local authorities have realized how tourism can stimulate economic and social development in the country. On the other hand, India is truly a country with a great potential regarding its location, natural diversity, rich historical and cultural heritage and, of course, vast sea spaces surrounding the land (7,517 kilometers long coastline).

In this way, tourism has been provided with a priority platform in the local strategies of economic development. In the meantime, it is not enough to succeed in traditional touristic entertainments. It is vitally important to be sensitive and responsive to the global trends and demands, and one of the broad avenues required to follow is now cruise tourism. While it is already highly popular and rapidly growing in the rest of the civilized world, especially in the North America, India has been missing out the potential it already possesses: first, it is located on the crossroad of the most significant international sea routes; second, its terrific coastline makes up more than seven and a half thousand kilometers of length; third, there are already natural seaports to start from; and, certainly, India has enough breathtaking destination not to fall apart in attracting tourists from the different corners of the world. Therefore, there is a unique opportunity to join this highly promising industry at the moment and to gain the winning positions until it has not been done by other companies. Herein, this report will scrutinize the existing market within cruise tourism industry; analyze its structure and value in order to see all the advantages and disadvantages of participation; study the strategies of operators already working in the field and the most crucial characteristics of the competitive environment in order to make clearer conclusions on the potential of the market and to work out probable recommendations for advance.

MARKET GROWTH AND DIRECTION

Statistical Highlights

It is common knowledge that India belongs to the Asia-Pacific region. This region is now effectively responding to the global cruise tourism activities. The South Pacific, Southeast Asia, Far East and Trans-Pacific territories, making up the Asia-Pacific region, have experienced a 134 per cent growth between 1992 and 2001 and the figure of income has reached 2.1 million nights, with a global market share of 3.5 per cent. The Indian Ocean and the Arabian Gulf are now strongly emerging, with the growth of 88 per cent in 2000, though the share was only 0.38 per cent of world night stays growing at that time. In fact, market share of cruise tourism is rather small: in 2000 there were only 0.056 million cruise visitors in India, which is only 2.11 per cent of all the 2.65 million tourists coming from different corners of the world to the country. The trends of cruise tourists in India in the first decade of the twenty first century can be seen.

Advantages of the Market

At the moment only 0.5 per cent of the India's foreign arrivals are constituted by cruise arrivals, but the overall increase in tourist visits is obvious and promising. It seems reasonable to present the structure of the cruise market as a combination of two spheres. On the one hand, India can be used as a worthy destination by the cruise operators from other countries, and thus it becomes necessary to develop all the services for tourists coming by cruise ships. This is a worthy field as the global operators and liners are passionately seeking new destinations, markets and itineraries. On the other hand, India can develop its own domestic cruise sector and provide cruise services for the population as well as for tourists coming with different purposes. It is achievable firstly due to the overall strong domestic tourism sector of the country. The structure can be also based on the criterion of the source of demand for the cruise tourism. These are four major segments: the foreign tourists; the Indian outbound tourists; the Indian domestic leisure tourists and the current cruise tourists (both international and Indian). In 2009 there were about 50,000 Indians set sail on different cruises. As the growth of market size was expected to reach 184,710 cruise tourists in 2011 and by the year 2030-2031 the size of cruise market is expected to become 1.2 million cruise tourists.

In fact, there are international cruise liners that are now interested in India and understand its great potential: the Star Cruises, the Royal Caribbean International, Princess Group, Dubai Cruise Terminal are among the leaders. These are already well-known companies and it is crucial to outrun them.

INDUSTRY DRIVERS

Frontline Stakeholders' Strategies

The frontline stakeholders of the cruise terminals in India are Ministry of Shipping, Central and State Ministry of Tourism, and private agencies. The segment of private agencies includes cruise lines and cruise operators, ship agents, tour operators, ship chandlers and provision suppliers. The most well-known port operator is Adami Ports in Gujarat. The most appreciated cruise operators at the moment are Goa Sea and River Cruises and the Kerala Backwaters cruise. The former is the most popular with the domestic tourists, while the latter is mostly preferred by the foreign tourists. The synergies of building cruise terminals are now explored by the hoteliers the Taj Group, the Oberoi Group, the Leela Palace and Resorts and others. As for large tourism entrepreneurs, these are the Muthoot Group and the Reliance Group.

The existing operators struggle for making the brand cruise India the umbrella brand, and the most spread messages are, on the one hand, concentrated on the convenience of multifunctional programme and, on the other hand, the attractiveness of destinations: 'more for less', 'value for money', 'diversity in harmony', 'must see', 'safe friendly'. Those operators who are more focused on domestic outbound tourists tend to base their circuits on foreign and exotic destination, while those operators who focus on tourists from abroad base their circuits on the historical values, world heritage and health.

Gaining Competitive Advantage

In order to gain competitive advantage, it would be rational to pay more attention to river cruises, as this subdivision is even less developed, but it can seriously complement and even strengthen the overall cruise tourism development. To become popular, these river cruises should connect the most fascinating and the most significant destinations within the continent. For example, the key destination of the Buddhist pilgrimage is Sarnath and it is situated at the bank of the Ganges River, the sacred river for the Indian nation. It would be useful here to examine the Inland Water Transport development plan proposed by the Indian Ministry of Shipping. The cruise destinations in the Indian Ocean are reflected.

In addition, there are two more sectors to cooperate with. These are ecotourism and rural tourism, both becoming popular at the moment, but still lacking enough investors and researchers. These two sectors are now at the priority platform in India and they are found highly attractive for foreign tourists, so it would be highly beneficial to apply their opportunities in the development of cruise itineraries.

In the meantime, the existing operators lack effective media campaigns, therefore leadership can be won by participation in various worldwide programmes and forums; to create visibility through indoor and outdoor advertising, audio- visual presentations and films, printed products (attractive leaflets, brochures, posters, hand-outs) and organize exhibitions, conferences and other events to promote the brand. There are a lot of other opportunities (like the International Sea Trade Shipping conferences and conventions, various trade shows and fairs, and so on).

COMPETITIVE ENVIRONMENT

Consumer Profiling

In 2008 the Indian government approved the Cruise Shipping Policy in order to develop the country both as Source and Destination Market, to stimulate cruise ship calls and passenger arrivals in a sustainable manner.

Further on, demographic characteristics of the Indian population are highly favourable for the development of the cruise tourism. As cruise is not a cheap entertainment, this sector is highly dependent on the nation's incomes and paying abilities. In 2004 the amount of the people referred to the middle class made up more than 150 million, while there are more than 200 rupee millionaires. It is also reported that 22 per cent of the Indians spend more than $2000 per trip when they travel abroad, and thus tourism here is the third highest revenue-generating market.

What is more, a number of surveys conducted among the Indian tourists and local population have shown that the advantages of cruise tourism make the sector rather appealing for both domestic and foreign tourists. According to the surveys, the best ports in India are Goa, Cochin and Mumbai, but at the same time there is still much to invest in to improve the conditions of the cruise entertainments.

Winning Consumers

To make the potential consumers switch from the existing operators, the new agent should have strong advantages. Many current complaints are connected with the harassment at the ports and other discomforts faced by the clients due to the lack of organization and order, lack of streamline clearance and baggage services at the customs. One of the methods to improve the situation is to provide more electronic equipment for dealing with all that passenger stuff in order to simplify the procedures of control and pass.

As viability of cruise terminals is highly significant for attracting and satisfying the tourists, there may be a need for support from the state. There may be applications to the local government for a kind of subsidy or other funding measures to overcome viability gap and legislation as for privatization of the ports may be changed or modified correspondingly.

FUTURE DEVELOPMENT

Potential of the Sector

The entry point, the first experience and thus the promotional platform of each cruise circuit is the cruise port. It is critical to create a positive image of a port when starting a cruise. The greatest potential for cruise tourism is probably possessed by the ports of Kerala, Goa and Chennai. However, Indian ports are just the factor which needs to be revolutionized in order to make the road for the cruise business free. Ports are naturally the core infrastructure requirement of the cruise tourism sector, and the Indian ports have to be improved to meet the international standards. Passenger services and commodities, linkages, conveniences, and amenities for the cruise tourists should fit the standards, and this condition is almost lacking today in India. The imperative for stimulating incomes in cruise tourism is to develop quality cruise terminals first of all. It has been calculated that in case of developing new berth, the investment would require about ₹. 105 crores (approximately $40 million) per each terminal, and in case of renovating the existing berth the investment would require ₹. 70 crores (approximately $20 million) per each terminal.

Favourable Conditions

To be more specific, there are certain locations where the building of the dedicated cruise terminals seems to be the most favourable. These are the port facilities at Mumbai, Cochin, Chennai, Mangalore, Tuticorin and Goa and Upgrade. The first two and the latter are associated with the beauties of such exotic places as Chennai and Lakshadweep and Andamans. Apart from that, it seem perspective to explore the potential of less popular ports including Vishakapatnam, Calcutta and Paradeep (the East Coast) and Porbandar and Kandla (the West Coast). Concurrently, there would be no excuse to forget about the well-trained personnel. The quality of service to 60 per cent depends on the level of the personnel, and to 30 per cent on the tangible resources. The rest 10 per cent are other mere factors. It would be beneficial to provide training programmes for every specialist engaged in the process, including the staff at information kiosks, travel agents and tour guides, shopkeepers and baggage handling staff as well as the entire crew serving at the ship. The key training points should be: awareness, accountability and transparency, knowledge and skill, communication and hospitability, safety and security. Environmental issues should also be taken to account.

Conclusions

The research has shown that India has a lot of opportunities for the development of cruise tourism. Geographical and demographic situation are favourable for the profitable cruise tourism business, and this fact is already realized my many international tourism operators and cruise liners. India turns out to be attractive as a destination for the foreign cruisers and at the same time it has much to offer as the starting point for its domestic tourists and guests of the country. In particular, India is rich in historical religious, spiritual and cultural sights; its nature conditions are unique and landscapes are really picturesque with its vast coastlines and virgin forests. Many of the areas are almost undisturbed and thus present incomparable opportunities for having rest and escaping from the burdens of civilization. Concurrently, the paying capacity of the Indian population is growing and disposable incomes make them more demanding and searching for diversity in leisure activities.

Despite those obvious advantages, the cruise industry is still in the infancy in India. The main obstacle on that way is weak development of the major ports, so there is an urgent need to reconstruct them and to make them serve as a perfect entry for each tourist going on a cruise trip. To build and to equip adequate cruise terminals at the strategically important ports, fund-rising programmes should be worked out and implemented, probably with the assistance of the state. The advantage is that the local government realizes the perspective of cruise business for social and economic development of the state and seems to be friendly and responsive to the initiatives in this field.

Recommendations

In order to succeed and stay competitive, it is necessary to care about the reinforcement of port development. The issues of security and facilitation should be addressed, and the terminal plans should be performed after consulting the world leaders in cruise industry. What is more, it would be beneficial to initiate further feasibility studies and structure bankable public-private partnership options. Further on, cruise design, themes and logistics should be linked to both foreign destinations and coastal destinations of India, and the dedicated funds intended for the hinterland tourism advancement should be received from the Ministry of Tourism, as it corresponds to the recently adopted programme of local tourism development. Moreover, it would be beneficial to concentrate on the development of river cruises and to cooperate with the operators of the rural and ecological tourism. One more step to take is to seek for alliance with other Indo-Asian shipping players.

2

Cruise Industry

Cruise Industry Overview

The cruise ship industry is the fastest growing segment in the travel industry and has had an annual growth rate of 8.0 per cent since 1980. Just imagine about 339 active cruise ships with well over 10.9 million gross tons and about 296,000 beds. In 2007, the worldwide cruise passengers grew to 12.9 million. According to the Cruise Industry Report 2012 by the Florida Caribbean Cruise Association, the 2011 passenger number was over 16 million, of which 11.2 million originated in North America. The forecasted numbers for 2012 forecast was 17.0 million worldwide, with the preferred destination being the Caribbean. The cruise lines continue to add new ships and exciting options to ensure continued growth. Today's ships offer a new generation of dizzying onboard innovations, including surf pools, planetariums, on-deck LED movie screens, golf simulators, water parks, self-leveling billiard tables, multi-room villas with private pools and in-suite Jacuzzis, ice skating rinks, rock climbing walls, bungees and trampolines. With all of this luxury and increase in passengers' numbers, the impact and the challenges in such areas as economic, socio-cultural, environmental, safety and security and taxation are a major concern.

ECONOMIC EFFECTS

These economic benefits arise from five principal sources: 1) spending by cruise passengers and crew; 2) the shore-side staffing for their local offices, marketing and tour operations 3) expenditures for goods and services necessary for cruise operations; 4) spending by the cruise lines for port services; and 5) expenditures for the maintenance. According to CLIA, the economic impact of the U.S cruise industry from 2005 to 2006 resulted in expenditures of $35.7 billion in gross output, a 10 per cent increase, which generated 348,000 jobs and paid out $14.7 billion in salaries. It should be noted that accommodation of large cruise ships in ports require a great deal of initial capital investment in infrastructure and maintenance costs, which is absorbed eagerly by the host port, not by the cruise line. It is recommended that to create a more balanced port development the cruise companies should contribute financially towards the local infrastructure costs, and also put a pause on increasing the size of new ships to allow the existing ports to still welcome new ships without incurring additional rebuild costs.

IMPACT OF POWERFUL CRUISE COMPANIES

Three main cruise lines, Carnival, Royal Caribbean and Star/NCL control around 35 per cent of cruise vessels, with Carnival controlling 22 per cent of that 35 per cent alone. If one adds to it the growth rate of 8 per cent annually, the net result is that the above three cruise companies exert a lot of power globally. Cruise business has become a revenue and profit churning machine and this is often with the exclusion or restriction of local providers. Arguably, cruise lines benefit the most from the activities associated with the passengers both onboard and off-board. There are minimal profits for the providers of local tourism services as cruise lines obtain all income from items sold on board such as souvenirs, rental of aquatic equipment, food and beverages, leaving the local tour operator with little profit. Tourism service providers also have to pay for promotion on board; videos, brochures and booths. A booth can costs up to U.S. $16,500.

Other income comes from "dream islands", cruise line's private island property and once again reducing the economic benefit to impacted communities. The cruise industry also has a strong lobbying group to push for policy and legal decisions in their favour and during the period from1997 to 2007, the Cruise Line International Association spent US$10 million on lobbying the U.S Congress. They try their hardest to avoid or minimize paying local taxes. For example, many of their ships go under the flags of convenience, Liberia, Bahamas and Panama and cross international borders, where they are exempted from paying certain destination taxes and pollution fees, and where it is difficult for the local jurisdictions to enforce these payments. This causes the local hotels to get angry as they are obligated to pay such taxes and it makes them less competitive and profitable than the cruise lines. One suggestion is for a new international standard where cruise ships are obligated to pay a local port tax and economic development contribution based on the size of the ship and number of passengers, payable while in port.

ENVIRONMENTAL EFFECTS

Cruise ships generate a number of waste streams that affect the marine environment, for example, sewage, graywater, hazardous wastes, oily bilge water, ballast water, solid waste and also emits air pollutants to the air and water. These environmental costs are significant but incalculable given that the cruise ship industry is largely unregulated. As an example, blackwater and graywater generate 15,000 to 30,000 gallons per day for a ship with 3,000 passengers, and 24 per cent of vessel solid waste worldwide comes from cruise ships. Unfortunately, the few regulations that are there are not always successful enforced. In 1999 Royal Caribbean paid a fine of US$18million for discharging oily bilge water in Alaska, the same amount was paid by Carnival Cruise Line in 2002 for dumping oily waste from five ships, and still not much has changed. Cruise ships have a positive image of glamour, even though they only represent a small percentage of the entire shipping industry worldwide, and because of this their environmental impacts are tolerated and continue to be unregulated.

LeAna B. Gloor's article on cruise tourism impact on Hilo in Hawaii illustrates the social, physical and environmental concerns. She states that while Hawaii is benefiting economically at unprecedented levels, it is also being impacted negatively on the environmental side of things at unprecedented levels. She advocates for a stronger legislation, more aggressive enforcement and more bills such as the Clean Cruise Ship Act.

SOCIAL AND CULTURAL EFFECTS

Interactions between resident and cruise passengers can have positive effects but at the same time, high frequency and density of cruise activities can restrict the available space for local residents and push them to adopt different moral and cultural standards. There are often negative reactions from the residents triggered by the cruise tourism in small ports, where the ratio of cruise tourists to inhabitants is high, in places such as Aruba, Antigua, Barbuda or Dominica. This leads to local resentment, overcrowding and lack of services such as taxis, beach space and available seats in restaurants on the cruise days, or lack of demand, and no work on the days when cruise ships are not in port.

This differs for ports such as Miami, Barcelona and European destinations, where the number of cruise visitors' ratio is small compared to other tourists and local residents. Another negative is that ships with flags of convenience have questionable labour and work safety standards and with no legal minimum wage enforced. Past efforts to have this changed by organizations such as the ITWF have failed. It is recommended that standard minimum wage, work hours and days of rest for cruise ship workers are established and enforced internationally.

HEALTH AND DISEASES

A number of recent studies have focused on the health risks and disease directly attributable to cruise ships with their high concentration of people from different countries. One such study looked at the risks and diseases caused by contaminated water and it showed that their water supply is very different from the water supplies on land. . The risks of contamination were much higher due to the way it was sourced during loading and also the dispersal on the cruise ship. The authors reviewed 21 documented outbreaks of waterborne diseases from various vessels and it was discovered that the bulk of the outbreaks were on cruise ships. Some other risk factors involved already contaminated water from the port to the ship and contamination in their storage tanks, which could be a result of poor maintenance and lack of disinfectants. The recommendations include the need for hygienic and a better comprehensive system to handling of their water supply from source to consumption.

This may be achieved in the future by the adoption of improved Water Safety Plans that cover the overall design of the water storage tanks, better internal operations and regular inspection and maintenance. Another study of waterborne diseases on cruise ships concluded that the overall decrease of gastroenteritis over a 10 year period prior to 1986 was directly attributable to the improved enforcement of the Vessel Sanitation Programme (VSP) of the Centers for Disease Control and Prevention. Another study from 2006 involved 43 outbreaks of Norovirus on 13 vessels. It is a known fact that cruise ship holidays create an environment where Norovirus spreads easily, so it was recommended that an active reporting system could function as an early warning sign, but more importantly steps must be taken to implement internationally accepted rules and guidelines for reporting, investigating, and controlling Norovirus and other diseases on cruise ships. A Los Angeles Times headline, February 4, 2012 stated: "Florida cruise ships riddled with Norovirus. Anyone surprised?"

SAFETY AND SECURITY

After the terrorist attacks on New York's World Trade Center, cruise related tourism became one of the safest ways to experience foreign travel. Yet, as P. Tarlow indicates in his rather somber study on cruise risks , that cruising is not immune to dangers ranging from virus outbreaks to terrorism to accidents. He lists a number of major disasters, terrorist attacks, robberies and on-board assaults to demonstrate his point. Cruise tourism can as well lead to incidents where the ship can become a trap, as the recent examples of the Costa Concordia grounding and Carnival's ship engine fire and subsequent stranding of passengers for several days at sea.

TAXATION

There are no common standards in the application of port taxes to cruises. Some ports charge levy that is reasonable, some excessive. Some ships pay, some do not. Another unresolved situation is that the cruise lines are continually allowed to operate under the "flags of convenience" (FAO), usually, Panama, Bahamas and Liberia. This allows them to be exempt from multiple tax responsibilities, it is easier for them to have lenient standards of safety, they undergo few environmental inspections, their operating costs are lower, and they recruit staff without adhering to international regulations. The most obvious is Panama, where the ship pays for each passenger landing in Panama, which further encourages the use the Panama FAO. A good recommendation would be to adopt an internationally binding comprehensive policy and standards related to taxes, fees, and as well address key areas of staff, passenger safety, and the ships' environmental responsibilities. Only then can we have a more sustainable, controlled development and operations of cruise lines where rules are adhered to rather than avoided.

HISTORY OR CRUISE INDUSTRY

The earliest ocean-going vessels were not primarily concerned with passengers, but rather with the cargo that they could carry. Black Ball Line in New York, in 1818, was the first shipping company to offer regularly scheduled service from the United States to England and to be concerned with the comfort of their passengers. By the 1830s steamships were introduced and dominated the transatlantic market of passenger and mail transport. English companies dominated the market at this time, led by the British and North American Royal Mail Steam Packet (later the Cunard Line). On July 4, 1840, Britannia , the first ship under the Cunard name, left Liverpool with a cow on board to supply fresh milk to the passengers on the 14-day transatlantic crossing. The advent of pleasure cruises is linked to the year 1844, and a new industry began.

During the 1850s and 1860s there was a dramatic improvement in the quality of the voyage for passengers. Ships began to cater solely to passengers, rather than to cargo or mail contracts, and added luxuries like electric lights, more deck space, and entertainment. In 1867, Mark Twain was a passenger on the first cruise originating in America, documenting his adventures of the six month trip in the bookInnocents Abroad. The endorsement by the British Medical Journal of sea voyages for curative purposes in the 1880s further encouraged the public to take leisurely pleasure cruises as well as transatlantic travel. Ships also began to carry immigrants to the United States in "steerage" class. In steerage, passengers were responsible for providing their own food and slept in whatever space was available in the hold.

By the early 20th century the concept of the superliner was developed and Germany led the market in the development of these massive and ornate floating hotels. The design of these liners attempted to minimize the discomfort of ocean travel, masking the fact of being at sea and the extremes in weather as much as possible through elegant accomodations and planned activites. The Mauritania and theLusitania, both owned by the Cunard Line of England, started the tradition of dressing for dinner and advertised the romance of the voyage. Speed was still the deciding factor in the design of these ships. There was no space for large public rooms, and passengers were required to share the dining tables. The White Star Line, owned by American financier J.P. Morgan, introduced the most luxurious passenger ships ever seen in the Olympic (complete with swimming pool and tennis court) and Titanic. Space and passenger comfort now took precedence over speed in the design of these ships-resulting in larger, more stable liners. The sinking of the Titanic on its maiden voyage in 1912 devastated the White Star Line. In 1934, Cunard bought out White Star; the resulting company name, Cunard White Star, is seen in the advertisements in this project.

World War I interrupted the building of new cruise ships, and many older liners were used as troop transports. German superliners were given to both Great Britain and the United States as reparations at the end of the war. The years between 1920 and 1940 were considered the most glamorous years for transatlantic passenger ships. These ships catered to the rich and famous who were seen enjoying luxurious settings on numerous newsreels viewed by the general public. American tourists interested in visiting Europe replaced immigrant passengers. Advertisements promoted the fashion of ocean travel, featuring the elegant food and on-board activities.

Cruise liners again were converted into troop carriers in World War II, and all transatlantic cruising ceased until after the war. European lines then reaped the benefits of transporting refugees to America and Canada, and business travelers and tourists to Europe. The lack of American ocean liners at this time, and thus the loss of profits, spurred the U.S. government to subsidize the building of cruise liners. In addition to the luxurious amenities, ships were designed according to specifications for possible conversion into troop carriers. Increasing air travel and the first non-stop flight to Europe in 1958, however, marked the ending of transatlantic business for ocean liners. Passenger ships were sold and lines went bankrupt from the lack of business.

The 1960s witnessed the beginnings of the modern cruise industry. Cruise ship companies concentrated on vacation trips in the Caribbean, and created a "fun ship" image which attracted many passengers who would have never had the opportunity to travel on the superliners of the 1930s and 1940s. Cruise ships concentrated on creating a casual environment and providing extensive on-board entertainment. There was a decrease in the role of ships for transporting people to a particular destination; rather, the emphasis was on the voyage itself. The new cruise line image was solidified with the popularity of the TV series "The Love Boat" which ran from 1977 until 1986.

1965: FIRST AFFORDABLE CRUISES

The 1960s saw the founding of the first of the modern powerhouse cruise companies, bringing down prices through competition. Princess was born in 1965, offering the first short, reasonably priced cruises on its Princess Pat, which sailed from California and down along the Mexican coastline. Norwegian Cruise Line went into business in 1966 providing the first budget Caribbean cruises on its Sunward and soon became the first cruise company offering packages including low-cost airfare. The Royal Caribbean Cruise Line debuted with the 724-passengerSong of Norway in 1970. Finally, Carnival opened in 1972, instituting their "Fun Ships" and quickly becoming a behemoth, absorbing nearly a dozen other lines including Cunard, Holland America, and Seabourn.

1977: FIRST BIG SHIPS ON THE SMALL SCREEN

As kitschy as it seems today, The Love Boat brought the notion of cruising (previously perceived to be only for the elite) to the masses. Viewers ate up the hijinks that top stars of the day got into with the fictional passengers and crew on a Princess cruise and booked their own vacations with hopes of running into cruise director Julie or maybe even Charo. The cruising frenzy was further fueled in 1984 by Carnival's Ain't We Got Fun ads starring Kathie Lee Gifford, the first to appear on television.

1980: FIRST MEGA SHIP

The '80s was the era of the size wars and the debut of the floating resorts. In 1980, Norwegian Cruise Lines introduced the first supership, the Norway. NCL bought the former S.S. Franceand spent $80 million converting it into a ship measuring in at 150 percent the size of its competition, capable of carrying 2,181 passengers and offering entertainment to rival Vegas shows. In 1988, Royal Caribbean's Sovereign of the Seas had a then-record-setting capacity of 2,350 passengers and was the first ship equipped with the now-ubiquitous multi-story atrium with glass elevators. The title "world's largest cruise ship" has continued to be passed from company to company ever since.

1996: FIRST CRUISE LINE WITH A PRIVATE ISLAND

Disney Cruise Line purchased the small Bahamian island of Gorda Cay and rechristened it Castaway Cay, spending more than a year expanding the beaches and installing a dock big enough for the line's megaships. They have been continually updating it ever since and in the summer of 2010 will debut a new waterslide platform, an expanded stingray habitat, and 20 new beach cabanas. And of course, this being Disney, the ship from the Pirates of the Caribbean movies is moored offshore. Holland America, Princess, Norwegian, and Royal Caribbean all followed suit and snapped up their own private islands in the Bahamas. Royal Caribbean actually has a second island, Labadee, off the coast of Hispaniola.

1999: FIRST SKATING RINK

Royal Caribbean debuted the first shipboard ice-skating rink on the 3,114-passenger Voyager of the Seas and ushered in the amenities war. Cruise lines continue to one-up each other with more and more outrageous forms of onboard entertainment like surf simulators and intricate waterslides. In 2003, Royal Caribbean was the first to add rock-climbing walls. In 2006, NCL installed bowling alleys on its Norwegian Pearl. In 2008, Celebrity was the first to feature 15,00 square feet of lawn space on Solstice. Launched in late 2009, Royal Caribbean's Oasis of the Seas became the biggest ship ever built with a capacity of 5,400 passengers, offering a zip-line, a park with outdoor cafes, the first onboard carousel in its Coney-Island inspired boardwalk, and performances of the Broadway show Hairspray.

2010: FIRST LOOK INTO THE FUTURE...AND THE PAST

This will be another year for firsts. Nine lines are launching new ships (all ordered before the recession). NCL is debuting the Epic, which will offer the first studio cabins for people traveling alone-without the onerous single-supplement fare add-on. The ship will also have the Epic Plunge (a 7-deck tube waterslide), 20 restaurants, and an Ice Bar made of, yes, ice. Seabourn will debut the Sea Cloud Hussar, the largest masted sailing ship in the world. Cunard's Queen Elizabeth will bring back the Art Deco décor of the grand old passenger ships of the 1920s to the 1940s. Princess, too, is returning to the nostalgia of the grand passenger lines, offering Bon Voyage parties. For four hours before the ship's departure, passengers can bring friends and family on board for a tour and lunch.

TYPES OF CRUISES

To most people, "cruise ship" implies a colossal white ocean liner loaded with all the pleasures of paradise and none of the punishment. This is an image that most public relations firms and travel and advertising agencies promote because it sells. Consequently, most job hunters are also sold on this image and only send applications to cruise lines they've heard about. However "Love Boat" types of cruise vessels (150 or more crew; 500 or more passengers) are only part of the cruise ship industry story. Those interested in working aboard a ship should consider all the options, from the biggest ocean liners to luxury river boats to specialty sailboats and yachts.

WORLD CRUISES

Large ships traveling the world over definitely have their appeal. In every port, spectators line up dockside to marvel at these giant ships. Staff making their way down the gangway are often interrogated by the curious crowds: "It must be a fabulous place to work! You're so lucky. I'd give everything to work there." Indeed, it's impressive to be the recipient of such awe.

Big ships also have the distinction of being out to sea for longer periods of time, circumnavigating the globe. They take passengers to places most others can only dream about, and do it in high style. Large cruise lines often reposition their ships according to seasons or to entice different clientele. For example, several cruise lines send ships up to Alaska in the summer, then reposition them to the Caribbean in the winter months.

How does a ship get from the pristine, glacier-clad waters of Alaska to the tropical, sun-drenched waters of the Caribbean? Most schedule a longer cruise trip through the Panama Canal and along the South America coastline to the Mexican Riviera, with stops that include ports in Costa Rica, Belize, Cozumel and Cancun. Heading east from the Panama Canal, a cruise ship might make stops in Aruba, Trinidad, or Barbados. Other ships leave Alaska and cruise to the Hawaiian Islands and then to Asia before swinging back around to the Caribbean. If working aboard a ship with marvelous amenities and fantastic ports of call is appealing to you, world cruise lines are worth investigating. However, keep in mind that working on a cruise ship for extended periods of time can result in a massive case of cabin fever, for which going ashore is the only cure. Time off will depend on your position and duties. Bigger ships have crews large enough to allow for a decent shore leave rotation so members can "escape" from passengers for a few hours.

Another characteristic of large cruise lines is that job duties aboard big ships are more specific. Actually, the situation is quite similar to the assembly-line system invented by Henry Ford. If one person builds an entire car, he or she will perform several tasks in the process. However, when 100 people are working on a series of cars, each person concentrates on a specific task, and, consequently, specialization for that skill occurs. Not only is this system more efficient, its simplicity allows each worker to perform the task at hand with fewer mistakes. A quality product is practically guaranteed each time. When a bar steward, for example, is assigned to a bar, he or she serves drinks in that bar only. That employee is expected to do nothing but serve drinks every night. Again, this ensures that the drinks are well-made and that customer service is excellent. There is potential to earn a lot of money in this situation (the benefits of serving 1,500 tipping passengers, for example), but it's also hard and often monotonous work.

RIVER AND BARGE CRUISES

More and more people are considering river and barge cruises as an alternative to oceangoing trips, or extending their cruise experiences to include these unique waterway vessels. Even if you are committed to working for the biggest and the best megaliners, take the time to read what we have to say about smaller cruise lines. It will only broaden your employment opportunities. Passengers find this form of cruising to have a more informal, intimate atmosphere, especially since some of the smaller river barges limit their cruises to a dozen passengers or so. This arm of the cruise industry has seen tremendous growth in the last decade. And who could argue with itineraries that include pampered rides along some of the world's greatest rivers? Some of these destinations include the Nile, Amazon, Volga, Yangtze, Mississippi, Columbia, Danube, and Rhine rivers.

The longest waterway in Europe is the newly opened Rhine-Main-Danube, which connects fourteen countries from Rotterdam on the North Sea to Sulina and Izmail on the Black Sea, offering passengers and crew incredible, ever-changing scenery most oceangoing cruises would be hard-pressed to match.

One of the grandest traditions in riverboating just might be the huge wooden paddlewheelers plying the rivers of the United States. These thoroughly modern boats, which carry up to 450 passengers, evoke an era of Victorian style and opulence that was the turn-of-the-century standard for all well-heeled passengers. Their classic wedding-cake composition, tall smokestacks, and luxurious amenities are reminiscent of the boats piloted by Mark Twain, causing him to remark, "The steamboats were finer than anything on shore. Compared with superior dwelling houses and first-class hotels in the valley, they were indubitably magnificent, they were palaces." Steeped in heritage, history, and adventure, paddlewheelers traverse rivers such as the Columbia, Mississippi, and Ohio with all the dining and entertainment options found on oceangoing cruises. Yet the experience is quite different from sailing on the open seas, where hurricanes and general bad weather can wreak havoc. Moreover, riverboat companies cruising U.S. waterways typically hire Americans for all shipboard positions. One employee who served as a customer service representative for a river cruise company described his work:

"Our cruise ship ran up the Columbia River from Portland, Oregon, through the Gorge all the way to the Snake River in Idaho. We did a little bit of everything on our boat. We served meals, cleaned the deck, cleaned guest rooms, and served drinks. It was a lot like working on a floating hotel, only on a much smaller scale with a really natural atmosphere. It was great being so close to our surroundings, and I think the guests and employees were a lot more laid back and interesting than the people on glittery cruise ships."

In contrast to large U.S. riverboats, European river vessels have long and low profiles with masts that fold down in order to clear the many bridges found along the way. Barges, which cruise primarily through European canals from April through November, are even smaller than their river counterparts. They serve mainly as first-class water hotels. Passengers go ashore on their own during the day, returning at night for a gourmet dinner. Despite their sometimes ungainly appearances, barges are highly sophisticated and beautifully outfitted with custom-built furniture, rich fabrics, and crystal service ware. Because of their popularity with North American passengers, European river and barge cruise companies have been known to employ English-speaking crews to handle a variety of duties. However, applicants should already be living in Europe to be seriously considered for employment with such a company. Most will not pay for an employee's transportation from the United States to Europe. Applicants who can speak German or French, in addition to English, will have a definite advantage as well.

SAILING AND YACHTING CRUISES

Working aboard sailboats and yachts offers a different environment from large ocean liners and even riverboats. Yachts and sailing ships generally have smaller crews, so each member is expected to perform a greater variety of tasks. If it is an open-water sailboat, the entire crew will likely need to know how to sail and be expected to work the riggings and lines. On such a boat, a deckhand might also serve breakfast, clean cabins, and lead tours ashore. Many people prefer this variety to the same daily routine of the larger ocean and river vessels.

Working aboard a large oceangoing vessel is much like working in a luxury hotel. On the plus side, they offer more space, facilities, and stability in rainy or cold weather situations. Aboard a small vessel, your relationship to the water will be more intimate, and bad weather will have a much more profound effect on both the crew and passengers. Many of the smaller lines are registered in the United States and hire American crews, even for their entry-level positions and housekeeping staff. Moving up the ladder on smaller ships is also a lot easier than with the big cruise lines. For example, to become a purser with a major cruise line might take five to ten years of prior ship experience. However, small vessels have been known to hire college graduates with hotel and restaurant or accounting backgrounds and make them pursers immediately. Some smaller excursion companies also hire their cruise directors straight from their hospitality staff, or from tour staffs in their land tour and shore excursion divisions. So even if your ultimate goal is to be a cruise director with a major line, small ships might be the best route to gaining the experience you need. Because of their ability to travel to remote, secluded areas, many smaller ships have found an appropriate niche for the environmentally aware '90s market: "eco-touring." Eco-tour itineraries typically involve some kind of nature and ecology-oriented cruises to primitive wilderness areas. Tours of the Northwest Passage along the British Columbia coast, Alaska, and numerous areas in the South Pacific and South America have become very popular. These cruises are a far cry from the luxury cruises featuring 1,200-foot ships with ballrooms and casinos. One eco-cruise director describes his ship this way:

"We use small, yacht-like cruise ships that carry no more than 100 people at a time. It's an intimate, naturalist, educational style of cruising-there's no band, and no discos, magicians, bingo, shopping, or casinos. We also don't have black-tie dinners. Our entertainment consists of educational tours and lectures on local history, marine biology, ecology, and botany."

Another eco-cruise veteran says:

"The focus of our trips isn't on our ship. The boat is essentially a base for our tour operations. Our clientele is younger and more adventuresome than the typical cruise ship guests, and we organize lots of really active hikes and trips at our destinations. The atmosphere is pretty informal, with a lot of interaction between the ship's crew and the passengers."

While the jobs for most small cruise lines aren't usually seasonal, they offer a great opportunity for someone who's willing to take some time off from school or their regular job and see interesting new places. These jobs are rewarding and give a great taste of life at sea, but they can be difficult. As one personnel officer puts it:

"It's tough work. You're on duty every day, ten to fourteen hours, seven days a week, with six weeks on and two weeks off. There's no place to go, no personal space, and not much free time. People are away from their home, their cat, their stereo, and their friends, and many people just aren't cut out for the job." But according to one long-time cruise manager:

"We have a lot of American crew on our ships that work as deckhands, stewards, or maintenance people. Usually they're recent college graduates looking for a break and are eager to see places like Baja or Alaska in a unique way. The work can be tough, but the camaraderie is great, and with little to spend their money on, they save almost all of their income."

Eco-cruises don't usually hire traditional cruise staff, at least not in the sense of the entertainment-oriented staffs of the large cruise ships. Instead, they tend to hire for more lecture-oriented positions-a cruise director on these ships is much more likely to be at the bow with a microphone lecturing on passing sights than introducing a comedy act.

Some companies, like Alaska Sightseeing/Cruise West, look for experienced tour guides, or people who have worked as shore expedition personnel, to fill their cruise staff positions. They're more interested in a person's communication and organizational abilities than particular academic knowledge. There is a growing need, though, for lecturers and people with knowledge of the environment and biology. In addition to lecturers and naturalists, companies specializing in eco-tours will often hire expedition leaders. According to one former expedition leader at a successful nature cruise company:

"Our itineraries were very flexible, because we had so many small, out-of-the way ports to visit and we had to really work around wind and weather conditions, find where the wildlife was, and work with the captain on all the scheduling. Basically, along with the captain, I decided where to go, and organized all of the shore side activities, the naturalist lectures, and the landings. It was pretty demanding, but I got fantastic management experience while traveling the world."

Small ships can be more personal as well. You often get to know the passengers by name. The drawback is it's not as easy to escape from your responsibilities. Having said that, if you don't like being around people, you should probably reconsider going to sea on a cruise ship of any size.

DEVELOPMENT OF CRUISE INDUSTRY

Cruise industry symbolizes a small part of the vacation business environment which itself is a very small portion of the leisure business. The cruise industry is attributed by extraordinary value proposition, great demand, favourable guest demographics, high guest fulfillment rate and positive supply vs. demand balance. The business has seen a large development over time and it is anticipated to grow more in the following years. Though, "in 2009, the development in business has turned down, but it is anticipated to lift up again as the global economy improves progressively from the recession. Seeing the development potential in cruise industry, the number of competitors has raised and the existing competitors will be growing their capabilities in the following years." The cruise industry has its roots dating back to the 1970s and this is the era that has been seen an enormous growth in the North American industry. It has been seen that there has been an increase of popularization that is considered as a key factor in the tourism sector with an increase in the cruising business becoming an important economic factor.

Cruise industry is an important example of the globalization having many destinations all around the world, the customers of cruising industry belong to various countries as well as the employees of the cruising industries are from various continents. In addition to this an important fact is that in the past there was an increased level of detachment from the rest of the societies and the countries that are now reduced along with an increase in an economic, legal, ecological and social implication. A crisis-resistant industry with a varied offer of airlift choices and ports that are more modernized have made people choose cruising as an option for having vacations as there is an increase in the consumers knowing the fact that cruising is more relaxing, eventful and an adventurous choice for more than a million consumers coming in to cruise from global destinations.

Cruising is now considered as a dynamic business that has been known for an increase in the products that it has offered with a development in potential markets. As observed there has been an average 8.5 per cent increase in the annual growth in cruising industry since the last 20 years, with an addition of almost 90 million passengers since the 80s. the reports have suggested that more than 60 per cent of the current customers have been generated in the last ten years . since that time there has been no slowing down as there were more than 13 and 13.5 million passengers between 2008 and 2009 as compared to 13 million in the year of 2007, and these increases are also being observed in the coming years.

An important part to be considered in the case of cruising industry is the capacity and since the last ten years and more there has been an increase in the capacity of cruise industry. The history has it that there were only 40 cruise ships in 1980s, with an addition of 80 vessels in the 1990s, with a 40 per cent increase between the years of 2000 and 2005. These years these fleets have joined newly designed ships that have caused a 25 per cent increase in the cruise ships.

Recently there has been an increased investment in newer and more innovative ships that have a capacity of more than 3,000 passengers. These ships promise to offer lower shipping and cruising rates thereby helping in developing a better economy of scale . Some of the activities that are offered by these ships include multi-story shopping centers, cafes, restaurants, art galleries. Thereby these ships offer more than just the cruising experience to the customers.

In the case of cruising ships it has been seen that there is a fleet that has a capacity to carry more than hundred cruise ships having the capacity of carrying more than millions of passengers. These ships travel and cruise through many geographical locations on the global scale that can cover more than 500 destinations worldwide. Of these, these days, Caribbean cruises are the most popular ones, than the Mediterranean cruises and European cruise ships that have reached destinations that include Barcelona, Athens and the Greek Islands, Amsterdam, the Scandinavia Fjords, Helsinki, and San Petersburg.

However, the North America is the main market for cruise trade. Though the area signifies the most mature marketplace of cruise business, with mainstream of travelers originating from the United States, it is still immature with large potential. Therefore, business players are working to raise their ship capabilities and lower berth capabilities to fulfill the increasing need of the business. "Europe is the 2nd largest marketplace after North America, symbolizing the fastest developing marketplace. The European cruise business continues to boost its share of the international cruise marketplace, with United Kingdom being the biggest shareholder in the European marketplace."

The major strengths of the cruise line market are its extreme desirability among customers. Cruises attract to the US citizens desire of adventure. The 2nd strength is that cruise lines industry has demonstrated a great capability to modify their product to fulfill famous social trends and extend into untapped marketplaces. The current trend to present a large range of entertainments and the current fame of "Theme Cruises" has been a worthwhile asset. The presenting of different priced cruises is also sign of the industry's capability to change and as a consequence expand their marketplace. The spreading out into foreign marketplace is further proof of this strength (Mancini, 2003). The cruise line market has shown the capability to not only discover new marketplaces, but to take over them as well. And the final benefit is that the cruise line business operates at 100 percent capacity.

The international cruise business is now looking towards Asia as a key development engine. The Asian cruise industry is increasing at a good growth pace. With the increasing middle class group and the growing interest of individuals in cruising businesses, this area gives ample development potential for the players. Being among the top ideal destination for passengers, the Australian and Singapore cruise market can witness large development in upcoming years. With an increase in the business of the cruising industry there has been an increase in the demand of better organizational structures and better planning and strategic structures that can increase competition on the global scale. These competitions are based on the potential markets that are being focused and that have been able to generate higher revenues with an addition of the markets from North America and Britain.

SAFETY AND SECURITY

Recently it has been found that the number of tourists worldwide who hire cruise vacations stands at approximately 13.4 million, symbolizing around 1.8 percent of the total global travel market, as anticipated by the World Tourism Organization. Roger Cartwright and Carolyn Baird, 2007 also mentioned that the far from being disheartened at this existing level of market portion, the business fully identifies the opportunities ahead as players expand into modern forms of cruises (containing the niche budget option); set their objectives on various demographic groups; and, head for new waters. (Cartwright and Baird, 2007)

Within one year there are more than 13 million passengers who enjoy the cruising each year and the main aim behind these cruises is to ensure the safety and enjoyment of the cruising customers. The help of extra protection provided by law enforcement agencies, FBI and U.S. Coast Guard, ensures the safety of the customers. In order to maximize the protection of the customers there are numerous codes that are to be followed by the cruise lines. CLIA policies have been recently approved that ensure an increased level of security. On an annual basis an examination known as Control Verification Certificate examination is conducted by the U.S. Coast Guard.

An important part of the cruising industry is a Security Committee that is composed of security officers. These security officers are responsible for meeting the law enforcement and intelligence agencies in order to discuss the issues that relate to ship security and intelligence assessments.

COMPETITION IN CRUISE INDUSTRY

Currently the cruise line business has been undergoing a period of huge development over the last 10 years. By some calculations, the cruise market in US alone has earned over $32 billion during 2005. Such income makes sure that the cruise business remains one of the very competitive across all marketplaces. Even smaller marketplaces have been experiencing a boost in cruise business operations. The Canadian marketplace has seen some ports increased over ninety cruise ship callings on a yearly basis and this is a large amount of traffic for a conventional smaller market. Therefore, the competitive profile for the business has boosted in terms of market share and competitive contention.

These days it has been seen that the cruise shipping volume is smaller as there are barriers associated with the entrance and exits along with higher costs of selling and purchasing the cruise ships. In addition to this there are higher investments needed in the managing cruise lines as there are influences of these purchases on the multiple strategies related to organizational and management of these cruise lines.

Important actors that have been identified in the case of increased and changing bargaining power and capability of the cruise industries in order to gain advantages of better economies include the size of the market that is effective in two different ways:

a. There are a lesser shipbuilders and technology developers in the cruising industry that are able to accept the prices that are offered to them;
b. There are a large number of suppliers and equipment thereby there is a great choice of bargain;

Thereby there are a lesser number of companies left that are more vary of the potential threats that are faced by the companies for the clientele in order to provide the customers with options as improved vacation strategies, sightseeing vacations, including thematic parks. There are many opportunities that have caused planning diverse strategies that can help the specialization in specific areas of business. Newly designed strategies have also helped in the development of better cruising products that help to serve massive consumer markets. There has been a great change in the marketing strategy along with a great change in the brand image that has caused an improvement in the commercial environment.

DISCUSSION

The cruise industry has been seen to be threatened by such events as Achille Lauro hijack in 1985, the Iraq and Kosovo wars, and September 11 attacks, and these include the process of restructuration and merging in the cruising sector. Among the cruising companies, Renaissance Cruises was among the first ones to file for bankruptcy in 2001, after this American Classic Voyages and ten well-known brand names, a result of which there was a cease in operations thereby leaving the market open for the largest cruise companies that include Carnival Corporation, Royal Caribbean Cruise Limited and Star Cruises. The Carnival Corporation, having a headquartered in Miami and London is considered as a leader in the cruising industry. This is the company that has over 12 cruise brands in North America, Europe and Australia operating more than 89 cruise ships, along with more than 65,000 shipboard employees and 170,000 guests all around the world.

It has been seen that the corporate offices of some of some of the cruise companies are located in the United States and Europe as the clients of these organizations. The companies have their fleets registered in the countries as Panama, Bermuda, Liberia, and Bahamas.

Some of the main revenues that are generated in this case are from the passengers and by the help of maintaining the clients that helps in the financial stability. On the other hand, it has been seen that the cruise fares play important roles in the commercial relations of the cruise industry. These days there is an increase in the number of items and services provided by the cruising ships for the customers. For instance as compared to the older days there is an increased number of spa and personal care services, shipboard stores and boutiques, photography departments and art auctions at prices that have been the cause of an increased competition. Some of these services are offered by the concessionaires and subcontractors. Other than these there are some Cruise companies that have started to introduce varied practices in order to build the customer base that makes them spend more money. These services include cybercafés, satellite telephone services, restaurants and bars, and diverse revenue-generating schemes in passengers' cabins that include the interactive multimedia and TV, minibars.

One of the main aims that are linked with cruising includes relaxing and having a vacation whereas there is one class of consumers that are more into enjoying all kinds of services that are being provided along with enjoying all the destinations. Thereby there has been an increase in the kind of activities that are being offered at the cruise ships that include gambling, videogames, adventure sports, computers, culinary workshops, and virtual reality centers, theme nights and so on.

On the other hand it has been seen that passengers on the cruise ships are also encouraged to participate in an increasing number of onshore activities. The marketing campaigns of these activities on the ships began in the 1980s and since that time there has been an increase in the number of excursion tours and port lecturers, contracted with local concessionaires and tour operators so that later on it can be sold to passengers onboard.

Cruising may last for several hours as the time increase when there is anchoring and the ship is docked. These dockings also provide different themes and a number of activities that include sightseeing, as there are sites that include natural, ecological and bio spherical locations. Along with these the destinations include wildlife viewing; adventure sports excursions, adventure tours, along with diverse environments that include natural environments; and historical places and cultural tours, museums and monumental heritages.

It has been seen that these days the cruise industry has been able to maintain good relationships with the land-based tourism industry. In addition to this the bargaining power has also increased in the recent years and these have impacts on the services and these bargaining powers have also provided additional income from selling of such products and services.

It has been estimated that there is an additional income associated with an arrangement of the On-shore excursions and visits to ports for many cruise companies. Thereby as a service it has been seen that passengers are provided with a map from which the passengers can select their destinations. These maps also include service shops that are associated with the cruise shops along with commercial establishments in a specific area..

In the year of 1990, it was seen that there were changes in these strategies provided to the passengers as there was an introduction of the concept of "Private Island". This concept was developed by Norwegian Cruise Lines and was later on adopted by other companies that were providing the cruising services in the Caribbean waters. These strategies have been the cause of additional incomes for these companies. Newer cruise companies have an additional control over some shops.

Other than onboard revenue, there are many alternative ways by the help of which cruise industries are making money having better economic results as there has been an increase in the economies of scale and there has been an improved in the management systems. Economic scales have also shown changes in the case of cruising industries as there has been an increase in the port-related activities with an increase in the port based activities. Thereby ports are now the source of an increased incomes even since the 9/11 attacks, as there has been a redesigning of the cruise routes as these routes are now closer to United States. These changes in routes have now caused a great change in the market trends in the case of Caribbean cities that have offered a reduction in the port charges.

One of the most important facts in this case illustrates the fact that cruise companies are now playing important roles in an economic development along with a port facilities and infrastructures.

FUTURE TRENDS

Within a short time, there has been an increase in the potential growth of cruise industry with an increase in the capability to move ships and fleets with an increase in the cruising demands. There has been an increase in the fuel price in the face of economic crisis, an increase in the terrorism, along with an increase in the political instability have been some of the most important challenges that are being faced by the cruise industries.

Since the last ten years, cruise companies have ordered new and improved ships on the daily basis. On the other hand, the new ships that have been ordered are the ones that the new ships have added additional 20 billion dollars with an addition of 85,480 berths in the cruising market. It has been estimated that until 2012 there will be an addition of 4.2 million passengers.

On the other hand, cruising companies including Royal Caribbean International have been ordering more innovative and luxurious ships that have additional capacities that also include Genesis-class vessels, and these have the cost of around $1.65 billion. On the other hand it has been seen that these new ships have an additional capacity of 5,400 passengers and 2,100 crewmembers. However one of the main changes that have taken place is that there are slower economic changes that have caused reconsideration in the business having a control over the costs and a reduction in the costs.

But there have been some studies carried out by the financial analysts and they have argued that there will be no effects of these economic changes on the passengers. There have been many arrangements made by these companies with additional fleets that are equipped with more innovative services and technologies. These services promise better services to the passengers as there has been an increase in the innovative ships that can offer better services and better environments to the passengers. Many cruise executives are convinced that the current economic situation has an advantage on the cruise companies.

DEVELOPMENT TREND OF CHINESE CRUISE INDUSTRY

As the global cruise tourism focused eastward, cruise travel is growing rapidly in China, showing a good momentum of development. In the "2012-2013 China Cruise Development Report", according to the China Cruise and Yacht Industry Association (CCYIA) Statistics: in 2012 Chinese cruise market accommodation had grown rapidly, and mainland China received total of 285 international cruise ships and an increase of 8.8 per cent, the immigration cruise tourists 660,000 passengers, an increase of 31.9 per cent. The number of cruise ships departing from Chinese coastal city was 170, with year-on-year growth of 19.7 per cent, and the number of domestic exit and entry cruise passengers was 420,000. The number of cruise ships visiting Chinese coastal city was 115, with year-on-year decrease of 4.2 per cent, and the number of international exit and entry cruise passengers was 240,000. According to CCYIA statistical bulletin, till the end of December 2013, the three major cruise ports in China (Shanghai, Tianjin and Sanya) had hosted 377 international cruise ships, 55.8 per cent higher than in 2012.

Among them 195 cruise ships in Shanghai, with an increase of 61 per cent; Tianjin, 70 ships, with an increase of 100 per cent; Sanya, 112 ships, with an increase of 30 per cent. A number of 1.168 million home and abroad cruise passengers were hosted in 2013, 97 per cent higher than in 2012. Of which host 759,000 passengers in Shanghai, with an increase of 113 per cent; 250,000 passengers in Tianjin, with an increase of 110 per cent, 159,000 passengers in Sanya, with an increase of 36 per cent. As shown in The number of international cruise ships hosted in China increases gradually by a ladder trend, especially the growing number of international cruise departing from ports in China. While the number of international cruise visiting China in recent two years has decreased. By 2020 China's cruise immigration reception tourists is expected to reach 4.5 million passengers, and China will become the world's fastest-growing emerging markets in global cruise industry.

From an economic point of view, based on average per capita GDP in China, some of China's cities already have the basic conditions for the development of cruise tourism. International cruise development experience has shown that when a regional per capita GDP reached 8000-10000 dollars, cruise consumption started, and when reached 20000 dollars cruise consumption would reach its peak then slowed down.

According to statistics, in 2013 the number of provinces in China which per capita GDP reached 10000 dollars was increased to 7, namely, Beijing, Shanghai, Tianjin, Inner Mongolia, Liaoning, Jiangsu, Zhejiang. Guangdong and Fujian are also close to 10000 dollars. The per capita GDP of Guangdong, Fujian, Shandong, is expected to exceed 10000 dollars in 2014, at that time, all China's eastern coastal provinces will enter 10000 GDP USD per capita rankings. Therefore, the development of China's economy with per capita GDP rising to cruise ship tourism development has laid a good economic base.

From the perspective of national policies, the government has promulgated a number of guidance which is conducive to the development of cruise tourism industry. In June 2008, the National Development and Reform Commission (NDRC) first proposed "the guidance on promoting development of the cruise industry in China", which pointed out that the focuses of development of the cruise industry are strengthening the construction of infrastructure, breeding domestic consumer market, perfecting the relevant laws and regulations, and research and development in cruise technologies. In October 2009, the Ministry of Transport issued an announcement: "foreign ship chartered to carry out multi-point anchored business in China." Foreign ship may be approved more than two consecutive anchored Chinese coastal ports.

December 1, 2012, the State Council issued "the Development of the Services Industry 'Twelve-Five' Plan". The "Plan" called for the strengthening construction and management of passenger terminals, marinas and parking area, developing ro-ro transport, sea tourism and yacht economy of the straits and the islands, encouraging port develop cruise economy which contains entertainment, leisure, dining and shopping. On July 1, 2013, the new edition of the People's Republic of China formally implemented the law on exit and entry Administration. According to the new regulations, foreign cruise travelers in accordance with the law on exit and entry management-related conditions can enjoy 24-hours transit visa policy as long as applied to the border authorities. Therefore promulgated policies and legal regulations enhanced the confidence of developing cruise tourism industry in China.

From the enterprise perspective, the rapid growth of the Chinese market makes the world's major cruise ship companies accelerate significantly layout in China, at the same time Chinese companies begin to get involved in the cruise industry's core sectors. Currently three major international cruise companies Carnival, Royal Caribbean and Star Cruises have entered the Chinese market. In January 2013, the wholly-owned subsidiary of ICBC-ICBC financial leasing company and Silver Sea Cruises focusing on global high-end cruise markets announced that both sides would cooperate in a five-star cruise ship "Silver Shadow" financial leasing business. The deal is the first time that domestic financial institutions entered into international high-end cruise markets.

On January 26, 2013, the first "Chinese Style Cruise", named "Henna" started her official maiden voyage at Sanya Phoenix Island international cruise port, indicating that the national brands of China formally entered the cruise market, which broke the monopoly of foreign cruise companies in the Chinese market. On February 10, 2014, Bohai Ferry Company of Hong Kong Limited, a wholly owned subsidiary of the Bohai Sea Cruises was allowed to set up. On February 12 Bohai Sea Cruises and Costa Cruises Ltd. signed a boat purchase contract at a price of $ 43.68 million to buy "Costa Voyager" cruise.

BOTTLENECKS OF THE CRUISE INDUSTRYIN CHINA

The explosive growth of cruise tourism makes cruise industry begin transiting from infancy to the development phase. But in the process of industrial development, China's cruise industry is also facing many problems. These problems become the bottlenecks of the cruise industry in China's future development.

Imperfection of Cruise Industry Chain

Cruise industry chain includes the upstream industry like cruise manufacture, cruise ship operating company, and the downstream industry like port services, tourism and trade industry. China's cruise industry profits mainly come from port services, tourism and trade. Through attracting foreign cruise ships anchored and travel agency sale cruise tickets to gain profits, not through the production and operation of cruise ships. However, the barriers to entry the cruise industry are mainly in operating and shipbuilding.

Due to the large cost of cruise manufacturing and long period of payback, China has no self - made cruise fleet at present. All the time, the cruise industry was monopolized by European countries (mainly Finland, Germany, France and Italy). Although the shipbuilding industry in coastal areas of China has developed well, it is mainly responsible for the shipping manufacturing. The designing and building of advanced cruise ship in China are still in blank, which requires difficult technologies and stringent standards. China has no specialized cruise operate enterprise now, because of higher registration fees required for the cruise, high cruise imported taxes, and lacking of experience in the cruise business management. Comparing with Japan cruise industry, it is found that the advantages of Japan shaped at the beginning of industrial development. At that time Japan considered cruise manufacturing and operation as the development strategy. As early as 2005, Japan had had 8 self-made cruises. The driving role of cruise manufacturing and operation for the entire industry is self-evident, which will change the passive situation of cruise tourism market in China, boosting the growth of tourism, transportation, catering and trade. Therefore, the cruise industry requires us to develop the upstream industry, from top to bottom , to stimulate the vitality within the industry and achieve industrial chain multiplier effect of 1+1>2.

Simple Investment Model

Cruise port and dock construction scale of investment are very large and the payback circle is up to 10-20 years. The cost of a cruise ship construction needs at least 5-7 million, which brings high demanding in the related financial services. In China cruise port and dock construction are financed by the State and local governments, and there are no related businesses in the area of large cruise liner manufacture. Single investment pattern and the shortage of fund have become another bottleneck restricting the development of Chinese cruise industry. An industry's development is inseparable from the support of funds.

If lacking of private capital injection, without good financial services supporting, and relying solely on the government's financial support, it is often not sufficiently stimulating market vitality. In 2011, Wenzhou private capital combined with Fujian, Hong Kong and Taiwan capital to purchase "stars of Asia" luxury liner, which marked the private capital first foray into the cruise industry. However, for the development of the whole industry, that capital is far from enough, needing greater range of capital strength, and improving cruise tourism industry's core competitiveness. Meanwhile, supporting financial and insurance operations should also be followed up in time.

Unsound Policies and Laws

Although it has promulgated some policies to support industry development, the macro-plan of whole industry as well as industry support policies are still absent. The cost of the cruise dock in China is 3-5 times higher than other Asian countries and European counties, which is one of the most important factors to prevent more international cruise ship docking in China. There are noticeable lag in the regulations. Most of the existing port fees are still in accordance with regulation in 1991, and some others reference to international standards for the transport of the goods. In the aspect of law, China lacks of unified international practice and security clearance procedures, besides the border inspection procedures vary in different port. At the same time, there are no relative behaviour regulation involved in sightseeing, leisure, dining and other code of conduct when passengers on the boat. China's law largely relies on international practices, such as "Athens Convention 1974", and some laws to regulate the passenger transport operation. As "Fighter ships" incident happens frequently, a very important reason is the lack of relevant legal norms. When majeure factors incident happens, the current laws cannot protect the interests of tourists, also cannot regulate visitor behaviour.

Immaturity of Main Cruise Consumers

Cruise travel is the emerging forms of tourism in recent years, just as a supplementary form of outbound tourists in China. Its main consumers still not mature. Derived from European aristocratic lifestyle of cruise travel, cruise culture in China is difficult for visitors to understand and get used to. Chinese tourists like venue wonders of sightseeing, and pay less emphasis on leisure, it is difficult to adapt to the relatively closed space in cruise. The habit of outbound tourism consumption is still delighted in luxury purchases. This mainly because that the ideology of visitors and spending habits are different from western country, meanwhile the current vacation system is not suitable, and the development of the relevant routes and advocacy efforts is far from enough.

In addition, from abroad experience in the development of cruise industry, civil society organizations can play a contributing role for the cultivation of main consumers and industrial development. However, China lacks of civil society groups and organizations. In China, Shanghai is the Center of cruise routes, headed north for "CJK" route, and south for Hong Kong, Macao and Southeast Asia. The product is relatively simple, relatively short range, lacking of attractiveness, so that the advantages of tourism resource in China's coastal city do not play well. When the form of leisure tourism in Western countries collide with traditional Chinese consumer attitudes and behaviour, it is very difficult to fit in, hence hinder the development of the cruise industry. Therefore, an urgent measure to foster positive market consumers is really necessary.

Acute Shortage of Professional Talents

Along with the world's leading cruise companies to seize the Chinese market, China cruise businesses sprout. The shortage of cruise professional talents has become an important bottleneck restricting the development of cruise tourism industry in China. At present, the gap of cruise talents is very huge, not only lacking of personnel and management team, but also lacking of cruise management experience. While facing difficulties in recruiting and training talents, the talent turnover is also serious. Just from the cruise service aspect, it requires a lot of highly qualified service personnel, who know foreign languages well, to realize staff and passengers matching ratio 1.5:1, even 2:1. The talents of cruise trade, marketing, manufacturing, and design are even more difficult to obtain. Foreign cruise lines often hunt talents from hotels and travel agencies or labour dispatch companies, or cooperate with counterpart school to train talents, but it is still struggled to meet the demand. The reasons include three aspects. First, Chinese traditional ideology; secondly, there is no good mechanism of training talent; thirdly, lacking of management experience and weak faculty.

COUNTERMEASURES AND SUGGESTIONS

Policies and Legal Norms

By Learning from foreign advanced experience of development in cruise industry, China can introduce the macro planning of the cruise industry. First of all, in terms of port development, China should form cruise home ports which take Shanghai as the center, Tianjin, Xiamen and Haikou as support ports. Meanwhile a number of ports of all should be developed, to encourage the economic development of the port and avoid duplication. Secondly, the government should introduce some relevant preferential policies, such as reducing requirements for cruise ship docked, optimizing the border clearance process, shortening the access gateway. Thirdly, taking full use of tax for whom plays a catalytic role in industrial development, at the same time expanding the scope of tax exemption and reducing procedures of tax rebates, cutting down the required import tariffs on the cruise ship.

Drawing from international current management practices, in line with China's national conditions, government introduces cruise tourism management regulations to regulate the tourism business behaviour and protect the interests of tourists. Cruise tickets should join the system of compulsory insurance and financial guarantees, thus clarify areas the responsibility of each other. In the aspects of cruise security management, the recommend is referring to "America 2010 Cruise Safety Act": Installing peephole, cameras and electronic delay door locks on the door of the passenger room; railing height is set on a cruise to reach at least 42 inches; issuing safety manual to cruise passenger; medical personnel must have higher education and formal qualifications, and also have received training in dealing with handling sexual assault cases.

Multi-Path Industrial Chain

Chinese cruise enterprises can be established through purchasing or chartering cruise. Government should reduce the opening fees of registration for cruise lines, pay attention to the cruise business qualification judgement, and encourage cruise manufacturing enterprises by financial support and preferential policies. China should actively learn shipbuilding technology and management experience of advanced countries; expand international exchanges, and strengthening the independent design and innovation. Cruise companies should cooperate with tourist attractions and travel agencies, making wide range of service like tourism, sightseeing, shopping, so that passengers can effectively enjoy the benefits. Through the improvement of port facilities, to create well-developed transportation hub, to expand the scope of radiation tourism, this consequently attracts more foreign cruise tourists.

Diversified Investment Mode

It is really necessary to break the current single pattern of cruise tourism industry investment, creating a good investment environment, and setting development fund of the cruise industry. In result this industry will attract more funds and investments. Firstly, government should implement various preferential policies within the cruise development experimental zone, and encourage three types of mixed ownership companies. One is the combination of public ownership and private ownership, which includes Sino-foreign joint ventures, national or collective joint enterprises and the private sector of the economy. Another is the combination of public ownership and individual ownership. The last one is mixed ownership consisting by public ownership within State-owned enterprises and collective enterprises. Secondly, travel agencies and other travel businesses cooperate with international cruise companies to broaden cruise market scale. Thirdly, set up pilot leasing companies of cruise ship finance in Shanghai and Tianjin, where are the cruise tourism comprehensive development experimental zone in China. In order to solve the problem of financing, bank financing, the cruise ship industry fund or trust products can be useful methods. Meanwhile cruise finance leasing companies shall be exempted from business tax, giving them benefits of turnover tax, stamp duty, and depreciation tax in accordance with international practice.

Actively Cultivate the Market Consumers

The cruise market should actively foster the cruise consumer culture emphasizing on quality and fitting in tourists' vacation mentality. Careful market research is also necessary, thus developing cruise lines and tourism products in accordance with Chinese culture and the culture of cruise. Cruise enterprises need to increase cruise travel propaganda, popularize cruise travel knowledge, so that to improve the understanding of tourists about cruise travel. Besides, cruise companies should enhanced cruise travel marketing, focusing on the cruise market segments. In the meantime, government should encourage establishing civil society organizations, which will play the role of advocating cruise and establishing industry codes.

ESTABLISH SCIENTIFIC TALENTS TRAINING MODE AND ENTERPRISE COOPERATION MECHANISM

As higher cruise personnel requirements, colleges and vocational training schools in China should lay emphasis on molding cruises staff with solid theoretical knowledge, excellent communication skills, smooth foreign languages and strong sense of service. Educational institutions should also pay attention to practice-oriented education, and cooperate with cruise companies to form coordinating relationship between the cruise talents and the demand of cruise enterprises. Implement "going out" and "bringing in" strategy. On the one hand, the managers, designers and constructor of cruise industry should learn the advanced theory and experience from Occident. At the same time, China should import experienced talents to guide the cruise operation, design and management. On the other hand, cruise staff in China should also actively explore and develop work methods and systems suitable for future.

RESPONSIBLE CRUISE TOURISM: ISSUES OF CRUISE TOURISM AND SUSTAINABILITY.

Cruise tourism is the fastest growing segment of leisure tourism, increasing 7.2 per cent annually since 1990, doubling every decade (Cruise Lines International Association [CLIA], 2010). While typically greatest in North America, growth is in recent years increasingly at a quicker pace elsewhere in the world. Between 2006 and 2009 passenger numbers in North America were virtually unchanged, compared to a 68 per cent increase (an average 17 per cent annually) outside North America (CLIA, 2010). Growth 'downunder' has been even greater. Carnival Australia reports a 26 per cent passenger increase between 2008/09 and 2009/10 a level of growth that will continue with the addition of ships to the company's fleet. New Zealand reports a 513 per cent increase between 1996/97 and 2009/10; an average 37 per cent per year.

This growth is in part a result of redeployment of older ships from North America to other parts of the world, including Europe, Asia, and Australia. The growth also reflects construction of ever-larger ships. Carnival Cruise Lines' and Royal Caribbean's first ships carried 1,024 and 724 respectively. Their newest ships carry 4,000 and 6,000 passengers, respectively (Klein, 2005a).

As the size of ships has grown, and the number of ships has increased, new ports have been established and existing ports have found ever-growing numbers of day-visitors. The growth for some has been phenomenal. Belize saw a 2,000 per cent increase in cruise passenger arrivals between 1999 and 2009 (an increase of 1,591 per cent in just four years between 1999 and 2003; Caribbean Tourism Organization, 2010; Klein 2005a). Over the same period, the Bahamas, Saint Maarten, and Antigua saw increases of between 110 per cent and 120 per cent (Bahamas logging more than 3.25 million passengers annually). It is not only the Caribbean. Cruise passenger arrivals in Victoria, British Columbia, and Seattle increased more than 1,000 per cent between 1999 and 2009 while arrivals in neighboring Vancouver decreased 5 per cent over the same time period.

Cruise tourism's growth has brought with it concern about environmental impacts, including the footprint left ashore by cruise tourists—the number of cruise passengers has grown more than 30 fold between 1970 and 2011, which poses a much greater environmental threat. As well, there are debates about the economics of cruise tourism—the value of cruise passenger spending and costs associated with infrastructure required to host ships, including cruise terminals that can cost $100 million or more—and about the impact of cruise tourism on local culture and society. These three areas of concern—the environment, economic benefits, and maintaining cultural integrity—are embedded in the concept of 'sustainable tourism.'

However, the question must be asked as to sustainable for whom. Corporations, including cruise lines, talk about 'best practices' as an example of sustainable practices; or they equate meeting or exceeding international regulations with sustainability. Directly impacted local communities and stakeholders are not normally included in the determination of sustainability. One way to put communities and stakeholders into the equation is to think in terms of responsible tourism. This chapter looks at select concerns about cruise tourism through a responsible tourism lens. The purpose is to demonstrate how this lens analyses the impact of cruise tourism. Data and insights incorporated in the article are generated from a range of sources, including dialogue with cruise industry executives and suppliers to the cruise industry; interactions with key actors and citizens groups in ports frequented by cruise ships; cruise industry, government, and non-governmental organisation (NGO) publications, studies, and reports; mainstream media reports; and the author's involvement as an expert witness in cases involving the cruise industry and in giving lectures around the world sponsored by universities, grassroots community groups, and NGOs.

RESPONSIBLE TOURISM

Responsible tourism emerges from the movement for sustainable tourism. Sustainability was defined in 1987 by the Brundtland Commission as 'development that meets the needs of the present without compromising the ability of future generations to meet their own needs' (World Commission on Environment and Development [WCED], 1987). Five years later, the Earth Summit's Agenda 21 offered a blueprint for sustainable development focusing on environmental issues and equitable distribution of economic benefits derived from development and tourism (United Nations Environmental Programme [UNEP], 2002). According to UNEP on Tourism (cited in the Responsible Travel Handbook, 2006):

Ten years after Earth Summit's Agenda 21, in 2002, the World Summit on Sustainable Development was convened. A preliminary report jointly prepared by four industry bodies (including the International Council of Cruise Lines) gave direction for the summit. The report reflected industry's interests and concerns, focusing more on best practices, certification programmes, and the economic benefits of tourism than on the inherent challenges to achieving sustainability. The primary focus when it came to cruise tourism was waste management practices and procedures. These were addressed solely from an industry perspective.

Immediately preceding the World Summit on Sustainable Development was the first International Conference on Responsible Tourism in Destinations (RTD). The conference shared the same concerns as sustainable tourism (*i.e.*, a focus on environmental, economic, and sociocultural impacts), but was grounded in ethics and human rights—companies are expected to do what is morally and ethically 'right' (McLaren, 2006) from the perspective of consumers and communities. It is not a matter of simply reducing negative impacts, but of mediating and/or ameliorating those that persist.

RTD concluded with the Capetown Declaration. It defined responsible tourism as:

- Minimising negative economic, environmental, and social impacts
- Generating greater economic benefits for local people and enhancing the wellbeing of host communities, improving working conditions and access to the industry
- Involving local people in decisions that affect their lives and life chances
- Making positive contributions to the conservation of natural and cultural heritage, to the maintenance of the world's diversity
- Providing more enjoyable experiences for tourists through more meaningful connections with local people, and a greater under standing of local cultural, social and environmental issues
- Providing access for physically challenged people
- Maintaining cultural sensitivity, engendering respect between tourists and hosts, and building local pride and confidence.

RESPONSIBLE CRUISE TOURISM

Responsible tourism has three broad areas of concern: (a) tourism's impact on the environment, (b) the equitable distribution of economic benefits to all segments of a tourist destination, and (c) minimising negative sociocultural impacts. These three areas shape the following discussion, with a view towards demonstrating how principles of responsible tourism may be applied to cruise tourism. As already indicated, the determination of what constitutes 'responsible' is vested with stakeholders involved in the development of tourism products and in those impacted by that development. Thus, when considering environmental responsibility, it may not be whether a company uses 'best practices' or follows international regulations, but instead the environmental impact on people of those practices. In the case of wastewater treatment for example, the issue is not whether cruise ships have installed advanced wastewater treatment systems (AWTS), but whether the effluent of these systems has deleterious effects. Similarly, when considering economic benefits of cruise tourism the focus may not be on whether a port community realises income but rather the degree to which economic benefits are distributed equitably between the cruise line and port and among the stakeholders and segments of society in the port.

ENVIRONMENTAL ISSUES

A cruise ship produces a number of wastestreams. Some, such as oily bilge water, ballast water, and air emissions from fuel are common to most ocean-going vessels. Other wastestreams are specific to cruise ships, such as the volume of human waste and grey water, solid waste, and incinerator emissions and ash. Three wastestreams will be considered here for illustration: wastewater treatment, air emissions from engines, and solid waste.

WASTEWATER TREATMENT

Many notable technological advances have been applied to cruise ships in recent years (Seatrade Insider, 2010a), including systems for treating the roughly seven gallons of sewage and 90 gallons of greywater per person per day. These new systems, however, can produce as much as 28,000 gallons of sewage sludge per week. While land-based tourism also produces greywater and sewage, treatment systems on board cruise ships are often less effective given the limited space available for the full suite of treatment systems commonly found on land.

Greywater (water from sinks, showers, galleys, etc.) has typically been discharged overboard untreated, which by international regulation is legal. Human waste typically has been treated by a Type 2 Marine Sanitation Device (MSD). A slow shift to AWTS began in the early 2000s after testing in Alaska demonstrated that MSDs failed to meet operational specifications: 79 of 80 samples from cruise ships were seriously out of compliance and posed an environmental risk.

These new systems (AWTS) were initially installed on ships deployed to Alaska. But they still have problems. Sixty per cent of ships permitted to discharge in Alaska state waters were cited for violating Alaska Water Quality Standards in 2008, logging 45 violations; 72 per cent were cited in 2009 with a total of 66 violations. The largest number of violations was for excessive levels of ammonia, but there were also violations for copper, zinc, biological oxygen demand, fecal coliform, pH, chlorine, nickel, and total suspended solids (TSS). In view of the poor results, the cruise industry successfully pressured the Alaska Department of Environmental Conservation to reduce the standards for wastewater; citizen groups in the state challenged the reduced standards in court (Bluemink, 2010). They argue that discharges from AWTS have deleterious impact on fisheries and on mammals depending on sealife for their survival, and disagree with the cruise industry's claim that 'dilution is the solution' (*i.e.*, the oceans are so vast that a bit of pollution will have little impact).

Alaska is unique—it is the only jurisdiction where onboard observers (Ocean Rangers) are placed on cruise ships permitted to discharge in state waters. Observers monitor waste treatment systems and regularly sample effluent. While these systems are likely to be installed on ships sent to Alaska, they are not necessarily on ships deployed elsewhere. There is variation by company. For example, Norwegian Cruise Line had AWTS on their entire fleet by 2008, whereas only one of Carnival Cruise Lines' 22 ships was equipped with this technology (Brannigan, 2008). The other major player, Royal Caribbean International, despite an assurance in May 2004 that it would have AWTS on all of its ships by 2008, still had 11 ships (almost half its fleet) without AWTS at the start of 2010 (RCI, 2010).

Despite AWTS not being installed on many of the world's cruise ships, the industry often says: 'Cruise Lines International Association members have a policy to treat all blackwater (sewage) prior to discharge anywhere in the world. Before discharge in U.S. waters, it is treated by an Advanced Wastewater Purification System, which produces an effluent cleaner than what is discharged from most Municipalities' (Hansen, 2010). While it can be argued that AWTS are an example of responsible practices, it does not appear responsible to claim these systems are more broadly used than they are. There is also no mention of what is done with greywater, of which there is a much greater volume, which is still frequently discharged untreated, and which some AWTS cannot treat.

Perhaps more troubling is that cruise ships have different practices based on the jurisdiction. Rather than adopt a common policy of responsibility applied across locations, practices are based on what regulations permit. For example, Celebrity Cruises' Mercury in 2005 dumped a half million gallons of sewage and untreated gray water into Puget Sound and the Strait of Juan de Fuca 10 times over nine days in September and October. The company initially denied the claim but it acquiesced when shipboard documents indicated otherwise.

It then appealed to state officials for relief from the $100,000 penalty because three of the violations occurred on the Canadian side of the international boundary and Washington did not have jurisdiction—the cruise corporation argued the discharges, while a violation of its Memorandum of Understanding (MOU) with Washington, were not illegal in Canada (McClure, 2006). The citizen backlash in Canada was predictable with some labelling British Columbia as the industry's toilet bowl. The Haida Nation, on the northern end of the Queen Charlotte Islands, convened Gaaysiigang—An Ocean Forum for Haida Gwaii, a conference and meeting with experts in January 2009 to address this issue specifically, exploring strategies to protect its territorial land and waters. Other First Nations have subsequently followed suit.

Practicing responsible cruise tourism would suggest having consistent practices, at the highest level of responsibility, across jurisdictions rather than variable practices based on what is permitted by one jurisdiction versus another. The issue is not what one can get away with, but what is responsible behaviour for the environment.

AIR EMISSIONS FROM FUEL

Air emissions from ship engines are an obvious source of pollution, resulting in an estimated 60,000 deaths worldwide each year, and estimated to grow by 40 per cent by 2012 due to increases in global shipping traffic. According to the US EPA, ocean-going ships that used Category 3 marine engines and operated in the US Exclusive Economic Zone (EEZ) in 2007 emitted 870,000 tons of nitrogen oxide, a key contributor to smog (US EPA, 2007). Cruise ships comprise 12 per cent of the world's commercial ships (Sutton, 2010), however, they pose a unique problem as they run auxiliary engines while in port to drive their onboard power plant. Some ports have introduced 'cold ironing' (a requirement that ships plug into the power grid for electricity while in port); however, the practice is still quite limited.

Conventionally a cruise ship's daily emissions are likened to the impact of 12,000 automobiles. A study published in 2007 raises an even greater alarm. It found that bunker fuel on average has almost 2,000 times the sulfur content of highway diesel fuel used by buses, trucks, and cars and that one ship can make as much smog-producing pollution as 350,000 cars (Waymer, 2007). This varies widely depending on the fuel being burned.

Current international standards set maximum sulfur content for ocean going vessel fuel at 4.5 per cent, making it easy for cruise lines to say they meet or exceed international regulations since bunker fuel averages 3 per cent sulfur content (low sulfur fuels such as on-road diesel have sulfur content as low as 0.0015 per cent). Limits will reduce to 3.5 per cent in 2012 and 0.5 per cent in 2020. To date, cruise lines have been resistant to using fuels below 2.5 per cent sulfur because of higher cost, except where cleaner fuels are required. Ships transiting the Inside Passage of Alaska and British Columbia, for example, typically use fuel between 1.5 and 1.8 per cent sulfur content (Montgomery, 2007).

Governments have recently taken action to curtail air pollution from ships. The European Community issued Directive 2005/33/EC requiring all ships while in European ports to use fuel with sulfur content of 0.1 per cent or less effective January 1, 2010. Six months later, provisions in Annex VI of the International Convention for the Prevention of Pollution from Ships (MARPOL) regarding Sulfur Dioxide Emissions Control Areas (Baltic Sea, North Sea, and English

Channel) placed a limit of 1.0 per cent sulfur content; the limit reduces to 0.1 per cent in 2015. Following developments in Europe, the US and Canada partnered to establish the North America Emission Control Area (extending 200 miles from the coast), which was ratified by the International Maritime Organization on March 26, 2010 (Lagan, 2010). It limits sulfur content in fuel to 1.0 per cent effective 2012 and 0.1 per cent by 2015.

The cruise industry argued against the emission control areas (ECA) in Europe (Seatrade Insider, 2010b). It also voiced concern about increased fuel costs associated with the North American ECA (Canadian Press, 2010) and asked that consideration be given to '... alternative means, such as scrubbers, that ships could use to meet emissions goals, and to take a piecemeal, rather than blanket approach. 'The ECA area should be tuned to prioritise those areas where urgency exists and the greatest health and environmental benefits can be achieved' (Stueck, 2010, p. A4). Ironically, while saying they support the health and environmental goals behind the creation of the ECA, cruise industry associations questioned the research on which the regime is based and warned it could hurt the Canadian and North American cruise sector insofar as ships relocating elsewhere.

Despite the increased cost, estimated to be between US$7 and $15 per day per passenger, principles of responsible tourism suggest cruise operators would embrace internationally sanctioned and locally legislated regulations in order to enthusiastically demonstrate their commitment to the environment. After all, using cleaner fuel compliments what has already been achieved through greater fuel efficiency, more efficient itinerary planning (including travel at slower speeds), and energy-saving practices on board. The public relations value of behaving consistent with their environmental image would appear to be a better payoff than a stance that contradicts claims of environmental concern and responsibility. The industry could demonstrate its moral high ground, consistent with underlying principles of responsible tourism.

SOLID WASTE

A cruise ship produces a large volume of non-hazardous solid waste, including huge volumes of plastic, paper, wood, cardboard, food waste, cans, glass, and the variety of other wastes disposed of by passengers. It was estimated in the 1990s that each passenger accounted for 3.5 kilograms of solid waste per day. With better attention to waste reduction this volume in recent years has been cut nearly in half. But the amount is still significant, more than eight tons in a week from a moderate sized cruise ship. Twenty-four per cent of the solid waste produced by vessels worldwide comes from cruise ships (Copeland, 2008). While land-based tourism also produces solid waste, cruise ships pose a unique problem given the amount of waste discharged at sea and, some would argue, the greater volume of waste per guest.

Glass and aluminum are increasingly held on board and landed ashore for recycling, but only when the itinerary includes a port with reception facilities; it is otherwise discharged at sea. Food and other waste not easily incinerated is ground or macerated and also discharged into the sea, legally beyond three miles from shore. These '... food waste can contribute to increases in biological oxygen demand, chemical oxygen demand, and total organic carbon, diminish water and sediment quality, adversely effect marine biota, increase turbidity, and elevate nutrient levels'. They may be detrimental to fish digestion and health and cause nutrient pollution (Polglaze, 2003). An additional problem with discharging food waste at sea is the inadvertent discharge of plastics. Under Annex V of MARPOL, throwing plastic into the ocean is strictly prohibited everywhere. Plastic poses an immediate risk to sea life that might ingest or get caught in it (Reid, 2007).

Solid waste and some plastics are incinerated on board, and then the incinerator ash is dumped into the ocean. Incinerator ash and the resulting air emissions can contain furans and dioxins, both found to be carcinogenic (Klein, 2009), as well as heavy metal and other toxic residues. For this reason Annex V of MARPOL recommends, but does not require, that ash from incineration of certain plastics not be discharged into the sea (US EPA, 2008). At the very least, incinerator ash should be tested before each overboard discharge in order to determine whether it should be categorised as solid waste or hazardous waste (US EPA, 2008).

Although cruise ships have reduced their volume of solid waste, the total amount is still significant. Royal Caribbean's commitment in 2003 to not dump any trash overboard is admirable (Fain, 2003), assuming it has been practiced. While companies have been adept at promoting what they do to be environmentally responsible, they are not always transparent about practices that to some may not be viewed as responsible. The first step towards responsible cruise tourism is that cruise corporations need to be more transparent about what they do and what they don't do. Stakeholders, consumers, and interested parties should be able to determine what systems operate on which ships and be informed about the environmental impact of each ship and each itinerary. Given the wide variation, whether it be between ships with AWTS and those without, or between ships on itineraries where there are recycling facilities versus those where there aren't, it is important that detailed information be available. Such transparency reflects a sense of responsibility. It also permits local communities and stakeholders to make informed judgements about whether cruise lines are behaving responsibly.

ECONOMIC ISSUES

Ports of call are a focal point of any cruise. They provide value to passengers and economic benefits to local merchants and tour providers. It appears on surface to be a perfect arrangement—everyone benefits. But on closer inspection there are issues. For example, economic benefits are not always distributed equitably between the cruise ship and the port. The issue is not that ports do not make money; they obviously do. It is whether the income generated exceeds direct and indirect costs and whether income distribution is responsible. A second issue of concern is that ports increasingly feel pressure to construct new cruise terminals and often compete with neighbors for business.

DISTRIBUTION OF BENEFITS

Belize is a good illustration. Passengers arrive by tender at Fort Street Village in the centre of Belize City. The village is contained by a wall and security fence and has within a range of shops and eateries/bars, many of which are found in other Caribbean ports (including Diamonds International, which until 2011 co-owned the Fort Street Village with Royal Caribbean). The retail space is expensive so few local merchants can afford to be there; there is a small crafts market for them in another area, but the rents again are relatively significant given the degree of income. The result is that merchants in the Fort Street Village have income, despite heavy overhead costs, but merchants outside do less well given the relatively few cruise passengers who venture independently from the Fort Street Village.

Most passengers take shore excursions. These are major money makers for the cruise ship, which holds back 50 per cent or more of what passengers pay on board for a tour. This creates two problems. First, a passenger spending US$50 for a shore excursion expects a $50 product, but the shore excursion provider only receives US$25. While the cruise ship walks away with its cut, the shore excursion provider must provide a quality product that pleases passengers and the cruise line while still retaining a small profit. If passengers are unhappy they will blame the shore excursion provider, unaware of the cruise line's cut, which can exceed 50 per cent; one cruise line retains 90 per cent of the cost of a shore excursion in St Vincent and the Grenadines; 80 per cent on an excursion in Halifax, Nova Scotia. Though not unique, in Charlottetown, Prince Edward Island an authorised taxi picking up a cruise passenger at the port must give 30 per cent of every fare to the cruise line (CBC, 2010). Those willing to pay the 30 per cent 'fee' have access to passengers while they are still in the cruise terminal; other taxi drivers are left behind the security gate entrance to the terminal. Those barred from cruise passengers question the equitability of these arrangements.

A second problem relates to the distribution of economic benefits within the port community/country. Again using Belize as an example, there were several speakers at the third International Conference on Responsible Tourism in Destinations in October 2009 who talked about a small hand full of individuals making money from cruise tourism, but that the majority of Belizeans realise little if any benefit. In fact, cruise tourism earns considerably less for the economy than traditional land-based tourism. A 2007 study found cruise visitors spent less than half as much per day as land-based visitors (US$44 vs. US$96). Cruise passengers accounted for 75 per cent of arrivals to Belize, but only 10 per cent of employment in the tourism industry (Centre of Ecotourism and Sustainable Development [CESD], 2006). While cruise tourism brings many more visitors, its economic impact is relatively small and concentrated in a few hands. The situation in Belize became more problematic in early 2011 when Carnival Cruise Lines announced it would no longer use locally owned tenders to transport passengers from the ship to shore. The cruise line insisted that tenders must accommodate at least 200 passengers. Many local tender owners fear going out of business, especially given the debt incurred to purchase vessels that previously met the cruise corporation's requirements. Subsequent to its initial demand, the cruise line called on tender operators to reduce their fees and it boycotted the port.

ECONOMICS AND CRUISE TERMINALS

As cruise tourism has grown, demand for terminal facilities has also expanded. Port cities without terminals build facilities hoping to attract cruise ships. This was the case of Prince Rupert and Campbell River, British Columbia: Campbell River's C$14 million terminal has been used rarely; Prince Rupert's C$12 million terminal has had less traffic than originally projected and expects little or no traffic in 2012 (250 News, 2010). Many existing ports are either expanding what they have or building new facilities. Some are based on assurances from a cruise line. That was the case for Saint John, New Brunswick, which spent C$12 million on a cruise terminal, specially built to accommodate Voyager of the Seas. It subsequently learned in August 2004 that one-third of its cruise ship passengers would be lost in 2005 because the ship was replacing Saint John with Bermuda (Klein, 2005a).

New, larger ships dictate renovations. The financial burden for construction and maintenance of these cruise facilities is often on local governments that may or may not recoup their investment—the Government of Jamaica is spending more than US$120 million on a new US$225 million cruise terminal at Falmouth. Like many other ports, they may end up subsidising the cruise industry. They feel forced to make investments, but at the same time are pressured to keep cruise passenger head taxes as low as possible (in the Caribbean considerably lower than fees paid by those arriving or departing by air). However, some ports appear to negotiate better deals than others. St Maarten received a $34.5 million loan from Carnival Corporation in 2007 for construction of a new pier. Royal Caribbean loaned it an additional $10 million for a fixed berth on the new pier. Given terms of the loans, agreed to passenger head taxes, and maintenance costs, the port is likely to end up subsidising the construction project—anticipated revenues will barely keep up with expenses. At the same time, Port Everglades (Fort Lauderdale) agreed to renovate one of its new terminals at a cost of $37.4 million in order to accommodate Royal Caribbean's Oasis of the Seas and Allure of the Seas, but in that case neither the port nor taxpayers will foot the bill. Royal Caribbean will instead pay for the work through a $5.70 surcharge on passengers when they leave and arrive. That's in addition to a $9.95 port user fee all passengers pay. The result is that while St Maarten has to pay for its new piers with existing port fees and is left at the margin with regard to generating enough income to cover all expenses, Port Everglades maintains its usual port fees and collects an additional fee to specifically cover construction costs.

An increasingly common arrangement that avoids this problem is that cruise corporations are building and operating their own cruise terminals. Carnival owns terminals in Cozumel, Roatan, Turks and Caicos, Long Beach California and elsewhere; controls a terminal in Savona, Italy; and in partnership with Royal Caribbean holds the concession for the cruise terminal at Civitavecchia (Rome). Royal Caribbean holds the concession for cruise terminals at Falmouth, Jamaica and Kusadasi, Turkey, and in partnership with Diamonds International owned the terminal in Belize. The effect of these arrangements is that income generated from cruise tourism increasingly goes into corporate coffers rather than local purses. As well, as was seen in Kusadasi, shops within the cruise terminal take business away from shops traditionally visited by cruise passengers (Klein, 2008). The economic value of cruise tourism to local constituents and stakeholders is dwindling while the cruise line's income increases. This does not constitute responsible tourism.

These corporate owned terminals in some regions compete with other ports and may factor in bargaining as nearby ports negotiate with the cruise industry. Ports are potentially played off against one another. This is certainly the case in British Columbia where five ports have been encouraged to build terminal facilities, yet the number of cruise passengers is not increasing. With alternatives, cruise lines are able to ensure they get the best possible deal while some ports win and others lose.

The difference between responsible tourism and sustainable tourism is relevant here. While these business practices might be considered sustainable from a cruise line's perspective, the moral and ethical slant of responsible tourism makes them problematic. Is it responsible to encourage ports to build terminals knowing they will be underutilised or left unused?

At the same time that a corporation is responsible to stockholders for generating profit, it has a responsibility to the ports and communities it visits. Port communities should receive fair, equitable, and widely disbursed benefits from cruise tourism. The issue here isn't that cruise tourism is doing nothing, but it can do more. Carnival Corporation's goal should be receiving a score of 10/10 for social responsibility rather than the 3/10 it received in 2004 on The London Times Corporate Profile (London Times, 2004).

SOCIOCULTURAL ISSUES

There is again a range of possible issues, but three will suffice for illustration: people pollution, homogenisation of the port experience, and authenticity of cultural experience.

PEOPLE POLLUTION

People pollution refers to the point at which the carrying capacity of a port is exceeded (Baekkelund, 1999). This has increasingly become a concern as the number of cruise ships has increased and the size of these ships have grown. In the 1990s, five ships calling at a port would have offloaded 10,000 passengers or less; today five ships could easily bring more than twice that number of passengers. The experience of passengers is impacted, however, more importantly local inhabitants are forced to deal with overcrowding and other problems associated with this growth. These problems are in many ways unique to cruise tourism given the short-term daily influx of large numbers of people and that land-based visitors stay at their resort or are disbursed more broadly across a region.

Curson (2009) describes the cruise passenger problem differently, calling it pack behaviour: This can be seen in most ports in Alaska that see 10,000 or more passengers a day in communities such as Skagway with a population of less than 1,000.

Cruise tourism takes its toll:

Crowds disrupt usual routines and the activities associated with cruise tourism can themselves be a problem. People living in Juneau, Alaska, complain of the constant sound of helicopters ferrying cruise passengers to glaciers or other sights. Residents in Victoria, British Columbia, complain about sail-away parties and horn toots after midnight when ships sail through a residential area as they leave the port. Lobster fishers in Prince Edward Island complain that ships pass over buoys and sever lines to which traps are attached, causing them to drift, with captive lobsters inside—a loss of the $100 trap and lobsters. Norfolk's Elizabeth River Run, which celebrated its 25th anniversary in 2003, was canceled in 2004 because it conflicted with a cruise ship visit. A benefit walk for multiple sclerosis in San Diego had to be relocated because of traffic concerns stemming from the arrival of a cruise ship. And pier expansion plans in Maui would have ended outrigger canoe racing, regattas, and other paddling events in Kahului Harbour and severely impacted traffic congestion had the government not backed off under staunch public pressure. These are impacts on quality of life. (Klein, 2008, pp. 99-100)

Quality of life is directly impacted by the volume of visitors. The United Nations Committee on Sustainable Tourism notes that when the social carrying capacity of an island is surpassed, cost of living increases along with overcrowding, traffic congestion, and noise pollution. A lower standard of living results for a significant segment of the population and an attitude shift occurs whereby the tourist is blamed for the majority of social problems (Baron, 1999). This describes in part the citizen backlash in Key West, Florida after cruise tourism exceeded the city's carrying capacity, negatively impacting traditional, land-based tourism and local residents alike, and contributing to the city's 'getting ugly' label by National Geographic Traveler in 2004. There were citizen forums, a lawsuit calling on the city to undertake a quality of life study, media and public relations campaigns, and demonstrations. The quality of life study was completed in 2005 and the number of cruise ship visits reduced (Klein, 2008). Unlike Key West, key decision-makers in many ports will accommodate as many cruise ships as want to come, and not seriously consider sociocultural impacts.

HOMOGENISATION OF THE PORT EXPERIENCE

The Caribbean is an example of a mature cruise destination. As such, ports have to a degree become homogeneous—jewellery stores, duty frees shops for liquor and other goods, and an assortment of tourist-oriented products. A number of companies (*e.g.*, Little Switzerland, Diamonds International, Colombian Emeralds, etc.) have stores in various ports. While this homogenisation may have economic value to the outside corporations that own the stores, it takes its toll on local people.

Take Ketchikan, Alaska. With a population of less than 8,000, it had 43 jewelry stores downtown in 2004; a decade earlier there were only a handful (Markell, 2003). 'Locals call the migrants who own and run these jewellery and curio shops taking over downtown the "Pirates of the Caribbean", since they follow the wake of the ships' and because many of these stores are owned by the same companies that own the stores on Caribbean islands. Not only have these stores changed the character of the downtown, which is largely boarded up from the end of one cruise season and beginning of the next, but the volume of cruise tourists makes the downtown unattractive to local citizens, who have to wait until the end of the season to again enjoy their quiet city. In addition, many store employees come from 'the lower 48 states', taking their savings with them at the end of the season.

It is essential that the growth of cruise tourism not have a negative impact on the quality of life of citizens in and around a port. If anything, the impact should be positive. As quality of life is a largely qualitative concept, the best indicator is people in and around the port—all walks of life and all segments of society. A responsible cruise operator works with a community to grow cruise tourism at a pace and in a manner that is mutually beneficial to all involved (not just a few stakeholders). They engage and listen to local people and provide as much economic benefit as possible to as wide a segment of the community as is possible.

SOCIOCULTURAL AUTHENTICITY

Concern is with whether visitors have an opportunity to interact with and to experience local culture, and that local cultures are treated respectfully. Here again the sheer volume of cruise passengers can compromise the experience for both. In Belize for example, locals warn visitors not to visit Xunantunich on 'cruise day,' one of the main Mayan sites in Belize for cruise passengers (Krohn, 2010). Passengers' experience of the sacred site is limited by both the length of time spent and by the number of other cruise passengers sharing the site—on most days the site is quiet. Cruise day is especially busy for the operator of the hand-cranked bridge that crosses the river to get to the Mayan site (quaint when crossing in a single vehicle on a lazy day), and for some of the craftspeople selling wares at the crossing point, but otherwise passengers stay on their bus and are whisked someplace else. There are many other sites and communities in other countries about which the same can be said—where the sheer number of passengers negatively impacts the quality of the sociocultural experience. Awareness that it is qualitatively falling short ideally paves direction for the cruise industry to redesign its product for better delivery. This challenge is ever-greater as cruise ships are larger, carrying more and more passengers to the ports they visit. But then again, the ship is increasingly the destination; cruise lines want there to be so much to do that passengers do not want to leave the ship while in port. It is clear that cruise tourism is not sensitive as it could be to local communities, their citizens, and the range of stakeholders.

Another issue regarding sociocultural authenticity is the knowledge and accuracy of information provided by onboard port lectures and those leading tours. Passengers tend to depend on these cruise ship employees for accurate information, however it frequently is limited or incorrect. According to a seasoned cruise lecturer there is a great deal of misinformation given by both cruise ship port lecturers and tour guides. But to be entirely fair, the misinformation ... starts not with the guides but with the cruise line brochures, where glowing prose and brightly coloured pictures (usually of Santorini's white houses and blue roofs) entice customers with fantasies of 'exploring' the ancient world. 'Wander down the back streets of Venice'; 'Visit Ephesus and walk in the footsteps of St. Paul'; 'Come to the Acropolis, the birthplace of democracy'. This inevitably entails their serving up some factoids though the ad writers are often unsure if the Parthenon is on the Acropolis or vice versa, or if the Parthenon is really the Pantheon. Pompeii, we are told, was buried in molten lava, all theaters are regularly upgraded to amphitheaters, and in one Silverseas brochure Imperial Rome was called Empirical Rome (suggesting that the barbarians who sacked the fifth century were a bunch of Emersonian transcendentalists). The point this is meant to illustrate is the need to accurately represent sociocultural sites and to take responsibility for accurately educating passengers about what they are about to experience. Cruise lines need to maintain standards. An example of failing short is something told to the author by a native Hawaiian in Hilo in 2003. He was among a group that was upset because Norwegian Cruise Line fired all of the Hawaiian musicians playing Hawaiian music on ships in Hawaii and replaced them with Filipino musicians playing Hawaiian music. The Filipino musicians cost less, worked more hours, and appear Hawaiian when dressed in Hawaiian shirts. Most passengers knew no different, but to the native Hawaiians it was an insult on multiple levels. This is another case of falling short of responsible cruise tourism.

SEEING THROUGH THE RESPONSIBLE CRUISE TOURISM LENS

Cruise tourism's pace of growth and the nature of its product presents many challenges to the industry and to ports and port communities. While it is easy to think about sustainability in terms of shipboard operations, when considering the interaction of cruise tourism with local communities the concept of responsible tourism may be more useful. One obvious reason is the mobile nature of cruise ships. Its passengers are day visitors and the ship itself is not part of the communities it visits. Impacts must be measured from the perspective of the port community. This becomes even more important as ships get larger given the greater volumes of waste and the increasing number of visitors. While some stakeholders may benefit, others may not. A focus on responsible tourism places priority on benefits being fairly distributed across a community. The goal of this chapter was to illustrate how principles of responsible cruise tourism may apply to issues faced by the industry. As seen with environmental issues, it was suggested there could be greater transparency about environmental practices in place and greater care in not generalising innovations on one set of ships to others with such innovations. There is no question that the cruise industry has made many strides when it comes to environmental practices. It shouldn't detract from its achievements by not embracing internationally sanctioned regulations such as emissions control areas and by not handling solid waste as well as they can. Royal Caribbean's 2003 pledge to not discharge any solid waste at sea is a goal to be sought. As well, the industry can be more transparent about its environmental practices, taking pride where achievements have been made and admitting where achievements have not been made.

Several areas related to the socioeconomic benefits of cruise tourism were also discussed. As was seen, the distribution of benefits between cruise ships and shore excursion providers appears to be tipped heavily in favour of the cruise ship. Not only is the shore excursion provider apparently short-changed, but their low level of income means others in the supply chain also receive less. The scenario around cruise terminals also appears to put port communities at an economic disadvantage vis avis the cruise industry. Cruise corporations are out to make a profit, and they do that very well, however they can do better at sharing the profits from cruise tourism with the ports on which they depend for attractions and entertainment for their passengers. This income needs to reach all segments of the society—not just the relatively few merchants and guides who come into contact with the passengers.

The final area discussed was sociocultural impacts: the problem of overcrowding, homogenisation of the port experience, and the need to honestly represent cultural and historical sites. The most immediate problem to address is the issue of overcrowding—people pollution. Ports and cruise lines together need to determine the realistic carrying capacity of port, port cities, and tourist attractions and then design itineraries and port calls that stay within these limits. A port can absorb only so many passengers at a time, and can tolerate only a certain number of days being inundated by cruise passengers. A responsible approach to cruise tourism would add these elements to the equation when cruise corporations or the cruise industry determines whether it is responsible.

Using the responsible tourism lens to view cruise tourism can be a useful exercise. It helps focus the analysis of 'sustainability' on the local community and stakeholders that are effected by cruise tourism. While it may be useful from a corporate perspective to think in terms of sustainability, viewing cruise tourism from the grassroots—the ground up—may be best accomplished with the responsible tourism lens. This shift in focus has yet to be adopted by academic researchers. There is limited research on the challenges posed to local communities and governments by cruise tourism, and virtually no research focusing specifically on responsible cruise tourism. It is an area that begs for attention, not only research focusing on how impacts of cruise tourism are viewed differently from an industry perspective versus from the viewpoint of stakeholders and effected citizens in ports of call, but in regard to the social and environmental policy implications of insights provided by that research.

3

Cruise Onboard Management

The good thing on this particular ship is that the Cabins and the Offices are on 2 opposite sides. The cabins are located forward, on a higher deck and the offices are on a lower deck at the aft of the ship. This means that the even the walk to the work place, passing through the ship, enables me to carry out my Hotel Manager duties by keeping note of my surroundings.

Passing through all public and behind-the-scenes areas such as Galleys, Provision Rooms, the Laundry, the Offices of the Department Heads, the Crew Area, Crew and Staff/Officers Mess is necessary for me to understand what is really happening on board the ship. I observe all activities, take corrective action where necessary and make myself available for questions/comments, especially from crew members who will never stop by the Hotel Managers office.

At the same time, this walk through includes my greeting and talking to guests, making sure they are enjoying themselves, listen to complaints and be present as a Ships Officer and representative for the Cruise Company. After the initial walk-through, and maybe breakfast, it is time to do paperwork, answering e-mails, reporting to the main office, dealing with requests and providing information. Almost every day I have meetings to attend, such as the Captain's Meeting, Hotel Manager Meeting, Revenue Meeting, conducting crew cabin inspections or a safety drill. Meeting with Department Heads to ensure a smooth operation, or the occasional "putting out fires" moments, making decisions in line with the company's guidelines and dealing with guest complaints or crew issues are part a regular party of my day.

After a busy morning, it is time for another walk through, especially during meal times, to see the galley and restaurant staff in full swing. Depending on what is going on on-board the ship, after lunch I can have a short break for either resting, going ashore or just enjoying some off-time.

For coffee-time and cocktail hour I must have another walk through, then there is more paperwork to be done and more e-mails to be answered. An important part of my job is to be present during dinner and eating with the guests. Being ready to entertain them and being available for conversations is also part of the job, as well as dealing with internal issues. Whilst this may sound like a nice, easy task, I can assure you it is not as simple as it sounds. Hosting a dinner table at least once every week means you are entertaining 8 guests. The menu is the same every week, and so are the questions of the guests. At one point, the waiter serving the Hotel Manager's table answered the questions for me, since he knew the answers perfectly and he gave me a chance to get at least a bite of each course which was served!

WORKING ONBOARD CRYSTAL CRUISES

CRYSTAL SERENITY AND CRYSTAL SYMPHONY

Signing on the Ship

Immediately upon boarding the ship, you will be required to "sign on" in the Crew Accountant's office. You will hand in your passport, medical papers and employment agreement. You will receive your crew card. Your crew card is your identification and must be carried with you at all times when going ashore and boarding the ship. A "Buddy" (a member of your department) will greet you and assist you in picking up you uniform, getting your cabin and safe key from the crew office as well as show you the emergency exits from you cabin and working area. Your "Buddy" will also help you familiarize yourself with the ship prior to sailing and take you to the Safety Meeting where you will receive your emergency card.

Safety Onboard

When joining one of our ships, it is mandatory that you attend a Safety Meeting for new, returning and newly promoted crewmembers. As a crewmember onboard, you will be given a job description for your normal duties. In addition to this, all crew members have a duty to perform in event of an emergency. In order to prepare for a hazardous situation, all crew must attend various emergency drills and special training.

Drug and Alcohol Policy

It is the policy of Crystal Cruises that our vessels be operated safely and with maximum concern for the environment. To this end, the use, sale or possession of illegal drugs; the misuse of legal drugs; and the immoderate or unauthorized use of alcohol are specifically forbidden onboard company vessels. Accordingly, Crystal Cruises Incorporated will not employ persons known to use drugs. All new crew members will have to take a drug test within the first 72 hours of joining the ship. All crew members are subject to random drug and alcohol testing.

Language on Board

The official, and therefore mandatory, language on board is English. English should always be spoken in the presence of guests – even when conversing with another crew member. All personnel must have demonstrated a good command of the English language prior to joining the ship. Crystal Cruises will evaluate your competence by conducting the Marlin English test.

Living Quarters

Depending on your position onboard, you will have to share cabin with a fellow crew member. All cabins have wall to wall carpet, telephone, TV and bathroom. Limited free space and living together with a fellow crew member may be a new and different experience. All crew members are expected to maintain a neat and professional appearance. Keeping your cabin clean, orderly and in good condition is everyone's responsibility.

Crew/Officers Mess

All meals are served in the Crew/Officers Mess. The meal hours are posted on board. Smoking is not permitted in any of the messes.

Laundry

There are several self-service washing and drying machines for the use of the crew. Laundering and dry cleaning of uniforms and working clothes will be paid by the company.

In-Port Manning

In accordance with International Maritime Law, approximately twenty-five per cent of the crew must remain onboard while the vessel is in port for responding to fires and other emergencies. These duties are rotational and assigned by the department heads.

Crew Facilities

The areas available for leisure time activities include a fitness room, swimming pool, deck for sunbathing and a Crew Bar. At appointed hours you will be able to shop in the ship's Gift Shop at special crew prices. The Crew Officer in cooperation with an elected Welfare Committee will be arranging crews' entertainment like films, games, crew parties, soccer games, table tennis and other activities. At the beginning of every cruise, you will receive a Crew Activity Calendar which lists all the upcoming events for the cruise.

Signing Off/Vacation

In general, sailing periods are between five and six months followed by approximately 2 months vacation. This is based on an established vacation plan worked out by the ship. Provided you follow this vacation plan, you will be guaranteed reengagement. Thereafter the company will pay repatriation expenses to the nearest commercial airport of your place of residence when going on vacation in accordance with the established vacation plan.

Wages

Each crew member will receive, free of charge, an OceanPay Visa debit card. This card is yours personally, for life. The OceanPay card account is a US dollar account drawn on a US bank. You will receive your pay via direct deposit (free of charge) in your OceanPay card account each month while you're working onboard and while on vacation (for those with paid vacation time). You can transfer the money from your OceanPay account to any bank account worldwide, make purchases or pay bills, or just leave the money in the OceanPay account.

EMPLOYMENT SCHEDULED CRUISE ONBOARD

What are the requirements for onboard employment? While specific position requirements depend on the job you are interested in, there are some essential requirements that all crew must meet to work onboard:

- Be 21 years of age or older
- Be able to pass a criminal background check
- Hold a valid passport
- Have a US C1/D visa (if you are not a Canadian or US citizen/resident)
- Have a Princess-specific pre-employment medical exam certificate
- Meet the English fluency requirements relevant to your position

What is a C1/D visa? Also known as a seaman's visa, some nationalities need this to work onboard a ship and travel to certain countries. This visa normally lasts between two and five years. You will be required to make an appointment at your nearest US Embassy to gain this visa; all paperwork for the appointment will be supplied by your manning agency. The cost of the first C1/D visa is at the crew member's own expense but visa renewal costs are reimbursed by the company.

How do I get a medical certificate? This extensive examination is at the employee's expense and can be conducted through one of Princess's recommended medical facilities—you'll be advised which one is closest to you. Once this is completed and approved by our corporate Medical department, you are cleared to travel and work onboard. Which ship will I be assigned to?

Shipboard employees are scheduled to vessels based on operational need. This means you could be assigned to any one of our vessels in the fleet depending on where a position is open at the time you are travel-ready. After your first assignment, we will be able to provide details about the next assignment after your leave period.

How do I get to and from the ship I am assigned to? At the beginning of each contract Princess Cruises will provide flights from your designated airport to your assigned ship. At the completion of your contract, Princess will arrange for your travel back home as well. It is your responsibility to get to the airport from your home, but from there we will provide any necessary accommodations and/or transportation to and from the ship.

Do I need travel insurance? While you are covered medically in Los Angeles and onboard the vessel, we suggest you purchase basic travel insurance to cover the cost of lost luggage or injuries that could result from shoreside activities.

How long will I be onboard? Contract lengths vary by position but range between four and ten months. After each contract you will receive approximately 60 days of vacation before your next assignment. Your daily work schedule while onboard will depend on your particular position, but you can expect to work seven days a week and anywhere between 10-13 hours per day.

Can I get off and go home during the contract? Time off during the contract is not permitted. In case of family emergencies, Princess Cruises does understand that additional time at home may be needed and does accommodate these requests on a case-by-case basis.

Will I have my own room? Accommodations vary depending on the ship and position. Those in non-management positions generally share a cabin with one to three other roommates whereas those in most management positions are entitled to a single cabin. Cabins include a storage space, TV, and DVD player. What is the power voltage in my cabin? All vessels have 120v US power and some vessels also have 220v European power. Can I drink alcohol onboard? Yes, alcohol is available for purchase during time off. However, Princess Cruises has a strict alcohol limit and at no time can a crew member be intoxicated.

Is there a drug policy? Princess has a zero-tolerance drug policy. All crew are subject to random and reasonable-suspicion drug testing. Violation of these policies will result in termination. Is there a curfew? There is no set curfew. However, crew who are out late should be respectful of other crew members and guests nearby. Can I bring a family member or friend onboard? Crew members who meet specific length-of-service criteria have the option of requesting "relatives travel," a benefit that allows family members to sail onboard for a limited period of time. Some restrictions may apply.

Will I have access to guest areas and amenities during my time off? While some officer-level positions do allow restricted access to guest areas, most facilities are for guests only. However, we have a variety of crew-only facilities, such as a crew pool, whirlpool, gym, bar, and Crew Club, which is a communal room where you can gather to watch movies, play games, sing karaoke, and much more!

Once onboard, how do I stay in touch with my friends and family back home? Postal mail services are available while onboard. You will also have access to computers in the crew training areas. Wi-fi Internet is also available in the crew areas if you choose to bring your own laptop or tablet. Princess offers discounted rates for phone and Internet cards so you can stay in touch with those at home. But remember that satellite capabilities are sometimes limited while the ship is at sea. Can I have mail delivered to the ship? You will be provided with mailing addresses for ports where mail can best be delivered. Is there an ATM onboard to use? There is an ATM in the guest areas; an ATM charge will apply. You can also cash checks in the Crew Office onboard to get cash.

Will I have to pay taxes? US citizens will have federal taxes automatically deducted and may be required to pay state taxes, if applicable. All other nationalities are responsible for filing their own tax forms upon returning to their home countries (as they are self-employed).

Can I send money home from onboard? You can wire money via the Crew Purser's office. Details are available onboard and rates may vary. How do I pay for items onboard? You will be provided with a bar account number, which is your personal number for the duration of your contract onboard each ship. As the entire vessel is cashless, even for guests, you will provide your account number at the bars, salon, and shops in guest areas. In the Crew Bar you can purchase a CrewCard and add money onto it for purchases. At the end of every month you will be required to settle your account.

How do I do laundry? There are crew laundry facilities where the washers and dryers are free of charge—you just provide the soap. You can also use the dry cleaning onboard, but there is a nominal cost.

What if I miss the ship in port? Crew members who miss the ship should contact the ship's Agent who will be at the port (the address and phone number are always in the Princess Patter, a daily newsletter for our guests). The Port Agent will arrange transportation to the ship's next port of call. However, it is the responsibility of crew to pay these transportation costs. Crew may be disciplined for the offence and could be terminated. Depending on the port all crew members are required to be back onboard half an hour to an hour prior to sailing time.

What happens if I get sick while working onboard? While onboard, all crew are medically covered and can visit the Medical Clinic for health concerns. If you need to be medically disembarked during your contract, Princess will provide transportation to a land-based medical facility and repatriate you back home. Can I visit the ports while working onboard? If you are not scheduled to work during the time the ship is in port, you can disembark the ship with your supervisor's approval. Occasionally, there are crew-specific activities or tours to participate in. Safety requirements dictate that a certain number of crew members be present on each vessel at all times. As such, there may occasionally be times when, although not scheduled to work, you will be required to remain onboard while the ship is in port.

How do I apply to work onboard? Princess Cruises recruits globally through authorized hiring partners. Once you contact the authorized hiring partner, you can get answers to questions regarding the application process and which positions are currently open in your region.

WORKING ON CRUISE SHIPS

The precarious position of cruise-ship workers was made apparent in 2000, when Premier Cruises went bankrupt and left hundreds of workers stranded in Halifax. They had to go to court to fight for their money that was on deposit with the cruise line (back pay and gratuities to be sent to family back home). The Canadian courts ordered they be paid more than US$745,000 in back pay, and, with the help of the International Transport Workers' Federation, they were able to return to their home.

The Premier Cruises workers who were in Barcelona were not as lucky. Twenty-eight women and 232 men were stranded for 10 weeks on the Seawind Crown, with no income and no means to leave. After eight weeks, the ship had virtually run out of fuel, water and provisions. It was running on one emergency generator, which supplied only minimal power and lighting. According to the ITF's European cruise-ship coordinator, Ruud Touwen, crew members were "stripping equipment, radios, and TVs and taking it to the town to sell." Their only subsistence was provided by the Port of Barcelona, charities, and other ships. The workers were finally repatriated by the ITF, though their back wages were lost.

The cruise industry experienced massive growth in the past two decades. Since 1980, occupancy increased almost 600 per cent, from 1.5 million to over 10 million passengers worldwide. As the industry has grown, it has also consolidated. Some companies have gone bankrupt. In 2000, three companies, reflecting four brand names, ceased operations. In 2001, another three companies reflecting six brand names went under. At the same time, the largest companies – Carnival Corporation, Royal Caribbean Cruises Limited, Star Cruises, and P and O Princess – have expanded and diversified through the purchase of other cruise lines. These four companies control almost 90 per cent of all berths on cruise ships. Carnival Corporation, which owns six brands, is the largest. It controls one-third of all berths. It had net profits of $1 billion each in the past two years, with gross revenues of approximately $3.5 billion.

The industry's growth has brought a need for more workers. Royal Caribbean International is owned by Royal Caribbean Cruises Limited. It operates 14 ships and has more than 30,000 berths (about 15 per cent of the North American cruise fleet). RCI estimates that it will need 12,000 new "hotel" employees for housekeeping and the dining room each year for the next five years to keep pace with expansion, and its need to replace staff who leave.

The majority of new workers will be drawn from under-industrialized countries in Asia, Eastern Europe, the Caribbean, and Central America. They are seduced by the idea of getting paid to travel the world on some of the most modern and beautiful ships. However, the image is not the reality. As the ITF reports, "below decks on virtually all cruise ships, there is a hidden world of long hours, low pay, insecurity and exploitation. Those who work continuously below deck, like in the galleys [ships kitchens], rarely see the light of day, let alone the shimmering sea of the Caribbean."

Most of the workers in the lowest-paid positions secure their jobs through a recruiting agent. Paul Chapman, an American chaplain associated with seafarer's missions, says seafarers often view the agent – not the captain or ship owner – as their employer. In his study of international seafarers, he says: "The agent becomes the seafarers' patron, someone to whom they remain loyal, despite abuses. The others in authority are strangers; seafarers often do not know the ship owner, and the officers who give day-to-day orders are often from another country and speak another language. It is the agent with whom the seafarers negotiate the terms of their contract, [and] in whose office employment agreements are signed." It is also the agent who forwards money to workers' families.

Using an agent increases the cost of securing employment on a cruise ship. The Wall Street Journal reported on one newly hired employee who had to pay a Croatian cruise-ship agent $600 to confirm his hiring. Carnival Cruise Line loaned him $1,400 for his ticket to the U.S. and the employee, suddenly in debt, "became, effectively, an indentured cruise-line employee, obligated to work for months to pay off his loan." The Miami New Times described a cook on Carnival's Paradise who gave a Bombay agency $2,000, which included airfare. That sum was almost a third of the $7,000 he would make during his 10-month contract. Jim Given is ITF's North American cruise-ship campaign director. He told me of an agency in Bucharest, Romania that charges prospective applicants US$500 simply for an interview, and an additional $1,000 to confirm their employment if they are hired. A Canadian company named Sea Cruise Enterprises was recently reported by Lloyd's List, a British-based international maritime newspaper, to be charging prospective shipboard employees US$57 simply to receive and transmit their resume to potential employers.

Under International Labour Organization regulations, these fees are to paid by the cruise line. However, that is not always the case. The scenarios above are common. Employees often accrue an enormous debt in order to get a job. In 1998, one such worker, a woman from Turkey who inadvertently learned she was going to be fired, jumped overboard as Holland America Line's Westerdam approached Vancouver's harbour.

Workers on cruise ships have contracts that run as long as 12 months. Most work 10 months, followed by a two-month vacation. They then return for another 10 months. This means long separations from family and friends. An Indonesian waiter on Holland America Line's Statendam told me he hadn't been home for the birth of any of his four children. Another worker said, "The first month after returning home, I sleep. The next month, I live with the knowledge that I will shortly be back on the ship." The pattern is the same, whether a worker is from Jamaica, Haiti, Indonesia, the Philippines, Turkey or Hungary.

Employees commonly work 10 to13 hours a day, seven days a week. A shipboard waiter may work as many as 16 hours a day, and often gets less than six hours of uninterrupted rest per night, well below international standards. It is common to find collective agreements on cruise ships that require all shipboard employees to work 80 hours per week. In a survey of shipboard employees conducted by the ITF in 2001, 95 per cent reported working seven days a week.

In addition to long hours, remuneration is low, by North American standards. According to the ITF, wages for salaried workers who receive no tips "can be as low as US$400 a month, rising to US$700 a month for skilled cooks and security guards." Those who receive tips have salaries that are even lower. Holland America Line, which employs primarily Filipinos and Indonesians in its hotel department, pays US$300 a month. This salary is higher than the industry norm, given the line's policy of "tipping not required." On ships where tipping is expected, waiters, busboys and room stewards can earn salaries as low as US$50 a month. In any case, almost two-thirds of those receiving tips earn monthly incomes of $1,000 or more. And then there are fees that some workers are forced to pay.

Celebrity Cruises deducts $7 a week from waiters' and busboys' salaries for breakage, for instance, whether or not they break anything. "If I break something I am punished by having to go to the storeroom in the lower decks to get replacements," an Indian waiter on Celebrity Cruises' Meridian told me. "Even if I am in the middle of serving, I must run down and get the supplies, which means my service may suffer and my tips will be lower."

Carnival Cruise Line requires workers who interact with passengers to pay a $50 deposit for their uniforms. According to the ITF, some companies charge employees a "security bond" of up to US$750, supposedly to stop desertion, or to cover the consequent U.S. immigration-service fine a company gets charged. The bond can extend the amount of work time a worker spends just covering expenses to six out of the eight or 10 months on board.

Cruise lines have typically restricted the ability of workers to engage in collective action by hiring staff from multiple countries, and from diverse cultural and ethnic backgrounds. In those few cases where workers have joined together, they have met with harsh resistance from the companies. In 1981, 240 Central American workers went on strike aboard a Carnival Cruise Line ship in Miami to protest the firings of two co-workers. The company ended the strike by calling the U.S. Immigration and Naturalization Service. The strikers were declared illegal immigrants, bussed to the airport and flown home, unemployed. In January 1986, Norwegian Cruise Line solved a sudden labour dispute aboard the Norway by loading 55 South Korean, Jamaican, and Haitian room stewards on buses at the Port of Miami and sending most of them back to their home countries.

Supervisors on cruise ships often tell seafarers who complain, "If you don't like it here, you can go home." Since the seafarer has already paid for the return trip, the threat is real and the seafarers know it will be carried out at their expense. Staff quickly learn to do their jobs and not to complain. A 27-year-old janitor from Saint Vincent, for instance, had his pay reduced from US$452 a month to US$37 while working for Carnival Cruise Line. He was clearly upset, and was not sure what prompted the reduction. But after five years with the company, he feared his supervisors would brand him a troublemaker if he complained. He endured the reduction in pay without question, rather than risk his job. By registering their ships in these countries, companies successfully avoid having to pay income taxes, and they also avoid having to abide by national labour laws – including health-and-safety legislation – and environmental regulations. They also avoid unions this way. The regulations that a ship must follow are those of the country where the ship is registered, and whose flag it flies.. Flags of convenience are clearly an economic benefit to a cruise line. They are also a benefit to the flag state. In 1995, Panama earned $47.5 million in ship-registration fees and annual taxes (five per cent of its federal budget), and another $50 million for maritime lawyers, agents and inspectors.

The Canadian government has been relatively silent on this issue. In the U.S., there have been regular calls in the U.S. Congress, and from the U.S. Coast Guard and the National Transportation Safety Board, that cruise lines operating from U.S. ports, carrying U.S. passengers, should be held to U.S. standards, regardless of where a ship is built, under what flag of convenience it is registered, and where its owners are headquartered. In addition, the ITF continues a campaign against flags of convenience on all ships, including freighters. So far, all efforts have had only limited impact.

"When I left [the] ship," a former cruise-ship bar waitress told Paul Chapman, "I finally had a phone conversation with the owner. He only laughed at me and said I was wasting his time...." The worker had called to complain about the ship's bar manager, who turned out, she told Chapman, "to be nothing but a constant source of trouble." On the second night aboard, he approached her about going to bed with him. "He was a disgusting creep," she says, "who just wouldn't leave us alone – and he was our boss. "I was very lucky that I had the money to get myself out of the rotten situation, but there are many who are not as fortunate. They have to stay and make the best of it, because they have families to support. [T]hat is the weakness which this disreputable cruise line exploits." And that is the kind of exploitation that the ITF hopes, one day, to put an end to.

NORWEGIAN CRUISE LINE JOB OPPORTUNITIES

Typical cruise ship employment entails work similar to positions in industries such as hospitality, restaurant, and entertainment. Job seekers wishing to work for Norwegian Cruise Lines may find roles in onboard casinos, restaurants, and even theaters. Customer service roles, duties as housekeepers and concierges as well as leading off-ship excursions comprise positions for which candidates may apply. Employees typically show interests in travel, pay attention to detail, display strong interpersonal skills, and work well in team environments.

Additional employment opportunities with Norwegian Cruise Lines fall into a variety of categories. In order to successfully run such a large enterprise, the cruise line company invariably needs engineers, mechanics, and technicians to service ships as well as medics, firefighters, and surveillance officers to keep passengers and crews safe. Such roles require further training, certification, and education in order to qualify for hire. Individuals looking for full-time and fulfilling employment may find careers in management readily available as well.

NORWEGIAN CRUISE LINE POSITIONS AND SALARY INFORMATION

Most positions available for entry-level workers require minimal to no hiring requirements outside of applicants standing at least 18 years of age. Additionally, job seekers must possess high school diplomas or equivalents. Perfect for seasonal workers such as individuals on school breaks, candidates may find employment in the following positions:

Guest Service Representative

Earning a starting hourly wage of around $12.50, a guest service representative works in various roles throughout the cruise ship. For instance, a guest service rep may work exclusively in the onboard casino. Employees receive inbound calls and assist with product-related questions, process reservation orders, and must maintain working knowledge of current promotions. Representatives support guest requests, including stateroom upgrades, enquiries about shipboard amenities, and any itinerary queries. Guest service reps must display exceptional interpersonal skills as well as the ability to handle high-volume calls with enthusiastic characteristics.

Surveillance Operator

A surveillance operator retains responsibility for the safety of people aboard the ship, including passengers and crew. Employees actively observe and report incidents while conducting real-time monitoring of assigned areas as well as utilize CCTV and monitoring equipment with regularity.

With salary packages starting around $11.00 an hour, a surveillance operator must maintain professional appearances at all times, work well in team environments, possess exceptional vision, and may require additional certifications before or after hire. Surveillance operators must also prove able to walk, stand, bend, twist, lift, and reach with relative continuity in order to receive hiring consideration.

Personal Cruise Consultant

Viewed as an outbound sales representative, a personal cruise consultant remains responsible for selling cruise line products and packages directly to consumers. Associates must promote products, including upgrading patrons to more luxurious packages, to prior customers and new cruisers alike. Maintaining strong client lists and rapports with regular customers, as well as in-depth knowledge of industry features, promotions, benefits, pricing, and typical itineraries, remain a must.

Previous sales experience may prove beneficial during the hiring process, though candidates with excellent verbal skills, the ability to multitask, and desire to work flexible schedules also qualify for hiring consideration. Personal cruise consultants make pay rates of $11.00 per hour.

TIPS FOR APPLYING

Norwegian Cruise Lines offers interested candidates a straightforward and relatively easy application process online via the company job portal. After registering e-mail addresses and unique passwords, applicants fill out personal information, work and education histories, and answer brief questionnaires. Job seekers may upload resumes and cover letters, as well.

As some positions prove seasonal, applicants should nail down availabilities ahead of time in order to come across more appealing to hiring personnel, if possible.

APPLICATION STATUS

Applicants may check statuses directly by logging in to view profiles on the company job portal. As the cruise line leader receives a multitude of applications for similar roles, wait times vary from a couple weeks to as long as a month. Hiring also takes place at varied times of the year, due to peak travel seasons. Contacting recruiters directly may yield little results as the company updates job statuses with frequency online.

BENEFITS OF WORKING AT NORWEGIAN CRUISE LINE

Along with seeing the world, exceptional pay rates, and various paid trainings, employees of Norwegian Cruise Lines frequently report access to work benefits packages. The cruise line company offers tuition reimbursement, service recognition programmes, and cruise discount programmes to both team members and immediately family. Additionally, eligible full-time and part-time employees cite access to medical, dental, and vision plans. A 401(k) retirement plan remains available for full-time associates in addition to paid time off for vacation, floating holidays, and sick time.

OTHER INFORMATION ABOUT NORWEGIAN CRUISE LINE

Norwegian Cruise Line partners with the Make-A-Wish Foundation to grant the wishes of children facing life-threatening medical conditions. The vacation company assists in booking the cruise and ensuring special accommodations. Tailoring each experience to the individual child, the cruise line bases wishes off the personal interests, which includes the honourary title of "Captain for the day."

THE MARITIME WORK SCHEDULE

When you work in this industry, where you are largely responsible for the navigation and upkeep of a vessel, you have to consider that working conditions and working hours might not always be ideal and to your liking. These jobs can be hazardous and require people who are detail oriented and conscientious, which is something that you have to consider before applying to work on a vessel and training at a maritime school or academy.

While some jobs require more than one member of the same position to take shifts on board, some industries only employ one of each type of crew member. This all depends on the number of hours at sea, the size and type of vessel you are working on. Your working conditions will vary greatly. On cruise ships you will have relatively good accommodation and meals and meet lots of interesting people while you work. You get to work in a more luxurious setting and the environment is also more relaxed, while on a commercial fishing vessel you are under more stress, you have to navigate through dangerous waters, make excellent time, and the environment is not exactly luxurious. The facilities mean that if you are a deckhand or in another position on the deck you have to endure storms, high winds and extreme temperatures out in the open, completely at the mercy of all the elements.

Your working hours also vary greatly especially depending on your specific job title, but all the maritime jobs from Captain to Deckhand all consist of long working hours. Aside from this, the entire crew will have to work in case of any emergency when called upon, even if it is at 3 o'clock in the morning. Some jobs have longer hours in the summer season, and some positions will consist of 24 hour shifts that rotate, so you have one day on duty, and the following day off. Each of the following positions have very diverse working hours, and completely different schedules according to the employers, size of the vessel, and the type of industry.

ENGINEERING CREW

Chief Engineer: The chief engineer usually works for 8 hours per day, but is always on call. When at sea for long periods of time the shift extends to weekends and holidays as well.

Designated Duty Engineer: This position sometimes requires you to work in 2 shifts of 4 hours each per day to perform various engine checks, but you will also work 8 to 16 hours or more 7 days per week depending on what vessel you are employed on and how long you are at sea for.

Assistant Engineers: You will work 8 or more hours in a day, working 7 days per week normally with a few days off in between, unless you are at sea, where you will work constantly for months and then receive a month or two off when you return to shore.

Engineer: The average for an engineer is 51 hours per week and this can be working in daily shifts, but also being on call.

Oiler and Wiper: These positions will be filled by more than one person usually giving you the opportunity to work in shifts of 12 hours each, although you will also be on call at all times if needed in an emergency situation.

WHEELHOUSE CREW

Master or Captain: As the leader of the entire vessel and its crew, captains are usually working full time for sometimes 3 months at sea, after which they will receive 3 months off. Sometimes masters will work very irregular hours depending on what is happening at any specific time at sea, and will rest whenever there is an opportunity.

First Mate, Chief Officer, or Chief Mate: This important job will also see you working irregular hours, but usually shifts are assigned, although you will be on call 24 hours a day. This job will also consist of sometimes 3 months at sea and then you will get 3 months leave.

Second and Third Mates: You will normally work in shifts while on board of about 12 to 16 hours per day, but are on call 24 hours a day.

Able Seaman Deckhand: There are various able seaman positions which means that shift work is offered and you can expect to be on duty for long hours, and can sometimes work for 4 to 7 days, and then get 3 days off (in a fishing environment).

Ordinary Seaman Deckhand: This position would also work in shifts of about 12 hours and you will get a certain number of days that you are on duty and then you get time off. This will normally depend on how long your time at sea is, but if you are on a cruise ship, you will still get time off after working for about 5 days, which you can spend on board, exploring ports, or you can spend them at home if possible.

Deckhands: On a commercial in-shore vessel, the deckhands can work anywhere from 5 hours to 16 hours per day and will normally get a day off during the week, especially if returning home each day. If you are based at sea, you will work for the duration you are at sea including weekends, and then you will receive a certain number of weeks or months off.

CRUISE ONBOARD CREDIT

We give you here a review of cruise deals with onboard credit included (packages, promotions, booking bonus), major cruise lines onboard credit benefits for shareholders (including on NCL, Royal Caribbean and Carnival ships) and useful tips on spending on cruise ships - what are the best "credit fun" buying options on board big cruise ships.

CRUISE ONBOARD CREDIT

Generally speking, the cruise ship onboard credit is a "cashless money" card used by passengers on the ship or on cruise lines private islands during the voyage. It's the amount you set up before sailing - a credit you can use onboard.

Most cruises operate on cashless system and each operation is done through a card (the same that you use to unlock your cabin). You can use the card to pay for services or goods you want onboard - at the end of trip you can pay the outstanding balance of the card.

Onboard credit is added to your cruise ship account. When you board the vessel, you give the line your credit card number and they open an account for you. The representative of the line will confirm your onboard credit or you will receive a card in your cabin stating you have onboard credit and its exact amount. Everything you get on cruise ships- from drinks and dinner wines, to boutique shopping and shore excursions and tours, will be accumulated on your account. You can track your scary account piling up on the TV in your cabin. If there is any dispute about your credit balance, you must take care of it before departing the ship at its Pursers Desk (usually located in the Lobby), as departing constitutes that you've agreed to the charges as listed by the line and then all will be charged to your credit card.

Why is the Cruise Ship Onboard Credit Offered?

Onboard credit on cruise ships is offered for various reasons with either cruise line packages, special and discounted deals, and often- as part of a promotion campaign by the shipping line (owner or operator) or by the travel agency. Ask the travel specialist you booked your voyage through for creative ways your onboard credit will work during your ship cruise vacation. Even if onboard credit is not offered with a package, you could ask your agent to purchase it before sailing. As a rule, pre paying for expected expenses makes the vacation more enjoyable. Does everyone in cabin get the charging privilege? Short answer - it's up to you. During check in you will determine who will have the onboard credit card charging privileges. If you don't want to use a major credit card with unlimited charging power, set up your account using cash. You may also set charging limits. Ask the line representative for all options available during check in. You can also request changes during your trip - again, at the Pursers Desk.

Cruise Deals with Onboard Credit

- Booking with a travel agent. Whether you work with a large online agency or with an individual travel agent, onboard credit is a common in the industry booking bonus. Most sites offer an average of $100 booking bonus per cabin, but this varies. The larger the agencies, the deeper their pockets concerning onboard credit. Loyalty is of great importance and if you have worked with the same agent for every cruise vacation, your shipboard credit is likely to raise over time.
- Booking by a specified deadline. $25 per cabin is the lowest average, but the amount ranges greatly. Luxury cruise lines provide onboard credit per couple of up to $1,000, and even beyond. Pay attention if the credit varies by the class of stateroom (cabin grade) and whether it's per person or per cabin.
- Booking a future cruise while on the ship. Lines do what they can to ensure their customers to sail with them again. Many ships feature a designated sales desk, with personnel educated to offer bonuses for "future cruise" bookings. Some find it the ultimate way to pick up

onboard credit for their next sailing. Celebrity offers up to $500 if you book a voyage onboard. Making a deposit towards an NCL Norwegian, you can earn $100 onboard credit to spend right on the trip you're on.

- Value-added deals. Subscribe to the e-mail list of a major line/operator, and you'll undoubtedly receive colourful promotions that will encourage you to book a vacation, with a great deal of incentives. The periodic promotions, usually the same that you can find on the line's homepage, almost always include a form of onboard credit.
- Price drops. If you notice that your fare has dropped, the line will often make up the difference through onboard credit bonus. This is kinda money back operation, but still beats paying higher fare and nothing in return.
- Referrals. Most lines boast referral bonuses for new voyages booked by first-timers. Don't just book the amazing deal yourself! Get your friends do the same and use their bookings to your onboard credit advantage. On board Royal Caribbean ships there is $25 per referred cabin booked. Princess deducts $25 as a discount, rather than offering a credit.
- Credit cards. Some of the cruise lines' credit cards (not all) allow passengers to turn their accrued points into onboard credit. This is turning cash spent into cash on their next cruise ship vacation. Return on this investment is relatively low. For example, the card of Royal Caribbean requires 10,000 points (equal to $10,000 - a point for every dollar) which is just $100 onboard credit. Have in mind that some credit cards are available only to North American residents.
- If something goes wrong. Not the best way for earning a credit, but when something goes wrong during a cruise (accident/incident, like skipping port calls, ship stranded, cruise illness outbreak, etc), or you are not pleased with the service, you may be compensated through future cruise credit offer depending on the situation.
- Loyalty programme offers. Treating return travelers well yields the return on investment. Shipboard credit is a frequent reward for loyal passengers. The more you sail, the more you'll be awarded. NCL Norwegian Latitudes Insider provides onboard credit of up to $250 on select sailings (Latitudes members only). Oceania boasts a tiered programme with $1,000 per cabin, for their most loyal customers (Diamond level).

CRUISE SHIP ON BOARD CREDIT FOR SHAREHOLDERS

Invest money in the brand if you love your cruise company. Most major lines offer shareholder benefits in the form of shipboard credit.

- Carnival Corporation (including Carnival, Costa, Cunard, Holland America, Princess, Aida, Seabourn, P and O and Ibero) offers up to $250 onboard credit per cabin for voyages 14 days/longer, $100 for cruises of 7-13 days, and $50 for sailings 6 days or less.
- RCCL - their brands (Azamara, Celebrity, CDF, Pullmantur and the largest Royal Caribbean) offer a similar to Carnival benefit, with $200 per cabin for voyages between 10-13 nights. $100 is offered on voyages of 6-9 nights, $50 for sailings less than 5 nights.
- NCL Norwegian has an offer of $100 onboard credit per cabin available to shareholders cruising 7 or more days, and $50 for voyages 6 days or less.

Remember to check the fine print and make sure you are eligible, as sometimes there are minimum share/stock requirements. Redeem your stockholder benefit and contact the line at least 2 weeks prior to sailing.

CRUISE SHAREHOLDER CREDIT BENEFITS

Travelers owning at least 100 shares of stock in CCL (Carnival Corporation) or RCL (Royal Caribbean) can receive onboard credits up to $250 during their next cruise vacation.

- *Azamara Cruises, Celebrity Cruises, Royal Caribbean Ltd., Royal Caribbean International:* Onboard credit is provided to shareholders who directly own (at time of booking) at least 100 shares of Royal Caribbean Cruises Ltd. To take advantage of this offer, the following items must be submitted:
- Name
- Home address, telephone number, e-mail address
- Ship and sailing date
- Confirmation number
- Crown and Anchor Society/Captain's Club number (if any)
- A photocopy of the shareholder proxy card or current brokerage statement that shows proof of ownership of a minimum of 100 Royal Caribbean Cruises Ltd. shares.
- *Carnival Corporation, Carnival Cruise Lines, Costa Cruises, Cunard Line, Holland America, Princess Cruises, Seabourn, Windstar:* Onboard credit is available to shareholders who hold at least 100 shares of Carnival Plc or Carnival Corporation. Tour conductors, travel agents cruising at discounted rates, employees or anyone traveling on reduced rates are excluded from the offer. The benefit isn't transferable and not combinable with other shipboard offer. It can't be used for casino charges/credits and gratuities that are charged to your onboard account. One onboard credit is allowed per shareholder-occupied cabin. Shareholders have to provide the following info to

the travel agent together with their initial deposit:

- Name
- Ship and sailing date
- Reservation number
- Proof of ownership of Carnival plc or Carnival Corporation shares (shareholder proxy card's photocopy, shares certificate, nominee statement, or current brokerage).

Onboard "Credit Money" Spending on Cruise Ships

Onboard credit is actually virtual cash. And there are few places onboard the cruise ship where you cannot spend it (though these vary by line). Ask line's representative about any onboard restrictions. Following are the most popular ways to spend the shipboard credit money on cruise ships:

- Specialty Restaurants. Ships continuously add new alternative dining venues. Your credit may be better than any specialty dining package, because these certificates are usually limited to specific restaurants. Use your own account to ensure that you choose the venues.
- A la carte items. There are a large variety of complimentary offerings onboard cruise ships. The unique treats at sea are fun but full of added fees. Use your onboard credit to forgo the buffet for Ben and Jerry's or regular for specialty coffee.
- Drinks. Alcoholic beverages are seldom found free of charge, unless you're cruising with a luxury line. Alcohol packages are a good deal, but if you need just a couple of beers, using shipboard credit is a better way.
- Shore Excursions. A significant (but pricey) part of cruise experiences are shore excursions. Applying your onboard credit to excursions provides a free way to embark on special shore experiences.
- Private islands. Onboard account applies to all purchases made when you make a port call to your line's private island (Cococay or Labadee with Royal Caribbean). This includes private cabana reservation.
- Spa Treatments. Onboard credit for spa applies to anything on the treatment menu - the list could be a long one. Wrapping in seaweed, painting nails purple, getting a trim for formal night. Onboard credit allows you to pamper with no need to have deep pockets.
- Photos. A formal night portrait is always in the gallery of every cruising family. Onboard credit can turn the photographer into your personal paparazzi, immortalizing you for generations to come.
- Souvenirs. Onboard credit is like a gift card, applicable to most purchases onboard. Designer stores make their appearance at sea, and why should you wait to buy the item you have always wanted? Buy it in the middle of ocean, and make any purchase memorable.

- Casino play. Casinos on some lines are off-limits if it comes to shipboard credit. Before hitting the slots, check if your cruise company allows it. The casino could double your onboard credit easily, or... lose it all. At least you'll have fun.
- Gratuities. Cruisers have to budget for onboard gratuities, unless they book an offer with prepaid service charge. Using shipboard credit for tips is not allowed on all lines, so check before the voyage in order to plan accordingly.
- Internet packages. Some travellers are terrified by the idea to be out of touch during their vacation. If you need to stay connected, Internet at sea is much expensive and difficult undertaking, but however, speed continues to improve. So, why don't you use your onboard credit and share some photos with an umbrella cocktail in hand?

If you have remaining onboard credit at the end of voyage, it's applied to your charge account. And in case there is still credit left (which is extremely unlikely), then you lose credit and you can't get the left over shipboard credit back as cash - it's a "use it or lose it".

CELEBRATE ON A CARNIVAL CRUISE

It's time to celebrate! What better reason to go on a cruise than for a special occasion or celebration. Each week thousands of guests are celebrating a wedding, birthday, anniversary, graduation, honeymoon, engagement, retirement or other special occasion onboard one of Carnival's "Fun Ships." The party can always be exciting whether it is planned months in advance or just spontaneously happens while sailing.

What's the secret to a good celebration on board? Simple, just let us know about your special event!

If you are cruising and know you would like to plan a celebration there are several options available for you. Contact your vacation planner and explore the possibilities. The opportunities are endless, from booking out a lounge with an open bar and hot and cold party food, to surprising someone with our stateroom decorations. Your vacation planner will help you set up the best night possible with all the trimmings. The more you would like to do or have, the more advanced planning is recommended; as there may be lounges that need to be booked or special flowers to order and we want to make sure everything is set and in place before you sail. However, there are also an onboard staff members and concessions onboard to actually cater to all of your last minute needs as well.

Formalities (or celebrations on the Carnival Dream) are great assets to cruising. You may order stateroom decorations, specialty cakes, champagne and strawberries, or simply surprise someone with a bouquet of flowers and sweets. We can also book parties onboard provided the lounge space is available (pre-booking recommended) for your special occasion. Everyone has a different celebration in mind but no matter how different the occasion our goal is the same… to make everyone feel special.

As a Cruise Director, I have been asked to participate in the "surprise" planning of many events and I always have a great time doing so. The best part of my job is seeing someone's face as they realize this is their memorable experience while feeling like the most special person onboard. I love planning engagements and helping someone literally, change their life.

So as an onboard expert – here are a few of my helpful hints:

1. Let us know before you go. We need the details (who, what, when, and how many people you are attending). Then we can help you decide if you want to have a big group event or a little quiet rendezvous.
2. Take the extra step onboard. Contact someone onboard who may be able to help with the small (but most precious) details. It's always good to see what the formalities shop has available and if the ship's Group Coordinator or Cruise Director may have any suggestions for the perfect touch.
3. While onboard check the ship's itinerary or Fun Time activities. This allows you to have plan your special event around a great activity happening on the day of your celebration. Deciding to celebrate on a "Cruise Elegant" night vs a "Cruise Casual" night, or even a daytime celebration will have vastly different atmospheres.
4. Take advantage of the ships luxuries. Most ships have a Steakhouse for fine dining and intimate experiences. Check into the couples spa packages or individual indulgences, plan a surprise appearance on the big screen during one of the live TV Shows or deck parties, or simply find out the best place on the ship to enjoy a peaceful sunset.

Whatever the occasion we know how special your day (or week) is to you and we are here to help. When you choose to cruise you choose a special kind of FUN experience. Get excited, please don't be shy and most importantly let us know all the details. We will do our best to help you plan and let you know what to expect, so the only person surprised is the "guest of honour."

ENGAGEMENT CELEBRATION VENUE

Celebrate your special announcement with opulent river views

You've said "yes", now you need to celebrate the big news with a fun and fabulous engagement party! As you and your special someone start planning your life together, start the celebration with a river cruise onboard The Crystal Swan.

You've said "yes", now you need to celebrate the big news with a fun and fabulous engagement party! As you and your special someone start planning your life together, start the celebration with a river cruise onboard The Crystal Swan.

Our friendly staff will ensure the details are perfect, from decorating the vessel in your chosen theme through to the final touches that represent you and your beloved best. We will help set the scene for a brilliant party that will surely stand out in everyone's memory so you can share the engagement excitement surrounded by those you love!

Combining the Luxury of a Quality Functions Venue with the Uniqueness of a River Cruise

The Iconic Crystal Swan is the only cruising vessel/venue that offers:

- Gourmet food and beverages
- Exceptional stability to ensure a smooth ride
- Fully enclosed temperature control for year round comfort
- Stunning 360 degree panoramic views of the City Skyline
- Professional and friendly crew add to your cruising experience
- Central city location

ENGAGEMENT RINGS AND WEDDING BELLS

Wedding season is fast approaching, and for those of you in need of inspiration, we want to help you dream up your perfect romantic occasion. It might be the most important decision you'll ever make, so allow us to help you show your loved one how much you really care.

ENGAGEMENT

Life's most important moments need celebrations that are unique. You may have been planning to ask this question for months, so how do you make sure that it's the perfect moment? Sometimes, it's good to keep things classic, and there's no better way to pop the question than over a beautiful meal.

Restaurants such as Murano serve up exquisite food in a sophisticated and intimate setting, so you can enjoy beautifully-crafted dishes with your new fiancé. Alternatively, why not enjoy a personal meal in your own luxury suite, and relish a champagne dinner together, delivered to your room by your very own butler.

Celebrity Weddings

A Celebrity holiday gives you the unique opportunity to combine your ceremony with the honeymoon of a lifetime. With itineraries covering some of the world's most desirable destinations, such as the Mediterranean, you can plan the perfect trip to complement your wedding.

Prepare to explore the stunning culture and gastronomy of Athens, or go trekking through the expansive rainforests of Singapore. Perhaps finish your trip in somewhere like Hawaii, and take a helicopter ride over Kauai before spending the days relaxing with your partner on an idyllic beach.

We're dedicated to ensuring your wedding runs smoothly, from flower-adorned ceremonies on our sun-kissedlawn club, to dazzling winter displays creating the picture-perfect festive wedding. Your personal event manager will be on hand to answer your questions at any time during the planning stage, so you'll have the support you need to plan your flawless wedding day.

Bridesmaids and Bachelors

If you're preparing bridesmaids celebrations, take a look at our bridesmaid tea party, where you can enjoy a range of delicious cakes, pastries and speciality teas with your closest friends, to say thank you. For the gentlemen's celebration, a cigar and cognac party offers a range of speciality cigars and a premium bar, the ideal extravagance for you and your best men.

For further indulgence, try a food and wine tasting for the chance to taste pure excellence whilst about food and wine pairings from around the world. If you have a discerning taste and wish to expand your knowledge of fine wines, the Riedel Comparative Wine Crystal Workshop uses the knowledge of sommeliers to explore the natural complexities of various wines from the world over.

Fine Jewellery

With so much choice, it can be overwhelming to choose the perfect piece of jewellery for that special person in your life. Whether you're buying a tasteful watch from TAG Heuer or Breitling, or a stunning accessory from Versace, our luxury shopping arcades hold some beautiful pieces, ideal for a tasteful but gallant romantic gesture.

Bvlgari

Founded in 1884, Bvlgari is a trendsetter and market leader in fine jewellery. With their headquarters based in Rome, they create beautiful, intricate pieces that couple the contemporary and traditional, in perfect harmony. Over time, Bvlgari's designs have shaped the way with which Italian jewellery has been created, and their signature large, bold pieces have become a trait of many other luxury Italian jewellers.

Omega

You may know Omega for their range of fine watches, but their jewellery is equally admirable, boasting clean lines and a sleek, contemporary style. One of their most timeless collections, Constellation was born over 30 years ago, and the collection's use of red and white gold has become one of Omega's most emblematic looks.

ONBOARD CREDIT: HOW TO GET IT, WHERE TO SPEND IT

Free. Money. Are there two more beautiful words in the English language? While money doesn't grow on trees, increasingly it can be found somewhere else — on the high seas. Call it an incentive, call it a bonus; whatever you want to call it, onboard credit lets you spend more freely with less guilt. You've paid your cruise fare, and now you can splurge on those enticing extras — Swedish massage, specialty restaurant, an excursion to swim with the dolphins — without busting your budget.

Not many need convincing as to why onboard credit — money automatically deposited into your onboard account— rocks, but finding out exactly how to get it and where you can spend it is a bit trickier. We found eight ways to hit the OBC jackpot (some more preferable than others) and offer even more suggestions on how to burn through it, although you probably have your own ideas already.

HOW TO GET IT

Value-Added Deals

If you've subscribe to the e-mail list of any major cruise line, you have undoubtedly received colourful promotions encouraging you to book your next cruise, with a number of incentives. These periodic promotions, which are usually the same ones you can find on the homepage of the cruise line's web site, almost always include some form of onboard credit. You can receive OBC just for booking by a specified deadline. The lowest average we've seen is $25 per cabin, for an inside cabin, but the amount can range greatly. For a luxury line, onboard credit offers can extend to $1,000 per couple and beyond. Pay attention to whether the credit varies by cabin class and whether it's a per-person amount or per cabin. Amounts are often staggered by cabin category.

Booking With Travel Agencies

Whether you work with an individual travel agent or a large online agency, onboard credit is a booking bonus common in the industry. Most third-party sites offer an average of $100 per cabin as a booking bonus, but again, this varies. The larger the agency, the deeper their pockets when it comes to onboard credit. Loyalty is noticed; if you've worked with the same travel agent for every cruise, your OBC amount is likely to build over time.

Booking a Future Cruise While on a Cruise

While they have you onboard, cruise lines will do what they can to ensure you'll sail with them again. To lure cruisers who are on the fence, many lines have designated sales desks onboard their ships, with personnel available to offer you something to make a future cruise worth your while.

Many vouch that this is the ultimate way to rack up onboard credit for that next sailing. Celebrity Cruises offers up to $500 per cabin when you book your next cruise onboard. If you make a deposit towards a future cruise on Norwegian, you earn $100 in onboard credit to spend instantly on the cruise you're already on.

Loyalty Programme Offers

Loyalty is key to cruise lines. While first-timers are a booming market, return cruisers are more than just bodies on a ship; they're brand ambassadors. From a business perspective, treating your loyal passengers well yields return on investment. That's why onboard credit is one of the frequent rewards for continued patronage. The more you sail, the more perks you'll likely be awarded. Oceania has a tiered programme, maxing out at $1,000 per cabin, for its most loyal cruisers (Diamond level). Norwegian's Latitudes Insider Offers is a promotion that doles out onboard credit up to $250 on select sailings to Latitudes members only.

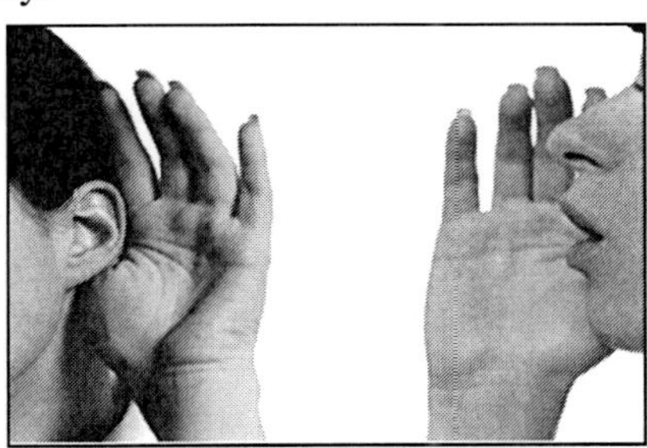

Referrals

Spreading the good word isn't a thankless endeavor. Most cruise lines offer referral bonuses for new cruises booked by first-timers. So don't just book that amazing cruise deal yourself; get your skeptical friends to do the same, and use their bookings to your OBC advantage. The amount tends to be $25 per every referred cabin booked; this is the case onboard Royal Caribbean. Princess, on the other hand, deducts $25 in the form of a discount, rather than offering it as credit.

Credit Cards

Some cruise line credit cards (but not all) allow you to turn your accrued points into onboard credit, turning cash spent into cash made on your next cruise vacation. The return on investment is relatively low with this method. Royal Caribbean's card requires 10,000 points (or $10,000, one point for every dollar) to equal just $100 in onboard credit.

Price Drops

You've booked and paid for your cruise, but you're still in the window of opportunity for the upgrade fairy to come knocking. If you notice that your cruise fare has dropped, many times the line will make up the difference through an onboard credit offer (within the 90-day window). This form of OBC is money back, rather than money gifted, but it still beats paying a higher cruise fare with nothing in return.

Become a Shareholder

If you love your cruise company enough to invest money in the brand, most major cruise lines offer a shareholder benefit in the form of onboard credit. Carnival Corporation (which includes Carnival, Princess, Holland America, Seabourn, Cunard, Costa, Aida, Ibero and P and O) offers up to $250 per cabin for cruises 14 days or longer, $100 for sailings of seven to 13 days and $50 per cabin for sailings six days or less. Royal Caribbean Cruises Ltd. (Royal, Celebrity, Azamara, Pullmantur and Croiseres de France) offers a similar benefit to Carnival, with $200 per cabin for cruises 10 to 13 nights, $100 offered on cruises six to nine nights, and $50 for cruises less than five nights. Norwegian Cruise Line has a cut-and-dry offer of $100 in onboard credit per cabin for shareholders cruising seven days or more, and $50 per cabin for cruises six days or less. Check the fine print to make sure you're eligible (sometimes there are minimum share requirements) and redeem your benefit by contacting the line at least two weeks prior to your sail date.

When Something Goes Wrong

It's not the best way to earn credit, but if something goes wrong on your cruise — ship is stranded, misses port calls, experiences a significant malfunction, or you're just generally not pleased with the service — one of the ways you may be compensated is through a future credit offer. The amount will vary depending on the situation.

WHERE TO SPEND IT

Think of your onboard credit as virtual cash, as there are very few places onboard where you can'tspend it (although these do vary by cruise line). It's always a safe bet to check the fine print or ask a cruise line representative about any OBC restrictions prior to that shopping spree. Here are the ways this credit might come in handy.

Shore Excursions

A pricey but significant part of many cruisers' experiences in port is shore excursions. While it might blow your credit out of the water, applying OBC to an excursion offers a free or discounted way to embark on a special shore experience.

Specialty Restaurants

Ships continue to add more alternative dining venues, and with the variety come cover charges galore. Avoid shelling out more clams for curated cuisine by using your onboard credit to dine where you like, without paying a dime more. In fact, your credit may be a better deal than a specialty dining package, as these certificates are often limited to specific restaurants. Using your own account ensures you choose the venues.

Spa Treatments

Many of us don't have the time or money to indulge in a little bit of me-time on a regular basis, but isn't that what a cruise is for? Onboard credit in the spa usually applies to anything on their treatment menu, and that list could be a long one. So wrap yourself in seaweed, paint your nails purple, or get a trim and a hot shave for formal night. OBC means you don't need deep pockets to pamper yourself.

Drinks

Unless you're cruising with a river or luxury line, alcoholic beverages are rarely found free of charge (not counting the Champagne during art auctions, of course). Sure, alcohol packages shave spending off your libations, but if you only need a couple of beers or one or two premium cocktails, using OBC is a better way to drink for free (and who doesn't love that?). Trying that cucumber-gin concoction or settling for an entire flight of rum will require fewer apologies to your wallet if you know that money is just the garnish atop your onboard account.

A la Carte Items

Sure there are still plenty of complimentary offerings onboard, but it's always what's not included that calls to us: Sometimes frozen yogurt just isn't as sweet as the gourmet gelato. The availability of unique treats at sea — a Starbucks latte or cupcakes the size of your head — is fun but fraught with added fees. Instead of feeling that dreaded nickeled-and-dimed sensation, use OBC as an excuse to forego regular for specialty coffees, or the buffet for Ben and Jerry's.

Private Islands

Just because you're on land, doesn't mean your OBC is null and void. If you're making a port call to your cruise line's private island — for example,

Labadee or Cococay with Royal Caribbean — then your onboard account applies to any purchases made there. This includes the reservation of a private cabana.

Souvenirs

Like a gift card, OBC is applicable to most onboard purchases, from a commemorative model ship to that toothbrush you managed to forget. Designer stores are making an appearance at sea, thanks to more brand partnerships. Why wait to buy the iPod or Coach bag you've always wanted? Buy them in the middle of the ocean, and make the purchase memorable.

Professional Photos

A long-held cruise tradition, formal night portraits are a staple in the gallery of every cruising family's home. If you've ever forked over for a family portrait on land, you know the endeavor isn't cheap. Onboard credit can be used to turn the onboard photographer into your own personal paparazzi, immortalizing your airbrushed physique for generations to come.

Internet Packages

Some long to be out of touch on vacation, and some are terrified by the idea. If you find the need to connect, Internet at sea has long been an expensive and rather difficult undertaking. As speed and bandwidth continue to improve, pricing remains a challenge. Use your nifty onboard credit to share photos of you with pina colada in hand.

Casino Play

What could be better than gambling with your own money? Gambling with someone else's money! On some lines, casinos are off-limits when it comes to onboard credit, so check if your line allows it before you hit the slots. That said, the casino could easily double your OBC with the help of Lady Luck — or lose it all, but at least you had fun, right?

Gratuities

Cruisers must also budget for gratuities, unless they booked an offer that has the service charge already prepaid. Again, using onboard credit for tips isn't allowed on all lines; check before the start of your cruise so you can plan accordingly.

COST-SAVING TIPS FOR A PRINCESS CRUISE

Consider booking your shore excursion with a third-party company that has an online presence.

A relatively small, 17-ship cruise line that prides itself on innovation — it debuted on TV's "The Love Boat," after all — Princess is part of the Carnival Cruise lines brand but caters to a more discerning crowd. Whether you book on board, late, early or somewhere in between, you can find a way to save on a stateroom, then use the balance for that important shore excursion or spa day.

Reposition Yourself

If your travel schedule is flexible and you do not mind a one-way cruise, consider taking a Princess repositioning cruise, a sailing that occurs when a ship changes ports for the season. Unlike other cruise lines, Princess does not list repositioning cruises on its web site's destination tab, which makes finding them tricky but not impossible with a little research. Look for one-way sailings that are offered just once a year. Princess repositioning cruises also tend to spend more time at sea, but when you consider the savings — up to 75 percent — the extra time at sea may be worth it. When budgeting for a repositioning cruise, make sure to add in the cost of flying home.

On Board with Savings

The cost of onboard perks, such as alcohol, spa days and casino nights, can really add up on a cruise. And when you combine these extras with the automatic gratuities for your steward and wait staff, the cost you pay at disembarkation may exceed what you paid for the cruise itself. Before setting sail, determine a daily budget for your onboard spending — including gratuities — and stick to it. If you're traveling on a tight budget, ditch the dining room for the buffet at dinner, which will save you on gratuities. Instead of purchasing an expensive bottle of wine at dinner, bring a bottle of your own. Princess permits one bottle of wine or champagne per person at embarkation, and your steward can provide the ice bucket.

One of the costliest Princess perks is the pickup laundry service, which can exceed hundreds of dollars for a few loads. Instead, do your own laundry in small batches with a small bottle of travel wash and dry your items on the clothes line in the shower.

When (and When Not) to Book an Excursion

Booking a shore excursion through Princess, while almost always more expensive than third-party excursions, is hard to pass up. Princess excursions come with the guarantee that the ship won't leave without you, and many travelers are wary of dockside, last-minute dealings. That said, many third-party companies are reputable, reliable and even offer the guarantee to return you to the ship on time. Book online before the cruise embarks and only with accredited companies that publish personal, recent reviews.

Book With a View

The next time you're traveling on a Princess cruise, consider booking your next trip from the comfort of your stateroom. Booking your next cruise at sea means a lower cruise deposit for any future cruise, and if you change your mind back on land, you can get a full refund. Princess also offers lower "book at sea" rates for Captain's Circle members.

Book Late

If you're a flexible traveler looking for a last-minute deal, Princess offers discounts on upcoming cruises within a four-month departure, with lower prices for cruises that sail within one or two weeks. You can find these deals through a link on the home page of the Princess web site.

Keep It on the Inside

An interior stateroom is the cheapest option on a Princess cruise, but the location of your stateroom is also key. If seasickness is not an issue, ask your travel agent for the lowest-category interior room, which is often on a higher deck in the stern of the ship. You may feel the ship sway on high-sea days, but for some this is an enjoyable, and even relaxing, part of the cruise experience.

Calling on Military Cruisers

Princess offers a substantial on-board credit for active and retired military personnel. You can use this credit on any Princess cruise itinerary. Keep in mind you'll need to apply for the credit 14 days before departure.

SAIL AND SIGN ONBOARD ACCOUNT

Sail and Sign is Carnival's cashless on board credit programme, which allows guests to charge on board purchases and gratuities directly to a personal account for convenience throughout the cruise. The Sail and Sign Card must be utilized for all money transactions on board as cash will not be an accepted form of payment. Personalized Sail and Sign cards will be provided to all guests (including minors) and are valid for use immediately upon boarding the ship.

Guest Services can provide guests with a balance update at any time throughout the cruise. In addition, guests can view their balance update at a Sail and Sign Kiosk or on their stateroom interactive television (in most ships but excluding Carnival Ecstasy, Carnival Elation, Carnival Fantasy, Carnival Fascination, Carnival Imagination, Carnival Inspiration, Carnival Paradise, Carnival Sensation and Carnival Sunshine).

On the final morning of the cruise, a statement detailing all purchases made with the Sail and Sign card will be delivered to the guest's stateroom. In our ongoing green efforts, the following ships will no longer deliver statements to the staterooms: Carnival Glory, Carnival Imagination and Carnival Magic; guests can view their statements at a Sail and Sign Kiosk, at Guest Services or on their stateroom interactive television.

Sail and Sign Accounts Opened with Cash or Traveler's Checks

- Guests may activate their Sail and Sign account on Carnival.com, My Cruise Manager - Online Check-In or on the first day of the cruise at embarkation.
- Guests must deposit cash (U.S currency) or Traveler's Checks at Guest Services on the first day of the cruise. The following minimum cash deposits are recommended:
  - 2 - 4 day cruise: $100 USD per person
  - 5 - 8 day cruise: $200 USD per person
  - 9 days or longer: $350 USD per person

Sail and Sign Accounts Opened with a Credit Card or Debit Card

- Guests may activate their Sail and Sign account on Carnival.com, My Cruise Manager - Online Check-In or on the first day of the cruise at embarkation.

- The guest's credit card or debit card will be swiped at embarkation with an initial hold placed on file as a deposit:
  - *2 - 5 day cruise:* $100 USD per credit card or debit card
  - *6 days or longer:* $200 USD per credit card or debit card
- Throughout the cruise, additional holds will be obtained as needed when the Sail and Sign Account exceeds the amount of deposit Carnival has on file.
- If a credit card is presented, this will reduce the amount available on the credit card for other purchases.
- If a debit/check-cashing card is presented, the hold will restrict the available cash in the checking account.
- Any remaining hold after the end of the cruise will automatically be released by the guest's issuing bank within a time period determined by the bank.
- If the guest replaces a credit/debit card previously used, the hold will remain on the account. This will reduce the amount of funds available on the credit/debit card account. The release of this/these hold(s) is entirely up to the issuing bank and can take from 3 to 7 business days after the cruise returns for the funds to be released.
- All charges will automatically be billed to the guest's credit card at the end of the voyage. The total amount will be applied to the credit card presented during registration.

Acceptable Cards

- Visa Card and Visa Gift Card
- MasterCard and MasterCard Gift Card
- An ATM/Debit Cashing Card may be used as long as it is a registered MasterCard or Visa Card.
- The Discover Card and Discover Gift Card
- American Express Card only
- Diner's Club and Diner's Club Gift Card
- JCB Card only

Note: Gift Cards may also be referred to as 'secured' or 'pre-loaded' credit cards or 'Travel Funds Card'.

Not Acceptable Cards

- Gift Cards and Travel Funds Cards issued by: American Express; Optima
- Keychain (mini) credit cards
- The American Express 'Persona Select'
- ATM/Debit Cashing Card other than those registered by MasterCard or Visa Card.

Use of a Credit Card by a Third Party

We accept credit cards belonging to a non-sailing individual. During the online check-in process, an authorization form is provided for guests who will be using a credit card belonging to an individual who is not on the cruise. This form will need to be filled out and printed.

At embarkation, the guest will need to present:

- The completed 'Letter of Authorization for Use of a Credit Card by Third Party/Guest' – the signature on the letter of authorization must match the signature on the back of the credit card.
- A legible copy of the non-sailing individual's credit card with signature (both sides – front and back). It is not required for the guest to carry the physical credit card with them onboard.
- A legible copy of the non-sailing individual's government issued photo ID with signature (example: Driver's License)

General Information

- Any enquiries regarding a Sail and Sign Account made after the cruise need to be referred to Guest Care (70530) for researching.
- The cardholding guest must be an authorized signer by the card-issuing bank.
- Each onboard expense account must have a designated account owner.
- The account owner may choose to authorize additional guests from his/her booking and guests in up to two other traveling staterooms. A guest may only be activated on one account.
- Every guest must be a member of an account in order to obtain a complete Online Check-In status.
- Account owners must be at least 18 years of age at the time of sailing and will be automatically assigned charging privileges to the account.
- Minors must have an account, but the account owner has the option not to allow charging privileges to their account.
- Cruise Service Gratuities will be charged to the account unless they are prepaid.
- The amount charged to the account for service gratuities will be deemed undisputed unless a request to modify is received prior to disembarking the ship. In addition, a 15 per cent beverage gratuity will be added to all beverage purchases.
- If the credit/debit card method of payment is selected, charges incurred by those authorized will be billed to the credit/debit account entered.
- Actual credit/debit cards must be present at the time of embarkation.
- The cardholder is responsible for amended charges discovered after the authorized guest (s) disembark vessel.

- Carnival will not be held responsible for any bank imposed overage or insufficient funds charges on debit/check cashing cards or credit cards.

Sail and Sign Refundable Overages

Refundable overages on a guest's Sail and Sign account will be refunded back in the same form of payment as was made for the initial deposit on the Sail and Sign account.

- *Credit Card:* If the guest uses a credit card for their Sail and Sign deposit, any refundable overages will be credited back to the original credit card account.
- *Debit Card:* if the guest uses a bank debit card for their Sail and Sign deposit, any refundable overages will be credited back to the original debit card account.
- *Carnival Gift Card:* If the guest uses a Carnival Gift Card for their Sail and Sign deposit, any refundable overages will be refunded in the form of a new Carnival Gift Card.
- *Cash Deposits:* If the guest uses cash for their Sail and Sign deposit, any refundable overages greater than $10 USD will be refunded via check mailed within 7 days after the cruise to the guest's home address on file. Overages less than $10 USD will be donated to St. Jude's Children's Hospital (excluding the Carnival Spirit and Carnival Legend in Australia). If a guest wishes to have the full overage in cash, they may retrieve it from one of the Sail and Sign Kiosks or the Guest Services Team. The refund checks will be reconciled by our shore side Refund Accounting team and distributed via PNC Bank (JPM Chase Bank for Carnival Spirit Australia guests).

4

The Cruise Industry: Hospitality and Travel

Cruising is hot, hot, hot, and not just when the weather turns sultry. Passenger loads have grown from a mere 500,000 in 1970 to 12.5 million in 2007 and an estimated 12.8 million in 2008. More than 80 ocean-going cruise lines with over 250 ships now visit some 2,000 destinations, and guests can choose from over 30,000 different cruises each year. Bookings have been expanding by 7.4 percent annually since 1990, the fastest growth rate in the hospitality industry.

Yet it has not all been clear sailing for the cruise sector. In 2001, some 10 million people booked passage on the world's cruise lines. The terrorist attacks of September 11 slashed that demand. In the following weeks, no fewer than seven ocean-going lines and one river cruise line either went out of business or filed for bankruptcy protection. Drastic price cuts brought business back—in the first half of 2002, ticket sales actually were up 4.3 percent over the previous year—but the discounts decimated profit.

The cruise industry entered a similar period late in 2008, when the worst chaos since the Great Depression struck the world's economies. As a luxury segment of the travel market, the cruises used to be relatively resistant to economic downturns; even in bad times, the rich can usually afford a vacation. Today, an easy majority of passengers are middle class, and they are not about to take a cruise when barely making ends meet and terrified that the next round of pink slips may put them out on the street. In December 2008, when it had become clear that the current recession was not just a minor downturn, Carnival Corporation reported that cruise bookings were running behind their pace a year earlier, even though prices were down.

That has changed dramatically, thanks to some of the most persuasive sales incentives the cruiselines have ever offered. Among the deals bringing timid consumers back to the ship: Carnival is offering discounts of up to 25 percent for bookings made up to three months in advance for cruises of up to five days and five months in advance for longer excursions.

On the Disney Wonder, passengers under 12 sail free for three-day voyages between March 12 and May 28. Holland America is offering low fares, 50 percent discounts on deposits and cruise tours, and 25 percent of the standard cancellation protection plan.

Seabourn is giving discounts of $1,000 per suite on top of early booking savings of up to 50 percent on all seven-day Mediterranean cruises in 2009, $1,500 per suite plus early booking savings of up to 45 percent on northern Europe/Scandinavia cruises, and a host of other incentives.

All this has been remarkably successful, given the state of the American economy. January 12, 2009, was the best booking day ever for Princess Cruises, with volume up 17 percent over the previous best. Expedia CruiseShipCenters reported that bookings made in January 2008 were ahead of the previous January by 14 percent. That money-saving "staycation" does not look so good when a cruise hardly costs any more.

However, the industry is not out of trouble yet. All these discounts are eroding profitability, and even they may not be enough to bring passengers onboard if the recession gets much deeper. In addition, capacity is rising faster than demand is likely to; at least 36 new cruise liners are scheduled for delivery between 2008 and 2012, with several more planned but not yet in the yards.

All this brings up obvious questions: How bad will the slump be? How long will it take the cruise industry to recover? How long will cruise prices remain depressed? How can cruise operators turn slow-growing demand into solid profits? How can they adapt to the challenges of a fast-changing world? We have some ideas. Here is how the most important forces affecting the cruise lines will play out:

U.S. ECONOMY

Nothing is as important to the cruise industry as the American economy. No less than 80 percent of cruise tickets are sold to Americans. One recent study found that only 20 percent of Americans have taken a cruise, but half dream of doing so. According to the Cruise Line International Association's (CLIA) 2008 Cruise Market Profile, some 51 million hoped to make that dream a reality between 2008 and 2010. Many of these potential customers may at least consider taking a cruise when they feel economically secure. But in bad economic times, the American cruise market shrinks, and it takes radical price cuts and other inducements to fill berths.

In early 2009, consumers are still afraid. They have reason to be. GDP shrank by 3.8 percent in the fourth quarter of 2008, and most analysts expect it to keep heading down for at least two more quarters. Home prices slid 12 percent in the last three months of 2008, the biggest drop on record; they were down again in January 2009. More than 100,000 homes were in foreclosure in the first month of the year. Employment numbers were even more terrifying. Employers cut nearly 600,000 jobs in January, bringing unemployment to 7.6 percent, the highest it had been in more than 16 years. Most forecasts say that it will reach double digits before the hemorrhaging stops. And if many working-class Americans think the economy feels worse than it sounds, they have good reason. If unemployment were still calculated as it was in the 1980s, the rate would already be about 17 percent.

The economic problems we expect to continue through much of 2009 and the slowness of the likely recovery thereafter will keep both prices and profits down until well into 2010. So this comes as good news: The current economic collapse should not last as long as many observers feared. In mid-February 2009, we believe that the economy will begin a new period of expansion before the end of the year. Growth will be slow at first, but by 2010 GDP growth should return to the area 2.5 to 3 percent, where it will remain for at least the next few years. This is important news for cruise lines whose potential customers have been finding it hard to commit themselves to a cruise vacation with steep discounts and other profit-killing incentives. This is one case where a rising tide floats all cruise ships.

Do note, however, that this analysis presumes that the Obama administration will follow its recently enacted stimulus plan with at least one more round of government spending and a much larger programme to stabilize and reform the American banking system. If the federal government does not find some way to employ several million people lost from other sectors of the economy and get the credit system working again, the downturn could be much longer, the dip in the cruise market more lasting and severe.

AGING POPULATION

Throughout the developed world, people are living longer and, on average, growing older. (Demographically, one does not necessarily imply the other.) Life expectancy in Australia, Japan, and Switzerland is now over 75 years for men and over 80 for women. In the United States, every generation has lived three years longer than the previous one. An 80-year-old in 1950 could expect 6.5 more years of life; today's 80-year-olds are likely to survive 8.5 more years.

As a result, and because birthrates are declining throughout most of the industrialized world, older people now make up more of the population than they used to. Their numbers will continue to grow. People over 65 were only 8 percent of the population in the developed world in 1950, but 15 percent in 2000, and will grow to 27 percent in the next half century, according to the Center for Strategic and International Studies. In Germany, people of retirement age will climb from under 16 percent of the population in 2000 to nearly 19 percent in 2010 and 31 percent in 2050. Japan's over-65 population, 17 percent of the total in 2000, will reach 22 percent in 2010 and nearly 37 percent in 2050.

This is important because older people are now the wealthiest segment of society, and the most likely to have the time for an extended cruise. According to the 2008 Market Profile Study conducted by the Cruise Line International Association, about 24 percent of Baby Boomers, now in their peak earning years, have taken at least one cruise, compared with only 19 percent in the over-60 group. However, well-to-do seniors generally take the longest and most luxurious cruises. Unlike younger, family- and budget-minded passengers, they tend to prefer smaller ships, giving up tennis courts and ping pong tables in return for all-out pampering. As the giant Baby Boom generation ages, the upper end of the cruise market can only grow rapidly.

The growth of the over-65 market will moderate the habitual seasonality of tourism, because retirees can travel off-season, and prefer to do so when it can save them some money. This should help to even out the cash flow of cruise operators. To serve these demanding customers, some cruise lines have adapted their ships to the needs of older passengers. Others should follow their lead. Obvious features for the elderly include safety handholds in bathrooms and showers, larger signs with easy-to-read type, and large, levered door handles for arthritic hands. Older cruisers also need special services such as help in moving their belongings and information about the physical demands of side trips. Such amenities will be increasingly important in the years ahead.

TOURISM GROWS

The number of Americans traveling to foreign countries (excluding Canada and Mexico) grew by 5 percent per year from 1981 through 1996. That expansion has slowed considerably in recent years, owing to fears of terrorism after 9/11, concern about possibly hostile receptions abroad due to the Iraq war, and to the weakness of the dollar on foreign exchange markets. Yet, Americans continued to drive the growth of the cruise industry until the global recession took the wind out of their sails.

Those American tourists soon will be joined by the growing middle classes of India and China. By 2013, China is expected to be the single largest source of international tourists in the world, displacing Americans, Japanese, and Germans as the planet's busiest travelers. (The target date was 2010 until the recession hit.) Already, more than 85 million Chinese are believed to be able to afford international vacations. By 2023, 100 million Chinese tourists will fan out across the globe. (Again, the pre-recession estimate was 2020.) If just 1 percent of them take a cruise each year, they will more than double the cruise market. Long before that, cruise lines will begin to offer cruises and on-board amenities suited to Chinese and Indian tastes, while native Chinese and Indian cruise lines will appear to serve their local market.

In recent years, short-distance activities have added to the bottom line of flexible, market-savvy cruise operators. These include shipboard meetings, brief "cruises to nowhere," scenic cruises during fall foliage season, and trips to nearby destinations—for example, from the Gulf coasts of Florida and Texas to Mexico. We expect similar cruise operations to appear in the Indian, Chinese, and Japanese markets.

One more source of change is the growing number of destinations for cruises. In addition to new resorts and adventure experiences, many passengers will be attracted by unique facilities such as the extraordinarily beautiful Bibliotheque, a recreation of the fabled Library of Alexandria, whose exterior walls are covered in passages from the Rosetta Stone. Another spectacular new destination is the Al Arab Hotel, a literally ship-shape 60-story edifice in Dubai where diners travel to the underwater, glass-ceilinged seafood restaurant by submarine. No fewer than 30 new hotels were scheduled to open in Dubai in 2008 alone. One slated for 2009 is more than 65 feet under water and accessible only by elevator. Serving these profitable niche markets will require small, luxurious ships suited to shallow ports and discerning cruisers.

HIGH TECH, HIGH TOUCH

The more dependent we become on technology, the more we require the attention of a friendly, courteous human being to soothe our jangled nerves. Fortunately, that very high-tech environment increasingly brings us the human contact we crave. The finest cruise ships now provide the best of both worlds, using technology to provide comfort, connectivity, and entertainment at sea and a large, well-trained staff to tend the passengers' every need.

For example, Hapag-Lloyd's opulent, German-speaking Europa offers a state-of-the-art "Cruise Infotainment System" that combines a capable PC and Internet connectivity with 24-hour video and audio on-demand in all suites. Outboard power pods pull the ship through the water with absolutely no vibration or noise. The two suites for the disabled provide electronically operated beds with hydraulic lifts. High tech all the way.

Yet the vessel's most spectacular features are the appointments provided for guests, including the attention of 1.7 highly trained crew members per passenger. Cabin stewardesses serve nearly every stateroom; the 12 premium accommodations have a butler. Deck stewards spritz sunbathers with cooling Evian water. Fresh flowers abound. Penthouse guests enjoy a fully stocked bar, hand-made chocolates, and caviar on request. No wonder Berlitz Ocean Cruising and Cruise Ships gives Europa five-stars-plus, the only ship in the world to attain that rating.

However, what may be the epitome of high-touch is found on the Seabourn line, where every member of the staff begins each cruise by studying photographs of the passengers. By the end of the second day, they can address every guest by name. It is a courtesy that astonishes many first-time passengers and is appreciated by all.

In the future, computer data mining will enable cruise lines to do the kind of personalized marketing to cruise passengers that is now being pioneered in hotels and resorts. Crew members will not only be able to recognize guests, but will "remember" what meals and entertainment cruisers enjoyed on previous voyages and be able to suggest appropriate activities for their current trip. Not every vessel, nor even every line, can hope to provide guests with that level of luxury and attention. Yet this is the balance all must work towards, a combination of high-tech conveniences with personal attention that leaves passengers feeling pampered—and eager for their next voyage.

ENERGY ECONOMY

Cruise ships will never be cheap to run, but at least they will not be burdened by high oil prices. The $140+ per barrel oil of mid-2008 was an aberration, brought on by a combination of rising demand from China and India, inadequate global refining capacity, and rampant speculation. New oil supplies coming on line in the former Soviet Union, China, and other parts of the world, and several new refineries will come on line in Saudi Arabia and Russia by 2012. In all, oil will generally remain in the neighborhood of $65 per barrel for the foreseeable future. That is a long way from the $25 per barrel the world was accustomed to as recently as the late 1990s, but it is a price that crude operators can live with.

It helps that cruiselines worked hard to improve their fuel efficiency during the bad times. Diesel-electric ships usually are designed to run at about 20 knots, but maintaining that speed means running the engines flat-out. Cruising just 1 knot slower can reduce fuel consumption by 5 to 10 percent. Most cruiseships now sail just a bit more leisurely than they could. Many have added monitors to make sure the engines run as efficiently as possible. Some have installed energy management systems to even out the peaks and valleys in electrical demand. And, of course, operators are reducing drag by making sure the hull and propellers are scrupulously clean. According to industry experts, doing everything possible to save energy on a cruiseship can cut fuel use by 30 to 40 percent. Given the lessons learned in 2008 and implemented since then, fuel costs should not be a serious problem for cruiselines in the foreseeable future.

CLEANING UP

Several years ago, a research vessel crossed the middle of the Atlantic, taking samples of what it found. When they reached land, the scientists told of packaging materials, clumps of tar, and even human waste, floating hundreds of miles from land. The report made headlines in newspapers and magazines across the United States.

Since then, scientists have recognized that garbage collects at the center of many circular current patterns in both the Atlantic and the Pacific. One such patch of floating debris in the north Pacific holds an estimated 100 million tons of trash, most of it plastic. Some 80 percent of this material comes from on land. Yet much of the remainder is believed to originate with cruiseships.

Gone are the days when vessels could casually dump their wastes near land. Yet it does happen. Ten years or so ago, Royal Caribbean, Norwegian Cruise Line, and Carnival all have been fined—in one case up to $27 million—for dumping oily bilge water, plastic trash, raw sewage, and even toxic chemicals. Crystal Cruises' Crystal Harmony was banned from Monterey Bay after dumping sewage and bilge water in October 2002.

U.S. regulations now ban discarding raw sewage and food wastes within three miles of shore and limit the amount of oil in dumped bilge water to just 15 parts per million. Yet, they allow gray water and treated sewage to be discharged anywhere. The average cruiseship produces more than 200,000 gallons of it per day.

Many cruise lines have gone a long way to clean up their act. Royal Caribbean has long processed all its bilge water on trips to Alaska. It even carries an environmental compliance officer on each trip there. Crystal Cruises switched to more expensive, less polluting fuel years ago and voluntarily reported the Monterey Bay incident. Modern cruise ships are equipped with extensive treatment plants for bilge water and sewage and with storage facilities for other wastes. Yet there is clearly room for improvement.

FI believes the rules for dumping waste at sea will be tightened drastically within ten years. Those rules will be enforced by satellite surveillance and other technologies. In the future, alarms will sound if wastes are dumped near land, and discharge of raw sewage and other noxious substances will be banned anywhere at sea. Eventually, new ships even may require double hulls in critical sections to prevent loss of toxic materials in a collision.

TECHNOLOGY IMPROVES TRANSPORT

Outboard power pods on ships such as the Queen Mary 2 are one relatively recent innovation; they propel ships efficiently, quietly, without vibration and make even the largest vessels far more maneuverable. Better stabilizers, satellite navigation, computerized controls, and even the computer-aided design systems that make it possible to build a new ship in two years instead of five all are improving the business of cruising.

At the same time, design innovations are helping to better the cruise experience. The sterns of Seabourn's Pride, Legend, and Spirit carry a water sports platform that extends to provide enclosed swimming and a marina for kayaks, peddle boats, wind surfers, and even a ski boat. (Thanks to this kind of amenity, these sister ships earned five stars from Berlitz.) On Queen Mary 2, one of the five pools has a retractable glass roof to combine the best features of indoor and outdoor swimming. Many other new technologies will be less noticeable, but equally appreciated by guests. Jerry Leeman, WW Food Service

Segment Manager at IBM's Retail Store Solutions division points out that technology is making it possible to personalize customer experiences in the grocery, retail, and food service markets. Cruise passengers will expect that same level of technology-driven personal care on shipboard.

In the years ahead, these and many other novelties will continue to make cruising more economical for operators and more pleasurable for their passengers. Expect to see floating islands that act as artificial ports, ocean-going condominiums for hard-core cruise enthusiasts, even more efficient engines and waste management systems, more small and modern coastal vessels optimized for the run to Alaska and the New England foliage season, and all manner of new amenities for guests.

CYBER-CRUISING

These days, you can take it with you, and pretty much have to. The Internet, that is. It's a rare user of e-mail who can stand to be away from his in-box for more than a day or two at a time, and many cruise passengers love being able to share vacations with friends and relatives almost as they happen. Hotels unable to offer 24/7 Internet access for guests already are losing revenues to those that can. There will be over 1 trillion Net users in the world by 2005, including a substantial majority of cruisers.

In response to this trend, many lines are providing more convenient Net access for their guests. Europa offers 24-hour Internet access free in every stateroom. Silversea is phasing stateroom Internet access into all its ships. Several ships have added Internet cafes, where passengers can surf while they graze. Five years from now, expanded Internet access will be standard fare on nearly all cruise lines.

IBM's Jerry Leeman points out that guests will also expect to be able to communicate through there PDA or cell phone to the on board ship customer information system. They will want to be able to check dinner reservations and plan activities anywhere aboard ship at any time. Cruise ships soon will require a "virtual concierge" to supplement their human staff. The exponential growth of the Internet has one more implication for cruise operators, one that some cruise executives we have talked with are reluctant to accept.

The Internet is revolutionizing the travel industry. An estimated 93 percent of travelers with Internet access now seek travel information online—and according to The Unofficial Guided to Cruises 2003 the amount of travel information available through the Internet has grown by 1,000 percent in just two years.

The Travel Industry Association of America says that 39 million travelers actually booked their trips over the Internet in 2002, up 25 percent from the previous year. Of those customers, 77 percent bought plane tickets, while 57 percent made hotel reservations and 37 percent booked rental cars.

This has had a big impact on some companies, especially in the airline market. Southwest Airlines reports that about 37 percent of its bookings are now made over the Internet. British Airways expected 50 percent of its bookings to arrive over the Internet this year. In Europe, about 90 percent of budget airline bookings now come through the Internet. According to Forrester Research, the number of households arranging leisure travel online will grow by at least 32 percent through 2007. At that point, Internet bookings will be worth nearly $50 billion.

Thus far, the cruise industry has lagged well behind this trend. Some 95 percent of cruise bookings are made through travel agents, and many industry executives expect that to continue. In announcing the recent promotion of Carnival president Bob Dickinson to CEO, the company used the opportunity to stress his close relationship with and commitment to travel agents. (He does advise them to put in more time on weekends, when customer calls are five times more common than during the business week.) Princess executive Dean Brown declares in the newsletter Cruise Week that "Cruise lines booking direct is one of the most distracting things that a retailer can look at." Only 5 percent of the company's business is booked direct, he adds, and travel agents provide at least one-fifth of new growth. Virtually every cruise line has a Web site, but many are little more than billboards designed to hone the corporate image.

It cannot last. Internet users are accustomed to the convenience of shopping online. They expect the companies they do business with to provide the information they need on the Net, where it can be browsed at will, 24/7. And as cyber-wary seniors begin to leave the market, they will be replaced by Net-savvy Gen-Xers and Dot-coms who have little patience with the stately pace of offline sales. The transition to Net-based marketing will largely bypass the luxury market, where customers prefer to have others do the tedious work of putting the travel package together. Two-earner families, those on a budget, and habitually informed consumers will take much more of the cruise shopping process into their own hands.

Ultimately, it may be that there are too few travel agents to meet the cruise lines' needs. The number of agents dropped from 35,000 to 26,000 in just the 18 months ending in June 2002—and that was before airlines eliminated commissions for sales on most domestic flights. Cruise lines cannot support all the world's travel agents on their own, and it seems that no one else has much interest in doing so.

This transition will be gradual, but it is inevitable. Five years from now, travel agents will be much less important to the cruise lines, while the Internet will account for a significant and growing portion of bookings. Only the extreme luxury market will be immune to this trend, as wealthy seniors continue to prefer the pleasure of being waited on by travel agents to the efficiency of online cruise shopping. Outside that niche, the only question is which lines will be early adopters of Internet sales and which will find themselves playing catch-up.

TIME IS PRECIOUS

Two-earner households just don't have much of it. Neither do affluent singles. In the United States, workers spend about 10 percent more time on the job than they did a decade ago, and the number is still rising. European executives and non-unionized workers face the same trend. In this high-pressure environment, consumers are increasingly desperate for any product or service that offers a taste of luxury—and many of them can afford to pay for it. There is no luxury tastier than a cruise.

Catering to this market will require some obvious adaptations: more short cruises, more three-day "cruises to nowhere," more departures from ports within driving range of their homes, still more attention to children's activities and facilities for the families of young, harried parents. (The average age of first-time cruise passengers is now under 40.) Given that Carnival Cruise Lines carried more than 300,000 children in 2001, while cruise ships are now being docked at lesser ports from Norfolk to Boston, it seems these changes are well in hand. Time has another aspect, which also presents opportunities for cruise operators. Older passengers often are concerned with "life milestones"—anniversaries, birthdays, and other opportunities for family gatherings. This is a clear market for brief, relatively inexpensive cruises. It is likely to grow as the economy improves and the retirement-age population grows.

BANG, YOU'RE DEAD!

They mean it literally, as suicide bombings and other attacks have proved from Saudi Arabia to Bali. Terrorism is a long way from dead, despite optimistic pronouncements from Washington in the weeks after the Iraq war. In fact, there is every reason to believe that Al Qaeda is reconstituting itself and a new round of large-scale attacks may not be far off.

To date, only one cruise vessel has ever been attacked by terrorists, the Achille Lauro in 1985. Yet a ship full of happy, prosperous vacationers is an ideal target for extremists. Some 94 percent of American travelers rate hotel safety as a prime factor in deciding where to stay. It would take just one incident to make terrorism a top concern for cruise passengers as well.

This is a growing concern also because cruise ships are increasingly being used as floating hotels. As early as February 2004, the Queen Mary 2 docked in Rio de Janeiro so that cruisers could enjoy carnivale, giving would-be terrorists access to a stationary target. And during the Olympics in Greece, many cruise vessels were moored in the harbour throughout the event to supplement scarce landside hotel space. Despite a $1.2 billion security programme that includes a new sonar system to protect the harbour against attack by submarine, this is one of the most obvious opportunities for a terrorist spectacular we have ever seen. That Greek authorities managed to defend these ships successfully was a very impressive accomplishment.

For cruise lines elsewhere, many other security measures already are in place. On-board bon voyage parties, once a normal part of cruising, have been eliminated, as only passengers are allowed on ship. Entering port in the United States, ships now pick up six "sea marshals" along with the pilot. Two remain in on the bridge, two watch over the engine room, and two patrol the remainder of the vessel. In Miami, divers from the local fire department carefully examine the ship for clinging mines. And a Coast Guard cutter leads the ship into port, watching for high-speed attackers such as the small boat that assaulted the U.S.S. Cole in Yemen.

In the years ahead, cruise operators will be forced to tighten security even beyond current standards. They will have to screen not only passengers, but everyone who has contact with the vessel—food loaders, baggage handlers, port pilots, and their own disgruntled employees and former employees. One thing they will not have to do is screen baggage, a job too expensive to handle at individual ships. That will be taken care of as people enter the dock, either by government employees or by private security firms under contract to the Department of Home Security or to industry associations. Already, some cruise lines have stopped the age-old practice of putting name tags on at the airport for fear that would-be terrorists will slip a bomb or hazardous material into a bag before it ever reached the ship.

Security is as important for small inland cruises as it is for ocean-going liners. On the Potomac, tour boats glide past within striking distance of the Kennedy Center, where a bomb could endanger 40,000 people. Many ships that cruise down the Mississippi and other waterways also pass within easy reach of populous, vulnerable targets. Tourists on these vessels undergo no security checks at all, but that is about to change. Coast Guard regulations scheduled to take effect on June 1, 2004, will require the screening of tour boat passengers.

All this represents a difficult adjustment for both cruise passengers and the companies that carry them. There is something about being treated as a potential hijacker that conflicts fundamentally with the sense of luxury and pampering that cruisers signed up for and cruise operators aim to provide. We will just have to get used to it. From now on, boarding a ship is going to look more and more like running the gauntlet at a busy airport. The alternative is even worse.

SAVVY CONSUMERS

A networked society is a consumerist society. Shoppers today can search the Internet for information about pricing, services, delivery time, and peer reviews of all manner of goods and services. Already, the monthly Internet newsletter CruiseReports delivers reviews of cruise ships, complete with passenger comments, directly to the reader's e-mail box. Over the next few years, this trend will sweep through the cruise industry as well. Disappoint one passenger, and thousands of potential customers will hear about it.

Norwegian Cruise Line showed how not to handle problems in April 2003, when ice in the Gulf of Finland forced Norwegian Dream to cancel stops at Helsinki, Tallinn, and—unforgivably—St. Petersburg, the high point of the trip. Passengers learned of the changes only when they checked in at Dover, and they were offered compensation of only $100 to $200 each, amounts that sent irate cruisers on stage to harangue fellow passengers in a near-revolt. As one dismayed agent commented, "They've come a long way to see St. Petersburg, and $150 ain't going to cut it." The Internet carried that tale around the world, no doubt in the words of the angriest customers.

A world of savvy, demanding, networked consumers requires still greater effort to give passengers the best possible cruise. It may be even more important to soothe their frustrations when something goes wrong.

SHOCK AND AAHS

Throughout the business world, institutions are undergoing what FI calls bimodal distribution: The big get bigger. The small survive, and some of them do quite well. But mid-sized competitors are squeezed out, because they are not flexible enough to prosper in niche markets and cannot achieve the economies of scale enjoyed by the Wal-Marts of their industries.

Similarly, purveyors of high-end luxury products flourish; look at any spectacularly good restaurant. The fast-food chains also make it; cheap, Spartan products fill a need for those who cannot afford better. But mid-priced family restaurants eventually go broke. We see this trend among auto manufacturers, computer makers, farms, banks, and very clearly in the airline industry. We are beginning to see it among cruise lines.

Those companies that failed or took refuge in Chapter 11 after the 2001 terrorist attack represent the vulnerable middle of the industry, underfunded and without the kind of core market it takes to survive. For the mass market, there is Carnival Cruise Lines; in the luxury end, there are Silversea and Carnival's subsidiary, Seabourn.

Carnival's ships are big, from roughly 85,000 to 110,000 tons, with stateroom capacities that range from about 2,100 to nearly 3,000 passengers. The atmosphere is relentlessly upbeat, with constant music and passenger games, but there is none of the emphasis on luxury typical of some other lines. The food is adequate, the cabins large enough, the glasses plastic, at least on deck and in the Lido Buffet. This is the McDonald's of the cruise industry, and it is spectacularly successful. Carnival's mass appeal has made it the largest cruise line in the world.

At the other end of the spectrum, we need to look at just one ship, the spectacular new Queen Mary 2, which sailed on its maiden voyage for Carnival's Cunard subsidiary in January 2004. This is the largest, fastest cruise ship ever built—150,000 tons, nearly a quarter-mile long, 100 feet taller than the Eiffel tower, able to carry 3,090 passengers across the Atlantic at speeds up to 30 knots.

Carnival set out to make the world's most luxurious cruising ship. The result, built at a cost of $780 million, is likely to provoke shock and "aah"s. Even its smallest staterooms offer 194 square feet of sumptuous appointments, its largest—two Grand Duplex apartments at the stern—can be combined with the penthouses above to create a single apartment with an unprecedented 8,288 square feet of floor space. Even the most modest accommodations, to whatever extent the concept of modesty applies to any part of this vessel, is equipped with a 20-inch television and attached computer keyboard providing digital video, music, and audio books on demand, with 24-hour e-mail access. There are 14 bars, ten restaurants, five swimming pools, a gymnasium, and a spa with 24 treatment rooms, and even a putting green.

In the words of one observer, "This is the ship God would have made if he had the cash flow." Carnival does, thanks to its firm hold on both the mass market and luxury ends of the cruise industry.

However, QM2 will not be the world's largest cruise ship for long. In fact, Royal Caribbean's new Mariner of the Seas already carries more passengers, 3,114, and the line has a 1,114-foot long, 3,600 passenger ship named Ultra Voyager scheduled for launch some time in 2006.

As this business grows more competitive, large and successful cruise lines increasingly will follow one of these models. Some will cater to relatively unsophisticated first-time passengers. Others will aim for discriminating cruise enthusiasts who can pay to be pampered. Smaller players will specialize in niche markets such as coastal cruises or expedition, nature, or adventure excursions. Mid-sized, mid-range operators will slowly disappear. That is just the way things are in the global economy.

COMPETITIVE ADVANTAGE

At both ends of the spectrum, the battle for market share will grow ever more challenging. That too is in the nature of worldwide competition. There are several tools and offerings that cruise lines will use to make it in this difficult environment.

One is specialized attractions for niche markets. Theme cruises already are popular. There have been highly successful trips specializing in adventure themes, astronomy, bridge, chess, computer science, education, film festivals, gays and lesbians, murder mysteries, and nudism. We will see many more such enticements in the future. In fact, the future itself could be a marketable theme, with lectures covering technology, medicine, economics, social issues, and other important, fast-changing fields.

Well-known celebrities, entertainers, and guest lecturers fall into this same category. Whenever someone writes a best-selling book, acts on a hit television show, or sings a pop song, they create a niche market for cruise lines. We would not be surprised to learn that the winners from American Idol already are booked on Carnival or one of its mass-market competitors.

YIELD MANAGEMENT

A key marketing technique just being adopted by the cruise industry is yield management. The basic idea is simple. Companies keep careful track of how their products are selling. If time is growing short and something needs to be moved out the door, it is discounted and advertised heavily until it sells.

This is basic marketing, computerized, turbocharged, and driven up-to-the-minute sales and inventory statistics. It can work remarkably well. In one typical case, after the SARS epidemic broke out in Asia, Crystal Harmony was abruptly repositioned to Los Angeles. Bookings were heavily discounted and sold out in just five days. Yield marketing cries out for the Internet, where prices can be changed around the world at the touch of a few keys. Predictably, some of its most effective practitioners in the travel industry are online discounters such as Expedia, Travelocity, and Orbitz. However, profit-minded cruise lines will want to bring this in-house, to route cash flow to their own balance sheets. This means that a dramatic expansion of Web sites and the adoption of Internet-oriented sales techniques are all but inevitable. In five to seven years, cruise operators will be every bit as dependent on Internet sales as the airline industry.

TEN TRENDS

In his feature, Budget Travel, Arthur Frommer recently surveyed developments in the cruise industry. He found ten trends, many of which paralleled Forecasting International's observations.

Here is his list:

- Continued discounting of ticket prices, often unannounced.
- A growing variety of ships, from multi-thousand-passenger megaships to 100-passenger vessels capable of visiting the smallest ports.
- More cruises from ports such as New York and San Francisco, which are within convenient driving distance for many passengers.
- A renaissance in freighter cruising, which ten years ago had almost vanished; today more than 40 freighters carry patient vacationers to a wide variety of ports not served by traditional cruise lines.
- New itineraries, particularly in formerly neglected areas such as Asia and Africa.

- More theme cruises for fans of music, history, murder mysteries, haute cuisine, and other specialized interests. This July, Norwegian Dawn will even carry what is being billed as "the first gay cruise with family values," led by former talk-show hostess Rosie O'Donnell.
- Many more cruises by luxurious sailing ship, a relaxed and relatively inexpensive alternative to traditional motor vessels.
- A wider variety of cruise lengths, with voyages stretching from three to seven nights up to 14 or 15, appealing to older travelers with plentiful free time.
- If cruising is hot, the Antarctic may be the hottest destination of all. Demand is so strong that vessels carrying up to 800 passengers are now plying this trade.
- Batteries, and a lot of other things, not included. Amenities from meals to miniature golf are being paid for separately, a trend that is sure to continue.

THROUGH 2010

It should be a good time for efficient, market-savvy cruise lines. Carnival CEO Bob Dickson reports that early in 2004 he had already seen a significant uptick in bookings from the lows of the recent recession. "Obscenely low pricing will not last," he predicts. "As demand rebuilds, pricing will go up." Forecasting International agrees.

Some of our other forecasts here may be more controversial. Yet if some of FI's views about the future of cruise lines appear to be radically different from current industry practices, most are simple extensions of current trends. They all grow directly from the market forces we see operating today. Tomorrow's cruise lines will be even more flexible, even more in tune with the needs of their changing, and growing, markets. As a result, we believe they will be some of the most dynamic and profitable companies in the world.

KEY TRENDS FOR THE CRUISE LINES

THE WORLD'S POPULATION WILL GROW TO 9 BILLION BY 2050.

Early versions of this report predicted that the world's population would double by 2050, and population growth has proceeded almost exactly on schedule. However, even this estimate may be too low. According to the Center for Strategic and International Studies, most official projections underestimate both fertility and future gains in longevity. Unfortunately, the greatest fertility is found in those countries least able to support their existing people. Populations will triple in the Palestinian Territories and Niger between 2000 and 2050 and will more than double in Yemen, Angola, the Democratic Republic of Congo, and Uganda. In contrast, populations in most developed countries are stable or declining. The United States is a prominent exception. Assessment: Demographic trends such as this are among the easiest to recognize and most difficult to derail. Barring a global plague or nuclear war—wildcard possibilities that cannot be predicted with any validity—there is little chance that the population forecast for 2050 will err on the low side. Implications: Rapid population growth in the United States compared with its industrialized competitors will reinforce American domination of the global economy, as the European Union falls to third place behind the United States and China.

To meet human nutritional needs over the next forty years, global agriculture will have to supply as much food as has been produced during all of human history. Unless fertility in the developed lands climbs dramatically, either would-be retirees will have to remain on the job, or the industrialized nations will have to encourage even more immigration from the developing world. The third alternative is a sharp economic contraction and lower living standards. A fourth alternative is the widespread automation of service jobs as well as manufacturing, to accomplish the work needed to support accustomed living standards. However, this requires development of a means other than wages to distribute wealth and to provide both a living income and a fulfilling occupation for workers and would-be workers displaced by machines and software.

Barring enforcement of strict immigration controls, rapid migration will continue from the Southern Hemisphere to the North, and especially from former colonies to Europe. A growing percentage of job applicants in the United States and Europe will be recent immigrants from developing countries. Implications for Hospitality and Travel: Rapid population growth, compared with other developed lands, will preserve America's place at the top of the global economy, with China taking second place from the European Union. This will help to keep the hospitality and travel industries growing rapidly.

] POPULATION OF THE DEVELOPED WORLD IS LIVING LONGER

Each generation lives longer and remains healthier than the last. Since the beginning of the twentieth century, every generation in the United States has lived three years longer than the previous one. An 80-year-old in 1950 could expect 6.5 more years of life; today's 80-year-olds are likely to survive 8.5 more years. Life expectancy in Australia, Japan, and Switzerland is now over 75 years for males and over 80 for females.

A major reason for this improvement is the development of new pharmaceuticals and medical technologies that are making it possible to prevent or cure diseases that would have been fatal to earlier generations. Medical advances that slow the fundamental process of aging now seem to be within reach. (This is a controversial issue within the medical community, but the evidence appears quite strong.) Such treatments could well help today's younger generations live routinely beyond the century mark.

Assessment: Demographic trends such as this are among the easiest to recognize and most difficult to derail. Barring a global plague or nuclear war—wildcard possibilities that cannot be predicted with any validity—there is little chance that the population forecast for 2050 will err on the low side.

Implications for Cruise Lines: Older people make up a growing segment of the cruise market. Because they form the wealthiest segment of industrialized societies, retirement-age consumers also are the most likely to take cruise vacations, particularly for the longest and most luxurious cruises. Younger travelers form a profitable market for family-oriented cruises. However, one of the biggest advantage of catering to them is the opportunity to build brand loyalty for their later lives, when they will be the most profitable cruisers.

Retired people are free to take trips when they wish, rather than when it suits an employer. They are beginning to even out the traditional seasonality of travel. Older passengers need amenities suited to their physical limitations. Examples include signs with larger type, lever door handles rather than knobs, safety grips in bathrooms and showers, and extra help with their luggage.

THE ELDERLY POPULATION IS GROWING DRAMATICALLY THROUGHOUT THE WORLD

Worldwide, the elderly (age 65 and over) numbered 440 million and represented 6 percent of the global population in 2002. Their numbers will nearly double by 2020 (and form nearly 9 percent of the total population) and more than triple by 2050 (becoming nearly 17 percent.) In the developed world, people age 60 and over made up one-fifth of the population in 2000 and will grow to one-third in the next half century. Throughout the developed world, population growth is fastest among the elderly. In the United States, there are 4.2 million people age 85 and up. By 2050, there will be 19.3 million. In Europe, the United States, and Japan, the aged also form the wealthiest segment of society.

Assessment: Again, this is a demographic trend, difficult to derail and unlikely to change while the massive Baby Boom generation remains on the scene.

Implications: Not counting immigration, the ratio of working-age people to retirees needing their support will drop dramatically in the United States, Germany, Italy, Russia, Japan, and other countries. This represents a burden on national economies that will be difficult to sustain under current medical and social security systems.

In the next two to three decades, shortages of health workers will loom large in "aging vulnerable" countries. The United States in particular will need at least twice as many physicians specializing in geriatrics as its current 9,000, as well as half a million more nurses by 2020. Suburban communities are likely to face a growing demand for social services such as senior day-care, public transportation, and other programmes for the elderly. This will place a growing strain on local government budgets. In the developing countries, where the elderly have traditionally relied on their children for support, this system will begin to break down as middle-aged "children" find themselves still supporting their parents while anticipating their own retirement. Implications for Hospitality and Travel: Seniors are not only the fastest growing segment of the population, they are the wealthiest. Few will be up to making an assault on Mt. Everest, but almost anyone can take a cruise or fly to Paris or Orlando for a long weekend with Mickey and the rest of the Disney gang. Fine dining, a tour of the links at St. Andrew's, or a visit to the tables in Vegas will appeal to some seniors and soon-to-be seniors.

As the older populations grow, the travel industry can only expand with them. In the process, it is likely to become more stable and less seasonal. Unlike the rest of us, most seniors can travel whenever the impulse strikes. Often, they do so when prices are down and crowds are thinner. In recent years, their off-season travel has begun to smooth the cyclical downturn typical of the hospitality and travel industry. Seniors will never eliminate seasonality, but the industry will find it less painful than in the past.

MASS MIGRATION IS REDISTRIBUTING THE WORLD'S POPULATION.

There are nearly 100 million international migrant workers in the world, according to the United Nations. About 30 million live in Europe, 20 million in Africa, and 18 million in North America. These figures include only the workers themselves, not their dependents. About 4 million people immigrated permanently to the countries of the Organization for Economic Cooperation and Development in 2005, 10.4 percent more than the year before. Immigration to Western Europe from Eastern Europe, North Africa, the Middle East, and the Indian subcontinent continues despite controls enacted in the wake of terrorist attacks. Immigration is quickly changing the ethnic composition of the U.S. population. By 2050, the number of Latinos in the U.S. will double, to 24.5 percent of the population.

Assessment: As native workforces shrink in most industrialized lands, economic opportunities will draw people from the developing world to the developed in growing numbers. Thus, this trend will continue for at least the next generation. Implications: Impoverished migrants will place a growing strain on social-security systems in the industrialized countries of Europe and North America. Similar problems will continue to afflict the urban infrastructures of China and India. Remittances from migrants to their native lands are helping to relieve poverty in many developing countries. Globally, these payments exceeded US$230 billion in 2005, according to the World Bank.

Significant backlashes against foreign migrants, such as the skinhead movement in Europe, will be seen more frequently in the years ahead. They will appear even in the most peaceful lands. For example, in Scandinavia, resentment against foreign workers is strong, in part because they can return to their native lands after three years of employment and collect a pension equal to the minimum wage for the rest of their lives.

- Since the terrorist attacks of September 11, 2001, and the rail bombings in London and Madrid, the large number of Muslim immigrants in Britain, France, and other European lands has inspired suspicion, and some persecution.
- Unfortunately, suspicion is to some extent justified. A tiny minority of Muslim immigrants have proved to be linked to terrorist groups, and some have plotted or carried out terrorist attacks. So have native-born Muslims and converts to Islam.

Implications for Hospitality and Travel: Barring enactment of strict immigration controls, rapid migration will continue from the southern hemisphere to the north, and especially from former colonies to Europe. A growing percentage of job applicants in the recipient lands will be recent immigrants from developing countries. This will compensate for a declining supply of entry-level and low-wage workers in the developed economies. Unlike post-retirement job-seekers, however, most new arrivals will be limited to relatively menial, behind-the-scenes jobs until they master the local language and adapt to the dominant culture of their new homes.

The market for relatively short-distance international travel should grow significantly in both the United States and Europe, thanks largely to their expanding foreign populations visiting their former homes. Routes between the United States and Mexico and Latin America will grow fastest, while those between Europe and the former colonies of Africa and the Middle East will not be far behind.

In the United States and Europe, foreign-born residents represent significant new markets for well-prepared foods from Latin America and the Middle East. Supplying this demand will fall to small restaurateurs at first, but the major chains can be expected to enter this field as soon as they are sure it will repay their investments. This trend will serve an aging population well, because it promises to introduce strong new flavours suited to the failing taste buds of older diners.

IMPORTANT MEDICAL ADVANCES WILL CONTINUE TO APPEAR ALMOST DAILY.

Research into human genetics, stem cells, computer-aided drug design, tissue transplants, cloning, and even nanotechnology promise to ease or cure diseases and injuries that do not respond to today's medicine. Radical new treatments for diabetes, Parkinson's disease, perhaps Alzheimer's, and many other disorders are expected to arrive within the next five to ten years.

Scientists even are beginning to understand the fundamental processes of aging, bringing the possibility of averting the diseases of old age, and perhaps aging itself.

Assessment: The flow of new medical advances will not slow in the next 40 years, and probably not in the next 75.

Implications: In the next ten years, we expect to see more and better bionic limbs, hearts, and other organs; drugs that prevent disease rather than merely treating symptoms; and body monitors that warn of impending trouble. These all will reduce hospital stays.

Outside the United States, transplants of brain cells, nerve tissue, and stem cells to aid victims of retardation, head trauma, and other neurological disorders will enter clinical use by 2012. Laboratory-grown bone, muscle, and blood cells also will be employed in transplants.

Expect also the first broadly effective treatments for viral diseases, experimental regeneration of lost or damaged human tissues, and effective ways to prevent and correct obesity. By 2025, the first nanotechnology-based medical therapies should reach clinical use. Microscopic machines will monitor our internal processes, remove cholesterol plaques from artery walls, and destroy cancer cells before they have a chance to form a tumor.

Forecasting International believes that cloning and related methods will be accepted for the treatment of disease, though not to produce identical human beings. Even without dramatic advances in life extension, Baby Boomers are likely to live much longer, and in better health, than anyone now expects. However, this trend could be sidetracked by the current epidemic of obesity, which threatens to raise rates of hypertension, diabetes, heart disease, and arthritis among Boomers if a cure is not found quickly enough.

However, a significant extension of healthy, vigourous life—to around 115 or 120 years as a first step—now seems more likely than no extension at all. The most significant question remaining, other than the scientific details, is whether it will arrive in time for the Baby Boom generation to benefit or will be limited to their children and descendents.

High development and production costs for designer pharmaceuticals, computerized monitors, and artificial organs will continue to push up the cost of health care far more rapidly than the general inflation rate. Much of these expenses will be passed on to Medicare and other third-party payers. Severe personnel shortages can be expected in high-tech medical specialties, in addition to the continuing deficit of nurses.

A growing movement to remove barriers to stem-cell research in the United States could speed progress in this critical field. This could be expected to produce new treatments for neurological disorders such as Parkinson's and Alzheimer's disease and many other illnesses now incurable or untreatable. It also would recover one aspect of America's lost lead in science.

Implications for Hospitality and Travel: This trend is responsible for the growing number of older, fitter seniors who remain able not only to travel, but to participate in relatively vigourous activities at their destination. Their numbers will grow rapidly as the Baby Boom generation reaches their retirement years. Accommodating the needs of healthy seniors will be a major priority for the hospitality and travel industry in the coming decades.

This trend also is a major source of medical tourism, in which travelers combine a vacation with low-cost, high-quality medical care in places such as India, Thailand, South Africa, or Eastern Europe. Medical tourism will bring India alone an estimated $2.2 billion per year by 2012.

THE PHYSICAL CULTURE AND PERSONAL-HEALTH MOVEMENTS ARE IMPROVING HEALTH IN MUCH OF THE WORLD, BUT THEY ARE FAR FROM UNIVERSAL

During the 1990s, health in the United States improved by 1.5 percent annually, based on such measures as smoking prevalence, health-insurance coverage, infant mortality rates, and premature deaths. Since 2000, health improvement has slowed to just 0.2 percent a year, largely due to personal choices. The global obesity crisis is a significant countertrend to the physical-culture movement. Poor diet, physical inactivity, and associated obesity contribute to 47 percent of diseases and 60 percent of deaths worldwide. However, health consciousness is spreading to Europe. For example, a recent poll found that two-thirds of Britons now spend more to maintain a healthy lifestyle than they did a decade ago, and three out of four say they enjoy leading a healthy lifestyle. Unfortunately, much of the developing world still worries more about eating enough than about eating well.

Assessment: This trend always seems a case of two steps forward, at least one step back. We expect it to continue for at least the next generation.

Implications: As the nutrition and wellness movements spread, they will further improve the health of the elderly. Better health in later life will make us still more conscious of our appearance and physical condition. Thus, health clubs will continue to boom, and some will specialize in the needs of older fitness buffs.

Diet, fitness, stress control, and wellness programmes will prosper. States will continue to mandate insurance coverage of mammography. By 2012, they will begin to require coverage of sigmoidoscopy and colonoscopy. By 2015,Congress will add coverage of many preventive-care activities to Medicare. The cost of health care for American Baby Boomers and their children could be much lower in later life than is now believed.

However, Asia faces an epidemic of cancer, heart disease, emphysema, and other chronic and fatal illnesses related to health habits. Like tobacco companies, producers of snack foods, liquor, and other unhealthy products will increasingly target markets in developing countries where this trend has yet to be felt. Continuing health improvements in the industrialized world will be accompanied by a dramatic rise in heart disease, diabetes, cancer, and other such "lifestyle" disorders in the developing lands. Chronic diseases related to obesity burden national economies and could thwart economic progress in developing countries.

Implications for Hospitality and Travel: Most cruise lines, high-end hotels, and resorts already have adapted to their guests' wish for nutritious, low-calorie meals, exercise facilities, and tobacco-free areas, particularly in the United States. Their peers in other lands will find themselves forced to make similar concessions to health consciousness in the next decade. This trend also means that hospitality and travel operators will be receiving more guests who are older, wealthier, and fitter, still able to indulge in vigourous activities that their counterparts of an earlier era would not have considered.

SOCIETAL TRENDS

SOCIETAL VALUES ARE CHANGING RAPIDLY.

Industrialization raises educational levels, changes attitudes towards authority, reduces fertility, alters gender roles, and encourages broader political participation. This process is just beginning throughout the developing world. Witness the growing literacy, declining fertility, and broad voter turnout seen in India over the last decade. Developed societies increasingly take their cue from Generation X and the Millennial generation (aka Gen Y or Generation Dot-com), rather than the Baby Boomers who dominated the industrialized world's thinking for most of four decades. Post-September 11 fear of terrorist attacks has led Americans to accept almost without comment security measures that their traditional love of privacy once would have made intolerable.

Assessment: This trend will continue for at least the next two decades in the industrialized lands and two generations in the developing world.

Implications: The growing influence of the post-BabyBoom generations will tend to homogenize basic attitudes throughout the world, because Generation Xers and especially the Millennials around the globe have more in common with each other than with their parents.

The highly polarized political environment that has plagued the United States since the 1980s will slowly moderate as results-oriented Generation Xers and Millennials begin to dominate the national dialogue. As national security concerns have begun to lose their immediacy, family issues are regaining their significance in American society: long-term health care, day care, early childhood education, antidrug campaigns, and the environment.

Concerns about health care, education, and the environment already are shaping the 2008 presidential campaign. Demand for greater accountability and transparency in business will be crucial for countries that wish to attract international investors.

Implications for Hospitality and Travel: Vacations also are becoming more active and participatory, as tourists become less interested in "go-and-see" and more eager to go-and-do. This is the trend behind the growth of adventure tourism and ecology-oriented travel. The trend is towards extreme quality, and convenience. Customers want constant pampering, luxurious accommodations, and fresh meals that seem like labours of love—all at a price that will not wound the consumer's conscience.

"Authenticity" is another key value. Tourists who go to see other lands, rather than surf their beaches, want to find unique natural and cultural features that survive as close as possible to their original form. Travel experiences that remind guests of Navajo Indian blankets with "Made in China" tags will leave visitors feeling that they might as well have visited their local mall instead.

PRIVACY, ONCE A DEFINING RIGHT FOR AMERICANS, IS DYING QUICKLY

Internet communications, a basic part of life for many people, are nearly impossible to protect against interception, and governments around the world are working to ensure their unfettered access to them. Corporate databases are collecting and marketing data on individual credit-worthiness, incomes, spending patterns, brand choices, medical conditions, and lifestyles. While privacy regulations bar distribution of much personal information in the European Union, restrictions in the United States are much weaker. Widespread surveillance of private individuals is technically feasible and economically viable, as tiny, powerful cameras now cost next to nothing. Increased surveillance has become socially acceptable in an age when many people fear terrorism and crime. Britons are caught on camera an estimated 300 times per day, Americans about 200.

Assessment: Pessimists could say that privacy already is a thing of the past; society is merely coming to recognize its loss. We believe that enough effective privacy survives outside the most authoritarian countries to justify noting its continued erosion. However, this trend could easily reach its logical conclusion within ten years. Implications: In the future, privacy is likely to be defined, not by the ability to keep information truly secret, but by the legal power to restrict its distribution. Even this limited form of privacy will be eroded as both government and private organizations find legal justification for their interest in personal information. Once access is granted to any type of information, it is unlikely ever to be rescinded.

Most surveillance provisions of the USA Patriot Act will survive, even if the law itself is repealed or modified. In the absence of a major terrorist event, most Americans will continue to consider privacy a "right," and privacy-related lawsuits are likely to proliferate as more people feel violated or inconvenienced by surveillance. However, courts will be unsympathetic to such suits for so long as conservative appointees dominate the bench.

In large and medium-size cities around the world, spaces that remain unwatched by video cameras will continue to shrink. Growing numbers of companies, and even private citizens, will encrypt their computer data. The number of criminal cases based on surveillance will grow rapidly in countries with the required technological sophistication and infrastructure.

Private citizens increasingly will use similar technologies to watch over government abuse, as in cases where bystanders have recorded police misconduct with their cell-phone cameras. Implications for Hospitality and Travel: Hospitality and travel operators are likely to find themselves facing more demands to watch for suspicious activities in travel destinations, or even to provide security agencies with information about their guests.

TIME IS BECOMING THE WORLD'S MOST PRECIOUS COMMODITY

In the United States, workers spend about 10 percent more time on the job than they did a decade ago. European executives and non-unionized workers face the same trend. In Britain, an Ipsos MORI study found that 32 percent of people who had not visited a museum in the previous year reported having too little time to do so; in 1999, only 6 percent had cited that reason. China's rapid economic development means its workers also are experiencing faster-paced and time-pressured lives. In a recent survey by the Chinese news portal Sina.com, 56 percent of respondents said they felt short of time. Technical workers and executives in India are beginning to report the same job-related stresses, particularly when they work on U.S. and European schedules.

Assessment: This trend is likely to grow as changing technologies add the need for lifelong study to the many commitments that compete for the average worker's time. As it matures in the United States, it is likely to survive in other parts of the world. It will not disappear until China and India reach modern post-industrial status, around 2050. Implications for Cruise Lines: Harried two-earner households are eager for any luxury they can find—and many of them can afford to pay for it. Many see a cruise vacation as the ultimate luxury. What many of them cannot afford is time. Growing numbers will take brief "cruises to nowhere," long-weekend coastal cruises, and short segments of longer cruises, preferably leaving from regional ports near their homes.

THE WOMEN'S EQUALITY MOVEMENT IS LOSING ITS SIGNIFICANCE, THANKS LARGELY TO PAST SUCCESSES.

According to some, though not all, studies, women have nearly achieved pay parity with men in the United States when factors such as educational level, responsibilities, and seniority are taken into account. Younger generations of women are better educated and are even more likely to be successful than their male peers. Generation Xers and Millennials are virtually gender-blind in the workplace, compared with older generations.

This is true even in societies such as India and Japan, which have long been male-dominated, though not yet in conservative Muslim lands.

Assessment: This trend is valid only in the developed lands. In the developing world, the movement towards women's equality is barely beginning. In the United States, the trend could be seen as complete, with women's equality now taken for granted and only mopping-up operations required to complete the process. However, we believe that the women's equality movement will continue to retain some importance, less with each passing year, until the gender-blind Generation X and Millennials accede to leadership in business and politics.

Implications: In most of the developed world, whatever careers remain relatively closed to women will open wide in the years ahead. Japan will remain some years behind the curve, owing to the strength of its traditionally male-dominated culture.

Women's increasing entrepreneurialism will allow the formation of entrenched "old girl" networks comparable to the men's relationships that once dominated business. The fraction of women entering the American labour force has leveled off in recent years. The percentage of female workers is likely to remain approximately stable until some force appears to begin a new trend. Demand for child care, universal health coverage, and other family-oriented services will continue to grow, particularly in the United States, where national services have yet to develop. Over the next twenty years, American companies may increasingly follow the example of their counterparts in Europe, whose taxes pay for national daycare programmes and other social services the United States lacks.

There is little sign of progress for women in much of the developing world. India is an exception, because growing literacy has given women the chance to earn income outside the home and, with it, gain value other than as wives and mothers. Implications for hospitality and travel: There are relatively few implications for these industries. Hospitality and travel operators have traditionally depended on women for much of their workforce, and especially in critical guest-contact roles. As a result, they have been relatively willing to pay women well and promote them into management positions comparable to those occupied by men.

DESPITE SOME XENOPHOBIC REACTIONS TO IMMIGRANTS, THERE IS GROWING ACCEPTANCE OF DIVERSITY

Migration is mixing disparate peoples and forcing them to find ways to coexist peacefully and productively. Because of this, the interaction of diverse cultures will continue to grow, both internationally and intra-nationally, throughout much of the world.

The Internet and other technologies promote long-distance communication and build links between distant, and disparate, people. The globalization of business is having a similar impact. However, in many countries there are powerful reactions against these changes. The growth of the German neo-nazi movement after unification in 1992 is one obvious example. American hostility towards undocumented aliens may be viewed as another.

Assessment: This trend applies most clearly to the West, where it will continue for as long as we can foresee. In other regions, including Japan and large parts of the Muslim world, it remains weak, if it exists at all.

Implications: Groups with highly varied customs, languages, and histories of necessity will develop ways to coexist peacefully. non-etheless, local conflicts will continue to erupt in societies where xenophobia is common.

Companies will hire ever more minority workers and will be expected to adapt to their values and needs. Much of the burden of accommodating foreign-born residents will continue to fall on employers, who must make room for their languages and cultures in the workplace. Public schools and libraries must find more effective ways to educate this future workforce.

Implications for hospitality and travel: Growing contact between countries and cultures in the United States and Europe should stimulate further demand for travel to foreign lands, where visitors can learn more about the cultures they have met, and begun to accept, at home. Companies in all industries, including hospitality and travel, will hire ever more minority workers and will be expected to adapt to their values and needs. Much of the burden of accommodating foreign-born residents will continue to fall on employers, who must both help them adapt to their new environment and make room for their languages and cultures in the workplace.

The more prosperous immigrant groups, such as those from Asia and the Middle East in the U.S., also represent valuable markets for specialized travel services. Expect growing demand especially for services aimed at the needs of Muslim travelers from Europe and the United States. Hotels, restaurants, and cruise lines all will have to be prepared to serve the special needs of religious, ethnic, and cultural minorities.

TOURISM, VACATIONING, AND TRAVEL (ESPECIALLY INTERNATIONAL) CONTINUE TO GROW WITH EACH PASSING YEAR

International tourism grew by more than 6 percent in the first half of 2007, thanks in part to global prosperity. By 2020, international tourist arrivals have been expected to reach 1.6 billion annually, up from 842 million in 2006. At that time, according to the World Trade Organization, 100 million Chinese will fan out across the globe, replacing Americans, Japanese, and Germans as the world's most numerous travelers. Some 50 million Indian tourists will join them. But put the target dates off to 2023, thanks to the recession of '08/'08.

Assessment: Travel seems to be in the DNA of the middle and upper economic classes. This trend will continue so long as national economies continue to generate new prosperity for the formerly poor.

Implications for Cruise Lines: The market for cruises will grow at least as fast as the travel market in general. If the American economy again begins to expand rapidly, rather than at the measured pace seen in early 2004, cruising should grow even more rapidly. Many consumers view cruising as one of the most desirable forms of vacation, even if they have never taken a cruise themselves. In affluent times, they will be even more inclined to indulge their wish for luxury by signing up for a voyage.

Within ten years, the number of Chinese and Indian cruisers will justify providing amenities, and even designing cruises, specifically for their tastes. By 2020, we expect to see several new cruise lines based in China and India and catering to the needs of local vacationers. The growth of tourism will inspire the development of many new destinations, giving cruise ships new ports of call to interest their passengers. Some of those destinations will be developed with the growing Asian tourist markets in mind.

13) Education and training are expanding throughout society.

Rapid changes in the job market and work-related technologies will require increased training for almost every worker, just as knowledge turnover in the professions requires continuous retraining and lifelong learning. Thus, a substantial portion of the labour force will be in job retraining programmes at any moment. All of the fastest growing occupations require some form of advanced training and continuous updating of job skills. In the next 10 years, close to 10 million jobs will open up for professionals, executives, and technicians in the highly skilled service occupations. In order to give those who cannot attend their classes a chance to educate themselves, the Massachusetts Institute of Technology has put its entire curriculum on the Internet, including class notes, many texts, and sometimes videos of classroom lectures. Other institutions are following suit.

Assessment: This is another trend at the beginning of its life.

Implications: Over the next two decades, the growing demand for education and training is likely to transform our working lives and educational systems around the world. In order to keep up with growing demands for education, schools will train both children and adults around the clock.

The academic day will stretch to seven hours for children so as to enable students to compete with their peers in other countries, who already devote much more of their time to learning, with predictable results. Adults will use much of their remaining free time to prepare for their next job. In knowledge-based economies, a region's growth prospects depend on its ability to generate and use innovation. This correlates roughly with the number of collegeeducated adults living there. Throughout the industrialized countries, this gives cities an advantage over rural and suburban areas. It is one reason upwardly mobile adults tend to move to the cities.

Skills are the most important factor in economic success today. Unfortunately, the people who need them most, the poor and unemployed, cannot afford schooling and therefore are least able to obtain them. Helping people overcome this disadvantage is a natural role for government.

As the digital divide is erased and minority and low-income households buy computers and log onto the Internet, groups now disadvantaged will be increasingly able to educate and train themselves for high-tech careers. Even the smallest businesses must learn to see employee training as an investment, rather than an expense. Motorola estimates that it reaps $30 in profits for each dollar it spends on training. Both management and employees must get used to the idea of lifelong learning. It will become a significant part of work life at all levels. Implications for hospitality and travel: Hotels and restaurants are likely to find this trend particularly difficult to cope with. Both need large numbers of relatively unskilled workers for both maintenance tasks and customer contact. Yet they have few opportunities to provide the kind of generally applicable training that most entry-level workers have come to recognize as the key to a better future. This is likely to make it difficult to compete with other industries for young, low-wage workers. Creating learning opportunities for young job seekers or finding some other way to motivate them will be a difficult challenge for the hospitality and travel industries, but this is a problem they urgently need to solve.

GENERATIONAL AND FAMILY TRENDS

FAMILY STRUCTURES ARE BECOMING MORE DIVERSE

In periods of economic difficulty, children and grandchildren move back in with parents and grandparents to save on living expenses. Many bring their own children with them. In the United States, one-third of Generation Xers have returned home at some point in their early lives. Among Millennials, the figure is even higher. The 2001 Census found that so-called "multigenerational households" are the fastest growing group in the United States. Yet the nuclear family also is rebounding in the United States, as Baby-Boomer and Gen-X parents focus on their children and grandparents retain more independence and mobility.

Same-sex households also are gaining new acceptance. At least five American states now permit same-sex marriage or have enacted domestic-partnership laws that provide similar protections. In this, they join such countries as Denmark, Germany, the Czech Republic, the United Kingdom, and most recently Switzerland. Many grandparents are raising their grandchildren because drugs and AIDS have left the middle generation either unable or unavailable to care for their children. This trend is strongest in sub-Saharan Africa, where there will be 25 million AIDS orphans by 2010.

Assessment: This trend will remain in effect for at least a generation in the United States, longer in the rest of the world.

Implications: Where many European countries have largely adjusted to this trend, the United States has not. Making that adjustment will be an important challenge for the next decades.

Tax and welfare policies need adjustment to cope with families in which heads of households are retired or unable to work. Policies also need modification for those who receive Social Security and work to support an extended family. In the United States, the debates over homosexuality and the "decline of the family" will remain polarizing for the foreseeable future. The next debate is likely to focus on granting parental rights to more than two parents, as when a sperm or egg donor wants a role in the life of a child whose official parents are the recipients.

Implications for hospitality and travel: Gays, lesbians, singles, single parents, and multigenerational families all have become lucrative markets for specialty cruises, group tours, and other niche services. They can only grow increasingly significant in the years ahead.

YOUNG PEOPLE PLACE INCREASING IMPORTANCE ON ECONOMIC SUCCESS, WHICH THEY HAVE COME TO EXPECT

Throughout the 1990s—effectively, their entire adult lives— Generation Xers, Dot-coms, and Millennials knew only good economic times. The economic downturn at the turn of the century seemed to them a confusing aberration rather than a predictable part of the business cycle. The current global recession is a frightening wake-up call. Yet, most expect to see growing hardship on a national level, but they both want and expect prosperity for themselves. In the United States especially, most young people have high aspirations, but many lack the means to achieve them owing to high dropout rates and ineffective schools.

Assessment: This trend appeared with the Baby Boom generation and has strengthened with the later cohorts. It will be interesting to see what develops among the children of the Millennials, something we find difficult to predict with any confidence.

Implications: Disappointed ambitions will be a major source of political unrest in the United States and many other countries in the next two decades. Most of the other countries seriously affected by this trend will be in the developing world or will be host to large numbers of disadvantaged immigrants.

Entrepreneurialism will be a global trend, as members of Generation X and the Millennials throughout the world tend to share values. Generation X and Millennial entrepreneurs are largely responsible for the current economic growth in India and China, where they are becoming a major force in the Communist party. In India, the younger generations dress and think more like their American counterparts than their parents. In China, the democratic fervour that spawned Tiananmen Square has been replaced by capitalist entrepreneurialism.

If younger-generation workers find their ambitions thwarted, they will create growing pressure for economic and social reform. If change does not come fast enough in the developing world, disappointed expectations will raise the number of young people who emigrate to the developed lands. In the United States, pressure will grow to provide more, and less burdensome, economic assistance to qualified high school graduates who cannot afford to go on to college. Pressure also will grow to make sure that all American students have access to an education capable of preparing them for college or a rewarding career.

Implications for hospitality and travel: Young people concerned with economic success may be even less willing to accept entry-level jobs, yet under-equipped to take on more demanding roles. This is likely to increase job turnover, even in non-menial positions. The most important asset for motivating and keeping these potential workers will be a strong training programme that gives them a clear path for advancement. Unfortunately, this may be difficult to provide.

GENERATION X, THE DOT-COMS, AND THE MILLENNIALS ARE GAINING SOCIAL AND ORGANIZATIONAL INFLUENCE

Members of each group—ranging from nearly 50 to the 20-somethings—have much more in common with their peers than with their parents. Their values and concerns are remarkably uniform throughout the world. Socially and in business, they are nearly colour-blind and gender-blind. Generation X is starting new businesses at an unprecedented rate, and the Millennial generation is proving to be even more business-oriented, caring for little but the bottom line. They will work for others, but only on their own terms.

Generation X and the Millennials thrive on challenge, opportunity, and training—whatever will best prepare them for their next career move. Cash is just the beginning of what they expect. Employers will have to adjust their policies and practices to the values of these new and different generations, including finding new ways to motivate and reward them.

However, they also have a powerful commitment to society. Gen Xers are mainstays of "voluntourism," spending part of their vacations on volunteer work. In a recent survey, 60 percent of respondents said they would be interested in doing scientific or environmental work while on vacation. Even more would be willing to teach English or another academic subject.

Assessment: As trends go, this is an evergreen. In ten years or so, we will simply add the next new generation to the list.

Implications: In values, cultural norms, political issues, and many other ways, this change of generations will be every bit as transforming as the transition from the World War II generation to the Baby Boomers.

Employers will have to adjust virtually all of their policies and practices to the values of these new and different generations, including finding new ways to motivate and reward them. Generation X and the Millennials thrive on challenge, opportunity, and training—whatever will best prepare them for their next career move. Cash is just the beginning of what they expect. For these generations, lifelong learning is nothing new; it's just the way life is. Companies that can provide diverse, cuttingedge training will have a strong recruiting advantage over competitors that offer fewer opportunities to improve their skills and knowledge base.

Generations X and Millennial are well equipped for work in a high-tech world, but they have little interest in their employers' needs. They have a powerful urge to do things their own way. As both customers and employees, they will demand even more advanced telecommunications and Internet-based transactions.

Implications for hospitality and travel: These generations have hard noses. Young business travelers may put up with delays when a massive snow storm arrives as they were ready to leave. They won't like waiting for hours because the airport's departure schedule is overbooked. Scheduling problems, faulty service, and other down-checks that today's consumers would accept with minor grumbling will have to be fixed, or tomorrow's travelers will plaster their disgust all over the Internet.

Millennials especially can be demanding. When they have a problem at an airline, they do not just bother the people at the airport ticket desk. They grab their cell phones and call or text the frequent flier department to apply pressure for a favourable resolution. Satisfying such customers will be a constant challenge. We have seen them arrive at a hotel without a reservation only to find that no rooms are available. Rather than accepting the situation, they called the chain's frequent-visitor programme to complain and ask whether a room might be available after all.

These generations will have no problem spending online sums that would have stopped their parents cold. They will not accept obstacles to their habit of shopping online and clicking "Buy" the instant their decision is made. This is especially important for the cruise market. If one cruise line is too stodgy to enable online booking—and stodgy, not exclusive, is how they will be perceived—then a more up-to-date operator will get their business.

Baby Boomers rebelled in the early-'60s, then adopted their parents' materialism and took it to whole new levels. Generation X, and particularly the Dot-coms and Millennials, have taken another path. They enjoy a Manhattan while surrounded by Rat-Pack retro elegance. Yet, they always pair indulgence with a self-deprecating humor that says it's not taken seriously. The most successful hotels will find a way to match that sense of feet-on-the-ground fun while providing impeccable service to older guests.

The new generations mean changes for restaurants as well. Although younger travelers are bringing home tastes for new cuisines, it may not be the foods of Uruguay or Nepal that next capture their imagination and limited customer loyalty. Unlike previous generations, the Xers and Dot-coms tend to mix and match. A typical meal might begin with old-fashioned Mexican nachos for an appetizer, then move on to a Thai fish dish with couscous from Algeria and a Chilean wine. Restaurants hoping to attract this crowd will need both imagination and broad experience with the world's exotic flavours.

The new generations could add a few points to the growth rate for hospitality and travel. They are enthusiastic travelers, willing to drop everything when a friend suggests an adventure. This may not make them the ideal employees by traditional standards, but it does make them great customers. Expect major growth in eco-tourism and "voluntourism," thanks to under-40 vacationers.

TWO-INCOME COUPLES ARE BECOMING THE NORM IN MOST OF THE INDUSTRIALIZED LANDS, ALTHOUGH IN THE U.S. THE TREND TOWARDS GREATER EMPLOYMENT AMONG WOMEN IS SLOWING

The percentage of working-age women who are employed or are actively looking for work has grown steadily throughout the industrialized world. In the United States, it has grown from 46 percent in 1970 to about 66 percent in 2005, compared with 77 percent of men. In Japan, a majority of households have included two earners since at least 1980.

In the United States, both the husband and the wife worked in 50.9 percent of married-couple families in 2003, according to the U.S. Bureau of Labour Statistics' Current Population Survey. This has declined since 1997, when it was 53.4 percent. However, families in which only the woman worked rose for the third straight year, to 6.8 percent, in 2003.

Assessment: In the industrialized nations, this trend has just about played out, as the number of two-income households has begun to stabilize. However, it will be a growing force in India and other industrializing lands for many years to come.

Implications: This emphasis on work is one big reason the richest 25 to 50 percent of the U.S. population has reached zero population growth. They have no time for children and little interest in having large families.

Demand for on-the-job child care, extended parental leave, and other family-oriented benefits can only grow. In the long run, this could erode the profitability of some American companies, unless it is matched by an equal growth in productivity. This also promotes self-employment and entrepreneurialism, as one family member's salary can tide them over while the other works to establish a new business.

Expect to see many families that usually have two incomes, but have frequent intervals in which one member takes a sabbatical or goes back to school to prepare for another career. As information technologies render former occupations obsolete, this will become the new norm. Implications for hospitality and travel: Two-career couples can afford to eat out often, take frequent short vacations, and buy new cars and other such goods. And they feel they deserve whatever luxuries they can afford. This is quickly expanding the market for travel and leisure activities. It will continue to skew the travel and hospitality markets away from traditional two-week vacations and towards three-day weekend getaways, "cruises to nowhere," and other forms of short-term pampering for pressured couples in need of a break.

ECONOMIC TRENDS

THE ECONOMY OF THE DEVELOPED WORLD IS GROWING STEADILY, WITH ONLY BRIEF INTERRUPTIONS.

When the United States catches a cold, the rest of the world gets pneumonia, or so economists used to say. Late in 2008, the United States has pneumonia. Home prices remain in free-fall, and the credit market has collapsed. Jobs are disappearing at a rate of more than 1 million every two weeks. Consumer confidence is plummeting. Most of the world is in recession. It turns out that 2008 and some of 2009 are one of the interruptions contemplated in the trend.

Looking abroad, we can see effects of America's problems. The entire European Union is in recession. China, Australia, India, Japan, and Russia are in or near recession. In all, the economies of the world seem a lot less healthy than they did a few months ago. Throughout the world, governments are scrambling to shore up lending institutions, stem the tide of foreclosures, restore the flow of credit, and provide jobs for the newly unemployed. These efforts will continue through 2009.

At that point, global economic growth will resume its accustomed rate, a bit more than 5 percent per year as of 2007.

Assessment: These trends have been revised many times since they were first codified in the late 1980s. Some trends have fallen out of the list as they matured or as circumstances came along to change them. Others have been added as they were recognized. This trend has remained a constant, and with each revision its effective period has been extended. To invalidate this trend would take a catastrophe on the order of the permanent loss of Middle Eastern oil from the Western economies. Not even the recession of 2008 and '09 rises to that level of destruction.

Implications for Cruise Lines: People take cruises when they feel economically secure and take less expensive vacations when they do not. In the next few years, many more people will feel they can afford to take a cruise. This is relieving the price pressure on cruise lines, so that fewer tickets will be discounted. This should improve profitability for the next several years.

THE GLOBAL ECONOMY IS GROWING MORE INTEGRATED

By some counts, only half of the world's one hundred largest economies are nation-states. The rest are multinational corporations. In the European Union, relaxation of border and capital controls and the adoption of a common currency and uniform product standards continue to make it easier for companies to distribute products and support functions throughout the Continent. The Internet also brings manufacturers effectively closer to remote suppliers and customers. Companies are increasingly farming out high-cost, low-payoff secondary functions to suppliers, service firms, and consultants, many of them located in other countries. Companies in high-wage countries also are outsourcing management and service jobs to low-wage countries. An estimated 3.3 million U.S. jobs are expected to migrate to India and China by 2015. Some 40 million jobs are believed vulnerable to outsourcing.

Assessment: This trend will continue for at least the next two decades.

Implications: The growth of e-commerce enables businesses to shop globally for the cheapest raw materials and supplies. In niche markets, the Internet also makes it possible for small companies to compete with giants worldwide with relatively little investment. This has brought new opportunities for quality-control problems and fraudulent cost-cutting by suppliers, as seen in the recent spate of tainted food and other products coming from China.

The Net also has created a generation of "e-preneurs" whose businesses exist largely on the Internet, with production, fulfillment, and other functions all outsourced to specialty firms. Demand will continue to grow for employee incentives suited to other cultures, aid to executives going overseas, and the many other aspects of doing business in foreign countries.

However, rising demand for foreign-language training is likely to be a temporary phenomenon, as more countries adopt English as part of their basic school curricula. Western companies may have to accept that proprietary information will be shared not just with their immediate partners in Asian joint ventures, but also with other members of the partners' trading conglomerates. In high technology and aerospace, that may expose companies to extra scrutiny due to national-security concerns.

Establishing overseas branches mitigates this concern by keeping trade secrets within the company, even while gaining the benefits of cheaper foreign labour and other resources. Economic ties can give richer, more powerful countries considerable influence over their junior partners. Thus far, China has been the most successful at wielding this "soft" power. This has given it the ability to undermine American foreign policy even as it secures its energy and raw-materials needs.

Implications for hospitality and travel: Online B2B sales and services will play a growing role in minimizing costs for all hospitality and travel businesses. For the same reason, some out-of-sight functions such as accounting may increasingly be outsourced to services in India, China, and Eastern Europe. However, most customer service operations will remain in the firm's home country, where quality is easier to oversee.

CONSUMERISM IS STILL GROWING

Consumer advocacy agencies and organizations are proliferating, promoting improved content labels, warning notices, nutrition data, and the like on packaging, TV, the Internet, and even restaurant menus. On the Internet, shoppers themselves have access to a growing universe of information about pricing, services, delivery time, and customer satisfaction. Japan, China, and other markets are beginning the same revolution that has replaced America's neighborhood stores with cost-cutting warehouse operations, discounters such as Wal-Mart, and "category killers" like Staples and Home Depot. As a result, consumer movements are springing up in countries where they have never existed. Consumer laws and regulations will follow.

Assessment: This trend seems likely to remain healthy for the at least the next 15 years.

Implications: Consumer advocacy agencies and organizations will continue to proliferate, promoting improved content labels, warning notices, nutrition data, and the like on packaging, TV, the Internet, and even restaurant menus. Europe, Japan, China, and other markets are undergoing the same revolution that has replaced America's neighborhood stores with discounters.

However, the cultural and political power of farmers and small shop owners has slowed this trend in some areas, particularly in Japan. Thanks to recent contamination of food imported from China, the U.S. Food and Drug Administration will be required to improve screening of incoming food products. However, it will not receive adequate funding to do the job effectively.

As prices fall to commodity levels and online stores can list virtually every product and brand in their industry without significant overhead, service is the only field left in which marketers on and off the Internet can compete effectively. Branded items with good reputations are even more important for developing repeat business. Consumer debt may be an even greater problem for Millennials than it has been for their elders. Implications for hospitality and travel: Fliers increasingly will expect quality service to go with their cheap seats. Airlines therefore will have to do a better job of getting their planes into the air on time, even if that means scheduling them for odd hours. Meals can remain optional, but if customers choose to buy them, they had better be good. And so on. We believe the consumerism of the past will prove to have been no more than prologue for the greater demands to come.

A good example is the new Terminal 5 at Heathrow, where nearly everything is bigger, better, and more luxurious. Check-in kiosks scattered throughout the spacious facility mean that waiting lines are no more than two or three deep. There are six lounges, a luxurious travel spa, more bathrooms than in older terminals, even showers for travelers.

There are 22 places to eat, from simple snack shops to high-end restaurants. There are designer clothing stores, a luggage shop and a luxury leather store, a computer shop, bookstore, six newsstands, and even a Harrod's. When Terminal 5 is fully operational, 80 percent of passengers at Heathrow will pass through it. Chances are that they will be glad to do so. Travelers are likely to be happier still when other air terminals are as convenient and comfortable as Terminal 5.

Cruise lines increasingly face similar pressures. The prestige-oriented days of booking through a travel agent are coming to an end. Today's consumers want value and convenience when buying a cruise package just as they do in any other form of shopping. That means picking through all the tours that seem appealing, selecting the one that gives the best possible value for the price, and buying it then and there.

In a networked, consumerist society, a respected brand is any chain's most important asset. This will be particularly significant for hotels and restaurants. A reputation for comfortable accommodations, pleasant surroundings, and top-notch service requires constant effort to establish and maintain. It can be lost in moments if a disappointed customer complains in the Internet's many forums and chat rooms. More than ever before, quality and service are all-important.

Consumer legislation and "bills of rights" are no more than reminders of business basics. The travel and hospitality industries exist to serve their guests. Companies that do it brilliantly will continue to prosper. Those that do not will find many new, fast-growing competitors eager to build a customer base at their expense. The essence of a consumer society turns out to be intense, endless competition to be the best in the industry.

RESEARCH AND DEVELOPMENT PLAY A GROWING ROLE IN THE WORLD ECONOMY.

Total U.S. outlays on R and D have grown steadily in the past three decades. In 2006, the United States spent about $330 billion on R and D. China has taken second place in the world's R and D spending, with a budget estimate at $136 billion in 2006. China says it will raise its R and D spending from about 1.23 percent of GDP in 2004 to 2.5 percent in 2020. R and D outlays in Japan have risen almost continuously, to nearly 3 percent of GDP, some $130 billion in 2006. R and D spending in the European Union (EU-15) amounted to $230 billion in 2006, about 1.9 percent of GDP. The European Commission has set a goal of raising R and D spending to 3 percent of GDP by 2010. In Russia, R and D funding is roughly 1.5 percent of GDP, up from just 0.7 percent in 1997; this amounted to about $26.25 billion in 2006. These figures do not include whatever clandestine military research escapes notice.

Assessment: This trend is stabilizing as developed nations, particularly the United States, devote more of their resources to less productive activities. We believe this is a temporary phenomenon. The trend will regain momentum in the years ahead. It will not fall off this list before the middle of this century.

Implications: This is a significant factor in the acceleration of technological change. The demand for scientists, engineers, and technicians will continue to grow, particularly in fields where research promises an immediate business payoff.

Low-wage countries such as China once took only low-wage jobs from advanced industrialized countries such as the United States. Today higher-paid jobs in science, technology, and the professions also are at risk. Countries like India, China, and Russia once suffered a brain drain as those with high-tech skills emigrated to highdemand, high-wage destinations. Today, many students and professionals spend time in the West to learn cutting-edge skills, and then return to their native lands to work, start companies, and teach. This promotes the growth of some developing countries while reducing the competitive advantages of the developed world.

Implications for hospitality and travel: Trend 22 is responsible for much of the acceleration in technological advances seen in Trend 34.

SERVICES ARE THE FASTEST-GROWING SECTOR OF THE GLOBAL ECONOMY.

Service jobs have replaced many of the well-paid positions lost in manufacturing, transportation, and agriculture. Most of these new jobs, often part time, pay half the wages of manufacturing jobs. On the other hand, computer-related service jobs pay much more than the minimum—for workers with sound education and training.

Service industries provide 79 percent of the GDP in the United States, 77 percent in France, 74 percent in Britain, 73 percent in Japan, and 70 percent in Germany. In each case, services are growing rapidly, other sectors less so, and they provide substantial majorities of private non-farm employment. Production and less-skilled jobs, in contrast, are disappearing. By 2014, the

United States is expected to have more chief executives than machine tool operators, more lawyers than farm workers.

Assessment: There is no foreseeable end to this trend.

Implications: In the United States, the growth of service industries is helping to deplete the middle class, as well-paid jobs in manufacturing are replaced by relatively ill-paid service positions, leaving a country of "have-a-lots" and many "havenots," but relatively few "have-enoughs."

Services are now beginning to compete globally, just as manufacturing industries have done over the last 20 years. By creating competitive pressure on wages in the industrialized lands, this trend will help to keep inflation in check. The growth of international business will act as a stabilizing force in world affairs, as most countries find that conflict is unacceptably hard on the bottom line.

Implications for hospitality and travel: This trend brings the opportunity to spin off peripheral functions to service firms that specialize in them. For example, there is no longer any reason for a major hotel to do its own laundry, wash its own cutlery, or even operate its own food service. All these functions can be farmed out to other companies and treated as an operating expense comparable to utilities. Many more such opportunities will appear in the years ahead, bringing still greater efficiency to the industries' core customer-service functions.

WOMEN'S SALARIES ARE APPROACHING EQUALITY WITH MEN'S—BUT VERY SLOWLY

In the 1980s and '90s, women's overall income in the United States was catching up with that of their male co-workers. More recently, it has stagnated. In 1995, university educated women earned 75.7 cents for every dollar earned by men, on average.

In 2005, it had fallen to 74.7 cents. During the same period, lower-income women continued to gain on their male peers, though very slowly. One reason may be that women are less interested than men in working 70 hours or more per week during their prime reproductive years, and growing numbers have chosen to stay home and rear their children. Women also appear to be less likely to choose and pursue a career on the basis of income. Studies that attempt to compensate for differences in factors such as education, occupation, experience, and union membership find much smaller income differences than others.

One reported that women receive about 91 percent as much as men. Another held that incomes are virtually equal when measured with appropriate rigour. Some studies also suggest that the pay gap has largely disappeared for women in the newest cohort of workers. This would make sense, given the nearly total gender blindness of the Millennials.

The same trend is visible in most other industrialized countries. According to the European Commission, women on the Continent earn 15 percent less than men, on average, down from 17 percent in 1995. In Britain, the gap was 20 percent, down from 26 percent. Japan is an exception to this trend. The gender gap there remains near 35 percent.

Assessment: In the United States, this trend may be in its last generation, thanks to the gender-blind values of the Millennials. In other countries, and particularly Japan, it may have another 30 years to run.

Implications: The fact that women's salaries are lagging despite higher academic achievement than men suggests that many college-educated women may be underemployed. Whether this is by their choice or occurs for some other reason has yet to be determined.

More new hires will be women, and they will expect both pay and opportunities equal to those of men. Women's average income could exceed men's within a generation. College graduates enjoy a significant advantage in earnings over peers whose education ended with high school. In the United States, some 65 percent of young men and women enroll in college after high school, but women are more likely to graduate. About 58 percent of college graduates are women.

To the extent that experience translates as prestige and corporate value, older women should find it easier to reach upper-management positions. This will blaze the trail and help raise the pay scale for women still climbing the corporate ladder.

Competition for top executive positions, once effectively limited to men, will intensify even as the corporate ladder loses many of its rungs. The glass ceiling has been broken. One-fourth of upper executives today, and nearly 20 percent of corporate board members, are women—far more than in any previous generation. Look for more women to reach decision-making levels in government and business. However, the remaining obstacles to women's advancement may explain why women now start businesses at roughly twice the rate of men. Implications for hospitality and travel: This trend has fewer implications for hospitality and travel than for most other industries. Barriers to women's advancement have been relatively small in hospitality and travel for many years, and women's pay has been much nearer to that of men in similar positions that is common in other fields.

WORK AND LABOUR FORCE TRENDS

SPECIALIZATION CONTINUES TO SPREAD THROUGHOUT INDUSTRY AND THE PROFESSIONS

For doctors, lawyers, engineers, and other professionals, the size of the body of knowledge required to excel in any one area precludes excellence across all areas. The same principle applies to artisans. Witness the rise of post-and-beam homebuilders, old-house restorers, automobile electronics technicians, and mechanics trained to work on only one brand of car. Modern information-based organizations increasingly depend on teams of task-focused specialists. For hundreds of tasks, corporations increasingly turn to consultants and contractors who specialize more and more narrowly as markets globalize and technologies differentiate.

Assessment: This process will continue for at least another 20 years.

Implications: In an information age, each new level of specialization provides greater efficiencies, reducing the cost of doing business even as it creates new opportunities. This should continue to make global business more productive and profitable for so long as it continues.

This trend creates endless new niche markets to be served by small businesses and individual consultants. It also brings more career choices, as old specialties quickly become obsolete, but new ones appear even more rapidly.

Implications for hospitality and travel: Again, the Implications for these industries parallel the common experience: greater business efficiency and the rapid proliferation of small businesses designed to provide the best possible service to niche markets.

THE TRADITIONAL AGE OF RETIREMENT IS LOSING ITS SIGNIFICANCE

Organization for Economic Co-operation and Development (OECD) data show that people are retiring earlier in the developed world. In 2004, less than 60 percent of the 54 to 60 age group in the OECD countries had a job. This varied from 50 percent in the earliest-retiring nations to 76 percent in the latest. According to Pew Research, as of 2006 the average American worker planned to retire at age 61 but actually did so at 57.8. These "retirements" may not be permanent. Americans in particular often return to work and delay complete retirement for several years. About one in five people, and 40 percent of seniors, say they plan to continue working until they die.

Assessment: In the United States, this trend will be complete in a generation. Where social safety nets are stronger, it is likely to continue through at least 2030.

Implications: Given the widespread shortage of retirement savings and investments, most Americans will delay retirement until they can no longer work, whether they wish to or not.

Since the penalty on earnings of Social Security recipients has been rescinded, more American retirees will return to work, and those not yet retired will be more likely to remain on the job. This trend will spread to other industrialized countries as the retirement-age population grows and the number of active workers to support them declines. People increasingly will work at one career, "retire" for a while (perhaps to travel) when they can afford it, return to school, begin another career, and so on in endless variations. True retirement, a permanent end to work, will be delayed until very late in life.

By 2015, we expect the average retirement age in the United States to be delayed well into the 70s. Benefits may also continue their decline, and they will be given based on need, rather than as an entitlement. Even though the Social Security programme has been the "third rail" of American politics, within five years, the retirement age will be moved back at least to 70 for early retirement and full benefits at 72.

Retirees will act as technical aides to teachers, especially in the sciences. In the long run, it may prove impossible to maintain the tradition of retirement, except through personal savings and investment.

Implications for hospitality and travel: Divide seniors into three groups:

- Those who can afford to do so are likely to retire early. They will spend much of their time traveling, eating out, and otherwise enjoying life. They will be a prime source of business for high-end hotels, resorts, and cruise lines.
- Those who are not quite so well-to-do but still can retire on time also will travel regularly but are likely to economize on accommodations, generally taking a trip to Orlando, rather than Paris, or a relatively brief Caribbean cruise, rather than a round-the-world trip.
- There will be many as well who really cannot afford to retire completely. These 0lder workers will partially make up for any future shortages of entry-level employees. The chance to remain in the workplace will reduce the risk of poverty for many elderly people who otherwise would have had to depend on Social Security to get by.

SECOND AND THIRD CAREERS ARE BECOMING COMMON, AS MORE PEOPLE MAKE MID-LIFE CHANGES IN OCCUPATION

Americans born at the tail end of the Baby Boom (1956 to 1964) held an average of ten jobs between ages 18 and 38, according to the U.S. Bureau of Labour Statistics. These job jumpers continue with short-duration jobs even as they approach middle age: 70 percent of the jobs they took between ages 33 and 39 ended within five years. In the United States, 23 percent of workers surveyed in 2004 reported being dissatisfied with their careers and considering a change of occupation. Seventy percent of Irish workers surveyed in 2004 also said they hoped to make a career change soon. Women and the 26-to-35 age group were most likely to report the desire to change careers. "Personal fulfillment" was the biggest reason cited for making the change.

Assessment: This trend will not disappear unless the pace of technological change slows dramatically—or we reach the so-called "singularity," when man's inventions grow so intelligent themselves that they entirely displace human beings from the workforce.

Implications: Boomers and their children will have not just two or three careers, but five or six, as dying industries are replaced by new opportunities.

"Earn while you learn" takes on new meaning: Most people will have to study for their next occupation, even as they pursue their current career. In many two-earner couples, one member or the other will often take a sabbatical to prepare for a new career. Self-employment is becoming an increasingly attractive option, as being your own boss makes it easier to set aside time for career development. This is especially true for Generation Xers and Millennials. Growing numbers of retirees will start their own businesses, both to keep occupied and to supplement their meagre savings with new income. This trend has already begun. Retirement plans must be revised so that workers can transfer medical and pension benefits from one career to the next—a change that has long been needed. We believe this will occur soon after the Baby Boom generation begins to retire in 2011.

Implications for hospitality and travel: These industries have obvious appeal for mid-life career changers. These first-time entrepreneurs start a substantial fraction of new one-off restaurants, travel destinations, bed-and-breakfasts, and business services. They will continue to be a source of creativity for hospitality and travel.

THE WORK ETHIC IS VANISHING

More than one-third of U.S. workers reported calling in sick when they were not ill at least once in the past 12 months, and 10 percent had done so at least three times, according to a 2004 survey by CareerBuilder.com. Job security and high pay are not the motivators they once were, because social mobility is high and people seek job fulfillment. Some 48 percent of those responding in a recent Louis Harris poll said they work because it "gives a feeling of real accomplishment." Fifty-five percent of the top executives interviewed in the poll say that erosion of the work ethic will have a major negative effect on corporate performance in the future.

Assessment: There is little prospect that this will change until the children of today's young adults grow up to rebel against their parents' values.

Implications: Both employers and voters must do their best to find candidates who can be trusted, but must expect to fail in their search. This makes safeguards against wrongdoing, both at work and in public lives, more important than ever. The new generation of workers cannot simply be hired and ignored. They must be nurtured, paid well, and made to feel appreciated or they will quickly look for a friendlier, more rewarding workplace. Training is crucial. Without the opportunity to learn new skills, young people will quickly find a job that can help them prepare for the rest of their many careers.

Implications for hospitality and travel: This trend will make it more difficult to ensure a high level of customer service in all industries. Since this is the core of hospitality and travel, they are likely to be hit harder than others by any decline in their employees' diligence.

LABOUR UNIONS ARE LOSING THEIR POWER TO SECURE RIGHTS FOR WORKERS AND TO SHAPE PUBLIC POLICY IN REGARD TO WORKPLACE ISSUES

Union membership has been falling for the past two decades. In the United States, some 20 percent of workers were union members in 1983. In 2006, just 12.0 percent of employed wage and salary workers were union members, down from 12.5 percent a year earlier. In Britain, where the Thatcher government broke union power in the 1980s, union membership has declined almost continuously, to 28.4 percent in December 2006. In South Korea, where organized labour once was invincible, no more than 11 percent of workers are union members. One reason for this decline is that companies are freely seeking and finding non-unionized workers around the world. They also contract out a growing proportion of business activities to non-union firms.

Assessment: In spite of determined, and occasionally successful, recruiting efforts in formerly non-union industries, union memberships and power will continue to decline for the next 15 years—until organized labour is little more than a fringe phenomenon. The trend will be reversed only if Washington and other national governments rescind pro-business labour laws and policies enacted in the last 20-plus years.

Implications: For large companies, this trend promises continued stability in employee wages and benefits. Unions eager to regain their membership will target any substantial industry or firm with less-skilled employees to organize. This could raise labour costs for companies that unions once would have considered too small to organize. In ten to 15 years, American labour unions will compete with AARP to lead the battle for the rights of late-life workers and for secure retirement benefits. They face an inherent conflict between the interests of workers in what once would have been the retirement years and those of younger members, who rightly see the elderly as having saddled them with the cost of whatever benefits older generations enjoy. Unions' political strength is also diminishing and is increasingly being surpassed by powerful blocs such as AARP, Hispanics, and African Americans. The old paradigm of unions vs. corporations is obsolete. In today's economy, workers negotiate alongside management, winning shared bonuses.

Implications for hospitality and travel: non-union segments of these industries represent an appealing "market" for union organizers desperate to shore up their memberships. Any major company in hospitality and travel can expect unions to focus on workers who have yet to be organized.

ENERGY TRENDS

DESPITE EFFORTS TO DEVELOP ALTERNATIVE SOURCES OF ENERGY, OIL CONSUMPTION IS STILL RISING RAPIDLY

The world used only 57 million barrels of oil per day in 1973, when the first major price shock hit. By 2004, it was using 83 million barrels daily, according to the U.S. Energy Information Administration. Consumption is expected to reach 97 million barrels daily by 2015 and 118 million by 2030. Much of this increase will be due to China, which is the second-largest user of oil in the world, and the fastest growing.

Assessment: Nothing is likely to reverse this trend in the next 25 years.

Implications: Oil prices now are high enough to provide an incentive to develop new fields, such as the Arctic National Wildlife Refuge and the deep fields under the Gulf of Mexico. Environmentally sensitive areas will be developed using new drilling techniques, double-walled pipelines and other precautions, that make it possible to extract oil with less damage to the surroundings. Any prolonged rise of oil prices to triple digits will erode support for environmental protections in the United States, leading to widespread development of whatever energy sources are most readily available, regardless of the long-term consequences.

Implications for hospitality and travel: For airlines, the rising price of oil has become a crushing burden. This more than any other single factor has driven the wave of industry consolidation in the last few years. It will continue to do so until prices stabilize.

For other hospitality and travel operators, energy costs represent a relatively small expense—significant, but much less so than staff paychecks and benefits. High oil prices are a problem that most of them can live with, at least temporarily.

CONTRARY TO POPULAR BELIEF, THE WORLD'S CONFIRMED OIL SUPPLY IS GROWING, NOT DECLINING

As a result of intensive exploration, the world's proven oil reserves climbed steadily since the 1980s and now hover at over 1.3 trillion barrels. Natural gas reserves stood at about 6.2 trillion cubic feet in 2007, about 1 percent more than a year earlier. Recent discoveries of major oil fields in Canada, Brazil, and under the Gulf of Mexico have substantially increased the world's known oil reserves.

Assessment: Talk of "peak oil," the suggestion that crude production has topped out, or soon will, is unjustified and, in FI's view, unjustifiable. Our best estimate is that the world has used about one-fourth of its recoverable oil, and almost certainly no more than one-third. This trend will remain intact until at least 2040.

Implications: Higher oil prices should make it cost effective to develop new methods of recovering oil from old wells. Technologies already developed could add nearly 50 percent to the world's recoverable oil supply.

OPEC will continue to supply most of the oil used by the developed world. According to the U.S. Department of Energy, OPEC oil production will grow to about 57 million barrels of oil per day by 2020. Russia and Kazakhstan will be major suppliers if the necessary pipelines can be completed and political uncertainties do not block investment by Western oil companies. Russia will grow into the world's second-largest oil producer by 2010.

Alternative energy sources face problems with economic viability. Barring substantial incentives, this will inhibit efforts to stem global warming for the foreseeable future. A generalized war in the Middle East after the United States leaves Iraq could drastically reduce the region's oil output. This is unlikely, but the probable impact of such a conflict is so great that the possibility cannot be ignored. The spread of fundamentalist Muslim regimes with a grudge against the West also could keep OPEC oil out of the American market. If the United States loses access to Middle Eastern oil, it will buy even more from Canada and Venezuela, tap the Arctic National Wildlife Reserve, and develop the deepwater fields under the Gulf of Mexico much faster than expected.

In a prolonged energy emergency, America also would be likely to develop its vast reserves of oil shale, which have long been economically viable at crude prices over $40 per barrel. New technology reportedly makes it profitable at any price over $17 per barrel. With enough shale oil to supply its own needs for 300 years, the United States could become one of the world's largest petroleum exporters. Developing shale would devastate the environment, but with crude oil prices in triple digits during a Mid-East war, the environment would be considered expendable.

Implications for hospitality and travel: There is at least some hope that oil prices will stabilize at livable levels within the next few years.

WHEN NOT PERTURBED BY GREATER-THAN-NORMAL POLITICAL OR ECONOMIC INSTABILITY, OIL PRICES AVERAGE AROUND $65 PER BARREL

New energy demand from the fast-growing economies of China and India has raised the floor that until 2004 supported oil in the $25 per barrel range. Nonetheless, the spike in prices to nearly $150 per barrel in mid-2008 was an aberration. At least four factors contributed to the bubble in energy prices: Perhaps 30 percent of the increase in oil prices to their June 2008 high stemmed from the long-term decline in the value of the U.S. dollar on foreign exchange markets. Another $10 to $15 per barrel represented a "risk premium" due to fears of instability triggered by the Iraq war and Washington's threats to attack Iran. Without those two factors, $145 oil would have been $100 oil. A worldwide shortage of refinery capacity helped to drive up the cost of gasoline, fuel oil, and other energy products. It appears that rampant futures speculation in the energy markets also helped to spur oil prices. None of these factors was permanent.

Assessment: The long-term trend towards stable energy prices can only grow stronger as the West reigns in consumption and alternative energy technologies become practical.

Implications for Cruise Lines: The single greatest "disposable" expense of running a cruise ship should remain under control. This will help to keep tickets affordable and profits acceptable.

GROWING COMPETITION FROM OTHER ENERGY SOURCES ALSO WILL HELP TO LIMIT THE PRICE OF OIL. NUCLEAR POWER IS GROWING RAPIDLY

In Russia, plans call for construction of twenty-six more nuclear plants by 2030, when 25 percent or more of the nation's electricity will be nuclear. China plans to build thirty reactors by 2020, quadrupling its number and bringing nuclear energy consumption from 16 billion kWh in 2000 to 142 billion kWh. Even the United States is weighing the construction of new reactors.

For transportation, ethanol is the most useful alternative to petroleum. Brazil already gets more than 40 percent of its fuel for cars from ethanol made from sugar cane. Renewable sources such as wind and solar power also are growing rapidly, but they are unlikely ever to make up more than a small fraction of the world's energy supply, save in areas where natural resources are plentiful. Iceland's drive to develop geothermal power is one example.

Assessment: This trend will remain in effect for at least 30 years.

Implications: Though oil will remain the world's most important energy resource for years to come, two or three decades forward it should be less of a choke point in the global economy. We should feed our stomachs before we feed our cars. Producing ethanol from switchgrass would cut the cost of corn by 20 percent, according to the Worldwatch Institute. This would significantly ease the global food crisis.

Solar, geothermal, wind, and wave energy will ease power problems where these resources are most readily available, though they will supply only a very small fraction of the world's energy in the foreseeable future. Declining reliance on oil eventually could help to reduce air and water pollution, at least in the developed world. By 2060, a costly but pollution-free hydrogen economy may at last become practical.

Fusion power remains a distant hope. Cold fusion also remains a long shot for practical power, but FI believes it can no longer be discounted. If the U.S. Navy's reports of successful experiments can be corroborated, power plants based on the process could begin to come on line by 2030. Implications for hospitality and travel: Save where there is an abundance of alternative energy resources, operators will continue to depend primarily on oil for their power. This will render them vulnerable to oil price shocks until a major alternative fuel source, such as fusion, becomes available.

TECHNOLOGY TRENDS

TECHNOLOGY INCREASINGLY DOMINATES BOTH THE ECONOMY AND SOCIETY

New technologies are surpassing the previous state of the art in all fields. Laptop computers and Internet-equipped cell phones provide 24/7 access to e-mail and Web sites. Flexible, general-service personal robots will appear in the home by 2015, expanding on the capabilities robotic vacuum cleaners and lawn mowers. New materials are bringing stronger, lighter structures that can monitor their own wear.

By 2015, artificial intelligence (AI), data mining, and virtual reality will help most organizations to assimilate data and solve problems beyond the range of today's computers. The promise of nanotechnology is just being explored, but real possibilities range from high-powered super-batteries to cell-sized health monitors. Ultimately, speculations that we are approaching the "singularity," the time when our artifacts become so intelligent that they can design themselves and we cannot understand how they work, may prove correct. At that point, humanity will be largely a passenger in its own evolution as a technological species.

Assessment: Technologically related changes in society and business seen over the last 20 years are just the beginning of a trend that will accelerate at least through this century.

Implications: New technologies should continue to improve the efficiency of many industries, helping to keep costs under control.

However, this increased productivity has retarded United States job creation since at least 2002. Other developed countries are likely to feel the same effect in the future. Technology made international outsourcing possible. It will continue to promote outsourcing to the benefit of the recipient countries, but to cause painful job losses in the donor lands.

New technologies often require a higher level of education and training to use them effectively. They also provide many new opportunities to create businesses and jobs. Automation will continue to cut the cost of many services and products, making it possible to reduce prices while still improving profits. This will be critical to business survival as the Internet continues to push the price of many products to the commodity level.

New technology also will make it easier for industry to minimize and capture its effluent. This will be a crucial ability in the environmentally conscious future. In 1999, a team at the technology organization Battelle compiled a list of the ten most strategic technological trends for the next 20 years.

Key technologies for 2020, as forecast by Battelle:

- Gene-based medical care, from custom-tailored pharmaceuticals to cloned organs for transplantation;
- High-powered energy packages such as advanced batteries, cheap fuel cells, and micro-generators;
- "Green integrated technology" to eliminate manufacturing waste and make products completely recyclable;
- Omnipresent computing with computers built into consumer products, clothing, and even implanted under the skin;
- Nanomachines measured in atoms rather than millimeters that do everything from heating and cleaning our homes to curing cancer;
- Personalized public transportation that integrates our cars into a coordinated transport network, automatically picking the fastest routes and bypassing traffic jams;
- Designer foods and crops genetically engineered to resist disease and pests and be highly nutritious;
- Intelligent goods and appliances such as telephones with built-in directories and food packaging that tells your stove how to cook the contents;
- Worldwide inexpensive and safe water from advanced filtering, desalination, and perhaps even extraction from the air;
- Super senses that use implants to give us better hearing, long-distance vision, or the ability to see in the dark.

Implications for hospitality and travel: Air travel will benefit more, and more immediately and directly, from new technologies than any other segment of hospitality and travel. New safety systems over the next decade are likely to include improved heads-up displays, en-route collision-avoidance equipment, and automated airport routing, both in the air and on the ground.

Better sensors will tighten airport security by recognizing explosives that slip past today's detectors. However, this equipment will not be installed until another Lockerbie-style bombing or a major hijacking renews up public demand for greater safety. These innovations will not be cheap. In-airplane safety systems will be mandated at the company's cost, while external equipment such as new satellites for the GPS system will be paid for by user fees.

New materials that sense their own condition are beginning to appear, particularly from nanotechnology research. They will be incorporated into critical aircraft components such as engine mounts by 2020. Soon after, skin alloys will alert mechanics to fatigue and incipient cracks. By 2018, the first supersonic business jets will take to the air, with 20-passenger models likely to appear around 2025. By 2030, efficient supersonic travel will replace first-class sections on long routes over water. Cruise lines face changes, too. Online travel agencies will account for only 9 percent of cruise sales in 2009, according to PhoCusWright. That will not long be true. Over the next decade, the most important technological development for cruise lines will be the continued growth of online booking. Early suggestions that cruise travel was too complex and expensive to book without human contact are fast proving to have been wrong. Carnival, Princess, Disney, and others have set up convenient and successful online booking systems for Net-savvy cruisers. Operators with less efficient sites, or none at all, will find themselves at a growing competitive disadvantage. Five years from now, the tradition of booking through a travel agent will have vanished, save in the extreme high end of the market—and there is room to wonder how long agents can survive to serve the luxury market after losing the rest.

Cruise lines hoping to do well in an increasingly Net-savvy marketplace will have to pay scrupulous attention to their reputation. Tales of poor service and disappointed travelers go a long way in online forums, chat rooms, and blogs, and they can take forever to disappear. An impeccable brand is the only assurance the online shopper has that his cruise investment will be money well spent.

The Internet has changed the cruise market in another way that dismays some operators. Bright European buyers are starting to check prices online and then buy from American agents, often at considerable savings. In one example, a trip through the Western Caribbean on the Costa Mediterranea cost £514 for a Class 1 inside cabin, or about $1,010, when booked through an agent in the U.K. Buying from an American Web site, the price was $569, or about £289. Thus far, some cruise lines are attempting to protect their profits by refusing to accept bookings except through agents in the customer's home country. That tactic is unlikely to work for very long.

For hotels, the biggest techno-trend is well recognized already. As database systems grow more sophisticated, operators are able to capture ever more detailed information about hotel patrons, from their choice of rooms to their dining preferences and local itinerary. This enables hotel staff to give returning patrons a highly personalized experience and all but guarantees return visits. This technology is quickly raising the level of play in the battle for customer loyalty. Cruise lines, resorts, and other destinations are quickly copying these methods.

On the negative side, long distance calling through the hotel telephone system once was a significant profit center. Cell phones have seriously eroded this business. The last of it can be expected to vanish now that the major cell providers all are offering unlimited calls for just $100 per month. Probably the biggest development for most sectors will be the growing use of RFID (radio-frequency identification) chips to track supplies, automate ordering, and make delivery more efficient, and therefore cheaper. One nascent restaurant chain in California features orderentry computers at each table. Customers use the terminal to read the menu, view each menu item, and place their order. They see human staff only when handing over their credit cards—before ordering—and when the food is delivered. Computerized ordering will not soon penetrate high-end restaurants or fast-food chains, but it will be welcome at midrange family restaurants, where savings are sorely needed. Also expect to see innovation at self-bussing restaurants, where patrons will deliver their plates and tableware directly to the maw of the automated washers.

Some of the most interesting new technologies for restaurants and food services will operate far behind the scenes. In laboratories around the world, scientists are building artificial "tongues" and "noses" more sensitive than human organs. Models now in development can distinguish among closely related wines, various cheeses and breads, and coffees. In the near future, food producers will use them to guarantee product quality. This innovation will provide restaurants with better, more consistent materials and give diners more predictable, and probably more satisfying, meals.

THE UNITED STATES IS CEDING ITS SCIENTIFIC AND TECHNICAL LEADERSHIP TO OTHER COUNTRIES

"The scientific and technical building blocks of our economic leadership are eroding at a time when many other nations are gathering strength," the National Academy of Sciences warns. "Although many people assume that the United States will always be a world leader in science and technology, this may not continue to be the case inasmuch as great minds and ideas exist throughout the world. We fear the abruptness with which a lead in science and technology can be lost—and the difficulty of recovering a lead once lost, if indeed it can be regained at all."

Although R and D spending is growing in raw-dollar terms, when measured as a percentage of the total federal budget or as a fraction of the U.S. GDP, research funding has been shrinking for some 15 years. In 2005, the United States spent about 2.68 percent of its GDP on R and D, down from 2.76 percent in 2001. Washington has often reduced the post-inflation buying power of its R and D funding request. In the FY 2007 budget, for the first time, it cut R and D funds in absolute dollars as well. Washington's neglect of basic science is being felt in many ways. Only half of American patents are granted to Americans, a number that has been declining for decades. Only 29 percent of the research papers published in the prestigious Physical Review in 2003 were by American authors, down from 61 percent in 1983.

More than half of American scientists and engineers are nearing retirement. At the rate American students are entering these fields, the retirees cannot be replaced except by recruiting foreign scientists. Between 25 percent and 30 percent of high school graduates who enter college plan to major in science or engineering. Fewer than half of them receive a degree in those fields. The number of U.S. bachelor's degrees awarded in engineering in 2005 was nearly 15 percent below the peak 20 years earlier

Assessment: This trend emerged from a wide variety of ill-conceived political decisions made over the last 30 years. It will take at least a generation to reverse.

Implications: If this trend is not reversed, it will begin to undermine the U.S. economy and shift both economic and political power to other lands. According to some estimates, about half of the improvement in the American standard of living is directly attributable to research and development carried out by scientists and engineers.

The Bureau of Labour Statistics predicts that the number of job openings in science and engineering will grow by 47 percent in the five years ending 2010—three times as fast as nontechnical fields. The United States will not produce nearly enough home-grown technical specialists to fill them. Demand to import foreign scientists and engineers on H-1B visas also will continue to grow.

Publicity about the H1-B programme, and about the offshoring of R and D to company divisions and consulting labs in Asia, in turn, will discourage American students from entering technical fields. This has already been blamed for shrinking student rolls in computer science. In 2005, China for the first time exported more IT and communications goods ($180 million) than the United States ($145 million.) Its lead has grown each year since then.

Implications for hospitality and travel: In the short run, this suggests that a growing fraction of the new technologies adopted by hospitality and travel businesses will originate with companies outside the United States. In the longer term, this trend could begin to reduce the relative wealth of Americans compared to the rest of the world. This may eventually cause a decline in per-capita spending by Americans on hospitality and travel, particularly outside the U.S. Loss of science-based prestige also could reduce America's appeal for some foreign travelers, discouraging tourism to the United States.

TRANSPORTATION TECHNOLOGY AND PRACTICE ARE IMPROVING RAPIDLY

The newest generation of aircraft, such as the Boeing 787 and future Airbus A350 XWB, are using lightweight materials and more efficient engines to cut fuel costs, stretch ranges, and increase cargo capacity. In the United States, two companies have even announced plans to build supersonic business jets and have them in the air by 2013 or so. One has already taken deposits for several dozen aircraft. At the same time, rail travel is getting faster. The new TGV Est line, which runs 300 km (180 miles) from Paris to Frankfurt, operates at 320 kph (198.8 mph) inside France, compared with 300 kph on other parts of the TGV system. China has begun to install a network of highspeed trains to compensate for its shortage of regional air transportation.

Assessment: These advances will continue at least through mid-century.

Implications for Cruise Lines: Outboard power pods, better stabilizers, improved satellite navigation and weather, and other technologies are making cruise ships faster, more comfortable, and more efficient.

Design innovations made possible by technology are creating new experiences for cruisers. These include extensible marinas and swimming areas and retractable glass roofs, as on the Queen Mary 2. In the future, much more ambitious innovations will be seen; artificial island ports and cruise ships the size of modest cities can be expected within 20 years.

THE PACE OF TECHNOLOGICAL CHANGE ACCELERATES WITH EACH NEW GENERATION OF DISCOVERIES AND APPLICATIONS

In fast-moving engineering disciplines, half of the cutting-edge knowledge learned by college students in their freshman year is obsolete by the time they graduate. The design and marketing cycle—idea, invention, innovation, imitation—is shrinking steadily. As late as the 1940s, the product cycle stretched to 30 or 40 years. Today, it seldom lasts 30 or 40 weeks. Almost any new consumer product can be exactly duplicated by Chinese factories and sold on e-Bay within a week after it is introduced. The reason is simple: Some 80 percent of the scientists, engineers, technicians, and physicians who ever lived are alive today—and exchanging ideas real time on the Internet.

Assessment: This trend will continue for many years. However, we may grow less able to perceive it. *Implications:* Subjectively, change soon will move so rapidly that we can no longer recognize its acceleration, save as an abstract concept. All the technical knowledge we work with today will represent only 1 percent of the knowledge that will be available in 2050. Industries will face much tighter competition based on new technologies. Those who adopt state-of-the-art methods first will prosper. Those who ignore them will eventually fail. Products must capture their market quickly, before the competition can copy them. Brand names associated with quality are becoming even more important in this highly competitive environment.

Lifelong learning is a necessity for anyone who works in a technical field—and for growing numbers who do not. In what passes for the long run—a generation or two—the development of true artificial intelligence is likely to reduce human beings to managers. Rather than making new discoveries and creating new products, we will struggle to understand and guide the flow of novelties delivered by creations we cannot really keep up with.

Implications for hospitality and travel: As new technologies arrive, hospitality and travel operators will be forced to hire more technology specialists and train other employees to cope with new demands. The next major development will be the spread of RFID chips throughout the hospitality and travel industry. Airlines, hotels, and restaurant chains all will need to hire technicians with experience in RFID to set up and monitor new, automated inventory and ordering systems, while everyone from chefs to warehouse personnel will need training in their use.

THE INTERNET CONTINUES TO GROW, BUT AT A SLOWER PACE

In mid-2007, Internet users numbered about 1.173 billion, up just less than one-fourth in three years. Most growth of the Internet population is now taking place outside the United States, which is home to only 19 percent of Internet users. In mid-2007, the most recent available data showed 162 million Internet users in China (12.3 percent of the population), 42 million in India (3.7 percent), and 86.3 million in Japan (67.1 percent.)

The growth of e-commerce also is slowing, with 2007 sales coming in at $116 billion Sales growth, as much as 25 percent per year in 2004, is expected to slow to 9 percent annually by 2010. The current recession may trim up to 2 percent off that pre-2009 forecast, but growth will continue at its expected pace thereafter.

Assessment: Internet growth will continue until essentially no one in the world lacks easy access to e-mail and the Web, about 30 years by our best estimate.

Implications for Cruise Lines: Vacationers accustomed to instant Net access will be increasingly unwilling to leave their e-mail at home. High-speed, 24/7 net access in all staterooms will be standard, as it is now for business-class and luxury hotels. This is a major force behind the growth of consumerism among potential cruise passengers. The Internet will be an increasingly important tool for the millions of potential cruisers in the Indian and Chinese travel markets.

TECHNOLOGY IS CREATING A KNOWLEDGE-DEPENDENT GLOBAL SOCIETY

More and more businesses, and entire industries, are based on the production and exchange of information and ideas rather than exclusively on manufactured goods or other tangible products. At the same time, manufacturers and sellers of physical products are able to capture and analyze much more information about buyers' needs and preferences, making the selling process more efficient and effective. The number of Internet users in the United States more than doubled between 2000 and 2007, to nearly 231 million, or 69 percent of the population. Yet the percent of the population online has remained almost unchanged since 2004. And while the percentage of Internet users in China is smaller than in the U.S., the number of users there passed the U.S. early in 2008.

Assessment: This trend will not reach even its half-way mark until the rural populations of China and India gain modern educations and easy access to the Web.

Implications for Cruise Lines: Internet cruise booking will become much more important to the industry, eventually displacing travel agents in all but the luxury market.

Cruise ships increasingly will require Internet connections in every room for 24/7 access to the guest's e-mail, either free or at a very modest price. Data mining can provide cruise lines with an opportunity for extremely personalized marketing, much as it already does for cutting-edge hotels and resorts.

ENVIRONMENTAL TRENDS

PEOPLE AROUND THE WORLD ARE BECOMING INCREASINGLY SENSITIVE TO ENVIRONMENTAL ISSUES AS THE CONSEQUENCES OF NEGLECT, INDIFFERENCE, AND IGNORANCE BECOME EVER MORE APPARENT

The World Health Organization (WHO) estimates that 3 million people die each year from the effects of air pollution, about 5 percent of the total deaths. In the United States, an estimated 64,000 people a year die of cardiopulmonary disease caused by breathing particulates. In sub-Saharan Africa, the toll is between 300,000 and 500,000 deaths per year. Pollution-related respiratory diseases kill about 1.4 million people yearly in China and Southeast Asia. And contaminated water is implicated in 80 percent of the world's health problems, according to WHO. An estimated 40,000 people around the world die each day of diseases directly caused by contaminated water, more than 14 million per year.

Though some debate remains about the cause, the fact of global warming has become undeniable. At Palmer Station on Anvers Island, Antarctica, the average annual temperature has risen by 3 to 4 degrees since the 1940s, and by an amazing 7 to 9 degrees in June—early winter in that hemisphere. Anticipating a three-foot rise in sea levels, the Netherlands is spending $1 billion to build new dikes.

Assessment: A solid majority of voters throughout the developed world, and even some in the developing lands, now recognize the need to clean up the environment, and especially to control greenhouse warming. They will keep this trend intact for at least the next 30 years.

Implications for Cruise Lines: Restrictions on dumping of refuse and waste will become much tighter in the years ahead, and will be much more strictly enforced. Ships will be forced to use more, and more capable, antipollution technologies. These will be a significant new expense for cruise lines.

WATER SHORTAGES WILL BE A GROWING PROBLEM FOR MUCH OF THE WORLD. IN MANY REGIONS, THEY ARE SEVERE ALREADY

The northern half of China, home to perhaps half a billion people, already is short of water. The water table under Beijing has fallen nearly 200 feet since 1965. Australia's Murray-Darling river system, which supplies water for 40 percent of the country's crops and 80 percent of its irrigation, no longer carries enough water to reach the sea without constant dredging. Salinity in the Murray is rising so quickly that the water is expected to be undrinkable in 20 years. There is worse to come. According to U.N. studies, at least 3.5 billion people will run short of water by 2040, almost ten times as many as in 1995. Ten years later, fully two-thirds of the world's population could be living in regions with chronic, widespread shortages of water.

Assessment: This trend will remain with us for the very long term.

Implications: Providing adequate supplies of potable water will be a growing challenge for developing and developed countries alike.

Such problems as periodic famine and desertification can be expected to grow more frequent and severe in coming decades.

In many lands, including parts of the United States, growing water shortages may inhibit economic growth and force large-scale migration out of afflicted areas. Climate change is expected to reduce the flow of Australia's parched Murray River by a further 5 percent in 20 years and 15 percent in 50 years. Water wars, predicted for more than a decade, are a threat in places like the Kashmir: much of Pakistan's water comes from areas of Kashmir now controlled by India.

Other present and future water conflicts involve Turkey, Syria, and Iraq over the Tigris and Euphrates; Israel, Jordan, Syria, and Palestine over water from the Jordan River and the aquifers under the Golan Heights; India and Bangladesh, over the Ganges and Brahmaputra; China, Indochina, and Thailand, over the Mekong; Kyrghyzstan, Tajikistan, and Uzbekistan over the Oxus and Jaxartes rivers; and Ethiopia, Sudan, and at least six East African countries, including Egypt, over the Nile. In the United States, repair of decayed water systems is likely to be a major priority for older cities such as New York, Boston, and Atlanta. Cost estimates for necessary replacement and repair of water mains range up to $1 trillion.

Implications for hospitality and travel: In the American Southwest, northern China, Australia, and other parched regions, water supplies will be a growing concern for hotels, restaurants, and other destinations. This is not likely to ease in the foreseeable future.

As water become ever more scarce throughout much of the developing world, regional instability could put otherwise attractive destinations off limits for Western travelers. Parts of the Middle East are the obvious candidates for future avoidance.

RECYCLING HAS DELAYED THE "GARBAGE GLUT" THAT THREATENED TO OVERFLOW THE WORLD'S LANDFILLS, BUT THE PROBLEM CONTINUES TO GROW

Americans now produce about 4.5 pounds of trash per person per day, twice as much as they threw away a generation ago. Seventy percent of U.S. landfills will be full by 2025, according to the EPA. Japan expects to run out of space for industrial waste as soon as 2008 and for municipal solid waste by 2015. In London and the surrounding region, landfills will run out of room by 2012.

Recycling has proved to be an effective alternative to dumping. As of 2005, Germany recycled 60 percent of its municipal solid waste, 65 percent of manufacturing waste, 80 percent of packaging, and 87 percent of construction waste, according to the Environment, Nature Conservation, and Nuclear Safety. Largely as a result, the number of landfills for domestic waste has been reduced from about 50,000 in the 1970s to just 160.

Assessment: The challenge of dealing with garbage will grow for so long as the world's middle classes continue to expand or until technology finds ways to recycle virtually all of the materials used in manufacturing and packaging. This trend will remain intact through at least 2050.

Implications: Recycling and waste-to-energy plants are a viable alternative to simply dumping garbage. This trend will push the development of so-called life-cycle design, which builds convenient recyclability into new products from their inception. Expect a wave of new regulations, recycling, waste-to-energy projects, and waste management programmes in the United States and other countries in an effort to stem the tide of trash. In the United States, it will of course begin in California, a jurisdiction often cited by policy forecasters as a bellwether of change. State and local governments will tighten existing regulations and raise disposal prices in Pennsylvania, South Carolina, Louisiana, and other places that accept much of the trash from major garbage producers such as New York. Trash producers in the developed world will ship much more of their debris to repositories in developing countries. This will inspire protests in the receiving lands.

Beyond 2025 or so, the developing countries will close their repositories to foreign waste, forcing producers to develop more waste-to-energy and recycling technologies. Ultimately, it may even be necessary to exhume buried trash for recycling to make more room in closed dump sites for material that cannot be reused. Waste-to-energy programmes will make only a small contribution to the world's growing need for power.

Implications for hospitality and travel: Hotels, resorts, restaurants, and other large-scale waste generators can expect to face the same kind of recycling requirements that many private homeowners have been complying with for years. This will increase handling expenses for recyclable bottles, cans, plastics, and paper, but it should ultimately reduce the cost of disposal.

This may bring even more scrutiny to cruise lines. Any ship caught dumping waste at sea can expect to bring its company catastrophic publicity, with a risk of boycotts. The rest may profit from advertising their "green" credentials, especially if they donate to ocean-oriented environmental groups.

PREFERENCE FOR INDUSTRIAL DEVELOPMENT OVER ENVIRONMENTAL CONCERNS IS FADING SLOWLY IN MUCH OF THE DEVELOPING WORLD

The Pew Research Center reports that less than one-fourth of respondents in any African country rated environmental problems as the world's most important threat. In Ethiopia, where desertification is at its worst and drought is a constant threat, only 7 percent did so. Beijing has made repairing the environment a national priority. Yet 70 percent of the energy used in China comes from coal-burning power plants, few of them equipped with pollution controls. The country intends to build over five hundred more coal-fired plants in the next ten years. Even Germany has committed to building more power plants fired by high-sulfur brown coal.

Assessment: View this as a counter-trend to Trend 40. It will remain largely intact until the poor of India and China complete their transition into the middle class, around 2040.

Implications: Broad regions of the planet will be subject to pollution, deforestation, and other environmental ills in the coming decades.

Acid rain like that afflicting the United States and Canada will appear wherever designers of new power plants and factories neglect emission controls. In India, an area the size of the United States is covered by a haze of sulfates and other chemicals associated with acid rain. Look for this problem to appear in most other industrializing countries.

Diseases related to air and water pollution will spread dramatically in the years ahead. Already, chronic obstructive pulmonary disease is five times more common in China than in the United States. As citizens of the developing countries grow to expect modern health care, this will create a growing burden on their economies.

This is just a taste of future problems, and perhaps not the most troublesome. Even the U.S. government now admits that global warming is a result of human activities that produce greenhouse gases. It now seems that China and India soon will produce even more of them than the major industrialized nations. Helping the developing lands to raise their standards of living without creating wholesale pollution will require much more aid and diplomacy than the developed world has ever been willing to give this cause.

Implications for hospitality and travel: All these problems will make the worst afflicted areas much less attractive to travelers in the coming years. They also will subject hotels, resorts, cruise lines, and other segments to new regulations designed to minimize their use of energy and to promote recycling and other environmentally friendly practices.

CONCERN OVER SPECIES EXTINCTION AND LOSS OF BIODIVERSITY IS GROWING QUICKLY

An estimated 50,000 species disappear each year, up to 1,000 times the natural rate of extinction, according to the United Nations Environmental Programme. By 2100, as many as half of all species could disappear. Eleven percent of birds, 25 percent of mammals, and 20 percent to 30 percent of all plants are estimated to be nearing extinction. Some 16,118 species are now listed as threatened (7,925 animal species and 8,393 plant and lichen species), according to the 2006 Red List of the International Union for Conservation of Nature and Natural Resources.

This is an increase of nearly 2,700 in four years. The real list is likely much larger, as the group has evaluated only 40,000 of the 1.5 million species on its list. The chief cause for species loss is the destruction of natural habitats by logging, agriculture, and urbanization.

Assessment: This trend has at least three decades to run.

Implications: Saving any significant fraction of the world's endangered species will require much more effort and expense than many governments find acceptable. For species such as corals, if the loss is attributable largely to climate change, it may not be possible.

Species loss has a powerful negative impact on human wellbeing. Half of all drugs used in medicine are derived from natural sources, including fifty-five of the top one hundred drugs prescribed in the United States. About 40 percent of all pharmaceuticals are derived from the sap of vascular plants. So far, only 2 percent of the 300,000 known sap-containing plants have been assayed for useful drugs. Most of the species lost in the years ahead will disappear before they can be tested.

The Indonesian economy loses an estimated $500,000 to $800,000 annually per square mile of dead or damaged reef. Australia may lose even more as degradation of the Great Barrier Reef continues.

The U.N. Intergovernmental Panel on Climate Change predicts that the Reef will be "functionally extinct" by 2030. Diverse ecosystems absorb more carbon dioxide than those with fewer species. Loss of biodiversity thus is a potential cause of global warming.

Implications for hospitality and travel: For the near term, environmentally conscious travelers will flock to endangered regions such as the Galapagos, the Great Barrier Reef, and the Amazon rain forests to witness their biological diversity while it is still available. However, in the long run the loss of coral and other extinction events will destroy the tourist appeal of some of the world's favourite destinations for environmental and adventure tourism.

URBANIZATION, ARGUABLY THE WORLD'S OLDEST TREND, CONTINUES RAPIDLY

Forty-eight percent of the world's population currently lives in cities, according to the Population Reference Bureau's 2006 World Population Data Sheet. By 2030, that figure will grow to 60 percent, as some 2.1 billion people are added to the world's cities. Cities are growing fastest in the developing world. In 1950, there were just eight megacities, with populations exceeding 5 million, in the world. By 2015, there will be fifty-nine megacities, forty-eight of them in less developed countries. Of these, twenty-three will have populations over 10 million, all but four in the developing lands.

Natural increase now accounts for more than half of population increase in the cities; at most, little more than one-third of urban growth results from migration.

Assessment: After surviving for some 3,500 years, this trend is unlikely to disappear in the next 50.

Implications: Cities' contribution to global warming can only increase in the years ahead. As the world's supply of potable water declines, people are concentrating in those areas where it is hardest to obtain and is used least efficiently. This trend will aggravate water problems for so long as it continues. Many more people will die due to shortages of shelter, water, and sanitation. Epidemics will become still more common as overcrowding spreads HIV and other communicable diseases more rapidly.

Since urban growth is now due more to natural increase than to migration, programmes designed to encourage rural populations to remain in the countryside may be misplaced. Education and family planning seem more likely to rein in the growth of cities.

Implications for hospitality and travel: Many cities in the developing world will become even more congested and polluted, reducing their appeal even when historical arts and artifacts might otherwise draw tourism.

MANAGEMENT TRENDS

MORE ENTREPRENEURS START NEW BUSINESSES EVERY YEAR

In the United States, about 9 percent of men and 6 percent of women are self-employed. These fractions have been growing in about two-thirds of the OECD countries. Many women are leaving traditional jobs to go home and open businesses, even as they begin a family. At least half of the estimated 10.6 million privately held firms in the United States are owned by women, employing 19.1 million people and generating $2.46 trillion in sales annually.

For the 14 years ending in 2003, the most recent period for which data is available, small businesses (those with less than five hundred employees) created 92 percent of the net new jobs in the United States, according to the

Census Bureau. The smallest companies, those with fewer than twenty employees, created 85 percent. However, jobs also disappear fastest from small companies, which are much more likely to fail than larger concerns. Though big-company layoffs have gotten the most publicity in the current recession, losses from smaller firms are likely to be even more severe.

Assessment: This is a self-perpetuating trend, as all those new service firms need other companies to handle chores outside their core business. It will remain with us for many years, not only because it suits new-generation values but because it is a rational response to an age in which jobs can never be counted on to provide a stable long-term income.

Implications: It is driven as well by the attitudes and values of Generation X and the Millennials and by the rapid developments in technology, which create endless opportunities for new business development.

Specialty boutiques will continue to spring up on the Internet for at least the next 15 years. This trend will help to ease the poverty of many developing countries, as it already is doing in India and China.

Implications for hospitality and travel: We can expect a wave of new hospitality and travel businesses to appear in the years ahead. Many will be new destinations in areas where the travel industry is just beginning to grow. Others will be specialty tour operators focused on either niche sports and other activities or on consumer groups with special needs, such as non-English-speakers, religious or cultural minorities, seniors, or all-female tour groups.

INFORMATION-BASED ORGANIZATIONS ARE QUICKLY DISPLACING THE OLD COMMAND-AND-CONTROL MODEL OF MANAGEMENT

The typical large business has reshaped itself or is struggling to do so. Soon, it will be composed of specialists who rely on information from colleagues, customers, and headquarters to guide their actions. Upper management is giving fewer detailed orders to subordinates. Instead, it sets performance expectations for the organization, its parts, and its specialists and supplies the feedback necessary to determine whether results have met expectations.

Assessment: This is a well-established trend. At this point, many large corporations have restructured their operations for greater flexibility, but many others still have a long way to go. This trend will continue in the United States for at least the next 15 years. The developing world may largely bypass this step in its new organizations and go straight to networked management structures.

Implications: This management style suits Generation Xers and Millennials well, as it tends to let them work in whatever fashion suits them so long as the job gets done. Downsizing has spread from manufacturing industries to the service economy. Again, this process encourages the entrepreneurial trend, both to provide services for companies outsourcing their secondary functions and to provide jobs for displaced employees. Many older workers have been eliminated in this process, depriving companies of their corporate memory. Companies have replaced them with younger workers whose experience of hard times is limited to the relatively mild recession since 2000. Many firms may discover that they need to recruit older workers to help them adapt to adversity. This too is driving the entrepreneurial trend. Many older workers find themselves self-employed by default, as they need income and cannot find work in their accustomed fields.

Implications for hospitality and travel: The growing demand for specialists to join in task-oriented teams will reduce the number of broadly experienced industry generalists needed by large hospitality and travel operators. Unfortunately, by relying on specialists for their expertise in relatively narrow aspects of company operations, it also will make it difficult to train promising staff members in the broad range of skills needed for promotion to higher management positions.

ORGANIZATIONS ARE SIMPLIFYING THEIR STRUCTURES AND SQUEEZING OUT PERSONNEL

Computers and information-management systems have stretched the manager's effective span of control from six to twenty-one subordinates. Information now flows from frontline workers to higher management for analysis. Thus, fewer mid-level managers are needed, flattening the corporate pyramid. The span of control could stretch again if computer science finally delivers on its long-delayed promise of artificial intelligence. Opportunities for advancement are shrinking, because they come within the worker's narrow specialty, rather than at the broader corporate level. By 2001, only one person in fifty was promoted, compared with one in twenty in 1987.

Assessment: In the United States, downsizing, restructuring, reorganization, and cutbacks of white-collar workers will continue at least through 2025. Its pace will not slow unless technology ceases to deliver new ways to replace human workers with faster, cheaper, more reliable hardware and software.

Implications: The current recession will be filled by another "jobless recovery" as companies squeeze still more productivity out of their existing workforce, rather than hiring new employees.

A typical large business in 2015 will have fewer than half the management levels of its counterpart in 1995, and about one-third the number of managers. Information-based organizations have to make a special effort to prepare professional specialists to become business leaders. Broad experience of the kind needed by a CEO no longer comes naturally during an executive's career.

Top managers must be computer-literate to retain their jobs and must make sure to oversee the increased spans of control that computers make possible.

Finding top managers with the broad experience needed to run a major business already has become difficult. It can only grow more so as the demand for specialization grows. This will reduce promotion from within and encourage companies to seek upper-level execs from other firms, and even industries. Executives increasingly will start their own companies, rather than trusting the old-fashioned corporate career path to provide advancement.

Ultimately, this trend will require a wholesale rethinking of the social contract, as it becomes difficult or impossible to create enough fulfilling, well paid jobs for human workers to support the population. The end of salaried work is not yet near, but it could arrive within the lifetimes of today's younger generations.

Implications for hospitality and travel: This trend could endanger the hospitality and travel industries' tradition of promoting from within. Because there will be fewer opportunities for promotion, it will be difficult to provide employees with the breadth of experience required of top executives. Thus, high-level managers are likely to come increasingly from competitors and from other industries. This is likely to increase the turnover of management personnel, who can no longer look forward to the rewarding careers that these industries once offered.

This also will force corporate managers to develop new ways to motivate their employees and provide them with the kind of experience needed to fill the few positions remaining at upper levels of the company.

GOVERNMENT REGULATIONS WILL CONTINUE TO TAKE UP A GROWING PORTION OF THE MANAGER'S TIME AND EFFORT

In 1996, the U.S. Congress passed regulatory reform laws intended to slow the spread of government regulations. Nonetheless, by 2001 more than 14,000 new regulations were enacted. Not one proposed regulation was rejected during this period. The Brussels bureaucrats of the European Union are churning out rules at an even faster rate, overlaying a standard regulatory structure on the national systems of member countries.

This is not all bad. A study by the Congressional Office of Management and Budget estimated that major federal regulations enacted in the decade ending September 2002 cost between $38 billion and $44 billion per year. However, the estimated benefits added up to between $135 billion and $218 billion annually.

Assessment: If the future holds an end to this trend, it is not yet in sight.

Implications: Regulations are necessary, unavoidable, and often beneficial. Yet it is difficult not to see them as a kind of friction that slows both current business and future economic growth.

The proliferation of regulations in the developed world could give a competitive advantage to countries such as India and China, where regulations that impede investment and capital flow are being stripped away, and health, occupational safety, and environmental codes are still rudimentary or absent.

However, there is a significant penalty for the kind of risk that comes from inadequate regulation. China pays an estimated risk penalty of 6.49 percent for international borrowing. Per capita GDP, access to capital, foreign direct investment, and other measures of a country's economic health all decline directly with a rising Opacity Index, which is heavily influenced by the lack of effective regulations to guarantee a level playing field for those doing business there. As a result, lands such as Russia will remain at a competitive disadvantage until they can pass and enforce the regulations needed to ensure a stable, fair business environment.

Implications for hospitality and travel: Airlines regulations will focus on safety and customer convenience. The most costly would be installation of an effective bomb detection system for checked luggage. It will be required only if an American flight is bombed. (It is far from impossible. Officials at the U.S. Transportation Safety Administration worry that a bomb could still be smuggled aboard as tiny parts, then assembled for use.) Other rules are likely to demand installation of more crashworthy seating, new user fees, and switching schedules to relieve peak-hour congestion.

A regulation proposed in February would require foreign-flagged cruise ships leaving from the U.S. to spend at least two days in a foreign port before returning, and at least one day in a foreign port for every two in an American port. The rule, proposed to limit competition for two American-flagged ships operated out of Hawaii by Norwegian Cruise Lines, would change itineraries for thousands of cruises. It might also devastate profits at American home ports. Juneau, Alaska, alone would lose an estimated $68 million in one summer. Forecast: This regulation is unlikely to pass scrutiny. If enacted, it will be rescinded quickly.

Hotels already are so well regulated that this sector should be relatively immune to new government-mandated complications. Relatively. Of course, any new rules that apply to restaurants will apply to hotel-based eating establishments just as they do to free-standing outlets.

Restaurant operators trying to avoid cluttering their menus with nutrition information are fighting a losing battle. Calorie counts, fat content, and other unpleasant details soon will be there for patrons to see when choosing their meals. And that sausage and pepperoni pizza will have a warning label that could scare the customer into a heart attack. This could easily sink the market for some traditionally popular—but unhealthy—dishes and raise demand for fish (omega-3 fatty acids), cruciferous vegetables (cancer fighters), and other "healthy" alternatives. We can expect significant menu revisions in the next few years. The biggest regulatory changes ahead for travel are the global move to biometric passports, prompted largely by Washington's fear of another major terrorist attack, and—within the U.S.—the REAL ID programme. According to plan, anyone seeking to enter the United States—including American citizens who have been out of the country—will need a biometric passport to get in. Countries from Switzerland to Singapore have adopted them in recent years. However, delays in pulling the American programme together have forced Washington to waive the scheme for some travelers.

Under REAL ID, before granting a driver's license, states must carry out extensive checks to confirm the applicant's identity. By 2014, anyone under 50 living in a state that does not provide compliant licenses will be unable to board an airliner or enter a federal building. Those over 50 can fly until 2017. Several states have said they will not comply with the programme, and their citizens now face being unable to travel by air.

Thus far, the Department of Homeland Security has backed down from a possible confrontation with these states, but we believe the REAL ID programme eventually will be enforced.

INSTITUTIONAL TRENDS

MULTINATIONAL CORPORATIONS ARE UNITING THE WORLD AND GROWING MORE EXPOSED TO ITS RISKS

The continuing fragmentation of the post-Cold War world has reduced the stability of some lands where government formerly could guarantee a favourable—or at least predictable—business environment. The current unrest in Iraq is one example. One risk now declining is the threat of sudden, extreme currency fluctuations. In Europe, at least, the adoption of the euro is making for a more stable financial environment.

Assessment: This trend will continue for at least the next 30 years, as companies in the developing world diversify into less developed markets.

Implications: It is becoming ever more difficult for business to be confident that decisions about plant location, marketing, and other critical issues will continue to appear wise even five years into the future. All long-term plans must include an even greater margin for risk management. This will encourage outsourcing rather than investment in offshore facilities that could be endangered by sudden changes in business conditions.

Countries that can demonstrate a significant likelihood of stability and predictable business outcomes will enjoy a strong competitive advantage over neighbors that cannot. Witness the rapid growth of investment in India now that deregulation and privatization have general political support, compared with other Asian lands where conditions are less predictable.

Although Russia has continued to attract Western investment, particularly in its energy industry, increasingly autocratic governance by the Putin regime and any successors could eventually discourage foreign companies from doing business there or require much more favourable terms to justify accepting the associated risks. Major corporations also can help to moderate some risks in unstable countries, such as by threatening to take their business elsewhere.

Implications for hospitality and travel: Unfortunately, multinational operations bring risks beyond those of national stability, or its absence. Some western firms have cut back or abandoned their operations in Russia, concluding that Moscow's capricious treatment of foreign concerns could be too costly to ignore. Others have found it difficult to deal with autocratic government and petty corruption in China. Primitive banking and legal systems, poor communications and infrastructures, and other such problems in developing lands can make it difficult for western firms to operate in the developing world. No industry is so exposed to these problems as hospitality and travel.

CONSUMERS INCREASINGLY DEMAND SOCIAL RESPONSIBILITY FROM COMPANIES AND EACH OTHER

Companies increasingly are being judged on how they treat the environment, their workers, and their customers. Many are changing their business practices as a result. For example, home-improvement retailers Home Depot and Lowe's have stopped buying wood from countries with endangered forests, while Nike now publishes its discoveries of worker abuse by offshore suppliers. Costco offers much better benefits than its competitors and has half the employee turnover rate as a result. In a 2005 survey of nearly 1,200 companies, 81 percent— and 98 percent of large firms—said corporate citizenship is a priority; 84 percent said that being socially responsible has improved profits. Once the business-friendly Bush administration leaves Washington, government intervention will rebound in sectors from finance to industrial chemicals. To avoid political backlash from the right, regulation is likely to be carefully targeted and limited, at least for a time.

Assessment: This trend is well established in the industrialized world, but only beginning in the developing world. It can be expected to grow more powerful as the no-nonsense, bottom-line-oriented Generation Xers and Millennials gain influence.

Implications: Once the current, business-friendly administration leaves Washington, government intervention will supplant deregulation in the airline industry (in the interest of safety and services), financial services (to control instability and costs), electric utilities (nuclear problems), and the chemical industry (toxic wastes).

In the United States, frequent incidents of political corruption may spread the demand for greater responsibility into the field of government and public service, although that is not yet clear. As the Internet spreads Western attitudes throughout the world, consumers and environmental activists in other regions will find more ways to use local court systems to promote their goals. Litigation is likely to become a global risk for companies that do not make the environment a priority.

Implications for hospitality and travel: This will bring still more pressure to minimize fuel consumption and cut air and noise pollution. The impact of jet exhaust on the ozone layer will continue to draw unwelcome publicity to air travel, but with little impact on seat-miles or the bottom line. Cruise lines whose itineraries permit may wish to add day trips to rain forests and other environmentally sensitive locations. Carefully managed excursions to poor areas are another possible option, if they can be structured to benefit the community. "Green" furnishings and supplies are the trend at hotels and resorts. Look for bamboo flooring in the rooms, eggs from free-range chickens in the kitchen, and a growing demand from guests for better worker benefits and pay. In all but extreme-luxury locations, hotels will save energy and water by providing fresh towels and linens only every other day, or when guests request them.

Even simple measures, like saving water by providing it only at the customer's request, can help to burnish a restaurant's eco-reputation. However, many necessary—or at least unavoidable— measures will be harder to accept. Demands for nutritional information on the menu eventually will become impossible to resist. They will be accompanied by calls for eco-conscious sourcing of foods and other supplies, better pay and at least minimal benefits for restaurant workers, and American-style work rules in offshore subsidiaries. Look at the pressure put on Nike to improve working conditions at the plants of overseas suppliers, and you see the future of the restaurant industry.

Trends such as eco-tourism and "pro-poor" tourism are just getting started. While tourists from China and India will still be eager to see Paris and Orlando, their more experienced peers from Europe and America will be looking for the last few elephants, coral reefs (before they are gone), and impoverished natives still living by the ways of their ancestors. However, they will want the people and sites they visit to benefit from their spending, not just the companies arranging their vacations.

ON AVERAGE, INSTITUTIONS ARE GROWING MORE TRANSPARENT IN THEIR OPERATIONS, AND MORE ACCOUNTABLE FOR THEIR MISDEEDS

Many different forces are promoting this change in various parts of the world. In the United States, the wave of business scandals in 2004, the exposure of child abuse within the Catholic Church, and other perceived offences by large organizations have inspired demands for greater transparency and accountability. China, rated by Kurtzman Group as the most opaque of the major nations, was forced to open many of its records as a precondition for joining the World Trade Organization. In India, a country often regarded as one of the world's most corrupt, the Central Vigilance Commission has opened the country's banking system to more effective oversight. Lesser "vigilance commissions" now oversee many parts of the Indian economy and government. More generally, wars against terrorism, drug trafficking, and money laundering are opening the world's money conduits to greater scrutiny. They also are opening the operations of nongovernmental organizations that function primarily as charitable and social-service agencies but are linked to terrorism as well.

Assessment: There are roughly as many reactions against this trend as there are governments, agencies, and individuals with something to hide. Yet, the benefits of transparency are so clear that the general decline of barriers to oversight is likely to continue until societies develop a consensus about how much—or little—secrecy is really necessary. We give this trend at least 20 years of continued vigour.

Implications: Countries with high levels of transparency tend to be much more stable than more opaque lands. They also tend to be much more prosperous, in part because they find it easier to attract foreign investment.

Greater transparency reduces the operational effectiveness of the world's miscreants. It impedes drug traffickers and terrorist organizations, as well as dishonest governments and corrupt bureaucrats. Implications for hospitality and travel: Like other companies, large hospitality firms are likely to face demands for more rigourous accounting practices and other transparency-oriented changes in their operations.

Companies based in lands such as China and India may find it more costly to borrow capital for expansion than those in the West. Western firms expanding into some of the developing countries also may find themselves paying unaccustomedly high rates for capital, particularly if they are forced to take on local partners.

INSTITUTIONS ARE UNDERGOING A BIMODAL DISTRIBUTION: THE BIG GET BIGGER, THE SMALL SURVIVE, AND THE MID-SIZED ARE SQUEEZED OUT

Economies of scale enable the largest companies to win out over mid-sized competitors, while "boutique" operations can take advantage of niches too small to be efficiently tapped by larger firms. We see the result in a wide range of industries throughout the developed world. In agriculture, banking, auto manufacturing, telecommunications, and many other sectors, the largest firms have been buying up their mid-sized competitors or driving them out of business. At the same time, hundreds or thousands of tiny operators have arisen in each industry to get rich by serving markets beneath the notice of the giants.

Assessment: Thanks in part to technology, this trend is likely to be a permanent feature of the business scene from now on.

Implications: No company is too large to be a takeover target if it dominates a profitable market or has other features attractive to profit-hungry investors.

No niche is too small to attract and support at least one or two boutique operations. Thus far, industries dominated by small, regional, often family-owned companies have been relatively exempt from the consolidation now transforming many other businesses. Takeovers are likely even in these industries in the next decade.

This consolidation will extend increasingly to Internet-based businesses, where well-financed companies are trying to absorb or out-compete tiny online start-ups, much as they have done in the brick-and-mortar world. However, niche markets will continue to encourage the creation of new businesses. In Europe as of 2006, no fewer than forty-eight small, no-frills airlines in twenty-two countries had sprung up to capture about 28 percent of the Continental market share. Only fifteen offered more than fifty flights per day.

Implications for hospitality and travel: FI expects airlines to continue merging for as long as there are airlines available to do so. At the same time, small startup airlines are appearing almost constantly, taking advantage of routes other niche opportunities that their predecessors either have not recognized or did not consider sufficiently attractive. In the United States, Delta and Northwest should be the next major union, as soon as their respective pilots can work out seniority concerns. United and Continental are likely to follow soon after. In Europe, Easy Jet has just completed its acquisition of GB Airways and TUI Travel's TUIFly is merging with Lufthansa's Germanwings airline. Air France wants a piece of the merged Delta/Northwest giant, if U.S. regulators will allow the deal.

We have long seen the same trend in the cruise industry. Royal Caribbean and P and O Princess joined forces in 2001. Four years later, diminutive Clipper Cruise Line announced its pending merger with Australia's Peregrine Adventures. And last year, Royal Caribbean/Celebrity spun off the new, upscale Azamara Cruises to compete with Oceania Cruises. There will be more such examples in the future.

Hotel chains have been merging constantly at least since Bowman-Biltmore bought United Hotels back in 1924. There is no sign the deal-making will stop in the near future. Given the weakness of the dollar, and of the American real estate market, we expect to see a wave of offers by European hospitality firms for their peers in the U.S.

In this aspect, the restaurant industry parallels hotels almost exactly. Mergers and acquisitions, startup and failures, change the industry almost too fast to follow. This is truly a universal trend. The implication for travel is the same as for all these sectors: Large companies will continue to snap up mid-sized competitors or, by outcompeting them, drive them out of business. At the same time, new companies will prosper in niche markets. Some will remain small and highly profitable for their owners. Others will grow until they attract the attention of the giants. A very few may become giants themselves. Look for the fastest turnover in the online travel search and marketing operations, where niche startups abound. All segments of hospitality and travel have been in ferment for as long as we can remember. They will remain in ferment long into the future.

TERRORISM TRENDS

MILITANT ISLAM CONTINUES TO SPREAD AND GAIN POWER

It has been clear for years that the Muslim lands face severe problems with religious extremists dedicated to advancing their political, social, and doctrinal views by any means necessary. Most of the Muslim lands are overcrowded and short of resources. Many are poor, save for the oil-rich states of the Middle East. Virtually all have large populations of young men, often unemployed, who are frequently attracted to violent extremist movements. During its proxy war with the Soviet Union in Afghanistan, the United States massively fortified the Muslim extremist infrastructure by supplying it with money, arms, and, above all, training. It is making a similar mistake today. The overthrow of Saddam Hussein and the American occupation of Iraq has inspired a new generation of jihadis, who have been trained and battle-hardened in the growing insurgency. In a now-declassified National Security Estimate, the American intelligence community concluded that Al Qaeda was more powerful in 2007 than it had been before the so-called "war on terror" began—more dangerous even than it had been when it planned the attacks of September 11, 2001.

Assessment: This trend may wax and wane, but it seems unlikely to disappear this side of a Muslim reformation comparable to those that transformed Christianity and Judaism.

Implications: Virtually all of the Muslim lands face an uncertain, and possibly bleak, future of political instability and growing violence. The exceptions are the oil states, where money can still buy relative peace, at least for now. These problems often have spilled over into the rest of the world. They will do so again.

In a 1994 terrorism study for the Department of Defence and other government clients, Forecasting International predicted that by 2020 a strong majority of the world's 25 or so most important Muslim lands could be in the hands of extremist religious governments. At the time, only Iran was ruled by such a regime. That forecast still appears sound.

Iraq is likely to become the next fundamentalist Muslim regime. Once American forces leave, Iran will support the establishment of a Shiite regime much like its own in Baghdad. There is a one-in-ten chance that this will set off a general war in the Middle East, as Sunni-dominated states intercede to protect Iraqi Sunnis against Shi'a domination. However, Iraq and Saudi Arabia already are negotiating to keep this situation under control. Any attempt to reduce the commitment of Western forces to the task of stabilizing Afghanistan will result in the restoration of the Taliban to power.

Implications for hospitality and travel: In Bangkok and Pattani, Thailand, hotel bombs kill four people. Another bomb shakes the Al Dera Tourist hotel, west of Gaza city. In Kabul, Pakistan, one journalist dies in a hotel bombing. In Islamabad, Pakistan, a restaurant bombing kills 20 people. In Baqouba, Iraq, a car bomb outside a restaurant kills at least 70. In Mumbai, three hotels and a restaurant are among 10 targets struck by terrorists. All these incidents happened in 2008—and outside Iraq it was a relatively slow year for terrorism.

In 1994, Forecasting International predicted that as government installations were "hardened" against attack, terrorists would turn to softer targets, and particularly those of the hospitality and travel industries. That forecast has been amply proved correct. Hotels, restaurants, and transportation facilities have become the preferred targets of both local and international terrorists.

The next generation of terrorists is now being trained in Iraq and Pakistan. As the American wars in those regions prove unsustainable, the most zealous among them will continue their war against their chosen enemies. Most will return to their home countries to attack local rulers. Others will focus on the United States and its allies in the Iraq war. All of them will continue to find hotels and restaurants easy targets with high publicity value. Some may attempt to attack passenger aircraft, while others will aim their bombs at public transportation. A few may even choose cruise ships, conference centers, or casinos as their victims of choice.

Terrorism will become more common in the future, not less so, and the hospitality and travel industries will remain appealingly vulnerable to attack.

[INTERNATIONAL EXPOSURE INCLUDES A GROWING RISK OF TERRORIST ATTACK

Terrorism has continued to grow around the world as the Iraq war proceeds, even as the rate of violence in Iraq itself has, at least temporarily, declined. State-sponsored terrorism has nearly vanished, as tougher sanctions have made it more trouble than it was worth. However, nothing will prevent small, local political organizations and special-interest groups from using terror to promote their causes. These organizations have found inspiration in the successes of Al Qaeda, and many have found common cause. The most dangerous terrorist groups are no longer motivated primarily by specific political goals, but by generalized, virulent hatred based on religion and culture.

On balance, the amount of terrorist activity in the world will continue to rise, not decline, in the next 10 years. This was seen in corrections to the State Department's April 2004 report on terrorism, which originally seemed to show a sharp drop in terrorist incidents. In fact, terrorist attacks had risen sharply since the invasion of Iraq, both in number and in severity.

Assessment: This trend is unlikely to change in the next decade and relatively unlikely to change in the next 20 years. A permanent end to the international terrorist threat would require a broad philosophical and cultural change in Islam that makes terrorists pariahs in their own communities. No such change is on the horizon.

Implications for Cruise Lines: Cruise ships are an ideal target for terrorists willing to sacrifice themselves so long as they can take large numbers of people with them. This represents a significant risk to the industry, particularly as government facilities and land-locked attractions become harder to attack.

Government mandates are likely to require even tighter security precautions on cruise ships. A successful attack on a cruise ship could stifle the industry's growth for several years.

INDUSTRY OVERVIEW: HOSPITALITY AND TOURISM

The hospitality and tourism industry has changed more than a little since the first motel, in San Luis Obispo, California, was opened in 1925. (Its rooms went for $2.50 a night.) Today, there are more than four million guest rooms in the country, and tourists and businesspeople spend about $550 billion each year on travel in the United States. The industry includes behemoths like Marriott, Hilton, Six Flags, and Disneyland and Walt Disney World, on down to out-of-the-way bed-and-breakfasts and roadside attractions like the Liberace Museum (in Las Vegas), the Cadillac Ranch (Amarillo, Texas), and the Dan Quayle Center and Museum (Huntington, Indiana).

Which means that the Gideons, who placed their first Bible in a hotel room in 1908, have a lot more work to do than they used to. But they're not the only ones. Today, the industry employs more than seven million people directly and even more than that indirectly. (For example, consider a waiter in a restaurant in Palm Springs, California, which is in the middle of the desert: His job wouldn't exist if it weren't for the fact that Palm Springs is a tourist destination.) Accountants, nurses, salespeople, lifeguards, park rangers, street cleaners, car rental agents, blackjack dealers, caterers, cruise directors, the actress in the Snow White costume, the clerk in the t-shirt shack, the tennis pro, the golf course groundskeeper-the industry employs these folks and many, many more.

Despite the size and complexity of the industry, today many of its arms are interconnected by technology. Computer systems now allow people to reserve airline tickets, rental cars, hotel rooms, and tours-all at the same time. These computer systems are called computer reservation systems (CRSs) or global distribution systems (GDSs).

Although many in the industry work in behind-the-scenes positions, those on the front lines-travel agents, front desk clerks, tour guides, and so on-must be enthusiastic and articulate. And in most any position, you'll need to have a love of service and a strong attention to detail. In the end, your job is about how satisfied you've made the customer.

RECOVERY?

It's been a very difficult few years for the hospitality and tourism industry. The economic recession has caused businesses, individuals, and families to cut back on their spending on travel, and fears of terrorism have made many folks even less inclined to travel. The results have included lower industry revenues, layoffs, and a tighter job market. Today, though, there are signs that people are starting to travel more and that the industry may be recovering. Industry analysts are expecting increasing demand for hotel rooms and seats on airline flights in 2004, with an increase in job opportunities in many sectors of the industry.

THE INTERNET

The biggest change in the travel industry in recent years has been the rise of the Internet. It used to be that you had to speak with your travel agent, or call hotels and airlines directly, to make your travel plans. But as Internet usage spread, it became possible to use the new technology to research destinations and compare prices yourself, or visit web sites that provide all that information in one place. Indeed, companies such as Expedia and Travelocity have become quite profitable doing just that. In 2003, 12 percent of lodging reservations were made online, and that number is sure to grow in coming years. One of the changes wrought by the Internet has been to make the travel agent and reservations clerk less necessary to making travel plans. According to industry experts, the Internet has also raised the number of rooms occupied per night-but it's also caused lower revenue per room, as the ease of Internet comparison shopping and Internet-only promos have increased competition among hospitality providers.

NICHE MARKETS

As in many other industries, the big players in the hospitality and tourism industry have become vastly more efficient due to technology and management advances in recent years. These days, smaller players just can't compete on price. So how can smaller hotels, motels, and tour operators compete with bigger players who pay half what they do for supplies? For many smaller players, the answer is finding a market niche that is not adequately served by the big players and becoming a specialist in providing services for that niche.

Although some market niches are already served by big industry players (think: golf resorts, or tour operators who put together trips to New York City to see Broadway plays), there are plenty of niches that smaller players focus on. For example, there are tour operators that focus on the gay male market, Christian- or Jewish-focused Jerusalem-tour packagers, back country-skiing tour guides, ecotourism resorts, and so on. If you love travel and have a passion for a certain place or activity, it's likely you'll be able to find a company that operates in that niche. The only problem is that many of these companies will be so small that they'll rarely have an open position for you to fill.

Hospitality and tourism is a big, hard-to-pin-down industry that actually consists of 15 or more specific sectors, including car rentals, restaurants, convention and meeting planning, airlines, State and National Parks, convention and visitor bureaus, and tour operators. That's way too much for us to look at here, though, so we'll stick to the following core sectors of the industry:

LODGING

The lodging sector, which serves both vacationers and business travelers and which made $103 billion in revenue in 2002, consists of hotels, motels, bed-and-breakfast providers, hostels, and the like: places where you can stay the night. Lodging types include budget accommodations (*e.g.*, EconoLodge, Super 8, and Motel 6), midpriced lodgings (*e.g.*, Sheraton, Marriott), and high-end luxury hotels (*e.g.*, W Hotels, Ritz-Carlton), as well as hostels, campgrounds, and bed-and-breakfasts. Major players in this sector include Carlson Companies, Cendant, Hilton, Marriott, Starwood Hotels and Resorts, Accor, and Choice Hotels.

RESORTS

These are destinations built around a specific activity (*e.g.*, golf or skiing), attraction (*e.g.*, Walt Disney World), or target demographic (*e.g.*, Club Med destinations for singles and families, respectively). Unlike the lodgings sector, this sector is focused squarely on the vacation market and includes timeshare accommodations. Big players here include Walt Disney Parks and Resorts, Club Med, Sandals, Fairfield Resorts, Bluegreen Corp., Intrawest Corp., Vail Resorts, and American Skiing Co.

GAMBLING

Las Vegas, Reno, and Atlantic City used to be the only places that came to mind when you mentioned the word "casino," but in recent years this sector has been growing in places from Louisiana to North Dakota and from Florida to California. Gaming businesses include casinos, riverboat casinos, racetracks, and racetrack casinos (or "racinos"). Casinos can be stand-alone attractions, or can be combined with lodging facilities (and in some cases, such as Vegas's New York New York, nongambling attractions) to make gambling resorts. This sector employed 351,000 people in 2002. Big players here include Harrah's,

MGM Mirage, Caesar's, Mandalay Resort Group, and Trump Hotels and Casino Resorts.

ATTRACTIONS

This sector comprises all the places you might visit as your primary destination while on vacation, as well as all those places you might stop to check out en route to your primary destination. In other words, everything from amusement parks (for instance, Disneyland) and roadside attractions (such as the Salem Witch Museum) to notable natural landscapes (the Grand Canyon), famous or historical buildings (Graceland, the Alamo), and in some cases entire towns or cities (Branson, Missouri). Big players in this sector include the National Parks Service, Walt Disney Parks and Resorts, Busch Entertainment Corp., Paramount Parks, Universal Parks and Entertainment, Six Flags, Cedar Fair, and ClubCorp.

TRAVEL AGENCIES AND TRAVEL PACKAGERS

Travel agents and packagers help travelers plan their business trips and vacations. Travel agents help business travelers and tourists plan and purchase everything from airline tickets and car rentals to resort stays and attraction tickets.

Travel packagers put together trips for individual tourists or groups of tourists, arranging for everything from hotel stays and restaurant reservations to tours guides, theater reservations, and sports lessons. Smaller travel agencies and packagers are more likely to focus on a single market, activity, or location. For example, one travel packager might focus on singles tours, another might offer only surf tours, and another may concentrate on tours of Asia. Major players in this category include American Express, Cendant, Expedia, Orbitz, Travelocity, Carlson Wagonlit Travel, WorldTravel, Maritz Inc., and World Travel Specialists Group.

CRUISE LINES

Cruise lines are included in this profile because while other modes of transportation, like airlines, are primarily about getting passengers from place to place, on a cruise ship the trip is the focus. Indeed, cruise ships are essentially floating resorts, with all the activities and amenities of resorts of every kind. Major players here include Carnival, Royal Caribbean, Norwegian Cruise Lines, Royal Olympic, and Star Cruises.

The outlook in the hospitality and tourism industry varies depending on the position and sector you're interested in working in:

- Opportunities in HOSPITALITY, which have been fewer than usual during the recent economic downturn, are projected to grow at a slightly greater rate than jobs overall between 2000 and 2010.

Of course, the hospitality and tourism industry is especially sensitive to the overall economy; when things are tough in the economy, businesspeople tend to travel less, and would-be vacationers tend to scale back their travel plans, if not cancel them altogether. Events of global significance, such as terrorist attacks and disease epidemics, can also hurt the travel business. Be aware that, occasionally, the industry will go into a downturn, and that when that happens nobody's job is completely safe. A final note: ADVENTURE TRAVEL is one particularly hot spot in the travel business these days. Competition is tough for positions in this sector, but jobs here should continue to grow in coming years.

JOIN THE INDUSTRY, SEE THE WORLD

In an industry built around travel, it makes perfect sense: Many in hospitality and tourism get great discounts on everything from hotel and airline rates to event tickets. Imagine a trip to an exotic location every year. Imagine staying in four-star hotels. Imagine having a suntan every winter. Your friends are going to be so jealous.

DO WHAT YOU LOVE

You want to work outdoors, way out in the desert, deep in the woods, or overlooking the ocean? There's a place in hospitality and tourism for you. You want to surf, or mountain bike, or work to preserve the environment? There's a place in hospitality and tourism for you. You want to sing, or dance, or act? Yep-there's a place in hospitality and tourism for you. Park rangers, lodging managers, golf pros, action-sports tour guides, and performing artists at theme parks and resorts-they all get to do what they love. And lots of their colleagues in more-corporate fields-such as sales reps, accountants, and travel agents-get just as much of a charge out of working in hospitality and tourism-out of working in a beautiful location or helping others go on the vacation of their dreams.

THE PAYCHECK

This is not an industry in which you're going to get rich. Of course, if you make it to the top of a big corporation in hospitality and tourism, you'll most likely be very comfortable. But in the years before that, while your friends who are bankers and doctors and lawyers and such are busy building their investment portfolios, you'll still be making a relative pittance. In other words: You're going to be so jealous of your friends.

THE STRESS

Customer service is the foundation of success in hospitality and tourism. And as anyone who's ever worked in customer service can tell you, that means one thing: stress. In most jobs in this industry, you'll almost always be facing deadlines. Say you're a housekeeping manager. Will all the rooms vacated this morning be ready for new guests at the 3 p.m. check-in time? They'd better be. Or say you're a travel agent.

Are there any luxury-hotel rooms available this weekend? If there aren't, you won't be receiving any commission. Or you're a tour guide, and one of your guests hasn't returned from the shopping excursion yet-even though the bus is supposed to leave in 3 minutes. Taking care of travelers with varying needs and varying levels of bossiness (not to mention varying levels of intelligence) can get the goat of the best of us.

You'll find the usual array of corporate positions within the hospitality and tourism industry: marketing executives, salespeople, accountants, HR specialists, and the like. But the majority of the career opportunities in the industry are in more customer service-oriented areas. Following are descriptions of some of those careers:

RESTAURANT MANAGER

Manages the daily operations of a restaurant. May require an associate's degree in a related area or its equivalent and at least 4 years of experience in the field or in a related area. Familiar with a variety of the field's concepts, practices, and procedures. Relies on experience and judgement to plan and accomplish goals. Performs a variety of complicated tasks. May lead and direct the work of others. Typically reports to a senior manager. A wide degree of creativity and latitude is expected. Salary range: $35,000 to $60,000.

EXECUTIVE CHEF

An alternate title for this position might be "boss of the kitchen." People in this position oversee everything from purchasing to menu planning to the details of food preparation.

Before you reach this level, you'll have to grind through years in lower-level food-prep jobs. If you aspire to this level, you'd be well-advised to attend a culinary institute. Salary range: $55,000 to $100,000.

CONCIERGE

This is the guy or gal at the hotel who focuses solely and relentlessly on making his or her employer's guests happy. You'll be arranging for guests' dry cleaning, theater ticket purchases, restaurant reservations, and more. To do this job, you've got to love serving guests, be a creative problem-solver, and know everything there is to know about your location. For example, you'll need to know whether and where there are Ethiopian restaurants in your location-and, maybe, where one might find a "technically illegal" game of poker, or how one might arrange to meet with a member of the opposite sex for an hour or two. Typical salary: $17,000 to $30,000, but a good concierge in an upscale hotel can earn a lot more via tips.

LODGING MANAGER

People in these positions manage the day-to-day operations of a hotel or motel. This means doing everything from managing the housekeeping, room-service, and reservations staff to managing the supply purchasing and inventory control. In addition, the lodging manager is ultimately accountable for anything that goes wrong at the hotel or motel, meaning that people in this position can basically be on call 24/7 for emergencies from computer breakdowns to on-site accidents. Salary range: $20,000 to $40,000.

MEETING/EVENT PLANNER

People in these positions plan meetings or special events (*e.g.*, company parties or industry conventions) for businesses and other organizations. These folks do everything from reserving hotel space for meeting or event participants to arranging for catering to negotiating rates and contracts with those hotels and caterers and other vendors. Salary range: $40,000 to $70,000.

TRAVEL AGENT

The travel agent helps customers understand their travel, lodging, and activity options,in addition to making reservations or purchasing tickets for everything from airline flights to car rentals. Agents have to have an understanding of one or more of the reservations technologies used in the industry: Sabre, Amadeus, Worldspan, or Galileo. They must also be good at selling and customer relations. More and more agents are getting a formal education in their field and getting certified by the Institute of Certified Travel Agents. Salary range: $25,000 to $50,000.

CORPORATE TRAVEL MANAGER

Folks in this job typically work for Fortune 1000 companies, in what's basically an in-house travel-agent position. In addition to handling reservations and ticket-purchasing responsibilities, some corporate travel managers are responsible for creating and maintaining corporate travel policies (which codify things like the rates that various levels of employees can pay for airline tickets and hotels, or which car rental companies employees can use). Salary range: $45,000 to $75,000. Some hospitality and tourism organizations offer internships or student co-op opportunities; these are generally the fastest entrée to full-time work in the industry. You can also go to school to learn about specific areas of the industry; Cornell, for instance, offers a renowned hospitality programme, and lots of vocational schools offer programmes for aspiring travel agents.

Here's what most employers look for when they hire at all levels:

- With the ever-increasing focus on keeping customers happy, you need to enjoy serving people and be perpetually alert as to how to serve them better.

- Can you work well in teams? There is a lot of teamwork in many of these jobs.
- How do you handle stress? Stress seems to be an ever-present factor in jobs in this industry, whether you're a chef, a travel agent, or a tour guide.
- Love your employer, love the experience it offers customers, love the prestige and cachet of your particular niche in the industry. The pay is low, the hours are long, and advancement is never easy. If you'd buy what your company is selling, you're a much stronger potential hire.

5

Passenger Security and Safety on Cruise Ships

Planning a vacation this winter? Each year, millions of people board cruise ships departing from U.S. ports. We have done work on the security and safety requirements for cruise vessels that may give you a better understanding of how cruise lines and U.S. agencies are supposed to protect you, the passenger.

CRUISE SHIP CRIME

One provision of the Cruise Vessel Security and Safety Act (CVSSA), enacted in 2010, required cruise lines with vessels that visit U.S. ports to report certain crimes that occur aboard their ships to the FBI and the U.S. Coast Guard. The U.S. Coast Guard maintains a web site to publish information on the reported crimes that are no longer under investigation by the FBI. *We found that the usefulness of some of the published data may be limited in three key ways:*

- *Completeness:* Not all allegations are reported, such as those where investigations are not opened.
- *Timeliness:* Crime data posted on the web site may represent incidents that occurred months or years in the past because of the lag between the time an alleged crime is reported and the time a case is closed.
- *Relevance:* Data posted on the web site lack context that could help the public compare cruise vessel crime rates to land-based crime rates.

We also found that some cruise lines are making efforts to improve reported crime data. In August 2013, several cruise lines began voluntarily disclosing alleged crime data on their web sites. Also, in July 2013, legislation was introduced to amend the CVSSA that would revise and expand crime-reporting requirements, among other items. Since these efforts were new or in process, it was too early for us to assess their long term impact.

Changes in Cruise Ship Safety since Costa Concordia Accident

The January 2012 grounding of the cruise vessel Costa Concordia off the coast of Italy resulted in the deaths of 32 passengers, raising questions, for example, about the procedures for safeguarding passengers in emergency situations. For example, although international maritime law requires all passengers to be evacuated within 30 minutes of an order to abandon a vessel, the Italian government reported that the evacuation of theCosta Concordia took more than 6 hours. The Italian government investigated the accident and reported in May 2013 on numerous lapses in emergency procedures and management, including problems with vessel evacuation, voyage planning, and emergency communication.

In response to the Costa Concordia accident, the Cruise Lines International Association (CLIA)—which represents over 98 percent of cruise lines in the United States—initiated a safety review to come up with new safety measures. The review identified 10 safety-related policies in 2012 that all member cruise lines adopted by July 2013, as you can see in the figure.

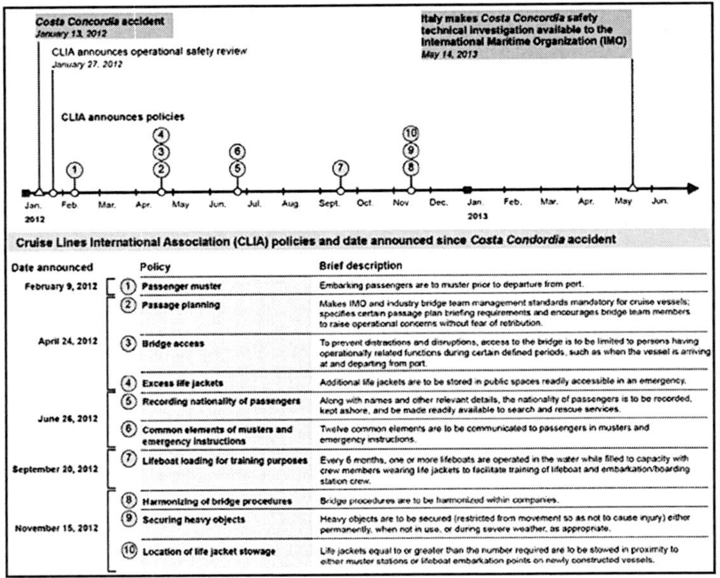

Cruise Lines International Association (CLIA) policies and date announced since *Costa Condordia* accident

Date announced	Policy	Brief description
February 9, 2012	(1) Passenger muster	Embarking passengers are to muster prior to departure from port.
April 24, 2012	(2) Passage planning	Makes IMO and industry bridge team management standards mandatory for cruise vessels; specifies certain passage plan briefing requirements and encourages bridge team members to raise operational concerns without fear of retribution.
	(3) Bridge access	To prevent distractions and disruptions, access to the bridge is to be limited to persons having operationally related functions during certain defined periods, such as when the vessel is arriving at and departing from port.
	(4) Excess life jackets	Additional life jackets are to be stored in public spaces readily accessible in an emergency.
June 26, 2012	(5) Recording nationality of passengers	Along with names and other relevant details, the nationality of passengers is to be recorded, kept ashore, and be made readily available to search and rescue services.
	(6) Common elements of musters and emergency instructions	Twelve common elements are to be communicated to passengers in musters and emergency instructions.
September 20, 2012	(7) Lifeboat loading for training purposes	Every 6 months, one or more lifeboats are operated in the water while filled to capacity with crew members wearing life jackets to facilitate training of lifeboat and embarkation/boarding station crew.
November 15, 2012	(8) Harmonizing of bridge procedures	Bridge procedures are to be harmonized within companies.
	(9) Securing heavy objects	Heavy objects are to be secured (restricted from movement so as not to cause injury) either permanently, when not in use, or during severe weather, as appropriate.
	(10) Location of life jacket stowage	Life jackets equal to or greater than the number required are to be stowed in proximity to either muster stations or lifeboat embarkation points on newly constructed vessels.

Fig. Timeline of CLIA Actions Relative to the Costa Concordia Accident.

Image excerpted from GAO-14-43

For example, one measure includes passengers doing their evacuation drills before the ship actually departs. Another includes additional life jackets that would be stored in public spaces so people would not have to go back to their cabins to get their life jackets if something happened suddenly. It is important to note at this point, though, that these are all being done voluntarily. The Coast Guard, so far, has not adopted any new regulations related to safety after the Costa Concordia accident.

SECURING HEAVY OBJECTS

CLIA's members recognize the differences in structure of vessels and operations which exist among the member cruise lines, and that the on board and shoreside management of each member line therefore determines its best practices under the circumstances presented.

CLIA's oceangoing members have adopted a policy to incorporate procedures into their Safety Management Systems to help ensure the securing of heavy objects either permanently, when not in use, or during heavy/severe weather, as appropriate. Under this policy, a person or persons are to oversee a deck by deck inspection to identify unsecured and potentially hazardous heavy objects. Integral to the procedures is a list of identified objects which have a significant potential to cause injury.

Shipboard personnel should apply good seamanship in identifying additional items to be secured. Attention should be given to muster stations, evacuation routes, and lifeboat embarkation stations as a ship emergency could give rise to conditions that differ from ship motions caused by heavy/severe weather.

Consideration should also be given to development of a guidance document to assist in the identification of heavy objects and the most adequate methods for securing them. An example of this guidance document is attached in the annex. This annex is only intended to provide an example for one method of implementing this policy.

Practices and procedures for securing heavy objects should be monitored by each Head of Department and/or as otherwise specified by the ship's command structure, and during routine shipboard inspections and audits. Heavy/severe weather should be clearly defined under the company policy taking into account the size of the ship, operational profiles, and other information. In defining heavy/severe weather, appropriate deference should be given to the judgement of the Captain.

Guidance document(s) should consider the following three elements, in addition to any other relevant information.

1. Heavy Objects. The following list is an example of some heavy objects that may be identified and secured in accordance with company policy. In this sample listing, the objects are grouped by those that should be permanently secured, always secured when not in use, and those to be secured in heavy weather.

Heavy objects that have been identified include, but are not limited to, the following:

- Heavy objects that should be permanently secured.
- Heavy plant pots, sculptures, TVs, cash machines, laundromat equipment, slot machines, and game machines such as in teen recreation areas.
- Display stands and racks.
- Treatment tables, heavy standalone product displays, treadmills, exercise weight racks, and weight lifting machines.
- Pianos, lounge speakers, and back-stage scenery equipment.

- Heavy objects that should be secured at all times when not in use.
- Trolleys and forklift trucks.
- Paint rafts, gangways, and deck trash containers.
- X-ray scanners.
- Cylinder heads, pistons, charge air coolers, heavy chemical containers, and heavy fan impellers.
- Gas bottles (refrigerant, oxygen, acetylene, CO_2, etc.)
- Heavy objects not otherwise secured that should be secured for heavy weather.
- Loose objects on display.
- Temporary decorations.
- Items brought aboard temporarily as part of shows.
- Materials/equipment onboard as part of repairs/refurbishment.
- Securing Methods.
- Consideration should be given to the strength and appropriateness of each point of attachment to which the heavy objects are secured.
- Consideration should be given to the following list of securing methods. Additional securing methods appropriate to the objects to be secured should be identified and used as necessary. Examples are as follows; however, additional methods should be identified and included as appropriate.
  - "Latch type gate hook and eye bracket mounted on bulkhead or vertical surface.
  - "Ratchet strap and eye brackets mounted on bulkhead or vertical surface.
  - "Rope secured to object and adjacent suitable securing surface.
  - "Contained in metal rack-type shelving system.
  - "Suction cup and bracket, ratchet strap, chain, etc.
  - "Permanent securing such as bolting to bulkhead or deck.
- Various. A list of specific heavy objects that have been identified by the company during surveys and inspections and that require particular attention.

RECORDING THE NATIONALITY OF PASSENGERS

The International Convention for the Safety of Life at Sea (SOLAS), Chapter III, Regulation 27 requires that all persons on board be counted prior to departure; details of those who have declared a need for special care or assistance in an emergency be recorded and communicated to the Master prior to departure; names and gender of all persons on board, distinguishing between adults, children and infants be recorded for search and rescue purposes; and that all of this information be kept ashore and made readily available to search and rescue services when needed.

To further facilitate the effective and immediate availability of key information in the event of an emergency situation, CLIA oceangoing members have adopted a policy that, in addition to the information required by SOLAS, the nationality of each passenger onboard is also to be recorded, kept ashore and made readily available to search and rescue services when needed.

FACTS ABOUT CRUISE SHIP SAFETY

All cruise ships must be designed and operated in compliance with strict requirements of international law and follow an extraordinary number of established rules and regulations to protect everyone on board. Every aspect of the cruise experience is heavily regulated and monitored under both U.S. and maritime law. According to CLIA (Cruise Lines International Association), a typical cruise ship has more than 60 safety, environmental and health inspections each year. Safety regulations are rigourous – and ships often go substantially above and beyond what is required. In recent years, safety-related technology processes have become more sophisticated. Cruise ship safety continues to improve as technology advances, and the industry learns from developing and evaluating best practices. As the industry has grown, regulators have updated and enhanced the safety requirements, including improvements in navigation equipment, shipboard safety management systems, life-saving equipment and training/certification standards.

The U.S. Coast Guard conducts periodic inspections for every cruise ship sailing from our ports. These inspections focus on crew training, fire safety, proper functioning of all safety systems and lifesaving equipment. Modern cruise ships are required to have state-of-the-art electronic navigational instruments, and most ships substantially exceed these regulatory requirements.

Ships are also required to have lifeboats, life rafts and life preservers for every person on board as well as additional capacity. The lifeboats are capable of being loaded, launched and maneuvered away from a ship within 30 minutes of a Captain's order. Safety drills in multiple languages are held prior to departure from port.

The average cruise ship, carrying 2700 passengers and 800 crew, has:

- 5 firefighting teams
- 4,000 smoke detectors
- 500 fire extinguishers
- 16 miles of sprinkler piping
- 5,000 sprinkler heads
- 6 miles of fire hose.

WHAT HAPPENS IF SOMEONE GET SICK ON A CRUISE SHIP?

Doctors on board international ships are trained and licensed with at least three years of clinical experience, including minor surgery and emergency care.

Modern cruise ships also have sophisticated medical facilities ranging from intensive care units to x-ray suites and laboratories for blood testing. If the ship's medical team feel they are not equipped to deal with a situation, outside resources will be called in to medevac patients to other medical facilities.

What About Norovirus?

Historic incidence rates of gastrointestinal illness aboard cruise ships are low; in fact, the vast majority of outbreaks occur in land-based settings.The cruise industry has taken steps to prevent sick passengers from bringing norovirus on board a ship and, in the rare instances of an outbreak, immediately employ numerous practices to mitigate its spread and treat ill passengers and crew.

CRUISE SHIP SECURITY

Cruise ships are like a small city where passengers are encouraged to forget their troubles and relax once onboard ship. It is natural for passengers on vacation to let their guard down, especially when out to sea in a resort-like setting. My advice: Don't let a false sense of security aboard a cruise ruin your vacation by becoming a crime victim. Before you ship out, take these preventative steps:

BEWARE OF YOUR LUGGAGE

Most complaints regarding theft, damage or loss involves the contents of luggage. Savvy travelers will make a written inventory of items in their luggage and photograph it in case of loss. Carry important items like medication, eyeglasses, and expensive jewelry in your hand luggage. Photocopy the contents of your wallet and your passport. Carry a copy in your hand luggage and leave one at home as back up. Keep luggage under your control until you check in with the cruise line. Once you turn over your luggage over to the ship baggage handlers you won't see it again for hours until it gets processed with a thousand other bags and is delivered to your cabin. A word to the wise, travel with sturdy plain-looking luggage. Expensive looking luggage may be targeted for its perceived contents. External bag tags should not list your full home address and telephone number. If they do, sophisticated home burglars will know that you are on a cruise and not be home soon.

Use durable luggage that is capable of being locked or secured and that will withstand being at the bottom of a pile of hundreds of other pieces of luggage without popping open. It is a good idea to add extra banding or airport plastic wrap or duct tape to your luggage locks to prevent anyone from opening your luggage without detection. Self-locking plastic tie-wraps work well for securing zippers on soft-sided luggage. You can buy these at any home improvement store for about a dollar. The reason for this is that smugglers have been known to slip drugs into luggage only to retrieve it later and maybe with force. Passengers have unknowingly transported cocaine that was slipped into their suitcase by baggage handlers only to be arrested later by port authorities. What explanation you would give to prove your innocence to a foreign government of why you are carrying drugs? If your luggage was properly sealed, you should see if it has been tampered with prior to opening it. Report any luggage tampering immediately to ship security before opening the case. Be sure to repack just as securely before you disembark and take similar precautions.

CABIN SECURITY

After you enter your cabin, and while the door is still open, always check inside the bathroom or closest before sitting down inside. Don't assume that your cabin is as secure as a hotel. Many people have keys to your cabin and your cabin door may be left standing open for hours while the cleaning crews or cabin steward services the room. Cabin doors locks are sometimes horribly outdated and are not re-keyed as frequently as hotel rooms. Obviously, don't leave valuable items lying around. It is a good idea to have inventoried your luggage and photographed expensive items at home before you packed them at home in case of loss. Since most ship passengers are set up on a charge account system, be sure to use the ship safe deposit box for storage of valuable items, papers, credit cards or extra cash. Use all locks on the cabin door including the night latch. Don't open your cabin door to strangers. Whatever the person wants can be expressed from the other side of the closed and locked door. Be sure to teach children about this important procedure.

Just like in a hotel, protect your cabin key and cabin number. Dishonest crew or passengers will look for the opportunity to snatch a loose key or one that is left unattended. When in port, be sure to leave your key with the registration desk before disembarking.

STAY IN PUBLIC AREAS

Once on board and out to sea, don't assume that you are totally safe from criminal acts. While there is little danger of an outside predator robbing or attacking you on a cruise ship, crimes can just as easily be committed by crewmembers or by fellow passengers. Many cruise lines hire transient and seasonal employees at low wages. Because of this, turnover is high and cruise lines struggle to keep a ship fully staffed. While most crewmembers are hardworking and honest people, you cannot assume that the ship has properly screened that nice cabin attendant, waiter or below deck crew.

A rule of thumb is to stay only in the public areas. On large cruise ships, security personnel are on board and will patrol in plain clothes. Occasionally, someone will monitor video cameras in key public areas. Unlike land-based resorts, the ratio of passengers and crew to security staff is often inadequate.

HAVE A FAMILY SECURITY PLAN

If you bring your children aboard, be sure to establish family rules in advance. Set curfews and restrictions...just like at home. Teenagers especially should be told never to accompany crewmembers into non-public areas nor should crewmembers be allowed inside your cabin. Being at sea can cause a false sense of security. Even though the crime incident rate per thousand is relatively low, there can still be predators on board. Ship nightclubs, casinos, swimming pools and jacuzzis are favourite spots for those looking for a victim.

You also need to keep your guard up with intoxicated passengers. Food and liquor consumption peaks onboard ships and cause bring out the worst in some people not used to it. Just because passengers are dressed up, doesn't mean they will act appropriately or not be overly aggressive. It is not unheard of for a ship passenger to slip a drug into your drink and take advantage of you just like on shore. There are pickpockets, purse thieves, and cabin burglars onboard waiting for you to let your guard down or become careless. There are also scam artists who will prey on rich women and men if given the chance.

Your family security plan for children should include bed checks, curfews, restrictions, and special meeting places. Beware of which children they hang out with, just like at home. Your children can be exposed to other children who use drugs or like to get into mischief, just like at home. Try to limit your child to ship sponsored activities in public areas. You should make contact with your children periodically even if they are supervised. Giving them the run of the ship while you spend hours in the casino or show is asking for trouble. Always have a backup plan and identify a ship crewmember as a contact person in case your child fails to show up or you get separated at a port.

LAWS MAY NOT PROTECT YOU

Although you boarded a ship in a US port doesn't mean that you are protected by our justice system. Most ships are registered in non-US countries and travel in territorial waters where US laws might not apply. The cruise industry does not report crime data consistently, if at all, to the FBI or have a database of ships with the most crime problems. Shipboard crimes sometimes fall into a "no man's land" of law enforcement. A crime can occur between two people of different nationalities, on a ship from a third country, and in the territorial waters of a fourth country. The governing law is the International Maritime Law and is not as well developed as US law. Reporting a crime on board a cruise ship doesn't mean anything will be done or that the crime will ever be investigated. The FBI is the only US law enforcement agency that can investigate a major crime but only if it occurs in International waters, otherwise crimes are reported to the jurisdiction of the closest foreign country and to the embassies of the parties involved. Prosecution of crime, in many cases, will be left in the hands of the local port authority where no one can predict the outcome.

Be aware that if you or your child gets into trouble on board a ship or in a port, you may be held accountable to the laws of a foreign country. The thing to do is to stay alert, be cautious, and stay safe while at sea. For details on the safety record of your cruise ship or how your ship will handle problems such are lost luggage or crime acts, contact the cruise line directly and ask for written disclosure of their policies and regulations. You can also contact the Cruise Lines International Association in New York City who represents the twenty five largest cruise lines for more information.

SAFETY AT SEA

The battle for more effective safety and security technologies onboard cruise ships, such as man overboard detection, is ongoing. Critics of the cruise industry say the corporations are circumventing their responsibility and the law when it comes to protecting their passengers. The cruise lines say they are safer than ever and consider the safety of human life their number one priority.

THE LAW

Sen. Blumenthal's strong criticism of the cruise industry did not begin with the death of Smook. In 2013, he and Sen. John D. Rockefeller (D-WV) introduced the Cruise Passenger Protection Act in the 113th Congress. The legislation would have required all cruise ships to establish medical training programmes for staff, install acoustic sounding devices to deter attackers, and install systems to alert crew members when a passenger has fallen overboard.

"In spite of the evidence that crimes, fires, mechanical failures, drownings, and mishandled medical emergencies occur with disturbing regularity on cruise ships, the industry continues to deny it has a problem," Rockefeller said in a July 2014 hearing. The legislation stalled, meaning that the Cruise Vessel Security and Safety Act (CVSSA), signed into law by President Barack Obama in 2010, remains the most comprehensive act governing cruise lines. The law outlines several provisions that cruise lines embarking and disembarking from the United States must adopt to ensure the safety and protection of passengers. The U.S. Coast Guard oversees the safety of U.S.-based cruise ships and is responsible for enforcing the CVSSA.

The CVSSA establishes several security measures for cruise ships, including that the rail height of ships be at least 42 inches above the cabin deck, and that each stateroom is equipped with portholes "or other means of visual identification" for security purposes.

The law also says each vessel should have technology that captures or detects someone falling overboard, and that each ship have an acoustical hailing device to provide communication capabilities around the entire vessel. Additionally, ships are required to maintain a video surveillance system and provide access to video records to law enforcement. In the event of a crime, under the CVSSA, cruise ships are required to provide security guides that instruct passengers on how to "prevent and respond to criminal and medical situations." If a crime is reported, the victims are to be given a hotline directly to the FBI, and if the crime is a sexual assault then they are to be given a medical exam. Cruise lines are also required to provide victims with contact information for the Coast Guard and the nearest U.S. consulate or embassy.

Crew members dealing with victims are also required to undergo training. Under the law, the FBI, the Coast Guard, and the Maritime Administration (MARAD) established model training standards that cover "crime prevention, detection, evidence preservation, and reporting of criminal activities," according to MARAD's web site. The agency provides a voluntary certification programme for cruise lines that want to submit their safety and training programmes for review.

But some argue that the law has not been thoroughly implemented or uniformly enforced. "I think the intent of the bill is there and the requirements are there, but they're not being enforced by the regulators," notes Ken Carver, who founded the International Cruise Victims Association (ICV) in 2006 after his daughter disappeared from a cruise ship. The nonprofit organization has been involved in several Capitol Hill hearings and backed legislation aimed at improving the safety and security of cruise ship passengers.

Members of government and victim advocates like Carver have been vocal about the shortcomings of the CVSSA. Some changes have been made, especially after the Government Accountability Office (GAO) released a report last year citing ways in which cruise lines had failed to implement the CVSSA. "Media reports about passenger personal safety while aboard cruise vessels—including those related to the January 2012 grounding of the cruise vessel Costa Concordia off the coast of Italy, which resulted in 32 deaths—combined with the increasing number of passengers taking cruises has raised questions about passenger safety and security," the report said.

Cruise companies must also comply with international law. The International Convention for the Safety of Life at Sea (SOLAS), governed by the International Maritime Organization (IMO), recently amended its regulations "to require musters [safety drills] of newly embarked passengers prior to or immediately upon departure," effective January 2015. The Coast Guard is proposing changes as well. This spring, the agency held a period for public comment on proposed changes to the CVSSA. According to the Federal Register, "the Coast Guard proposes amending its passenger vessel regulations to implement the Cruise Vessel Safety and Security Act of 2010 with respect to deck rails, systems for detecting or recording falls overboard, and for recording evidence of possible crimes, hailing devices, security guards, sexual assault response, and crime scene preservation training."

Lisa Novak, public affairs officer for the Coast Guard, says the comments will serve as a guide for amending the existing law. "While those comments cannot change the standards that Congress has already set through the CVSSA, they may suggest ways in which the details of implementation might be modified and improved, or suggest additional measures that Congress or the Coast Guard should take to improve cruise vessel industry safety," she tells Security Management. Novak adds that the provisions of the law are not "self-executing," meaning that the agency cannot directly require the cruise vessel industry to take action until the provisions are incorporated in the Coast Guard regulations that apply to the industry. "Some of the CVSSA standards do not contain details that industry will need in order to properly implement the standards," she explains. "The Coast Guard is proposing regulatory amendments that would incorporate the CVSSA standards and supply the necessary details of implementation."

Another organization that requires cruise lines to comply with industry standards is the Cruise Line International Association (CLIA), which represents 62 percent of the globe's ocean-going and river cruise vessels. Bud Darr, CLIA's vice president of technical and regulatory affairs, maintains that each cruise line is doing its best to follow the letter of the law. "The safety and security of our guests is the top priority for cruise lines, and our members maintain a rigourous set of policies and procedures that are tailored to their specific operations and designed to safeguard passengers and to provide an immediate and effective response to any shipboard incident," he says.

However, when it comes to proposed changes to the law, Darr stresses they are ready to comply. "It's a continuous process for us...we are very actively pursuing a wide range of potential safety enhancements, many of which were our proposals, and that's an ongoing process."

SAFETY MEASURES

The safety measures covered in the CVSSA include high-tech systems to deter threats and detect imperiled passengers, as well as policies and procedures to reduce crime. However, they have been only partially implemented. The Coast Guard notes that "the industry does not universally meet the requirements of the CVSSA at this time." Deterrence. Among its provisions, the CVSSA outlines measures to outfit cruise ships with security technologies designed to deter threats, such as pirates. As mentioned above, the law requires that all cruise ships "be equipped with a sufficient number of operable acoustic hailing or other such warning devices to provide communication capability around the entire vessel when operating in high-risk areas" as determined by the Coast Guard.

In ICV's public comments submitted to the Coast Guard, it emphasized the need for better acoustic hailing and warning devices. According to Mark

Gaouette, former director of security for Princess Cruises and Cunard Cruise Lines, "acoustic hailing devices are an important part of the ship's resources to confront small vessel threats at safe distances before they become threats close to the ship."

While the Coast Guard currently allows public address (PA) systems to satisfy this requirement aboard ships, Gaouette says "the ship's PA does not have the technical capability, nor was it designed to be audible at great distances from the ship." He cites an incident off the coast of Somalia in 2005 in which pirates attempted to attack the Seabourn Spirit, operated by Carnival Cruise Lines. Using a long range acoustical device (LRAD), the Seabourn Spirit successfully warded off the pirates. He and other advocates say that all ships should be required to keep such technology on board.

Man overboard. CVSSA requires man overboard detection technology on each ship. Specifically, the law says that "the vessel shall integrate technology that can be used for capturing images of passengers or detecting passengers who have fallen overboard, to the extent that such technology is available." Gaouette points out that the way the bill is worded leaves cruise lines with the option of "capturing images" of a passenger falling overboard, as opposed to detecting someone falling over and having time to save them. "The person in the water has no chance of survival—and I underscore no chance of survival—if they're not detected," he notes.

According to the Coast Guard's proposed changes to CVSSA, "the technology to reliably detect persons or objects as they are in the process of going overboard is not yet readily available for use at sea.... Based on industry data provided by cruise lines, we estimate that costs would range from $62,500 to $700,000 per ship in order to comply with the CVSSA requirements." But the Coast Guard also wrote that it anticipates "the cruise industry will focus on using capture systems rather than detection systems."

Most cruise ships meet the letter of the law by training CCTV cameras on either side of the ship, according to Gaouette. Even those ships with CCTV cameras that simply capture a person falling overboard have to later review the footage to ascertain the exact circumstances surrounding the incident. This can happen hours after the event, when passengers discover that a friend or loved one is missing.

However, Darr of CLIA says he is "not aware of any member ship that has entered or left the United States that is not in compliance with the CVSSA's self-executing provisions." Jim Walker, a Miami-based lawyer who has represented several victims of cruise ship crime, points out that alcohol consumption has been a major factor in many man-overboard cases. He says that many passengers who become ill after drinking too much will often lean over the side of the railing, causing some to actually fall overboard. As mentioned previously, in 2011 the CVSSA was amended to stipulate that rail heights be no less than 42 inches, but that did not solve the problem. According to the GAO report, there are two aspects necessary to detect someone going overboard in real time. The first, image capture, is currently available by using CCTV and thermal imaging. The second part, algorithms that can quickly determine when someone has gone overboard and sound an alarm, is not ready, according to the cruise industry. CLIA has noted that some of the problems with real-time detection include extreme weather, surface glare, and vessel vibrations.

Victims' advocates insist that a solution can be found. Gaouette suggests that the Coast Guard have an open call for developers of the technology to bring their products forth to be vetted, and then have the agency choose the top three systems, "and the cruise lines will have to back one of these technologies."

CLIA as an organization does not keep track of man overboard statistics, but Darr says individual cruise lines voluntarily report such incidents on their own web sites for transparency. In addition, the law allows cruise lines to conduct their own security assessments and place CCTV cameras accordingly. "The placement and number of cameras that are in place as part of that video surveillance will vary significantly from ship to ship," he notes.

Ross Klein, a professor of sociology at Memorial University of Newfoundland in Canada, runs a blog titled Cruise Junkie that chronicles overboard incidents on cruise ships. In 2013, he testified before the Senate Commerce, Science, and Transportation Committee that between 20 and 25 people have gone overboard each year since 2009. But Klein testified at the hearing that several such cases are not reported by cruise lines, including if they are rescued or intentionally jump over, because these incidents do not meet the definition of a "missing person" in the CVSSA.

Crime prevention. Victims' advocates say they are especially concerned about the level of crime that goes on during cruises, and that the CVSSA doesn't go far enough in enforcing accurate and timely reporting of incidents. Two wildly different pictures of crime statistics are painted by cruise lines and by industry critics. For example, in 2011, victims reported 563 incidents of crime aboard cruise ships. But cruise line web sites only documented 102 of those crimes, according to statistics compiled by Klein. The FBI data was given to him under a Freedom of Information Act (FOIA) request.

Much of that discrepancy arises from the way in which the CVSSA defines a criminal act. According to the law, a financial theft is "theft of money or property in excess of $10,000." Other criminal acts are defined as "homicide, suspicious death, a missing United States national, kidnapping...assault with serious bodily injury," or "tampering with the vessel."

Carver notes this wording leaves many acts of a criminal nature out of the picture. "You can rob somebody for less than $10,000 and no action is taken...and they don't have to report it," he says, adding that if a person suffers a sexual assault that does not result in "serious bodily injury," it doesn't have to be reported either.

Some of the reporting problems happen after law enforcement is notified. According to the law, victims of crime must immediately be given a hotline to the FBI from aboard the ship. But Walker says the law enforcement agency doesn't necessarily act on those cases. "They may be great at dealing with white collar crime but they'll just say that they're not interested in getting themselves involved in bar fights and people smashing each other with beer bottles or women who are raped," says Walker.

CLIA stresses that cruising remains safer than being on land, statistically. "Despite the way that it may be portrayed in the media, crime is rare on cruise ships and it's a fraction of any real corresponding crime rates on land," Darr notes. He says any crime allegations are reported and proper investigations are conducted, "but at times, just as on land, those investigations reveal that either the claim is unsubstantiated or it's just not sufficient to support a criminal prosecution. That's no different than any other legitimate criminal situation that you might face."

According to CLIA's web site, "The reporting procedures require that when an alleged crime is reported, cruise lines notify the FBI, the U.S. Coast Guard, the country under which a ship is registered, and local law enforcement authorities." But CLIA goes by the CVSSA's definition of crime, leaving out robberies under $10,000 and other acts not within the scope of the law.

Walker's firm represented victim Laurie Dishman, who was raped by a cruise line employee in September 2006 while on a Royal Caribbean ship. She testified at a congressional hearing in March 2007 that there were only three security guards for thousands of passengers on board the cruise. After reporting her sexual assault, she said that crew members sat on the bed where the rape occurred when questioning her, and instructed her to place any evidence she thought would be useful for the investigation in a trash bag. Based on testimony like this, the 2011 amendments to the CVSSA now mandate crime-scene-preservation training for crew. But Carver questions whether the one-day training programme required by the law is sufficient.

"What they came up with was a programme that's eight hours, with three hours on how to preserve a crime scene," Carver notes. Outlook. The Coast Guard has not announced when it will implement changes to the CVSSA based on the public comments it receives.

In the meantime, the cruise industry keeps on growing. More than 24 million passengers are expected to take a cruise by 2018, according to industry statistics, and the industry was worth $37 billion at the end of 2014. The concern among advocates is that without more regulation, the threat to security and safety on cruise lines remains. For threats such as piracy or terrorism, "the potential for mass disaster with a cruise line is far greater than with an airline because you have these floating cities with thousands of people," Walker says.

Darr notes that CLIA and the cruise lines are committed to making improvements, and that passengers are its top priority.

"When it comes to our mandatory policies we have set up a system which works quite effectively where each CEO of each cruise line has to personally sign every year saying that all of the policies...have been implemented successfully on their ocean-going cruise ships," he explains. "With or without government intervention we will continue to raise the bar on ourselves and make changes in safety in a wide variety of ways."

HIMES INTRODUCES CRUISE SHIP PASSENGER SAFETY LEGISLATION

Representatives Jim Himes (D-CT), Doris Matsui (D-CA), Ted Poe (R-TX) and members of the Congressional Victim's Rights Caucus, introduced bipartisan legislation yesterday to increase the safety and security of cruise ship passengers.

The Cruise Passenger Protection Act (CPPA) would build on the passenger safety measures put in place by the CVSSA, which was signed into law in 2010, by clarifying and strengthening the crime reporting requirements and the video surveillance requirements, and improving medical standards.

"This is a personal issue for me because it has profoundly affected my district and Connecticut," said Rep. Himes. "In 2005, George Smith IV of Greenwich went missing while on his honeymoon cruise in the Mediterranean Sea. Since George's disappearance, his family has been fighting tirelessly to improve safety on cruise ships and to protect cruise ship passengers. The fight continues today with the Cruise Passenger Protection Act. This bill bolsters current law with tighter crime reporting, expanded video surveillance equipment and record-keeping requirements, and streamlined tracking and public reporting of alleged crimes on cruise ships. It is safety improvements like these that will help prevent more avoidable tragedies."

"The Cruise Vessel Security and Safety Act was signed into law by President Obama in 2010, and was a critical first step in putting protections into place for the thousands of Americans who unknowingly put themselves at risk when they go on a cruise," said Rep. Matsui. "The Cruise Passenger Protection Act, which I am pleased to introduce today with my colleagues Representatives Ted Poe and Jim Himes, will continue to build upon the security and safety measures aboard our cruise ships and ensure that consumers have access to accurate information and victims are given the support and resources they deserve. I am grateful to the survivors and the victims' families who by sharing their stories have brought national attention and Congressional action to this important consumer safety issue." "The passage of the Cruise Vessel

Security and Safety Act in 2010 was a turning point for the safety and security of cruise passengers," said Rep. Poe. "The Cruise Passenger Protection act will go even further and build upon that success by putting in place stronger requirements to protect victims of crime and hold their perpetrators accountable." "Out of their deep concern for the welfare, safety and security of all U.S. citizens who travel on cruise ships, Reps. Doris Matsui, Ted Poe, and Jim Himes have introduced new legislation which will provide greater protection for those passengers," said Kendall Carver, Chairman of International Cruise Victims (ICV). "All members of ICV sincerely applaud this bipartisan effort to advance these much needed reforms. Rep. Matsui's passionate interest came about when one of her constituents, Laurie Dishman, sought her assistance. Rep. Poe, as Chairman of the Victim's Caucus, has played a meaningful role in providing support to victims of crime at sea. Rep Hines strong interest is in support of the Smith family, who lost their son. Their leadership resulted in the passing of the historic legislation known as the Cruise Vessel Security and Safety Act of 2010. ICV is most appreciative of their continued support to further enhance these safety requirements."

Specifically, the CPPA would:

- Ensure a cruise vessel owner notifies the FBI within four hours of an alleged incident.
- Ensure that if an alleged incident occurs while the vessel is still in a U.S. port, the FBI must be notified before that vessel leaves the port.
- Require vessel owners to also report an alleged offence to the U.S. Consulate in the next port of call, if the alleged offence is by or against a U.S. national.
- Clarify that vessels must have video surveillance equipment in all passenger common areas, and other areas, where there is no expectation of privacy.
- Allow individuals access to video surveillance records for civil action purposes.
- Mandate that all video records are kept for 30 days after completion of the voyage.
- Direct the Coast Guard to promulgate final standards within one year detailing requirements for the retention of video surveillance records.
- Transfer authority for maintaining the internet web site of alleged crimes on cruise ships from the Coast Guard to the Department of Transportation.
- Require that the web site breakout the crimes that are reported against minors and alleged "man overboards" incidents.
- Direct the Department of Transportation to conduct a study to determine the feasibility of having an individual on board each passenger vessel to provide victim support services

- Require integration of technology that can both capture images and detect when a passenger has fallen overboard.
- Ensure medical standards that would require a qualified physician and sufficient medical staff to be present and available for passengers, crew member basic life support training, accessible automated defibrillators, and that the safety briefing includes important emergency medical and safety information.
- Ensure that should a U.S. passenger die aboard a vessel his or her next of kin could request the vessel to return the deceased back to the United States.

SAFETY ON CRUISE SHIPS

One question that is foremost in potential cruisers'' minds seems to be "Is cruising safe?" Since 9/11 there have been new reports about cruise ships being the target of terrorists and of "massive" outbreaks of the Norwalk virus. If you believe everything you read in the newspaper or see on television, you might never leave your house!

The cruise industry''s highest priority is to ensure the safety and security of its passengers and crew. During the past two decades, North American cruise lines have maintained the best safety record in the travel industry while transporting more than 90 million people throughout the world. Cruise ships have, for the most part, always adhered to very strict security guidelines and practices. While the cruise lines and governments around the world have tightened and refined security after recent events, cruise ships have always been relatively secure.

Immediately after the terrorist attacks of September 11, cruise lines implemented what they call "Level 3" security measures, as outlined by the U.S. Coast Guard''s "Security for Passenger Vessels and Passenger Terminals" regulations. These measures include:

- Screening of all passenger baggage, carry-on luggage, ship stores and cargo; intensified screening of passenger lists and passenger identification; close coordination with the U.S. Immigration and Naturalization Service and other federal agencies to ensure that any passengers or crew suspected of being on the INS "Prevent Departure" list are promptly reported to the federal authorities.
- Restricting access to any sensitive vessel areas, such as the bridge and the engine room.
- Implementing onboard security measures to deter unauthorized entry and illegal activity.
- Requiring all commercial vessels to give 96 hours notice before entering U.S. ports. Previously, ships had to give 24 hours notice.
- Maintaining a 100-yard security zone around cruise ships.

ONBOARD SAFETY

A cruise ship is a "controlled-access environment" which means that, when a ship is in port, there are only one or two ways passengers and crew can enter the vessel. These entry points are manned by security personnel and ID"s are checked and, usually, packages and belongings must pass through an X-ray machine while passengers and crew pass through metal detectors. It is highly unlikely that anyone would be able to board the ship that doesn"t belong there.

Crew and port officials examine every shipment of supplies that are brought onboard and every piece of luggage that goes on the ship is thoroughly inspected by an x-ray machine. While the ship is in port, personnel are posted on deck to keep watch. Security onboard varies from line to line and ship to ship. Some cruise lines hire former military and naval personnel to implement and oversee their security, whiles others hire private security firms or former law enforcement officers. In the past, most security measures were intended to deal with passenger disturbances, but the focus now is on maintaining a safe and secure environment, eliminating or minimizing the threat of harm to passengers, crew and ship.

Most cruise ships today have an automated system linked to the ID card/ room key issued to each passenger upon embarkation. This system enables security personnel to know, at the touch of a button, who is on or off the ship at any given time. There are also surveillance cameras placed throughout the ship enabling security personnel, officers, staff and crew to visually monitor virtually every area of the ship.

All cruise ships carry a team of dedicated fire-fighters, and additionally, all ship"s personnel are trained in shipboard fires and undergo training and drills regularly. The average response time in an emergency is a matter of minutes, as members of the trained firefighting teams and firefighting equipment lockers are located throughout the ship. In the unlikely event of a dangerous fire, passengers are loaded into lifeboats to await a rescue ship which in most cases arrives within a matter of hours. It is the passenger"s responsibility to pay attention to the lifeboat drill when boarding and to know their muster station. When passengers follow instructions and remain calm everything works well. Additionally, Coast Guard personnel monitor firefighting and abandon ship drills on all cruise ships.

Individual cruise lines have their own criteria for determining their travel itineraries. However, the ability to ensure the security of the ship, passengers, and crew is a critical factor all cruise lines consider. The cruise lines obtain information from a variety of government and private sources on the countries and ports their clients visit. The decision as to which ports ships will visit is based on a variety of factors, one of which is security. A risk analysis of the port is conducted to ensure that the port authority and regional law enforcement are aware of, and will comply with, requirements for ensuring the security of the ship while it is in port, and passengers while they are ashore as guests in their country.

COMMON SENSE HELPS

Statistically, cruise ships are safer than hotels and resorts when it comes to fires and violent crime. However, it is in your best interest not to abandon common sense just because you board a cruise ship for a wonderful vacation. For example, don''t leave valuables lying around in your cabin. Put your wallet and valuables in the cabin''s safe or the purser''s safe. Be sure to use all the locks on the door when you are asleep. Protect your cabin key and cabin number. Do not invite strangers into your room. Don''t go into areas marked "No access." Don''t get drunk and sit on the railing. Take your common sense with you when you go ashore. Reading up on local customs and dangers before you go is always a good idea. Don''t dress flamboyantly, wear expensive jewelry or flash wads of money around. It is best to wear an under-the-clothing money belt but, if you must take a purse, be sure you can wear it with the strap across your body. Men, if you must carry a wallet, keep it in a front pocket and put a little money in each pocket. Keep cameras and purses in your lap when dining, not hung on the back of the chair or on the floor. Beware of that handsome stranger offering to change your money at a better than market rate. It''s most likely a scam! Watch out for groups of kids who are often well-organized gangs of pickpockets. One will distract you while another lifts your wallet. Even that gypsy lady with a baby (often only a doll) will distract you while a partner strips you of your belongings. It''s best to take only one credit card ashore with you.

Before you leave home, make a few copies of your passport, driver''s license, credit cards and travel documents (such as airline tickets) and leave a set with a trusted friend or family member at home. Be sure to have a copy of the credit card company''s contact number in case of lost or stolen cards. Pack the copies in a different place than you have the original documents. Leave the copies in a safe place on your ship and take a copy of your passport ID page with you when you go ashore.

Cruise lines exist to provide a safe, relaxing and enjoyable vacation experience for the cruise passenger. Good cruise ship security is almost transparent and quietly effective. With a little common sense and vigilance, anyone should be able to have a safe cruise vacation.

COAST GUARD PROPOSES NEW RULE ON CRUISE SHIP SECURITY

A proposed rule is underway attempting to improve safety and security for Americans on cruise ships. The U.S. Coast Guard's proposal addresses issues such as systems to detect or record falls overboard, crime prevention and criminal evidence-gathering, response to and treatment of sexual assaults, height of deck rails and security guides.

The rulemaking started with the passage of the Cruise Vessel Security and Safety Act of 2010 (CVSSA), signed by President Obama. The rule implements the bill by amending passenger vessel regulations. The bill's requirements apply to ships that sleep at least 250 passengers and that pick up or drop off passengers in the United States. It does not apply to vessels making coastal trips. In passing that bill, Congress determined that sexual and physical assault were the top crimes investigated on cruise ships by the Federal Bureau of Investigation (FBI) in the previous five-year period. In addition, passengers can disappear from vessels and don't understand their vulnerability to crime on cruise ships. They lack information about their legal rights or whom they contact after a crime. It is difficult for crime investigators to look into and document crime scenes aboard vessels. Getting reliable data is difficult because multiple countries are involved when a crime occurs at sea.

Many of the provisions of the bill are already in place and have been part of Coast Guard safety inspections. Examples include requirements for 42-inch-high deck-edge guard rails, peep holes, security latches and time-sensitive keys in every passenger and crew cabin and a security guide for passengers. There is a requirement for communication access for sexual assault victims including a private phone line and a computer with Internet access. Specific supplies and training must exist for medical staff responding to sexual assaults and limiting crew access to passenger rooms.

According to the proposal, 147 cruise vessels will be impacted with a cost to the industry and government of $79.1 million over 10 years. In 2013, 21.3 million people worldwide took cruises. Almost 11 million of those were Americans, according to Elinore Boeke, spokeswoman for Cruise Lines International Association (CLIA). This organization, which represents nearly 60 major cruise lines worldwide, declined to comment on specifics of the latest proposal. "We appreciate the Coast Guard putting forward this proposed rule for review, and CLIA and its members are evaluating it in detail," Boeke said. William Doherty, director of maritime relations at Nexus Consulting Group and ex-safety manager for Norwegian Cruise Lines, said the law is weak, with shortfalls in enforcement, financing and prosecution. "The rules are based on a sloppy foundation," Doherty said. "There are no enforcement teeth in the law."

Several specific sections of the proposed rule have raised concerns. One major issue is that the proposed training course for crime scene investigation is too short, according to some critics. The rule would require at least one crewmember to be trained in crime prevention, detection, evidence preservation and reporting. The U.S. Maritime Administration has begun certifying companies that will provide this training. This crewmember can be a mariner or a vessel security officer, but this is not a requirement.

A model course developed in 2011 by the Coast Guard, FBI and the U.S. Merchant Maritime Academy specifies eight objectives for students: to identify ways of preventing and detecting potential crimes; develop knowledge of emergency procedures; recognize security and safety risks; learn techniques used to evade security systems; recognize, without discrimination, the characteristics and behaviour of those who might be security and safety threats; understand the responsibilities of law enforcement, vessel security officers and medical staff; secure a crime scene until law enforcement officers take over; and understand reporting requirements to document serious crimes. The course described is scheduled for eight hours. Recertification would be required every two years.

Coast Guard personnel gather at a railing during a cruise ship inspection at Juneau, Alaska, in 2012. The new regulations call for higher, safer rails to prevent falls overboard.

"It is absurd that you can teach somebody in eight hours" the skills needed for this position, said Ross Klein, a professor at the Memorial University of Newfoundland who writes and testifies about cruise ship safety. Klein is concerned that this training is not enough for crime victims to make a strong legal case. "The people who are doing security work need to be trained as security professionals and their work needs to stand up in a court of law," Klein said.

"We believe that the instruction is adequate to meet its intended objective," said Coast Guard spokesman Lt. Jason Kling. "We understand that some suggest that the scope should be broader to encompass law enforcement duties/responsibilities/authorities that could adversely affect a criminal investigation."

Another issue is how crews should detect people falling overboard. The proposed rule gives cruise companies three options. They can use image capture systems, such as video or thermal technology, to record any person falling overboard; a system that immediately detects overboard falls and sounds an alarm; or a combination of the two methods. Man-overboard detection systems use combinations of thermal cameras, radar and infrared sensors and video analysis to detect a fall and alert the crew right away.

The notice of proposed rulemaking states that, based on responses from CLIA, the industry will predominantly use image capture systems. "However, the technology to reliably detect persons or objects as they are in the process of going overboard is not readily available for use at sea," the rule states.

Jamie Barnett, president of International Cruise Victims (ICV), said the technology is ready and the Coast Guard did not contact the five companies that submitted proposals for man-overboard detection systems.

"It is apparent from the proposed regulation's language that the technology does not need to capture an image, but must detect the event and sound an alarm," Barnett wrote in a letter to a U.S. congressman. When asked why the Coast Guard did not independently check the reliability of the new systems, Kling said, "The Coast Guard does not have the expertise to assess these products." Another concern is whether cruise ships that make short stays in the U.S. are covered by the proposed rule. "Any cruise ship that leaves from or arrives in the United States must be covered by the CVSSA with no exceptions as suggested in the proposed regulations," said Kendall Carver, chairman of ICV.

"Any contact with a U.S. port — U.S. residents should be subject to the act." Carver fears that cruise ships might use this exception to avoid the law. However, exempting those vessels does not apply to American passengers. "Temporary ports of call would be best described as those where people are not checking into or out of their cruise ship," said Kling.

HOW SAFE IS YOUR CRUISE SHIP?

It's been rough seas for the cruise industry over the last few years, especially with January's Costa Concordia tragedy that killed 32 people off the coast of Italy.

While the incident put into focus legitimate security concerns on board ships, it also prompted cruise lines, which have long claimed to be one of the safest ways to travel, to collectively ramp up – and promote – their safety initiatives. Over the past few months the Cruise Lines International Association, which represents 26 cruise lines, and the European Cruise Council have rolled out new policies, including two this week, that tighten up onboard safety and evacuation procedures.

But what about other potential dangers that lurk on board, including crime? Travelers will be happy to know that, in this area too, there have been moves to tighten safety measures. After sexual assaults on ships became a concern, Congress passed the Cruise Vessel Security and Safety Act of 2010, which required that cruise companies report serious crime and missing persons to the FBI when they involved a U.S. citizen. Previously, cruise ships voluntarily provided crime statistics to the FBI, but they weren't made public. Now, a tally of those crimes are reported online.

The CLIA maintains that passenger and crew safety is its top priority, comparing a cruise ship to "a secure building with a 24-hour security guard." Ships are equipped with security cameras and have "sophisticated security departments run by former federal, state or military law enforcement officials and staffed by competent, qualified security personnel," said David Peikin, CLIA director of public affairs, in an e-mailed statement to FoxNews.com. In addition, following the recent rash of onboard illnesses, many cruise lines have added sanitizing stations to their fleets and require passengers to use hand sanitizer after re-boarding and before meals.

But cruise ship crime remains one of the most hotly contested aspects of passenger safety. According to Peikin, it's "extremely rare. The industry's strong collaboration with all relevant authorities on crime reporting is well-established and the FBI, the U.S. Coast Guard and criminology experts have repeatedly commended our record in this area in testimony to Congress."

Not so, says Ross Klein, a professor at Memorial University of Newfoundland in Canada who studies issues involving cruise ships and has testified several times about cruise safety. His web site, Cruisejunkie.com, includes extensive data such as accident reports, fines from environmental agencies and ship inspection scores from the Centers for Disease Control and Prevention. According to analysis of crime statistics, Ross maintains that a person is twice as likely to be sexually assaulted on a cruise ship than on land.

"I don't want to be sensationalistic and say that a crime is definitely going to happen on any particular trip, but it happens frequently enough that you have to take precautions," Klein said, noting that cruise ships should be treated as "floating cities" and that passengers need to take an active role in protecting themselves while onboard. "Don't take an elevator by yourself. Avoid public restrooms at night. If you're taking any children aboard a ship, particularly female children, you have to 'street smart' them."

James Walker, another Miami-based attorney who advocates for cruise passengers, noted that about one-third of the approximately 75 sexual assault or molestation charges against major cruise lines that his firm has handled in the last decade involve minors. "Parents leave the child alone or with another child in the cabin, when they are going to the late seating in the dining room, or see a show or go to the casino, and a cabin attendant uses his key card and gets back into the cabin," Walker said.

"The other locations for cases we handled where children are abused are in or around the child activity centers including bathrooms." Despite the increased regulations and reporting, a vocal contingent of cruise experts claims that cruise lines aren't doing nearly enough for passenger safety – or transparency with crimes that occur on their ships. "I think people should take cruise vacations – it's a good value for their money," said Charles Lipcon, a Miami-based maritime attorney and author of Unsafe on the High Seas: Your Guide to a Safer Cruise. "But when something goes wrong, it's horrendous. And the thing I find disappointing is that when something does go wrong, [cruise lines] don't go out of their way to help the victim. Instead, they go out of their way to protect themselves."

The industry has come under recent fire from groups such as the International Cruise Victims Association when several media outlets learned that the FBI and the U.S. Coast Guard changed language in the Cruise Vessel Security and Safety bill right before it was passed into law to make it easier for cruise lines to withhold statistics about crime. Walker and other critics charge that far fewer crimes are being listed on the public database and that the industry is touting a false safety record.

But even with such risks, cruising remains a popular choice for travelers. And while the Concordia disaster has nothing to do with the Cruise Vessel Security and Safety Act, passengers report feeling safer on board. On a cruise aboard the luxury liner m/s Paul Gauguin in Tahiti this spring, David Porter and his wife, Carol, of Scottsdale, Ariz., who run the travel web site TheRoamingBoomers.com, noticed a "clear change" in how muster drills were conducted compared to previous cruises he'd taken on larger ships.

"You didn't leave the dock until every single person was accounted for, and you knew where the safety vests where and which boat you were to be on," Porter said. "I thought that was good. It always struck me as peculiar that you were on a ship headed out to sea and you had no idea what to do or where to go if something happened. I'm surprised cruise lines didn't do this earlier."

SAFETY AND SECURITY

Our commitment to maintaining a safe and secure cruise holiday environment. P and O Cruises is committed to maintaining a safe and secure environment onboard our ships to enable everyone to enjoy a great cruise and to take home only wonderful holiday memories. Our policies, procedures, staffing and security arrangements are designed to ensure our guests can be confident our top priority is ensuring their safety and security.

These arrangements include:

- Strict policies on the Responsible Service of Alcohol along with colour-coded cruise cards with photo-ID to prevent under-age drinking and warnings that it is against the law for anyone – even a family member – to buy alcohol for a child
- A 'zero tolerance approach' to any excessive behaviour that affects the enjoyment of other passengers with the likely disembarkation of offenders at the next available port
- Hundreds of CCTV cameras strategically located in the public areas of all ships in the P and O Cruises' fleet
- Trained security personnel onboard and strict procedures including crime scene preservation in the event that this is required

IMPORTANT SAFETY INFORMATION

Shortly after you have embarked, as a requirement of international law you will attend a mandatory guest emergency drill. During this drill, clear instructions will be provided which must be followed in the event of an emergency, including how to find your muster station, the essential actions you must take in an emergency including how to wear your lifejacket. In the meantime, for your own safety please read the following and refer to the safety notice behind the door in your room. On the day you embark, a safety video is available for viewing on your room television. We recommend that you make the time to watch it.

The General Emergency Alarm, which is used to call guests to their Muster Station, is seven or more short blasts, followed by one long blast on the ship's alarms and may be accompanied by the same signal on the ship's whistle. If you hear this signal, whether the ship is at sea or in port without having been warned that an exercise is taking place, you should go quickly to your room, collect your lifejacket, warm clothing, head covering, sensible footwear, any medication you may require, plus your cruise card for identification and proceed to your Muster Station. Please walk quickly and quietly, and on stairways and in alleyways keep to the right to allow other guests and crew to pass. The use of lifts is prohibited, as in the event of a power failure you may be trapped.

If you have mobility difficulties and feel that you may need assistance in an emergency, please tell your room steward and Reception today in order that special arrangements can be made. Please carry your lifejacket until you are at your Muster Station and to avoid accidents, please do not allow the lifejacket tapes to trail on the floor. In the event of an emergency, low location strip lighting will switch on automatically. If the visibility in your area is reduced so that you cannot see the normal exit signs, you should keep close to the floor and crawl if necessary.

Follow the illuminated strip and it will lead you to an exit. Your assigned Muster Station is marked on the Safety Notice, which is located behind your room door. When you reach your Muster Station, please keep as quiet as possible in order to hear any instructions which may be passed over the public address system, or by the officers in your Muster Station. Please ensure that all phones are switched off before entering the Muster Station. If you would like more information about our emergency procedures, please ask at Reception for a copy of our information sheet.

LIFEJACKETS

Lifejackets are stored in your room. There are small lifejackets provided for children. If your children have not already been issued with these jackets, please ask your room steward to supply them. There are also spare lifejackets stowed in lockers on deck.

FIRE

Fire is one of the most serious hazards at sea. Cigarette ends, cigars or matches should not be thrown over the ship's side as these may be drawn into a ship's side opening and cause a fire. Smoking is only permitted in specified outdoor areas and ashtrays are provided accordingly. All rooms and private balconies onboard this ship are designated non-smoking. If you should discover a fire, please raise the alarm by activating one of the red manual fire alarms located throughout the ship and advising a member of the crew.

ROOM FIRE DETECTION AND ALARM

Rooms are equipped with alarms by either buzzer or via the telephone system or a combination of both. If a fire is detected near your room, the buzzer will sound or your room phone will ring. You will hear a message instructing you to vacate your room by the nearest, safest possible exit. Please follow this instruction immediately.

Man Overboard

If you see a person fall overboard, throw them a lifebuoy and alert the nearest crew member by shouting "man overboard, man overboard". If there are no crew members in the vicinity, immediately dial Reception (speed dial) from any onboard phone.

Reporting Security Incidents

To report a security incident or emergency onboard, please immediately dial Reception (speed dial) from any onboard phone or contact your nearest crew member.

Room Safety

Do not leave items on balcony As your safety is our highest priority, we would like to remind you of some important precautions you must take while in your room or on your balcony. Never use candles, naked flames or any other burning material either in your room or on your balcony.

Tender Safety

For your own safety in the ship's tenders please:

- Read the "Tender Safety Notice" at the head of the gangway.
- Note smoking is not permitted while in the tenders
- Keep your hands and arms off the side of the tender as it comes alongside the ship or wharf
- Follow the instructions given by crew members
- Remain seated while in the tenders
- Wait until instructed by the ship's staff before getting in or out.

Accident Prevention

Do not sit or stand on ship rails

Please take time to review the suggestions given below for your personal safety:

- Never hold the frames of open doors as the ship's motion may cause the door to close on your hands or fingers.
- Careful attention is necessary when moving around the ship, as the pitching and rolling motion may cause you to slip.
- Never sit or stand on the ship's side rail or balcony rails
- Always hold the handrails when going up or down stairs, or while moving about the ship
- Please secure baggage or other movable objects in your room/suite
- Deadlights (the heavy steel plates over port-holes) must remain closed and can only opened by your steward
- Please take caution when on open decks, the ship's speed and locations may cause strong winds across the decks which can easily

reach 30 knots even on relatively calm days. Retain a firm hold on all exterior doors when passing through them.

- Open decks are slippery when wet due either to inclement weather or the daily routine ship cleaning. Use caution when walking in these areas, and rubber soled shoes are suggested.
- Rubber soled shoes should be used at all times when the ship is pitching and rolling. They are also recommended for some tours and when going ashore in the ship's tenders
- Raised thresholds are common on ships, particularly at fire doors, exterior doors and/or adjacent to bathroom facilities, including the bathroom in your room. Please take care when walking through all such locations as there are high steps and raised thresholds throughout the ship
- Do not attempt to raise or lower top bunks. Ask your steward(ess) to do this for you
- Children under nine years old, must never be allowed to sleep or play on top bunks
- Ladders must be used to climb and descend bunks
- The lifts are automatic and therefore unattended. Never place hands between closing doors
- Children under 12 are not permitted to use lifts unless accompanied by an adult
- Never leave your children unattended on a room balcony
- Do not stand on chairs or stools for any reason
- To avoid trip hazards, remember to switch on your light
- Do not leave valuables unattended in public areas of the ship. If you lose any items onboard, please visit Reception before you disembark. Any items (excluding clothing) unclaimed within three weeks of your cruise return, may be donated to charity. For hygiene reasons, unclaimed clothing will be destroyed onboard.

Pool Safety

- The area around swimming pools and spas may be slippery due to guest usage. Please take particular care in these locations
- Never leave your children unattended, particularly when they are using the swimming pool or spa
- There are no lifeguards on duty
- Please do not jump or dive into the pools
- No alcohol is allowed in the pools
- There is no access to pools or spas when they are netted
- If you see anyone in difficulty, please throw them a life ring, assist if possible and call Reception

Illicit Substances

P and O Cruises reserves the right to search your person and/ or luggage for any illicit substances and to deny boarding or, disembark any persons in possession of illicit substances. We are sure that you will appreciate that this security is in the best interest of all concerned.

Noise and Behaviour

While we encourage you to enjoy your cruise, for the comfort of other guests, please avoid making excessive noise in your room or in the corridors. If you seriously inconvenience or jeopardise the safety or enjoyment of any guest onboard, the Captain has the right to confine or put you ashore. P and O Cruises accepts no liability for this serious action or for any loss incurred (including repatriation expenses) and no refunds are available.

Smoking

Smoking, including cigar, e-cigarettes and and pipe smoking is only permitted in the designated open deck areas. Please note, all rooms and private balconies onboard this ship are designated non-smoking. Guests under 18 years of age are not allowed to purchase tobacco products. We are proud to offer this refreshing smoke-free environment for the safety and comfort of our guests. A $300 cleaning fee will be added to your onboard account if we find evidence of smoking in your room.

RESPONSIBLE SERVICE OF ALCOHOL

In the interests of guest safety and security onboard, we adhere to a strict Responsible Service of Alcohol policy. We also take a 'zero tolerance' approach to any excessive or irresponsible behaviour that can offend or affect other guests. This is all part of our commitment to making sure everyone onboard enjoys a great cruise so that you take home only wonderful holiday memories. We're particularly strict about underage drinking onboard – that's why minors get their own colour-coded cruise cards. Guests must be 18 years or over to purchase or consume alcohol. Please remember, it's against the law for anyone – even a family member – to buy alcohol for a child. Photo Identification may be requested. Any alcohol purchased ashore will be confiscated and will need to be collected before you disembark. Our senior officers and security staff will deal firmly with alcohol-related issues or excessive behaviour including the possibility of those involved being disembarked. It's really about everyone enjoying the magic of cruising but always being considerate of others by acting responsibly.

Ship's Security

Keep your cruise card close

In order to prevent unauthorised persons boarding the ship, you are required to:

- Carry your Cruise Card with you when going ashore.
- Produce your Cruise Card at the gangway when you leave and return to the ship
- Ensure that you also have a Government issued picture ID with you before leaving the ship
- Do not accept and bring onboard any parcels or packages from strangers
- Please note, you may also be asked by our Security Staff to open parcels or handbags which you are carrying
- Under no circumstances are guests allowed to enter crew living or working areas, even if invited by a member of the ship's staff. Some areas of the ship, such as the Galley are occasionally open for inspection on particular escorted tours.

Safety and Security when Ashore

The safety and security of our guests is our most important responsibility and P and O regularly communicates with various government agencies and officials to ensure you have a safe and enjoyable holiday experience. Unfortunately, terrorism, crime and civil unrest are a potential concern in many countries.

Therefore, we encourage you to consider the following safety and security recommendationswhen going ashore in any port:

- Travel with others and stay in open public places.
- Dress down conservatively and minimize the amount of jewellery you wear
- Take care of handbags, cameras and valuables
- Be aware of your surroundings and the people around you
- Use discretion when handling cash publicly. Separate money for small and large purchases to avoid showing a large amount of cash. Have gratuities ready
- Do not provide personal information to persons you do not know
- Exercise extra caution when exploring during the hours of darkness
- Do not accept rides from unofficial taxis; look for certification and proper licenses
- If confronted by a criminal, just remember that money and valuables can be replaced
- Consider going ashore on a P and O tour or other organized group; independent guests touring on their own should be particularly vigilant
- Do not leave drinks unattended when in bars or restaurants
- Do not travel in rural or deserted roads and areas

- If you are involved in an auto accident, only stop in locations you consider safe in order to exchange vehicle information
- Keep well clear of any gathering crowds or demonstrations.

Responsible Service of Alcohol (RSA) Explained

Crew members receive compulsory training in ₹A policies and procedures with refresher training every two months along with training to recognise signs of intoxication in passengers. No commissions are paid to staff on alcohol sales and crew members can face disciplinary action including dismissal for failing to prevent under age or intoxicated passengers from being served alcohol. Passengers are also prohibited from bringing alcohol onboard. Any alcohol found is confiscated and not returned until the end of a cruise.

'Zero Tolerance' Approach to Excessive Behaviour Explained

Our security personnel undergo specialised training. They are alert at all times for anyone displaying inappropriate behaviour that can affect the enjoyment of other passengers. Numerous CCTV cameras located in public areas operate on a rolling 24-hour basis as part of overall security monitoring onboard our ships. Senior officers and security staff will deal firmly with alcohol-related issues or cases of excessive behaviour. Any passengers who offend in this regard can be disembarked from the ship to return home at their own cost.

The guiding principle is that everyone should be able to enjoy the magic of cruising while always being considerate of the comfort of others.

Prevention and Response Guide

Although it's unlikely you'll ever need to report an incident while you are onboard a P and O Cruises' ship, it is still important to know what to do just in case. Incidents or allegations of criminal activity should be reported directly to the onboard Security Department by dialling 000 or by contacting the Reception desk. Any situations where medical assistance is required should be reported to the Medical Department by dialling 000 or by contacting the Reception desk. P and O Cruises has agreed Protocols with law enforcement agencies in Australia and the Pacific Islands for the reporting of crimes and serious incidents at sea.

When Special CARE is Needed

We have specially trained CARE teams onboard and onshore to assist passengers and their families in the event of a traumatic incident or experience. A streamlined process is also in place to deal with customer complaints including guidelines for response times and handling. A toll free number is advertised in cruise literature for passengers wishing to contact Customer Relations and our landside emergency number is answered 24 hours a day.

Ebola Virus Safety Policy

At P and O Cruises the safety and health of our guests and crew is our top priority, and we understand that media coverage of the Ebola virus and related cases has raised concerns among some travelers.

In order to safeguard our guests and crew, screen for any guests or crew who have recently visited or traveled through Liberia, Sierra Leone or Guinea within 21 days of the cruise departure date. We also screen for any guests who have had physical contact with or helped care for a person suspected of having Ebola or diagnosed as having Ebola within a minimum of 21 days before embarkation. Additionally, we are monitor bookings for any guests coming from these countries. To assist in these efforts, we require all embarking guests, crew members and ship visitors to complete a mandatory health screening questionnaire upon embarkation. If deemed necessary, some guests may also be asked to submit to further medical screening prior to being allowed to board. Please be aware, based on our assessment, you may be denied boarding. We greatly appreciate your understanding and cooperation.

Please be assured that P and O Cruises does not have any ships calling in any countries for which the Centers for Disease Control (CDC) has issued Level 3 Travel Heath Notices, and none of our crew members are from these areas. We have robust medical protocols that are consistent with public health recommendations. Our medical staff is fully engaged and monitoring the situation closely, along with our colleagues in the rest of the travel industry. The cruise industry is in close, frequent contact with the CDC and the World Health Organization (WHO) for updates and guidance.

IMPETUS FOR SAFETY REQUIREMENTS

To understand where we are today with respect to passenger vessel safety, we should look at the lessons the past has taught us. The 100th anniversary of the sinking of the RMS Titanic in April 1912 is only weeks away. The Titanic tragedy prompted overwhelming international response which resulted in the first Safety of Life at Sea Convention, also known as SOLAS 1914. This first version focused on lifeboats, emergency equipment, and radio watches. Improvements to the Convention made in 1929, 1948, and 1960 added requirements for subdivision, stability, machinery, firefighting, lifesaving, communications, and navigation systems. SOLAS is the key international maritime agreement focused on safety.

For the most part, large passenger vessels visiting the United States before the 1960s were in liner service, with the primary purpose of transporting passengers from one part of the world to another. With the advent of commercial airlines, the international passenger vessel industry evolved from transportation to entertainment, and liners became cruise ships. In the 1960s, a number of serious cruise ship fires, involving heavy loss of life, brought the issue of cruise ship safety to the attention of maritime authorities worldwide. These fires involved the older passenger ships Lakonia, Yarmouth Castle, and Viking Princess, which had superstructures that contained some combustible materials, allowing the rapid spread of flames and total destruction of passenger spaces.

In May 1966, the Maritime Safety Committee (MSC) of the Intergovernmental Maritime Consultative Organization (IMCO), now called the International Maritime Organization (IMO), met to consider measures to improve the fire safety of passenger vessels. The committee first directed its attention to the problem of fire safety in older passenger vessels and crafted the 1966 amendments to SOLAS 60, which included additional fire protection standards for existing passenger vessels. Congress showed great interest in this work, especially since the Coast Guard had conducted a Marine Board of Investigation into the 1965 Yarmouth Castle fire. On November 2, 1968, Public Law 89-777 (R.S. 4400(c); 46 U.S.C. 362(c)), Fire Safety Standards for Foreign and Domestic Passenger Vessels, came into effect, which required the Coast Guard to verify that foreign cruise vessels complied with the 1966 fire safety amendments.

In 1968, the United States unilaterally required all passenger vessels with overnight accommodations for 50 or more passengers to meet the 1966 fire safety amendments or U.S. passenger vessel requirements. The Coast Guard promulgated Navigation and Vessel Inspection Circular 2-68, which provided implementing guidance on how to conduct a control verification examination on foreign flag cruise ships, specifying that "this verification may necessitate a degree of plan review, removal of panels, ceilings, etc., in addition to the testing of construction materials." On August 26, 1983, Public Law 98-89 provided additional authority for the Coast Guard to verify that foreign flag cruise ships embarking passengers in U.S. ports comply with SOLAS convention requirements.

The Coast Guard made improvements to its vessel examination programme in 1985 and 1993, which further expanded examination requirements and provided much more detailed guidelines for control verification examination procedures on foreign cruise ships. Since 1993, cruise ship designs have continued to evolve, growing in size and complexity with the capability of carrying thousands of passengers and crew, and the Coast Guard has frequently updated guidance for plan review and control verification examinations necessary for foreign cruise ships operating out of U.S. ports. Last year, there were 143 cruise ships, sailing under foreign registry, that operated out of U.S. ports and carried over eleven million passengers.

MODERN STANDARDS FOR CRUISE SHIPS

Over the past decade, the international shipping community, through the IMO and with Coast Guard leadership, has moved decisively towards a proactive approach to passenger ship safety. With cruise ships growing progressively in size and capacity, in May 2000, the IMO agreed to undertake a holistic examination of safety issues pertaining to passenger ships, with particular emphasis on large cruise ships. The outcome of this proactive initiative is an entirely new prevention and survivability based regulatory philosophy for the design, construction, and operation of cruise ships.

The U.S., through the efforts of the Coast Guard, has taken a very active leadership role throughout this initiative, putting forward many of the recommendations for action taken by the various IMO Sub-Committees. The effort identified a number of areas of concern related to cruise ships, and resulted in substantial amendments to major IMO conventions, including SOLAS, International Convention for the Prevention of Pollution From Ships (MARPOL) 73/78, International Tonnage, Standards for Training, Certification, and Watchkeeping (STCW) and Load Line conventions. These conventions provide internationally-accepted standards for the design, construction, outfitting, and operation of ships. They address surveys, structures, stability, machinery, fire safety, lifesaving equipment, communications, navigation equipment, safety management, maritime security, pollution prevention, crew competency, watertight integrity, and safe loading.

Significant improvements under the five main pillars of the initiative entered into force in July 2010:

- *Prevention:* Amendments to the STCW Code and supporting guidelines focus on navigation safety and resource management;
- *Improved survivability:* New SOLAS requirements for the "safe return to port" concept address essential system redundancy, management of emergencies, and casualty mitigation, including the new concept of dedicated shipboard safety centers to manage emergencies;
- *Regulatory flexibility:* Amendments to SOLAS provide a methodology for the approval of new and innovative safety technologies and arrangements;
- *Operations in areas remote from SAR facilities:* Guidelines on external support from SAR authorities, as well as guidance to assist seafarers taking part in SAR operations have been developed; and finally
- *Health safety and medical care:* Guidelines on establishing medical safety programmes, and a revised Guide on Cold Water Survival.

Other recent improvements include stability and survivability of cruise ships through new probabilistic subdivision and damage stability regulations, and flooding detection systems; improved voyage planning, particularly in remote and high latitude areas; and voyage data recorders. As a separate initiative, stemming from the 2006 fire aboard the Star Princess, significant improvements have been made to the fire safety features of external areas on cruise ships. Overall, the past decade has been an enormous leap forward in cruise ship safety measures and has been largely proactive as opposed to reactive to casualties as has generally been the case in the past. Coast Guard's leadership in the international community with respect to cruise ship safety measures and our support to foreign casualty investigations evidences our dedication to U.S. passenger safety whereever our citizens embark on cruise ships.

THE SAFETY, SECURITY, AND ENVIRONMENTAL PROTECTION NET

The IMO conventions form the bases for the international safety, security, and stewardship net designed to ensure consistent standards across the world wide fleet of cruise ships. The owners and operators, flag states and port states each have distinct roles in ensuring compliance with those standards. Flag states have the primary responsibility to ensure vessels of their flag meet international and domestic standards. They often achieve this through recognized third party organizations who certify that vessels meet design, construction, operating, and manning requirements throughout the life of the vessel.

Port states verify substantial compliance with international standards and ensuring compliance with applicable domestic requirements for vessels of all flags calling in their ports. As the port state authority for the U.S., the Coast Guard has established a robust control verification programme that subjects cruise ships calling in U.S. ports to a much higher level of scrutiny than other foreign flag vessels, and much higher than any other port states require for foreign flag cruise ships in their ports.

COAST GUARD CONTROL VERIFICATION PROGRAMME FOR FOREIGN FLAG CRUISE SHIPS

The Coast Guard has a very robust port state control programme for cruise ships. All foreign flag cruise ships arriving in the United States that embark passengers or make a U.S. port call while carrying U.S. citizens as passengers must participate in the control verification process. Cruise ships that return to U.S. service after a prolonged absence are treated as if they had never been in service in the U.S. and must undergo the entire process again.

The Coast Guard control verification programme includes initial, annual, and periodic examinations for foreign flag cruise ships calling in our ports. It includes concept review during the very earliest stages of design, pre-construction plan review by Coast Guard naval architects and fire protection engineers, mid-construction inspections at the builder's yard by Coast Guard marine inspectors, an initial operational inspection of the vessel upon completion of construction, and at least annual inspections while the vessel is in service in U.S. ports. This regime allows the Coast Guard to determine that the vessel is in substantial compliance with all applicable international and domestic standards. The engineering review of plans for structural fire protection arrangements provides a great level of assurance that shipboard fire safety arrangements meet international standards. After review, these same engineers visit the ship and confirm that the actual arrangements on the vessel are the same as those shown on the structural fire protection plans. No other port state provides this level of attention to detail for cruise ships. On the basis of this initial examination, the Coast Guard issues a certificate of compliance that allows the vessel to operate in U.S. ports.

The annual examination ensures that foreign cruise ships continue to maintain all the systems the Coast Guard previously examined during the initial exam in proper operating condition and that the flag administration has performed annual renewal surveys as required by SOLAS. Inspectors focus on firefighting, lifesaving, and emergency systems and witness a comprehensive fire and boat drill by the crew. In addition, inspectors examine the vessel for modifications that would affect the vessel's structural fire protection and means of escape. They also check for modifications completed without the vessel's flag administration approval. After a satisfactory annual examination, the Coast Guard re-issues a certificate of compliance.

Periodic examinations are also conducted, typically midway between the annual examinations. These examinations are limited in scope and build on the more comprehensive annuals, and they are intended to ensure vessels are being operated in a safe manner. The periodic examinations focus on the performance of officers and crew, with specific attention paid to their training on and knowledge of the ship's emergency procedures, firefighting, lifesaving systems, and performance during the drills. To ensure the overall material condition of the ship has not appreciably changed since the annual examination, inspectors randomly select sample items for examination. Inspectors also vary the scope of the examination depending upon the material condition of the vessel, the maintenance of the vessel, and the professionalism and training of the crew. At every Coast Guard examination of a foreign cruise ship, the inspectors will determine whether the vessel is in substantial compliance with the international convention standards.

As a result of the Costa Concordia incident, I have directed Coast Guard field inspectors to witness the passenger muster required by SOLAS whenever they are onboard a cruise ship conducting an initial, annual, or periodic examination. Our personnel will witness these musters either immediately before or during vessel departure from port. I am pleased to see that the cruise industry associations announced a new emergency drill policy requiring mandatory muster for embarking passengers prior to departure from port.

INVESTIGATIONS

Foreign vessels operating in U.S. waters are required by U.S. law to report accidents immediately. Upon accident notification, we proactivly investigate to determine causes and issue safety recommendations to prevent recurrences. It is a continuous improvement process which incorporates lessons learned from accident investigations to enhance cruise ship safety and ensure compliance with national and international laws.

After the Costa Concordia incident, the Coast Guard immediately offered technical expertise and support to the Government of Italy's marine casualty investigation. The Coast Guard's expertise in marine casualty investigations will prove helpful as we move forward with the investigation. Currently, Coast Guard teams are conducting interviews with the U.S. passengers to ascertain the vessel's crew level of preparedness and response. Information gained from the Costa Concordia investigation may assist in identifying marine casualty causal factors that could have broad application. It is long standing practice to cooperate in all manner of accident investigations involving different flag and coastal states and the Coast Guard routinely acts in this accord.

SEARCH AND RESCUE (SAR) AND MASS RESCUE OPERATIONS (MRO)

The Coast Guard has maintained a good relationship with the cruise lines regarding search and rescue and medical evacuations. For the Coast Guard, a Mass Rescue Operation involving a cruise ship casualty offshore, with potentially thousands of passengers and crew forced to evacuate into lifeboats and the water, presents our greatest search and rescue challenge. Working with cruise line and passenger vessel companies, the Coast Guard continues to develop and improve SAR and MRO contingency plans. In addition to internal Coast Guard SAR plans, the Coast Guard holds a copy of cruise ship SAR plans and is able to incorporate the cruise ship plans into our overall SAR planning in the event of an emergency. The Coast Guard also meets periodically with cruise line medical personnel to discuss plans for medical emergencies, which pays dividends during actual medical evacuations. For example, many of the 857 medical evacuations performed by the Coast Guard last year, were conducted from cruise ships. evacuations last year.

In addition to working directly with cruise lines, Coast Guard has been working in partnership with the passenger vessel industry associations, including Cruise Lines International Association and the Passenger Vessel Association. Coast Guard works with the associations to develop, coordinate and represent Coast Guard policies and positions related to passenger vessel mass rescue plans, coordination, and exercises. Recently, Coast Guard led a Department of Homeland Security sponsored interagency table top exercise for Federal agency representatives involving a cruise ship emergency in the Arctic. Mass rescue planning involves support from many of our Federal agency and State partners. In 2002, Congress appropriated funding for 22 permanent billets for the Coast Guard's Passenger Vessel Safety Specialist/Mass Rescue

Operation Programme. These billets provide the Coast Guard with increased capacity and capability to help coordinate and promote passenger vessel prevention plans, manage risk and maintain a state of readiness in response to the impressive growth in foreign and domestic passenger vessels over the past decade. Planning for a mass evacuation of a cruise ship carrying thousands of passengers and crew involves intense preparation and extensive coordination to meet the varying types of emergencies that could arise.

Coast Guard passenger vessel safety personnel at each of our Districts assist in the conduct and coordination of Coast Guard mass rescue exercises. Over the last five years, the Coast Guard conducted thirty-six mass rescue exercises involving passenger vessels, three of which involved a cruise ship. The Coast Guard has an agreement with CLIA to include an actual cruise ship as part of these exercises every two years. Since 2007, CLIA has fulfilled this partnership agreement by providing a cruise ship every other year for a full scale exercise. The purpose of these exercises is to assist the Coast Guard, other Federal, state and local search and rescue authorities and cruise ship industry partners in exercising mass rescue plans, practice interagency/industry cooperation and coordination and identify ways to improve the overall response to a major maritime disaster.

Mass rescue exercises have been structured around a five-year cycle. In 2010, the Coast Guard directed that, at a minimum, each Coast Guard District conduct and/or participate in one discussion based (*e.g.*, seminar, workshop, game, or tabletop) and one operations based (*e.g.*, drills, functional, full scale) mass rescue exercise over a five year period. To meet this exercise requirement, beginning this year, the Coast Guard has planned a five-year mass rescue exercise series known as "Black Swan.

" The exercise series will begin this year with a cruise ship seminar in New Orleans, followed by a functional drill in 2013, also in New Orleans, and full scale mass rescue exercises in Miami in 2015 and Norfolk in 2017. The scope of these exercises provide a valuable opportunity to identify and resolve the difficulties associated with rescuing hundreds or thousands of people at once. It is also a chance to address the unique challenges posed by off shore mass rescues.

The Black Swan mass rescue exercise series will focus on the exercise of Coast Guard mass rescue plans, coordination with other authorities and industry partners, notification and information processes, personnel accountability, embarking thousands of survivors on rescue ships from the water, lifeboats and rafts, and rescued passenger and crew support.

CRUISE SHIP SECURITY AND CRIME

September 11, 2001 spurred the development of the Maritime Transportation Security Act (MTSA) and the IMO International Ship and Port

Facility Security (ISPS) Code, both of which are rigourously enforced by the Coast Guard. Prior to the MTSA and ISPS, only the cruise ships that visited the U.S. and cruise terminals were required to have security plans in place. The requirement for cruise ship and facility security plans in the United States had come into effect as a result of the 1985 Achille Lauro terrorist incident in the Mediterranean Sea, resulting in the murder of Leon Klinghoffer - a wheel-chair bound U.S. citizen.

The Coast Guard examines every cruise ship that visits the U.S. for compliance with MTSA and ISPS requirements at the same time it carries out annual and periodic examinations. Overall, cruise ship compliance records have been extremely good, with only three security-related detentions in approximately 1,800 security examinations since July 2004. Notwithstanding this security compliance regime, there have been serious incidents and crimes that have affected U.S. citizens aboard foreign-flagged cruise ships, however, this has led to an increased focus on protecting our citizens both in port and while they are at sea. In 2010, Congress bolstered passenger safety and security with respect to such incidents and crimes by enacting the Cruise Ship Security and Safety Act of 2010 (CVSSA). Since then, the Coast Guard has worked diligently to implement the provisions of this act.

The CVSSA prescribes security and safety requirements for designated cruise ships and is the authority for a rulemaking now under development by the Coast Guard. CVSSA amended Title 46, United States Code, by adding passenger vessel security and safety requirements, and crime scene preservation training requirements for passenger vessel crewmembers. CVSSA addresses many areas that affect personal safety and security, including: ship design; better public access to information about crime aboard cruise ships; improved precautions, response, medical care, support for victims of sexual assault; preservation of evidence necessary to prosecute criminals; and more consistent and complete reports about criminal activities. A large number of these requirements went into effect when the President signed the legislation on July 27, 2010; however, there are areas that require implementation through the publication of regulations.

Thus far, the Coast Guard has completed the following actions with respect to implementing the CVSSA:

- In June 2011, the Coast Guard published policy establishing guidelines for Coast Guard Marine Inspectors examining cruise vessels for compliance to include physical requirements, such as: rail heights; door peep-holes as one commonly sees on hotel doors, which allow cabin occupants to see who is outside before opening their cabin door; and the passenger security guide.
- The Coast Guard established an internet-based portal to facilitate electronic submission of crime reports.

- The Coast Guard established a web link to publish cruise ship sexual assault and criminal activity data received from the the Federal Bureau of Investigation (FBI) in accordance with the act:
- An Inter-agency workgroup consisting of Coast Guard, FBI, and the Maritime Administration personnel completed development of a model course addressing crime scene preservation standards and curricula. In July 2011, the Coast Guard published policy promulgating training standards and curricula for the certification of passenger vessel security personnel.

CLOSING

As I close, let me emphasize that the Coast Guard places the highest priority on vessels that embark passengers in the United States; and embark U.S. passengers world-wide. We have a strong and effective port state control programme for foreign cruise ships and ensure that vessels that visit the United States are in substantial compliance with applicable international and domestic standards. We participate in casualty investigations, even those taking place overseas, and we lead efforts at IMO to improve maritime safety, security, and environmental protection standards.

Furthermore, we have one of the best Search and Rescue programmes in the world and we work closely with the industry on SAR planning and medical evacuations. We have efforts underway to plan for mass rescue operations. We are taking measures to implement the CVSSA. We have accomplished much, but additional work must take place.

As a result of the Costa Concordia incident, we have also put into place a regime to witness passenger musters as part of our mandatory vessel examination programme. As the investigation unfolds, the Coast Guard will capture lessons learned and incorporate them into our safety regime. The Coast Guard also looks forward to continued cooperation with this committee, passenger victims groups, and the passenger vessel industry to maximize cruise vessel safety, security, and environmental protection. Although we are not asking for, or recommending to Congress, new legislation at this time, we may do so in the future once we have had the opportunity to review the Costa Concordia investigation.

SO, JUST HOW SAFE IS YOUR SHIP?

IN the wake of the Costa Concordia catastrophe on Jan. 13 that killed at least 17 people and raised troubling questions about the ship's captain, many tourists are wondering: How safe am I on a cruise? Well, the chance of dying in a cruise accident is small. From 2005 to 2010, about 100 million passengers took cruises, and there were 16 deaths attributed to marine accidents, according to the Cruise Lines International Association.

But the Concordia, which ran aground off the Tuscan coast of Italy a few hours after departure, has the cruise industry on the defensive. "All of our members recognize the seriousness of these events," said Christine Duffy, president of the Cruise Lines International Association, in a press briefinglast month. Still, no regulatory changes have actually been made, though there has been plenty of discussion about the growing size of ships and the 24-hour window after boarding in which ships must run safety drills.

Continue reading the main story

At the time of the deadly wreck, just off the coast of Isola del Giglio, about 3,200 passengers and 1,000 crew members were aboard the Costa Concordia, a massive vessel owned by a subsidiary of Carnival Corporation. Some travel industry experts say the sheer size of the Concordia and other cruise ships may pose greater evacuation challenges because of the large number of passengers, but cruise officials point out that regulations have kept pace with the size of the ships. Evacuation routes and safety equipment, including the size and number of lifeboats, are "scaled in accordance with the increased size of the vessel," said Capt. William Wright, a senior vice president at Royal Caribbean International, at the briefing convened by the Cruise Lines International Association.

There is no indication that size was a factor in the Concordia accident, but the 24-hour window for safety drills is being scrutinized. Some critics argue that the window should be tightened so that passengers will be better prepared in case an emergency strikes early on, as it did on the Concordia. Unlike airplane safety announcements, which take place before takeoff, cruise drills aren't required before the ship leaves the dock. The Concordia passengers who had boarded before Civitavecchia had already been through the drill, but nearly 700 passengers who joined the ship there had not. The next drill had been scheduled for the following day.

While the Carnival Corporation said it will do "a comprehensive audit and review" of safety procedures, at least one other cruise line, Prestige Cruise Holdings, the parent company of Oceania Cruises and Regent Seven Seas, has announced that it will hold drills on the day of departure. Previously, those drills were occasionally held the next morning. The Concordia tragedy has focused attention on safety and operating standards, but there are other concerns that passengers should keep in mind.

VIRUSES

Cruise passengers are more likely to get a stomach bug than face shipwreck. Last year, there were 14 outbreaks of gastrointestinal illnesses on 10 ships, affecting hundreds of passengers, according to the Centers for Disease Control and Prevention. The illnesses included the highly contagious norovirus.

Cruise companies increase cleaning and disinfecting procedures if there is an outbreak, including scouring "high-touch" areas of ships, like banisters and elevator buttons. But such measures can't prevent a sick passenger from infecting others. According to the C.D.C., the best defence against catching a stomach bug is simple: keep washing your hands, avoid shaking hands during outbreaks and use alcohol-based hand sanitizers.

CRIME

Crime on cruise ships has become such an issue that in 2010 Congress passed the Cruise Vessel Security and Safety Act. The law mandates reporting of kidnappings, sexual assaults and other crimes and requires vessels to be equipped with cabin peepholes and video surveillance systems, among other security measures. Last year, the Federal Bureau of Investigation closed 16 investigations involving crime on cruise ships, 13 of which were sexual assaults, according to data posted online by the Coast Guard. But that doesn't represent the total number of incidents reported to the F.B.I., including any still-open or pending prosecutions.

While it's easy to let your guard down on a cruise, travelers shouldn't assume they're safe just because they're onboard, said Charles R. Lipcon, author of "Unsafe on the High Seas" and a maritime lawyer who handles cases involving personal injury, cruise-line sexual assault and wrongful death claims. Sure, a cruise may feel like a floating party — and no one has to drive home — but drinking too much can compromise your judgement.

"I like to tell people, don't leave your common sense at the dock," Mr. Lipcon said. "That's typically what people do, and overdrink and get themselves into a risky situation."

FIRE

Even though modern cruise vessels are designed with smoke detectors and sprinkler systems, fire is a risk. Last year, a fire aboard a Hurtigruten cruise ship off the coast of Norway killed two people, injured nine others and forced the evacuation of nearly half of the 262 people aboard.CruiseShipFires.com, a

Web site dedicated to documenting blazes, explosions and other accidents on pleasure vessels, has photographs of similar events, including an engine fire on the Carnival Splendor in 2010. No passengers were injured, but the fire stripped the ship of its power, knocking out its operating systems and leaving its 3,300 passengers without air-conditioning, hot food or water.

Most of those fires started in the engine room in the lower part of the ship, said Janet Huggard, editor of CruiseShipFires.com and its sibling site,CruiseBruise.com, devoted to publicizing crime, injuries and other incidents on ships. She recommends avoiding cabins below deck. "Higher is better in almost all cases for evacuation purposes," she said.

FALLING OVERBOARD

Although falling overboard is rare, it does occur. Last year at least 22 people went overboard on cruise ships and passenger ferries, according toCruisejunkie.com, which lists cases reported by the media on its Web site, including passengers who jumped. One of the requirements under the Cruise Vessel Security and Safety Act is that ships must be equipped with rails not less than 42 inches above the deck, and with alarms and other technology to help signal and locate passengers who go overboard.

As a general rule, pay attention to safety announcements and make sure you try on your life jacket and know where your muster or lifeboat station is located. If you are traveling with friends or family, have a contingency plan so you know how to find one another in the event of an evacuation. "It is unlikely that something will happen," said Ross A. Klein, who has written books on the cruise industry and operates Cruisejunkie.com, "but it is better to have a plan if something does happen than to be drawn into a hysteria when an emergency situation presents itself."

CRUISE PASSENGERS 'NOT PROTECTED FROM SERIOUS CRIME'

Fig. Increasingly Cruise Ships are Choosing to Register in Countries Like the Bahamas.

The UK's Shipping Minister Mike Penning has told the BBC that cruise passengers may not be properly protected if they become victims of serious crime on board. Mr Penning has told BBC Radio 4's Face the Facts that when cruise ships are on the high seas and serious crime takes place on board, current international law prevents him from providing British passengers with the level of protection they would expect on land.

"I don't have any powers on the high seas," he explained. "Our legislation and international legislation does not mean that I can put a policeman on to a ship in the middle of the Caribbean - no-one has the power to do so."

Increasingly cruise ships are choosing to register in countries such as the Bahamas, Bermuda and Panama. Their ships then sail under the flags of these nations. So, if a British citizen becomes a victim of crime at sea, it is the police force of that country that will investigate.

In the recent case of Rebecca Coriam from Chester, who disappeared last March while working on a cruise ship, only one police officer from the Bahamas was sent to investigate. That, the family say, was only because they insisted on a police investigation.

"I was appalled when I first heard of Becky's case," the minister said.

The Bahamas Maritime Authority has 50 cruise ships registered under its flag. BMA chairman Ian Fair defended their record, saying: "We haven't had any major issues. We have a specific inspector, who's an expert in this area, who is available to handle any matters the BMA requires the police to handle."

Rebecca Coriam is one of 18 people who vanished from cruise ships last year - two more have gone missing this month. In the past fortnight, in two separate incidents, two crew members have been charged with raping under-age girls - aged 14 and 15.

William Gibbons, director of the UK Passenger Shipping Association, which represents the major cruise lines, said such incidents were of concern. "But they are very, very rare," he stressed.

"Any proved incident is one incident too many on board a cruise ship. Life at sea is much more secure and safe than ashore because we are operating in a controlled environment - we know who's on board the ship."

MOMENTUM FOR CHANGE

However, one person who will not be on board is a police officer, even though the ship may be carrying up to 9,000 passengers and crew. Cruise ships do have security officers but they are paid employees and according to Geoff Furlong, a former Scotland Yard detective who worked for six years as a security officer in the 1990s, this can cause a conflict of interest.

When he was investigating a rape on board a cruise ship in the Caribbean, it had to be abandoned. "I sealed the cabin, I told the steward on duty that the cabin was to remain locked and to remain untouched, it required forensic examination… and when I woke up, I was informed that the mattress involved on the bed had been dumped overboard."

Geoff Furlong also claimed that security officers may not have the relevant training in taking statements, securing crime scenes and gathering evidence. According to William Gibbons, security officers are properly trained but he said: "You don't have a ratio of security officers, it's down to the company and depends on the size of the ship."

He was unable to tell the programme what the training entailed.

Nevertheless, concern about security on cruise ships is growing internationally because when serious incidents like disappearances and rapes occur, if there is a police investigation at all it will be by a small, foreign force. The cruise companies agree that the system is not perfect, but "momentum is growing" to change the situation, which will mean changing international law. Not before time, said Britain's shipping minister.

"International law isn't clear at all, which is why at the last session of the International Maritime Organisation we, with the support of lots of other countries, put through recommendations that we needed to change international law," said Mr Penning, "to say that legally at sea, you're entitled to the sort of protection that you and I would expect at home."

CRUISE SHIPS OFFERING PASSENGERS A FALSE SENSE OF SECURITY

The disappearance of a couple from the cruise ship Carnival Spirit off the NSW coast on Wednesday night puts the spotlight on the dark side of an industry that is increasingly popular with Australians. Keri Phillips looks at the risks you don't read about in the glossy brochures. Australians are enthusiastic cruisers. According to industry figures a record 623,294 Australians took a cruise in 2011, a 34 per cent increase on 2010.

Australian cruise passenger numbers have almost tripled in the past five years, with the average annual rate of growth over that period exceeding 23 per cent. Ross Dowling, Foundation Professor of Tourism in the School of Marketing, Tourism and Leisure at Edith Cowan University in Western Australia, says that the growth reflects the fact that cruising has become cheaper and more accessible.

'There never used to be cruise ships based here in Australia but ten years ago we started to have the odd cruise ship being based here in some of the mega-ports like Sydney or Melbourne, maybe Brisbane,' he said. 'Over the last decade, we also have now got home porting, so that we've got ships based in Adelaide and Darwin and also Perth, et cetera, right around Australia. The cruise ships of today are absolutely massive, they're huge, and so on the economy of scale that's brought down the real cost of cruising. So probably 10, 20 years ago, really cruising was for the seriously rich people, and then it became a little bit more affordable and maybe for the cashed-up retirees. Today cruising is a very cheap form of travel.'

Ships are dangerous places and I always feel that most people leave their common sense at the dock. They get on these ships and they think that it's a totally controlled environment, which it isn't. They think they have a lot of security, which they don't—it's a false sense of security.

CHARLES LIPCON, MARITIME LAWYER

Professor Ross Klein, a Canadian sociologist and the author of many books and papers about the cruise industry, says that most people who sign up for a cruise have an unrealistic view of the safety of the onboard environment.

'Safety has really two or three different dimensions. Certainly one dimension—and that was in Australia made particularly salient by the Dianne Brimble case—is the issue of the personal safety of passengers; that is, safety from sexual assault and from other crime. The data I have, and this is from the cruise industry itself, indicates that the rate of sexual assault on a cruise ship is roughly 50 per cent higher than the rate of sexual assault on land.'

'The other alarming point is that those who are sexually assaulted, more that 18 per cent of those—perhaps as high as 30 per cent of the victims—are young children, girls under the age of 18. And the risk is in part from the crew of the cruise ship—50 to 75 per cent of the cases of sexual assault are perpetuated by crewmembers—but also they're potentially victims from other passengers. So I would always advise parents who are taking their children aboard a cruise ship to treat a cruise ship as though they were going to any major city—to London or to New York city, anywhere in the world.'

Other kinds of crime can occur on cruise ships, as was the case of George Smith, an American on his honeymoon who disappeared from a cruise in the Mediterranean. Charles R. Lipcon, a maritime lawyer based in Miami, Florida, says Mr Smith was last seen in one of the ship's bars.

'The husband was last seen drinking with his wife at the bar around midnight and then they made friends with, like, three Russian fellows, who apparently were seen walking George back to his cabin around three or four in the morning. The next day George was missing and outside the cabin down below was a big bloody area. And he was gone. And that occurred when the ship was sailing from Greece to Turkey, it occurred on board a Bahamian-flagged vessel, and since he was an American citizen you had US laws applying, you had Bahamian laws applying, you had Greek laws applying and you had Turkish law applying. And all of the governments handled it like it was a hot potato—nobody wanted to handle it and they all said, 'Oh, you do it,' and that government would say, 'No, you do it.' Nobody really wanted to get involved. So the murder was never solved.'

While millions of people have happy, incident-free holidays on cruise ships every year, Mr Lipcon agrees that most people form their impression of the cruise ship environment from glossy brochures.

'Ships are dangerous places and I always feel that most people leave their common sense at the dock. They get on these ships and they think that it's a totally controlled environment, which it isn't. They think they have a lot of security, which they don't—it's a false sense of security. And then people are over-served and they over-drink and you're on a ship with a lot of strangers and a lot of bad things can happen. There's a lot of crime on board ships—much more than the cruise lines would like their passengers to know—and when a crime does occur, the cruise lines rather than trying to help solve the crime are busy trying to protect themselves from being sued in a lawsuit.'

6

The Economy of Cruise Industry

As the American economy continues to improve and the U.S. dollar reaches new heights, the cruise industry is experiencing positive effects. Travelers are much more willing to spend their discretionary income on travel and companies like Royal Caribbean, Carnival, and Norwegian Cruise Line are bracing for growth by building new ships and adding unique destinations.

THE GROWTH OF THE CRUISE LINE INDUSTRY

In 1990, approximately 3.77 million passengers were carried on cruise ships around the world. That number remained fairly stagnant until the turn of the century when the total number of cruise passengers jumped to 7.49 million. Fast forward 15 years later and the projected total for this year is somewhere around 22.24 million passengers. It's a steady uphill climb and one that industry experts and financial analysts believe will only increase over the next five years.

North America has always represented the largest contingency of passengers, estimated to account for approximately 13 million of the 22.24 million passengers this calendar year. However, Europeans are also interested in cruise vacations, with around 5.76 million predicted to cruise this year alone. From 1990-2019, the compound annual growth rate is somewhere around 6.55 percent. However, it's possible that this healthy growth rate is stunted by a lack of new ships and unique destinations. Understanding this, the cruise line industry has big plans for resurgence.

CONSUMER PERCEPTIONS IMPROVING

According to an article by Rob Lovitt of Today.com, consumer sentiment regarding the industry as a whole is on the rise. "The perception of the industry has recovered to pre-disaster levels among the general public, and surpassed them among those who have cruised in the last 12 months." Lovitt attributes lower gas prices, lower unemployment rates, and rising home equity as the culprits for this rebound. He quotes Charlie Funk, co-owner of a Brentwood, Tennessee travel agency, who says, "A change of $1 a gallon adds up to about $750-$800 a year in savings so the psychological impact is substantial."

But it's not just the revitalized economy that's breathing air back into the sails of the cruise line industry. Another major factor is the improved perception. It's been more than two years since the Carnival Triumph broke down and stranded more than 4,000 passengers - and three years since the Costa Concordia experienced 32 fatalities in Italy.

PLANS FOR GROWTH AND EXPANSION

This year alone, seven new ships are being added to the worldwide fleet - increasing capacity by 18,813 passengers. In 2016 and 2017, a whopping 15 more ships will be launched - increasing capacity by another 39,637. The financial impact of the new ships from 2015 and 2016 is believed to hover somewhere around $3.6 billion. But the expansion isn't limited to the next 36 months. Carnival is planning to grow its 10 million annual passengers to a staggering 13 million by 2022. Norwegian Cruise Line is anticipating a 50 percent capacity increase over that same time period - the largest in the industry.

Of the new ships launched this year, Royal Caribbean's Anthem of the Seas is by far one of the more highly-touted additions (although it's nearly identical to its sister ship, Quantum of the Seas, which was released six months prior). The ship features a skydiving simulator, bumper cars, surfing simulator, an extendable arm that reaches out 300 feet above the sea for 360 degree views, a state of the art fitness center, and plenty of restaurants and bars. In October of this year, Norwegian Cruise Line will add its most highly anticipated ship to an already impressive fleet. The Norwegian Escape will have a capacity of 4,200 passengers and will travel to the Bahamas, Caribbean, and Mediterranean. It will have a private section with keycard access, 55 suites, a courtyard with a retractable roof and swimming pool, 82 studio cabins for solo travelers, and plenty of fine dining opportunities.

NEW DESTINATIONS ENTICE BORED PASSENGERS

Another problem the cruise line industry has faced over the past decade is that many passengers are bored with the same destinations. While still beautiful, the Caribbean is overpopulated with cruise ships and no longer offers unique experiences to travelers. In response to this, many companies are offering unique itineraries and new destinations. For example, Iceland is becoming a very popular destination. There are 415 cruises booked for this year, a 36 percent increase over 2014. Some of the cruise ship companies visiting the capital city this year include Royal Caribbean, Norwegian Cruise Line, Princess, Holland American, and Disney.

Southeast Asia - and countries like Cambodia, Vietnam, and Myanmar in particular - are experiencing incredible growth numbers. This year, research suggests 2.17 million passengers will be transported from cruise ships to Asia.

This is a combination of both large cruise liners and smaller river cruise ships. Other hot new cruise destinations include India, United Arab Emirates, Norway, Australia, and the scenic Northwest Passage. However, don't be surprised if this list gets longer in the months and years to come. New ships mean more passengers, which ultimately calls for a wider variety of destinations and ports.

GROWTH TO CONTINUE INDEFINITELY

Over the next five to seven years, growth within the cruise line industry will be steady and widespread. As large names like Royal Caribbean and Norwegian Cruise Line continue to lead the way, others will follow. And regardless of whether or not you enjoy traveling on cruise ships, this rapid expansion is good news for everyone. If nothing else, it's indicative of a healthier global economy.

THE ECONOMICS OF CRUISING

A friend asked me a question the other day, and it's the one I dread the most: What is the best cruise to take? It's an impossible question that has no answer – but one that I find people are asking more and more. And its origins lie in the ever-shifting dynamic of the cruise industry itself. Before 9/11, the cruise industry was a different beast. Prices were, on average, higher. The marked decrease in the tourism sector hadn't occurred yet, and the global economic turndown of 2008-9 wasn't even on the radar.

But there was also a difference in the average cruise passenger. In 1998, for example, there were no rock-climbing walls on cruise ships, and certainly no ice-skating rinks (though that would come a year later.) Dining tended to be fixed, with set times for lunch and dinners at an assigned table, with a dedicated wait staff that was yours for the week. You could, perhaps, draw the conclusion that people cruised for the sake of cruising.

Fig. Golden Princess Off Cabo San Lucas, Mexico in 2008. Three Years Later, Cruise Ships Would Stop Calling on the Mexican Riviera Due to a Combination of Rising Crime – and Unprofitable, Rock-Bottom Fares.

After September 11, 2001, the amount of cruise lines, travel agencies and airlines that went under is nothing short of astonishing. Renaissance Cruises is probably the best example of a company that was extremely successful, yet woefully overextended. None of their itineraries left from U.S.-based home ports, and with no one wanting to fly, the company folded just two weeks after the attacks. Charter airlines, like Canada 3000, went belly-up, despite having done record business on September 10.

Cruises leaving from ports close to the borders of the United States became immensely popular as a result. The cruise industry re-tooled their itineraries, but they also started re-thinking their ships. Mindful of the need to attract new passengers, they started to actively target vacationers who would normally chose an all-inclusive resort or a weekend in Vegas over a cruise. It was a smart idea, one that would launch an unprecedented building boom.

Fig. Alaska was Hit Particularly Hard by Rock-Bottom Fares a Few Years Back. While Consumers Love a $300 Per Person Trip to the Last Frontier for a Week, Cruise Lines were Obviously Less Enthusiastic.

Fast-forward to the global economic turndown in 2008. People had less money to spend overall. Fuel prices were skyrocketing north. And cruise lines found themselves with a lot of berths on a lot of ships that needed to be filled every seven days. So, they dropped the price. And dropped it. And dropped it again.

It worked – the ships started sailing full. But like the airlines, they were making little – if any money. The passengers basically paid the fuel bill. To turn a profit, cruise lines had to convince them to buymore.

How do you get passengers to buy more? You convince them to dine in specialty restaurants with a set cover-charge. You introduce extra-cost drink packages. You create entirely new events and slap a modest charge on them; something people won't think about. And even if they do, there's no choice: the cruise line has to stay in business, and a captive audience wants to enjoy themselves.

Fig. Norwegian Cruise Line has, Quite Successfully, Pioneered the use of Additional Cost Specialty Restaurants as a Way to Offer their Guests More Dining Choices than Ever.

Once again, it worked – remarkably well. People complained, yet continued to purchase and even enjoy these extras. But it did create one problem that seems to be more persistent now than ever, and that is this: cruisers today want it all: great wines. Great food. Great service. Amazing entertainment. Constant stimulation. And they want it all for less than you'd pay per-night at a Best Western. My friend asking what is the "best cruise" is rather symptomatic of the issue facing cruise lines today. The public believes there's one single line that's the best along with one single ship that's the best and a single destination and itinerary that's the best. And they want only the best – but that's very subjective. In an attempt to answer her question, I said Silversea was nice. Because let's face it, they're pretty awesome. The food is stellar, the service is personable, and the drinks are complimentary. What could be better? I said. She countered by saying she didn't want to pay a lot of money. Actually, she said she wanted a "cheap cruise." A cheap cruise that's the best!

Fig. River Cruising is More Popular than Ever – but Still Faces a Hurdle when it Comes to Educating Customers about the Value of Paying more up-front in Order to Get more Features and Amenities Onboard.

Like a good wine, there's nothing that says only expensive cruises can be enjoyable. One of my personal favourite cruise lines is Norwegian Cruise Line, which places emphasis on dining when you want, where you want and with whom you want. They've got more entertainment, dining, and bar options than you could possibly experience in a week, and their resurgence is nothing short of fantastic. If I were Adam Goldstein – head of Royal Caribbean – I'd sleep with one eye open. But that's not to say Norwegian is right for everyone. Some people prefer Holland America Line for their classic elegance and, let's face it, affordability. Some people swear by Carnival, and for good reason: you don't get to be the most popular cruise line in the world by alienating your guests.

But the couple who loves Lindblad Expeditions won't like Carnival, just like the couple who enjoy river cruising probably won't be booking Oasis of the Seas anytime soon. There's exceptions, sure, but you're dealing with products that are very, very different and don't really translate.

Fig. Airlines Found Out the Hard Way that Increasing Additional Fees – Known in the Industry as "Unbundling" – Raises the Ire of Passengers. Yet, Costs have to be Covered, Particularly in an Age when Most People will Book the Cheapest, Rock-Bottom Fare – Regardless of the Additional Charges.

Airlines discovered the hard way that excess fees rile customers. But their hands were tied: John Q. Public won't pay another $50 for his airfare, so we'll have to nail him for his seat and his checked bag. Maybe even his carry-on. But if he'd just cough up the extra cash up-front, we wouldn't have to!

The same is true for many cruise lines; you only have to look at how Disney and Royal Caribbean are trying to sexy-up their inside staterooms by creating virtual portholes and balconies – thus charging higher fares for them – to see the results. I'd like to hope a shift in public perception is there – but I just don't think it is. As long as cruisers demand rock-bottom pricing, cruise lines will be forced to roll out more additional revenue generators.

Yet, people just want to know what the single best cruise in the world is. And they still want it for next-to-nothing.

CRUISE INDUSTRY CONTRIBUTES TO ECONOMY

As the U.S. economy continues to recover from the global recession of 2008-2009, the cruise industry is doing its part. The industry experienced a strong rebound from 2009 to 2010. And, during 2011, the industry continued to be an economic bright spot with a total impact on the U.S. economy of $40.4 billion, according to an independent study commissioned by the Cruise Lines International Association (CLIA).

Spending in the U.S. by cruise lines, their passengers, and their crew members totaled $18.9 billion during 2011, according to the study. Cruise industry employment grew to 350,000 jobs that paid $16.5 billion in wages to U.S. workers. Those wages and salaries showed an encouraging year-over-year increase of 8.3 percent, too. While approximately 80 percent of the economic boost provided by the cruise industry is concentrated in ten states – most of them, not surprisingly, along the coasts – the study said the economies of all 50 states benefit in some way from the North American cruise industry. Florida's economy gained the most during 2011: the state received nearly 9 million visits from cruise passengers and crew members, with direct spending of $6.7 billion. Other states that benefit most from cruise industry spending include California, New York, Texas and Alaska.

The positive economic effect of the cruise industry was also felt in Canada. According to the Atlantic Canada Cruise Association (ACCA), the cruise industry provided more than $82 million in direct economic impact to the region during 2011, with more gains projected for 2012. The ACCA estimated direct spending by passengers and crew members in 2011 at $42 million.

The CLIA report also confirmed that the U.S. is the driver of the cruise industry not only in North America, but worldwide. Americans accounted for 63.5 percent of the 16.5 million cruise passengers around the globe during 2011. U.S. ports also handle 60 percent of all global cruise embarkations. So, for the benefit of vacationers and economies everywhere, cruise on! Talk with your Cruise Holidays personal cruise expert soon to make arrangements for your next cruise vacation.

CRUISE SHIPS AND GLOBAL CAPITALISM: THE INDUSTRY'S SHIFTING POLITICAL ECONOMY

Millions of people have come to connect in different ways with the globalizing cruise industry, from passengers to employees, from locals at its various destinations to managers and owners. The industry has grown tremendously in recent decades, earning massive profits for its major stockholders. Yet whereas some social groups have benefited, others have been disadvantaged or sidelined by the industry's changing structures. Like many other sectors of global tourism, the cruise ship

industry has become adept at repatriating more and more value from passenger spending, while at the same time maintaining a web of local and regional alliances and relations that benefit from the industry. As Robinson explains: "The major portion of tourist earnings is captured by transnational capital without entering the host country to begin with, going to the TNCs that control air travel and the tour operators and travel agents that organize and coordinate the global tourist traffic."

The major companies in the cruise industry have come to embody what it means to be 'transnational'—circumventing national borders and manipulating local economies in order to enrich the very few and sell "exotic" experiences to privileged sectors while at the same time generating very little benefit for those they exploit to achieve these ends. Below I delve briefly into several fundamental changes that have taken place in the industry in the epoch of global capitalism.

1. A variety of organizational and technological advancements have been used to streamline and heighten the exploitation of labour. The most important of these has been 'flags of convenience', a practice that allows companies to flag their ships from countries other than the location of ownership. This allows for lower registration fees, tax dodging, and heightened freedom to employ cheap labour. Traditionally (during and before the 1960s and '70s), cruise ships were part of a national line (Greek Line, Italian Line, Cunard Line, etc.) that was flagged in that country. Most if not all workers were from that country. With the advent of flags of convenience in the 1970s and '80s coinciding with the growth of companies such as Carnival, company owners could use labour from wherever they wanted and increasingly avoid labour laws and environmental regulations. A number of small developing countries, with little to no enforcement measures, provide flags to ships around the world. Clearly the

national and supranational laws enabling this practice ushered in changes to labour practices, which some labour organizations and civil society groups such as the International Transport workers Federation (ITF) in their campaign against flags of convenience and the ITF and War on Want's 2002 'Sweatships' campaign, have attempted to challenge. However, as the data below shows, the share of foreign-flagged (or 'flag of convenience') ships has expanded massively in recent decades.

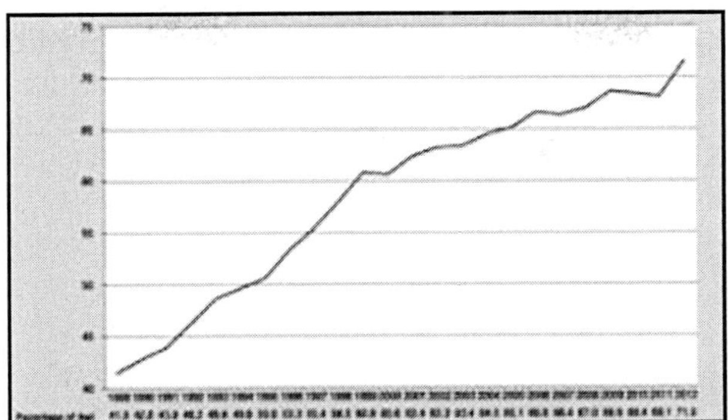

Fig. Global share of foreign-flagged fleet* (Beinning-of-year figures, precentage deadweight tonnage, 1989-2012). * Estimate based on available information of commercial seagoing vessels of 1,000 gross tons and above.

2. Another change has been the development of much larger cruise ships. Large ships in the 1970s weighed 20,000 to 30,000 tons, while by the first decade of the 21st century they reached 220,000 tons. This has provided further impetus to the creation of new port facilities able to accommodate the larger ships. Larger ship capacities (from less than 1,000 passengers in the 1970s to more than 6,000 in the 2000s) also mean that fewer vessels are required for the same number of tourists.
3. Cruise ship companies have also gained unprecedented rights and powers. To attract TNCs active in global tourism, state officials in regions such as the Caribbean have lowered taxes and regulations and allowed the industry to operate relatively unhindered. Cruise ship tourism thus has come to provide only minimal tax income to states.This transition in the industry's relationship with states is accompanied by a move away from traditional ports and state-run local port authorities. Nowadays, cruise companies are no longer at the mercy of local authorities and can more easily capture passenger spending at manufactured tourist sites, spending that in the past would have often been more directly connected with the local economy. The structure of new company-owned ports or enclaves in older ports (with fences and gates) also keep passengers inside "the port," only leaving on company-controlled bus tours or with approved taxi companies. According to an expert in the field, this is very different from twenty or thirty years ago when cruise ship passengers had far less controlled experiences.
4. A growing number of subcontractors, local shore excursion providers, and taxi companies competing for business have allowed cruise lines to maximize their profits by squeezing local economies. Competition between subcontractors and companies working in the tourist industry helps contain costs for the cruise lines. Importantly, subcontractors

and small businesses that link into the industry and depend on it economically have also become important for advocating on behalf of the cruise industry, with tour excursion providers and taxi operators, for example, mobilizing to lobby on the industry's behalf.

5. Cruise ship companies have further entwined with global capital flows through IPOs and partnerships with venture capitalists. Leon Black (Apollo Management) established Prestige Cruise Holding, which controls NCL, Regent Seven Seas, and Oceania; Carnival went public in 1987 by offering 20 per cent of its stock; Royal Caribbean went public in 1993. This, alongside major technological and organizational advancements, has allowed for tremendous growth in industry revenue (as the data below depicts): Royal Caribbean annual revenues of 3.4 billion USD in 2002 grew to nearly 7.7 billion in 2012; Carnival Cruise Lines revenues in 1990 were 1.25 billion and by 2013 had reached nearly 15.5 billion.

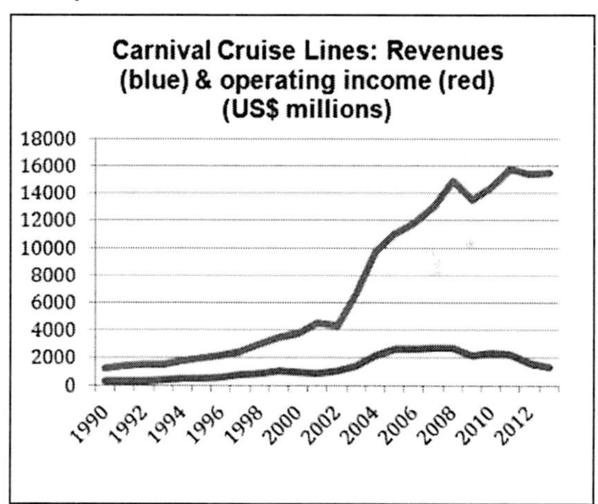

6. The industry and its major owners and managers have become increasingly transnationally oriented, seeking out profits and advantages around the world through a web of partners, subsidiaries, and financial transactions. For example, while the Cruise Royal Caribbean Company maintains its official corporate headquarters in Miami, it is officially incorporated in Liberia. While it has come to be geared towards upper and middle class clientele, it has investors, customers, and employees from around the world. According to Forbes, the company is valued at US$ 9.4 billion. Expanding to regions worldwide as the North American and Caribbean markets became saturated; the cruise industry has recently opened new markets in Asia (especially in China, Vietnam and Thailand), Australia and New Zealand, the Middle East (Dubai), and in parts of Africa. The industry's expansion has occurred alongside its increasingly finely tuned public relations and 'corporate responsibility' strategies.

Cruise ship companies are part of a huge and expanding global industry, yet they are on an economically, socially, and environmentally unsustainable trajectory. The shifting social relations and productive activities that undergird the industry have meant exploitation and disadvantages for too many. The industry has become increasingly monopolized by a handful of larger companies, driving smaller competitors out of business or acquiring them. Meanwhile, labour in the industry has become more socially alienated with low waged workers (from a increasingly wide variety of nationalities) on board the vessels whose activities are more and more standardized, monitored, and micro-managed.

CRUISE INDUSTRY CONTINUES GLOBAL GROWTH

PASSENGERS UP 77 PER CENT IN LAST DECADE

Data released by the Cruise Lines International Association (CLIA) on 15 September, show that worldwide, cruise industry expenditures generated US$117 billion in total economic contributions, supporting the employment of 891,009 full-time equivalent employees with total wages of US$38.47 billion. The report is the first to assess the worldwide economic impact of the cruise industry. Commissioned by CLIA from Business Research and Economic Advisers (BREA), The Global Economic Contribution of Cruise *Tourism 2013 found that:*

- 21.31 million cruise passengers embarked from ports around the world
- 55 per cent of global passengers are sourced from North America (11.82 million), including 10.92 million that reside in the U.S.
- 30 per cent of passengers reside in Europe (6.4 million), including 1.73 million from the UK and Ireland, and 1.69 million from Germany

- Also enjoying cruise vacations are travelers from Australia (833,000 passengers), Brazil (732,000), and China (727,000)
- The average length of a cruise is 7 days, with 3-4 port calls
- The cruise industry generated nearly 115 million passenger and crew visit days at ports around the globe; cruise ship passengers and crew spent an average of US$126.93 each port day

While North America is still the dominant source market, its proportion of total passengers has fallen over the past decade as Europe and the Rest of the World has generated faster passenger growth. Europe's share of the market has risen from 22.5 per cent in 2003 to 30.0 per cent in 2013 while the share of the Rest of the World rose from 9.0 per cent to 14.5 per cent over the 10-year period. "The cruise industry is truly global, bringing together a diverse mix of international passengers and crew to experience exciting itineraries, multiple destinations, and exceptional holiday vacation value on every continent," said Christine Duffy, CLIA President and CEO. "With so many fun options and a high return on vacation experience, it's not surprising that the popularity of cruise holidays continues to grow.

This study shows that the cruise industry's growth is also generating increased jobs, income, and revenue in all regions of the world." "The figures published today show that nearly 45 percent of the industry's 2013 global output was generated in Europe," said Pierfrancesco Vago, Chairman of CLIA Europe and Executive Chairman of MSC Cruises. "Unquestionably, the cruise industry today is a key contributor to Europe's economic recovery, creating real jobs and growth at a time when both are hard to come by. With more Europeans choosing to cruise, more tourists cruising in European waters and more cruise ships being built in European ship yards, the weight of our industry in Europe can only continue to increase in years to come." The economic impact of cruising is greatest in island destinations. For example, Vanuatu saw an estimated $34 million Australian dollars injected into its economy last year from cruise tourism, with an estimated further $18 million in indirect economic benefits, according to a recent study.

The study, jointly funded by Carnival Australia, the Australian Government and World Bank Group member IFC, shows the cruise industry also provides more than 3000 employment opportunities to the Pacific island nation. But there are worries that passenger numbers can overwhelm some destinations, and the environmental impact of cruising is also a concern. The debate over damage caused to Venice from large cruise ships, as well as the impact of huge cruise ships on the visitor experience of other tourists, has led to the Italian government stepping in to ban the largest ships from the centre of the city from next year. And as climate change opens up more of the Arctic to shipping, some commentators warn on the social and environmental risks of the growing cruise industry there.

CONTRIBUTION OF ALASKA PARKS AND WILDERNESS TO THE ALASKA ECONOMY

What is the economic contribution of wilderness to Alaska's economy? Tourism by nonresidents is the primary link that we consider between wilderness and the Alaska economy, although subsistence harvests and resident recreation clearly generate value for Alaskans. Here, we synthesize and apply existing data and research. We do not consider global ecosystem services provided by park lands and waters, nor do we assess activity that is not captured within the Alaska economy.

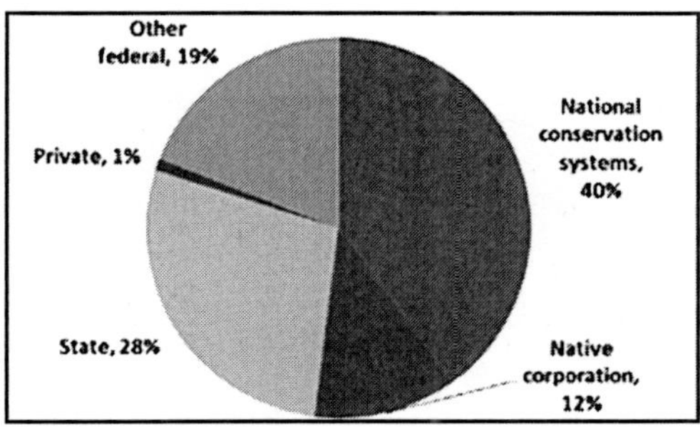

Fig. Alaska Lands by Ownership Status.

The allocation of Alaska's 375 million acres. Approximately 40 percent are in federal conservation units, and approximately 38 percent of these 150 millions acres are designated wilderness. The Alaska National Interest Lands Conservation Act (ANILCA) of 1980 added most newly designated conservation units in the form of national wildlife refuges. The second most important category of additions was new national parks and preserves.

WILDERNESS AND TOURISM

The Alaska visitor industry is the only private sector basic industry that has grown almost continuously since statehood and continues to grow. Almost 1.6 million visitors came to Alaska in summer 2011, and 91 percent of them came primarily to see the state's mountains, glaciers, and wildlife (McDowell Group 2012). Alaska's visitor industry accounted for an estimated 37,800 full- and part-time jobs from May 2011 to April 2012, including all direct, indirect, and induced employment. Estimated peak employment was 45,000. These jobs resulted in total labour income of $1.24 billion. Visitors spent $1.7 billion in Alaska, most of it in the summer months (McDowell Group 2013).

While these economic impacts cannot be completely attributed to the presence of designated wilderness, wilderness characteristics are a significant driver of Alaska visitation. In the summer 2001 Alaska Visitor Statistics Programme (AVSP) Visitor Opinion Survey, specific questions regarding wilderness were included. For over 80 percent of respondents, Alaska's wilderness character and the opportunity to see or spend time in wilderness places influenced their decision to come to Alaska and was an important factor in trip planning. Wilderness was also important to a decision to visit Alaska again in the future by 73 percent of respondents.

Protecting the wilderness character of Alaska was also important to 87 percent respondents. Most also of strongly supported rationing the use of popular wilderness areas to protect the natural environment (80 percent) and animal populations (84 per-cent). Rationing use to protect opportunities for visitors to be alone and away from crowds was also supported (47 percent) but not as strongly.

Fig. Bear Viewing at Katmai National Park and Preserve.

Data from summer 2012 confirms that Alaska tourism activity revolves around Alaska's national parks, especially Denali (433,000 visitors) and Glacier Bay (359,000 visitors) (McDowell, 2013). Our analysis of summer 2001 expenditure diaries collected by AVSP suggests that more than half the total amount spent by tourists in Alaska comes from people who visit Denali.

Visitors to Denali in summer 2001 stayed in Alaska for an average of fourteen days, while all other visitors averaged only eight days. Denali visitors spent $2,300 per party per trip, compared with only $1,100 spent by all other visitors. Similarly, visitors to Katmai National Park and Preserve also spent more days in Alaska and had higher expenditures per trip than the average Alaska visitor (Fay and Christensen, 2010). Several other studies confirm the economic significance of other parks and wilderness areas in Alaska. Fay and Christensen (2010, 2012) found that Katmai National Park and Preserve generated $52.1 million in annual visitor spending, providing approximately 650 jobs and $24.3 million in labour income.

Criteria	Importance				
tbd	Most	Very	Medium	Somewhat	Not
Importance of the wilderness character of Alaska in making the decision to visit Alaska	16	27	20	20	17
Importance of the possibility of seeing or spending time in wilderness places in making trip plans	12	12	24	24	18

Criteria	Strongly disagree	Disagree	Neutral	Agree	Strongly agree
The opportunity to visit or see wilderness would be important to my decision to visit Alaska in the future	2	4	21	39	34
I do not think the wilderness character of Alaska is important to protect	50	37	8	2	3
Use of popular wilderness areas in Alaska should be rationed if needed to protect the natural environment	2	4	14	49	31
Use of popular wilderness areas in Alaska should be rationed if needed to protect natural animal populations	1	3	13	43	41
Use of popular wilderness areas in Alaska should be rationed if needed to protect opportunities for visitors to be alone, away from crowds	4	12	37	31	16

Fig. A Cruise Ship Navigates Through Glacier Bay National Park and Preserve.

Goldsmith and Martin (2001) used a time-series approach to assess the effect of Kenai Fjords National Park on the growth of the economy of Seward, Alaska. They found a number of indications that the tourism industry grew rapidly throughout the 1980s and sustained the Seward economy through the 1990s: "Most of the economic growth, particularly since 1990, has been driven by the visitor industry. Although there is no direct way to track this industry, employment in trade, services, and transportation—the sectors that provide the most visitor-related jobs—grew at an annual rate of 5.9 percent. Retail sales from summer visitors have grown at a 9.9 percent annual rate (inflation adjusted) since 1987. Park tourism is a $52 million-a-year business for Seward."

Goldsmith, Hill, and Hull (1998) analyzed the economic activity associated with the Alaska Peninsula, Becharof, Izembek, and Togiak Wildlife Refuges. They found that these four refuges supported 3,225 average annual jobs and $127 million of personal income in 1997. Commercial fishing accounted for about 90 per cent of the jobs and income. The remaining 362 jobs were attributed to sport fishing, refuge management, subsistence-related activities, and hunting. If subsistence activity were treated as wage labour, it would equate to an additional 750 jobs, and the authors estimated that subsistence also generated more than $50 million in net economic value.

One of the earliest and most thoughtful studies of the effects of wilderness on tourism was the master's thesis done by Larry Bright (1985). Bright attempted to measure changes in tourism use patterns resulting from the creation of six designated wilderness areas within the Tongass National Forest. He collected primary data directly from tourism business operators.

Bright was very careful not to read too much into his survey results. Nonetheless, he concluded: "I have come to the conclusion that designation [of Misty Fjords Wilderness] has played a significant role [in the increased use of the area]....The dramatic jump in Misty Fjords use occurred during and immediately following the designation (1980/81), while use in surrounding areas continued to grow at a much slower pace. Some of the most convincing evidence supporting the designation effect comes from the operators themselves. Every Misty Fjords operator I interviewed stated that they used its official designation promotionally. The operators offering services in 1980 told me that the designation gave them a nationally recognizable name to advertise. (p. 33)" Bright also proposed that wilderness designation was likely only one of six distinct inputs to the increased production (and consumption) of tourism in southeast. Designation as a special area was one (p 68).

The others, in Bright's own words, were:

- Access—a site must be reachable within a reason-able amount of time and by a reasonable mode of transportation . . . In most cases, boat or plane are the two most reasonable mechanisms of transportation.
- The tourists must be "reachable"—there must be an available market in which the tourism operator can "peddle the goods." If cruise ships did not stop in Ketchikan and provide a market, scenic flights of [sic] Misty Fjords would not have developed to the present day level.
- A single, dramatic attraction—like a large glacier (Hubbard), many glaciers (Glacier Bay), or an outstanding salmon stream (Situk).
- Promotional skills and equipment—in many parts of Southeast boats or planes must be available to access an area. As well as the

equipment, individuals must be present with the promotional skills to initiate a tourism enterprise.

- Facilities—probably less a factor in Alaska than in other parts of the U.S. (p. 68)

Haley, Fay, and Angvik (2007) found that proximity to national parks was the strongest predictor of the number and variety of businesses in small rural Alaska villages with populations less than 1,400 people, places where wage income is especially scarce. This study's conclusion echoes other studies using U.S. data. These studies show that rural areas endowed with natural resource amenities, such as wilderness, experience higher regional economic growth rates (Deller et al. 2001, Rasker et al. 2004). Both the amount and proximity of public land was correlated with faster economic growth of adjacent areas (Rasker et al. 2004). Recent studies of western counties and states have shown that population, income, and employment growth increased as the percentage of wilderness increased, and the West's popular national parks, monuments, wilderness areas, and other public lands offer its growing high-tech and services industries a competitive advantage (Headwaters Economics 2012; Holmes and Hecox 2004).

Fig. Buses in Denali National Park and Preserve Carry Thousands of Tourists into the Park Each Summer.

MAXIMIZING THE ECONOMIC VALUE OF ALASKA WILDERNESS

Both economic theory and the evidence to date suggest that to maximize the long-term economic benefits of conservation lands, Alaskans and federal land managers will need to do three things. The first and most important task is to protect the "Alaska difference"—those fundamental attributes of Alaska's large intact ecosystems and their wilderness character. This is easier said than done. It is almost inevitable that individual residents, businesses, and visitors will, consciously or not, chip away at the integrity of Alaska's wildness. In some areas the degradation has been rigourously measured (Twardock et al. 2010). Second, Alaskans must be somewhat patient. Time is on our side when it comes to extracting economic value from wilderness. The global supply of wilderness is decreasing while the demand for Alaska nature-based tourism is growing. Taken together, these shifts in supply and demand mean that the "effective price" of Alaska's wilderness is likely to steadily increase.

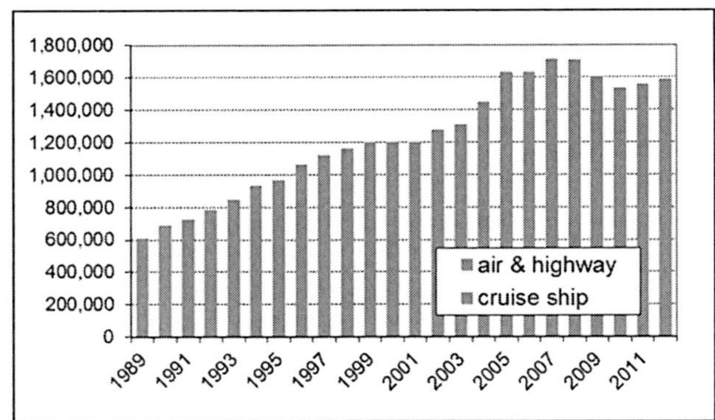

Fig. Alaska Summer Visitor Arrivals by Major Transportation Mode.

Finally, it is important to remember that wilderness and conservation lands are just one of many required inputs to tourism, subsistence, and fish production. Other important inputs include environmentally benign physical access, business talent, and capital investment in supporting infrastructure. Innovative transportation options that can bring more people into the Alaska wilderness with less environmental impact are a good place to start. Cruise ships could be powered by natural gas. Double-decker Denali buses might increase road capacity without affecting wildlife (assuming they can be accommodated without major road reconstruction). Increasing opportunities for remote rural gateway communities to participate in park planning could also help local residents to capture more jobs and income from their neighboring lands (Fay et al. 2005). Looking ahead, it is clear that Alaska's wilderness ecosystems will become increasingly valuable assets in a crowded urban world. If Alaska's wildlands, wildlife, and ecological integrity are cared for with respect, the contribution of wilderness and conservation lands to the Alaska economy and to people everywhere will be significant, positive, increasing, and enduring.

7

Understanding the Impacts of Cruise Tourism and their Remediation Costs for Small Island Communities

INTRODUCTION

Tourism remains one of the most important industries for Greece and her islands; the World Travel and Tourism Council reported that tourism in Greece contributed €12bn, or 6.5 per cent of total GDP for the nation. Furthermore, tourism directly supports 330,500 jobs, representing 8.8 per cent of total employment.

With an anticipated 5 million cruise tourists visiting Greece this year, significant numbers of day visitors arriving via cruise ships have the potential to contribute substantially to local economies. Quantifying the economic contribution of cruise tourism remains problematic, however, since it comprises business transacted with locally-owned leisure facilities, restaurants, retail shops, visitor attractions and the like, plus charges levied by port authorities (handling charges and taxes), and charges imposed by cruise operators that cruise tourists pay to partake in port excursions. These last are usually paid in advance of the visit, and typically include transport, entry to attractions, and refreshments. Such payments will eventually trickle through as a reduced sum for local businesses, for services rendered, but what can be construed as a high price to the cruise tourist will in fact be greatly reduced when it reaches the host economy.

For Chios, tourism in general is an important contributor to the local economy, and cruise tourism is surprisingly significant, with day visitor numbers approaching those for leisure tourists arriving by air. Ashcroft and Associates describe Chios as having an increasing appeal, particularly for cruise tourists. Chios can be considered atypical, when compared to other Greek Island destinations such as Corfu, Rhodes, Kos, Crete or Santorini; it is at an early stage of tourism and especially cruise tourism development, and decisions must be made as to the extent to which the host community will seek to develop the industry. Critical in such decisions is an understanding of the level of benefit to the island's economy, and the impacts in terms of sustainability.

RESEARCH METHODOLOGY

A useful starting point when considering issues of sustainability is Elkington's [1994] vision of Triple Bottom Line (TBL) accounting, often summarised as "people, planet and profit". Here, an activity is only said to be sustainable (which is to say, viable in the long term) if it is socially just, environmentally benign and commercially sound.

This definition has been widely adopted, and the Venn diagram that shows sustainability existing only at the confluence of all three issues is well known – but on its own it does not provide a means for practitioners to pursue sustainability. According to MacGillivray [2004] for sustainability to occur "economic, environmental and social balance sheets must all be in the black", yet the toolsets to measure environmental and social harm lag far behind the level of accuracy and wide understanding found in the assessment of economic performance.

Mitchell et al [2007] found that TBL reporting promoted sustainability thinking within organisations, but trade-offs between the different TBL dimensions remained difficult. (In a sustainable tourism context, for example, this might mean choosing between job creation and natural habitat destruction, when considering the construction of facilities.) Adams [2006] states that trade-offs between TBL elements are a flawed concept because governments and businesses will always tend to prioritise the economic. It can be argued that it is human nature for a system to tend towards further environmental or cultural degradation over time – at the risk of "killing the goose that lays the golden eggs." Middleton and Hawkins [2012] concur, warning that tourists can destroy the natural environment that attracted them to the destination in the first instance, if their tourism activities are not managed sustainably.

In this study, trade-offs have not been attempted; final decisions rest with the host community, after all. Instead, each component of the system has been examined to identify the scale, value and growth potential of the industry (profit), the environmental strain it imposes upon an island community (planet) and the social impacts upon the hosts (people).

Graci and Dodds [2010] acknowledge that it is important to establish just who the principal stakeholders are in the area of sustainable tourism, and more importantly for this study, in relation to island destinations. In this context we use Freeman's [1984] definition of a stakeholder, as a person or group who may hold an interest in the ability of an organisation to exercise actions involving the destination and possibly influence change. Several authors argue that qualitative research in tourism is an evolutionary practice and well recommended. When taking this approach Veal argues that it is possible to obtain a more comprehensive account of the situation in tourism related scenarios, involving individual feelings and thoughts, as opposed to the limited amount of information obtained from a larger study that quantitative research can reveal. Veal also argues that individuals absorbed in tourism experience situations are best positioned to interpret their account of the situation in a qualitative type of information gathering. In view of such recommendations, qualitative research was carried out among local businesses. Graci and Dodds recognise local businesses as being the 'grass roots' of the tourism industry, especially in an island destination [2010] since local businesses, as stakeholders, work to ensure that a high proportion of the income generated from tourism reaches the local economy, and that it is distributed across the island community.

Empirical research was carried out through in-depth personal interviews with a variety of local business owners, citizens and officials, in a non-directive manner. An interview guide was formulated, featuring semi-structured, broad, open-ended questions aimed at obtaining comments illustrating the experiences and opinions of the interviewees. In total, eighteen interviews were conducted, obtaining contributions from local residents, café and shop workers, taxi drivers, law enforcement and local officials. The stakeholder interviews allowed the researchers to catalogue the concerns of the interviewees, in terms of the ways that cruise tourism affects the business, social and natural environment of an Aegean island community.

ASSESSING THE SOCIAL IMPACTS OF CRUISE TOURISM

The social aspects of sustainability vary from one business proposition to another, but might include issues such as health and safety, consumer rights, participation in local democracy, fair dealing with consumers and suppliers, equal opportunities, infrastructure and access to services, culture and heritage; a list of potential impacts that remain difficult to measure or assign a value to.

The interviewees reported a number of social issues. By far most commonly identified, from 16 of the 18 interviewees, was that cruise tourism is affecting the opening hours of businesses in the port area. This represents a recent change; before the economic crisis tourists were left with little to do when shops closed mid-afternoon, but now their business is considered more valuable. The extended opening hours are something of a grey area, legally, but closure is not enforced.

Taxi drivers were also reported to be working a lot on days when there was a cruise ship in port, and some interviewees reported that road traffic congestion was an issue on those days. Interestingly, all interviewees rejected the idea that cruise visitors have a negative affect upon their everyday life; in fact residents rarely interacted with cruise tourists, who tended to take coach tours around the island. An emerging cultural influence on Chios comes from the growing number of Turkish visitors who also arrive by sea, as day visitors or on a two-day cruise from Izmir. Interviewees generally failed to distinguish between Turkish day visitors and more conventional cruise tourists. The emergence of this market segment has led to new signage appearing on the streets and within shops, where staff have started learning Turkish, and organising related cultural events.

Overall, respondents had relatively little to say that showed cruise tourism in a negative light. Local businesses appreciate the extra revenue, and reported that they cope with the influx of tourists by arranging to have extra staff on duty on 'cruise days'. It was also reported that the short period for which cruise day visitors stay meant that bars and cafés could still serve residents as usual.

ASSESSING ENVIRONMENTAL IMPACTS FROM CRUISE TOURISM

When questioned about environmental impacts, the great majority of interviewees saw no environmental problems at all. Just two reported that cruise ships "pollute the sea" and none mentioned problems of air quality, or climate change. It may be significant that the region is often subject to strong winds, and thus any smoke that the engines of a ship generate will rapidly be dispersed. In any event, 'green' issues seem not to be considered, beyond the two respondents who took exception to the discharging of waste that they assumed to take place.

The relevant marine environmental convention, MARPOL, specifies conditions under which the discharge of food wastes, certain cleaning agents, sewage and grey water are permissible– although one respondent's statement that "they empty their tanks just outside our port" is unlikely to describe the discharging of sewage, as a minimum distance of 4.8km from shore is specified for such material.

METRICS FOR THE ENVIRONMENTAL IMPACT OF CRUISE HOLIDAYS

To some extent, environmental impact can be quantified, although this remains highly complex. A common option is to consider the 'carbon footprint', based upon the emissions of greenhouse gases that are associated with the provision of a good or service, and the corresponding risk of climate change. Ward [2010] suggests a figure of 960kg CO_2 per passenger, for a one-week cruise (not including travel to and from the ship). For comparison, annual CO_2 emissions for a person living in Greece are around 8,400kg.

The cruise vessels that call at Chios appear to produce substantially higher CO_2 emissions per passenger. Le Levant, a cruise ship that regularly visited Chios in 2011, is reported to consume 14 tonnes of heavy fuel oil (HFO) per day; using the standard conversion factors published by DEFRA [2012] this quantity of HFO equates to 53,717kg of CO_2 and equivalent greenhouse gases emitted, or 597kg per passenger, per day – and more if full occupancy is not achieved.

Le Levant carries just 90 passengers in luxury and at speed; calculations based upon a typical large cruise ship – of the kind not currently seen at Chios – broadly confirms the Ward [2010] figure for CO_2 per passenger, although it should be noted that these basic calculations are for energy use only and do not include food, services, excursions, and the like.

Sustainability calculations based purely upon climate change potential are limited in that they do not address other environmental issues such as toxicity, habitat destruction or the consumption of scarce material resources – nor the other component parts of the TBL, such as social issues. Another key problem when calculating the environmental harm of tourism is that measurements tend to be attributed to the country where emissions occur, rather than being associated with the nationality of the citizens who visit. This does not affect calculations of environmental degradation at the global level, but can serve to conceal the source of climate change. An additional source of complexity is that some environmental problems are global in nature, such as CO_2 emissions, while others are more local, *e.g.* affecting water or air quality.

Addressing one example of the latter, EU Legislation (Directive 2005/33/EC) imposed a limit of 1.5 per cent sulphur in HFO used by passenger ships serving the EU with effect from 2010, and further limiting the sulphur content of fuel used when berthed to 0.1 per cent. Sulphur occurs naturally in crude oil, and can be present in HFO at up to 4.5 per cent by weight, but the sulphur dioxide (SO_2) resulting from combustion is known to cause many health problems, plus acid rain.

Further sulphur reductions are planned for 2015 and 2020, compelling ship operators to use more expensive, low-sulphur fuels.

Despite the lack of concern about gaseous emissions from those interviewed, the potential for environmental harm is huge, as the data on shipping in Greek waters in Tzannatos [2010] show. Passenger ferries and cruise ships are considered together because the vessels tend to be similar in terms of their performance; taken together they accounted for 18 per cent of ship movements in Greek waters, and 390,633 tonnes of HFO consumed in 2008.

Even with low sulphur fuels substantially reducing the local air quality problems, the global issue of climate change remains: based on the DEFRA [2012] conversion factors this fuel usage implies the emission of greenhouse gases equivalent to 1.47 megatonnes of CO_2 – and there are other emissions of concern as well. Vogtländer et al [2002] identified seven different classes of emission (acidification, eutrophication, heavy metals, carciogens, summer smog, winter smog and climate change), and proposed a common denominator in the form of "prevention costs at the norm". It may be that an adapted form of this mechanism could be used to assign a cost to the various forms of damage that occur as a result of cruise ship operations, perhaps with the ultimate aim of levying taxes and using money obtained for remediation or offsetting – but we have yet to consider the environmental harm that occurs when passengers come ashore, causing soil erosion in sensitive sites that endure high footfall, or engaging in hazardous or resource-intensive activities during excursions. Fortunately, the low numbers of cruise passengers seen on Chios at present are unlikely to be doing damage that cannot be repaired by natural processes.

EMERGING IMPROVEMENTS TO CRUISE SHIP ENVIRONMENTAL PERFORMANCE

On the technical side, some efforts have been made to improve the 'green' performance of cruise ships: some cosmetic, and some more practical. Fitting low energy lighting and heat-reflecting glass help to reduce the fuel consumed for on-board electricity generation, while "cold ironing" (using a shore-based electricity supply while docked) can further reduce emissions.

Tzannatos [2010] and Kalli et al [2009] also reported favourably on the use of a seawater-based scrubber to reduce SO_2 emissions, it being permitted to continue to use fuels with higher sulphur content with this technology in place to treat emissions.

Less conventional attempts to make cruise holidays more 'green' have included the addition of solar panels, sails, and even the introduction of biodegradable golf balls, made from surplus lobster shells; MARPOL classifies conventional golf balls as waste plastic, and prohibits their 'discharge'. Lobster shell golf balls provide an example of how a leisure activity can once again become sustainable, through re-engineering, but there is a danger that the small changes make good press, while failing to address the real problems.

ASSESSING THE BUSINESS IMPACTS OF CRUISE TOURISM

The responses from interviewees regarding the business impacts of cruise tourism on Chios were overwhelmingly positive. Stakeholders were pleased at the additional business generated by cruise ships, although one negative comment concerned a cruise ship that arrived complete with bicycles, allowing the visitors to tour the island without having completed a business transaction with local companies. As cruise ships become increasingly sophisticated, this kind of competition with local leisure amenity providers may become a significant problem.

The business issue that was most commonly discussed concerned the inadequacy of the present-day port. When a cruise ship is berthed within the port, it can prevent access for other vessels, and the larger cruise ships cannot gain access to the port at all, but must transfer passengers to and from shore by tender. The strong winds in the region can make this activity difficult or impossible on some days.

As a result, there is considerable interest in the development of a more suitable port, most likely at Mesta on the west of the island. Naturally, the proposal is unpopular with the businesses in the port area of Chios that would suffer if cruise visitors were to land elsewhere.

THE LIFE CYCLE OF CRUISE TOURISM

An aspect that needs approaching with caution when considering sustainability (literally, the ability to continue an activity) is that a business activity may flourish only for a brief time. Those who invest in developing a tourist destination may be disappointed to find that numbers cease to expand, and ultimately decline – with consequences in terms of the monetary investment and materials that have been expended on development, which will ultimately have social and environmental consequences.

It is useful, therefore, to determine the stage of development at a destination, when assessing the impacts of tourism (and specifically in this case, cruise tourism). Many authors recognise Bulter's [1980] Tourist Area Life Cycle (TALC) as being a valid model to explain how a destination develops over time, moving through the stages of involvement, development and consolidation with a corresponding growth in tourist numbers.

Graci and Dodds [2010] caution that the TALC cannot provide a typical evolution of an island destination, especially in a planning context. Choy [1992] and Agarwal [1997] support this, arguing that the exact angle of ascent in the TALC graph cannot be determined as "one size fits all". Indeed, there is evidence to support a very different tourist area life cycle occurring on Chios in comparison to Rhodes, despite the islands being of a similar size and in close proximity.

Rhodes evolved with the first charter flights in the early 1960s, attracting large numbers of tourists originating from UK and European consumer markets searching for an inexpensive packaged holiday. For summer 2013 Rhodes is expecting to attract in excess of 1.3 million tourists arriving by air, with a further 600,000 arriving as cruise tourists on 33 large capacity cruise ships, participating in day visit activities. These vast numbers of tourists in their various forms exceed the carrying capacity of the island at the height of the season, degrading the tourism product and over-stretching the infrastructure and natural resources. Obviously, day cruise visitors also cause a noticeable 'spike' in the load that tourists impose upon the destination.

Chios is largely unknown to the mass tourist markets of Europe, and instead attracts affluent Greek families, often with holiday homes, and Turks visiting on short excursions from the nearby Turkish mainland, only 10 km away. The island is expected to see fewer than twenty cruise ship visits during the 2013 holiday season, from five different ships with a maximum capacity of only 450 passengers– although it is worth noting that Seabourn, in particular, describe this as an 'ultra luxury' cruise product, which may increase the value of each passenger to the local economy.

Of course, a cruise tourist arriving at the island only stays for a few hours, but contributions from this source can be significant, if a fair share is allowed to permeate through to the host community.

When utilising Butler's [1980] TALC to determine the maturity of the destinations, Rhodes can be seen to be in the 'consolidation' stage, and arguably bordering on stagnation as the destination regularly reaches over-capacity, degrading the tourism product.

In comparison, Chios has developed so as to attract a very different kind of higher spend consumer, albeit in limited numbers. In addition to the low level of visitors, comments from stakeholder interviewees confirm Chios to be at the 'involvement' stage of Butler's [1980] TALC. The tourism industry on Chios has developed at a much slower pace, and the island lacks the infrastructure that would be needed to serve the mass market, although in consequence much of the coastline remains in a highly desirable, undeveloped state that has largely escaped tourism.

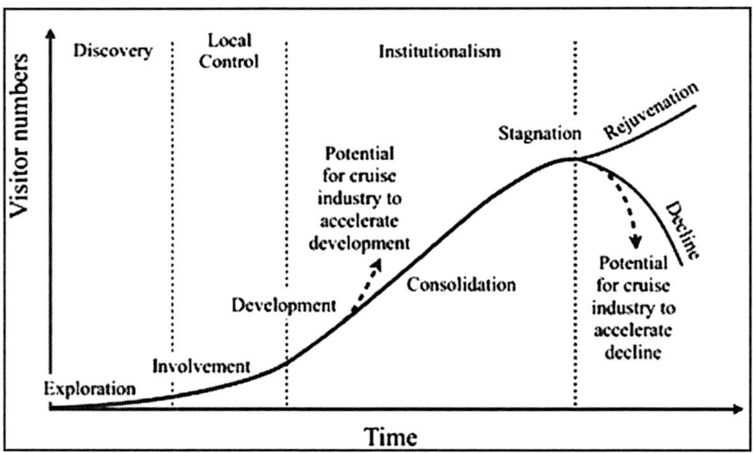

Fig. Tourist Area Life Cycle Showing the Cruise Industry's Potential to Accelerate Development, and Decline.

Cruise tourism should be pursued with caution, as its appeal as a sustainable income generator is questionable. It has the potential to skew the TALC because the mobile nature of the cruise product can overcome the normally slow process of development and consolidation. If a destination becomes popular, cruise visitor numbers can increase rapidly by the simple expedient of changing cruise itineraries from one season to the next:

Destination-specific investment would remain relatively small, allowing cruise operators to sample a destination, and move elsewhere if it proves insufficiently profitable. In this sense, cruise ships are superior to land-based development, but introduce considerable variability that may leave local businesses struggling to meet capacity requirements without taking on considerable financial risk.

In addition to the TALC theory, there are further established concepts that can be utilised to develop an overall image of the development of tourism on Chios. Cooper et al [2008] highlight that when searching for the allegations of socio-cultural impacts in tourist destinations, one of the major impacts on the host community occurs when they come into any kind of contact involving communication with tourists, either arriving to stay overnight or, it can be argued, via a cruise ship. This activity is reported as being a direct impact that can lead, over time, to irritation.

Brida et al [2012] have completed focused research involving destinations receiving cruise tourism, utilising successfully the fundamental theories devised by Butler [1980] and Doxey [1975] to determine the social-cultural impacts of tourism in Messina, Sicily.

In Chios both the TALC and Doxey's Irritation Index can be utilised to demonstrate that not only is the island destination at the 'involvement' stage, the responses from the local host community taking part in the primary interviews, acknowledge 'euphoria' per the Doxey Irritation Index. Largely as a result of the continuing economic crisis in the Eurozone which has impacted many businesses in Chios, the host population is increasingly reliant on tourism and in particular, on the cruise tourist to supplement their income and the local economy.

It appears that cruise tourism on Chios is developing towards the next stage of both the TALC and Doxey's Irritation Index models, although other authors have argued that these models are only reliable when utilised retrospectively. In the case of Chios it seems reasonable to suggest that an accurate prediction can be made, in that the economy is moving towards reliance on tourism and consolidation, involving the cruise tourism industry in particular. The cruise industry may ultimately become a major cause of annoyance amongst the host population, particularly if larger cruise ships are able to land greater numbers of cruise tourists on the island in the future. Cruise tourism could develop to attract numbers that would test the carrying capacity of the island, as has been seen on Rhodes.

CONCLUSIONS

Chios is at a pivotal stage in its development, and the importance of cruise tourism has been magnified by wider economic issues. The islanders must resolve some difficult business decisions if they are to invest in a major port development, and even if successful in this they run the risk of substantially altering the character of the island.

It appears that stakeholders are largely unaware of the negative impacts that a large increase in cruise tourism could inflict on their island, and their lives. The host population were found to have only a limited regard for maritime environmental issues, and the current social impacts were largely considered to be of minor importance and easily addressed. Meanwhile, the people of Chios remain well-disposed to tourism, and few perceive any significant risk. As a result, developments that will permit increased cruise tourism appear likely.

Whilst an attractive solution in the short term, and especially in the current economic climate, the fostering of cruise tourism on Chios ought to be undertaken with care – taking into account the luxury positioning of the current product, and aiming to maintain or increase local revenue per passenger even as numbers increase. Offering a rare example of a largely unspoiled destination, it should be entirely possible to derive further income from both cruise operators and passengers. Even when considered on a purely business level, investing in new port infrastructure is risky because there are no guarantees that with such facilities in place the island will attract larger cruise ships in sufficient numbers to repay the initial investment. Furthermore, there will be social changes for some in the host community, in the form of longer working hours and highly seasonal work, plus issues of congested roads and crowded amenities, while the environmental impacts of increasing cruise tourism in general will be borne by the much wider (or even global) community.

IMPACT OF TOURISM IN COASTAL AREAS: NEED OF SUSTAINABLE TOURISM STRATEGY

This chapter discusses the issues and impacts associated with coastal tourism, the current status of related environmental affairs and a forecast of tourism in the future. The article concludes by providing suggestions for future management of coastal tourism.

Since the 1992 Earth Summit in Rio de Janeiro, there is increasing awareness of the importance of sustainable forms of tourism. Although tourism, one of the world largest industries, was not the subject of a chapter in Agenda 21, the Programme for the further implementation of Agenda 21, adopted by the General Assembly at its nineteenth special session in 1997, included sustainable tourism as one of its sectoral themes. Furthermore in 1996, The World Tourism Organization jointly with the tourism private sector issued an Agenda 21 for the Travel and Tourism Industry, with 19 specific areas of action recommended to governments and private operators towards sustainability in tourism.

SPECIFIC SITUATION OF COASTAL AREAS

Coastal areas are transitional areas between the land and sea characterized by a very high biodiversity and they include some of the richest and most fragile ecosystems on earth, like mangroves andcoral reefs. At the same time, coasts are under very high population pressure due to rapid urbanization processes. More than half of today's world population live in coastal areas (within 60 km from the sea) and this number is on the rise. Additionally, among all different parts of the planet, coastal areas are those which are most visited by tourists and in many coastal areas tourism presents the most important economic activity.

In theMediterranean region for example, tourism is the first economic activity for islands like Cyprus, Malta, the Balearic Islands and Sicily. Forecast studies carried out by WTO estimate that international tourist arrivals to the Mediterranean coast will amount to 270 millions in 2010 and to 346 millions in 2020 (in 2000 around 200 million foreign visitors per year).

Main Sources of Impact

- Residence in the coastal zone
- Fisheries and aquaculture
- Shipping
- Tourism
- Land-use practices (Agriculture, Industrial development)
- Climate change

Resulting Problems

- Loss of marine resources due to destruction of coral reefs, overfishing
- Pollution of marine and freshwater resources
- Soil degradation and loss of land resources (*e.g.* desertification and salinification due to excessive water use, overuse of fertilizers, erosion)
- Air pollution
- Loss of cultural resources, social disruption
- Loss of public access
- Natural hazards and sea level rise
- Climate change

Fig. Recreational Snorkellers Harassing a Whaleshark.

Fig. Tourists Sunbathing on a Beach Used by Loggerhead Turtles (Caretta Caretta) for Nnesting, some with Beach Umbrellas which can Hurt Turtle Nests.

For further details see: Sustainable Tourism Management in Coastal Areas and WWF on Tourism Pressure

HOW DOES TOURISM DAMAGE COASTAL ENVIRONMENT

Massive influxes of tourists, often to a relatively small area, have a huge impact. They add to the pollution, waste, and water needs of the local population, putting local infrastructure and habitats under enormous pressure. For example, 85 per cent of the 1.8 million people who visit Australia's Great Barrier Reef are concentrated in two small areas, Cairns and the Whitsunday Islands, which together have a human population of just 130,000 or so.

Tourist Infrastructure

In many areas, massive new tourist developments have been built - including airports, marinas, resorts, and golf courses. Overdevelopment for tourism has the same problems as other coastal developments, but often has a greater impact as the tourist developments are located at or near fragile marine ecosystems.

For example:

- Mangrove forests and seagrass meadows have been removed to create open beaches
- Tourist developments such as piers and other structures have been built directly on top of coral reefs
- Nesting sites for endangered marine turtles have been destroyed and disturbed by large numbers of tourists on the beaches

Careless Resorts, Operators, and Tourists

The damage doesn't end with the construction of tourist infrastructure. Some tourist resorts empty their sewage and other wastes directly into water surrounding coral reefs and other sensitive marinehabitats. Recreational activities also have a huge impact. For example, careless boating, diving, snorkeling, and fishing have substantially damaged coral reefs in many parts of the world, through people touching reefs, stirring up sediment, and dropping anchors. Marine animals such as whale sharks, seals, dugongs, dolphins, whales, and birds are also disturbed by increased numbers of boats, and by people approaching too closely. Tourism can also add to the consumption of seafood in an area, putting pressure on local fish populations and sometimes contributing to overfishing. Collection of corals, shells, and other marine souvenirs - either by individual tourists, or local people who then sell the souvenirs to tourists - also has a detrimental effect on the local environment.

Cruise Ships: Floating Towns

The increased popularity of cruise ships has also adversely affected the marine environment. Carrying up to 4,000 passengers and crew, these enormous floating towns are a major source of marine pollution through the dumping of garbage and untreated sewage at sea, and the release of other shipping-related pollutants.

THE CASE OF CRUISE SHIP TOURISM

A development that has turned out to be a severe problem for many coastal areas in the last decade is the increase in cruise ship tourism. The cruise ship business is the segment that has grown most rapidly during the last decade. While world international tourist arrivals in the period 1990 – 1999 grew at an accumulative annual rate of 4.2 per cent, that of cruises did by 7.7 per cent. In 1990 there were 4.5 million international cruise arrivals which had increased to a number of 8.7 million in 1999. Particularly for many islands in the Caribbean, cruise tourism is an important market segment. In the period from 1990 to 1999 there was an increase from 13.71 million international tourist arrivals to 20.32 million (CTO). Meanwhile the number of cruise passengers increased from 7.75 million to 12.14 million in the same period. This means that in 1999 almost 2/3 of all arrivals to the Caribbean were cruise passengers.

Problems

- Discharge of sewage in marinas and nearshore coastal areas.
- The lack of adequate port reception facilities for solid waste, especially in many small islands, as well as the frequent lack of garbage storing facilities on board can result in solid wastes being disposed of at sea, and being transported by wind and currents to shore often in locations distant from the original source of the material.
- "Tar balls" on beaches indicate that oil tankers and other ships dump their oil and garbage overboard (despite laws against such practice), while pollution off Florida and in the Gulf of Mexico is causing serious concern.

- Land-based activities such as port development and the dredging that inevitably accompanies it in order to receive cruise ships with sometimes more than 3000 passengers can significantly degradecoral reefs through the build up of sediment. Furthermore, sand mining at the beaches leads to coastal erosion.
- In the Cayman Islands damage has been done by cruise ships dropping anchor on the reefs.
- Scientists have acknowledged that more than 300 acres of coral reef have already been lost to cruise ship anchors in the harbour at George Town, the capital of Grand Cayman.
- The potential socio-cultural stress produced by cruise tourism needs to be mentioned as well, since it means that during very short periods there is high influx of people, sometimes more than the local inhabitants of small islands, demanding food, energy,water, etc. and possibly overrunning local communities.

IMPACTS

Environmental Impacts

Tourism can create great pressure on local resources such as energy, food, land and water that may already be in short supply. According to the Third Assessment of Europe's environment (EEA, 2003), the direct local impacts of tourism on people and the environment at destinations are strongly affected by concentration in space and time (seasonality).

They result from:

- The intensive use of water and land by tourism and leisure facilities.
- The delivery and use of energy.
- Changes in the landscape coming from the construction of infrastructure, buildings and facilities.
- Air pollution and waste.
- The compaction and sealing of soils (damage and destruction of vegetation).
- The disturbance of fauna and local people (for example, by noise).

Impacts on Biodiversity

Tourism can cause loss of biodiversity in many ways, *e.g.* by competing with wildlife for habitat and natural resources. More specifically, negative impacts on biodiversity can be caused by various factors.

Socio-Cultural Impacts

Change of local identity and values:

- *Commercialization of local culture:* Tourism can turn local culture into commodities when religious traditions, local customs and festivals are reduced to conform to tourist expectations and resulting in what has been called "reconstructed ethnicity"

- *Standardization:* Destinations risk standardization in the process of tourists desires and satisfaction: while landscape, accommodation, food and drinks, etc., must meet the tourists expectation for the new and unfamiliar situation. They must at the same time not be too new or strange because few tourists are actually looking for completely new things.This factor damages the variation and beauty of diverse cultures.
- *Adaptation to tourist demands:* Tourists want to collect souvenirs, arts, crafts, cultural manifestations. In many tourist destinations, craftsmen have responded to the growing demand and have made changes in the design of their products to make them more attractive to the new customers. Cultural erosion may occur in the process of commercializing cultural traditions.

Cultural clashes may arise through:

- *Economic inequality* - Between locals and tourists who are spending more than they usually do at home.
- *Irritation due to tourist behaviour* - Tourists often, out of ignorance or carelessness, fail to respect local customs and moral values.
- *Job level friction* - Due to a lack of professional training, many low-paid tourism-jobs go to local people while higher-paying and more prestigious managerial jobs go to foreigners or "urbanized" nationals.

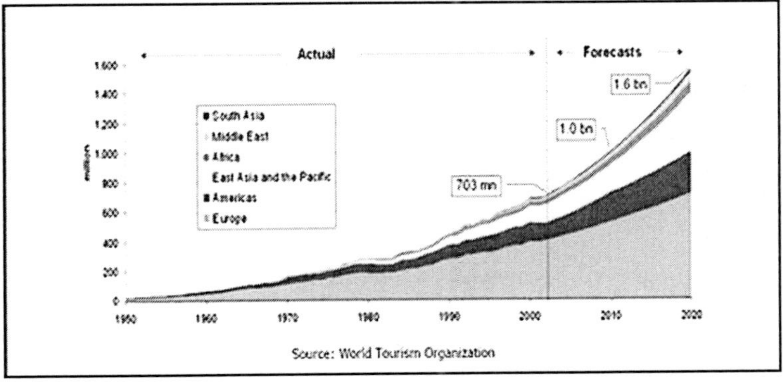

Fig. UNWTO's Tourism 2020 Vision Forecasts that International Arrivals are Expected to Reach Nearly 1.6 Billion by the Year 2020. Of these Worldwide Arrivals in 2020, 1.2 Billion will be Intraregional and 378 Million will be Long-Haul Travellers.

BENEFITS OF SUSTAINABLE COASTAL TOURISM

Economic Benefit

The main positive economic impacts of sustainable (coastal) tourism are: contributions to government revenues,foreign exchange earnings, generation of employment and business opportunities.Further information on economic contributions of tourism can be found on the web site of the World Travel and Tourism Council.

Contribution to Government Revenues

Government revenues from the tourism sector can be categorised as direct and indirect contributions. Direct contributions are generated by income taxes from tourism and employment due to tourism, tourism businesses and by direct charges on tourists such as ecotax . Indirect contributions derive from taxes and duties on goods and services supplied to tourists, for example, taxes on tickets (or entry passes to any protected areas), souvenirs, alcohol, restaurants, hotels, service of tour operators.

Foreign Exchange Earnings

Tourism expenditures, the export and import of related goods and services generate income to the host economy. Tourism is a main source of foreign exchange earnings for at least 38 per cent of all countries (World Tourism Organisation).

Employment Generation

The rapid expansion of international tourism has led to significant employment creation. Tourism can generate jobs directly through hotels, restaurants, taxis, souvenir sales and indirectly through the supply of goods and services needed by tourism-related businesses; for *e.g.* conducted tour operators. Tourism represents around 7 per cent of the world's employees (World Tourism Organisation). Stimulation of infrastructure investment Tourism can influence the local government to improve the infrastructure by creating better water and sewage systems, roads, electricity, telephone and public transport networks. All this can improve the standard of living for residents as well as facilitate tourism.

Contribution to Local Economies

Tourism can be a significant or even an essential part of the local economy. As environment is a basic component of the tourism industry's assets, tourism revenues are often used to measure the economic value of protected areas. Part of the tourism income comes from informal employment, such as street vendors and informal guides.

The positive side of informal or unreported employment is that the money is returned to the local economy and has a great multiplier effect as it is spent over and over again. The World Travel and Tourism Council estimates that tourism generates an indirect contribution equal to 100 per cent of direct tourism expenditures.

Direct Financial Contributions to Nature Protection

Tourism can contribute directly to the conservation of sensitive areas and habitats. Revenue from park-entrance fees and similar sources can be allocated specifically to pay for the protection and management of environmentally sensitive areas.

Some governments collect money in more far-reaching and indirect ways that are not linked to specific parks or conservation areas. User fees, income taxes, taxes on sales or rental of recreation equipment and license fees for activities such as hunting and fishing can provide governments with the funds needed to manage natural resources.

Competitive Advantage

More and more tour operators take an active approach towards sustainability. Not only because consumers expect them to do so but also because they are aware that intact destinations are essential for the long term survival of the tourism industry.

More and more tour operators prefer to work with suppliers who act in a sustainable manner, *e.g.* saving water and energy, respecting the local culture and supporting the well being of local communities. In 2000 the international Tour Operators initiative for Sustainable Tourism was founded with the support of UNEP.

ENVIRONMENTAL MANAGEMENT AND PLANNING BENEFITS

Sound and efficient environmental management of tourism facilities and especially hotels (*e.g.* water and energy saving measures, waste minimization, use of environmentally friendly material) can decrease the environmental impact of tourism.

Planning helps to make choices between the conflicting interests of industry and tourism, in order to find ways to make them compatible. By planning sustainable tourism development strategy at an early stage,prevents damages and expensive mistakes , thereby avoiding the gradual deterioration of the quality of environmental goods and services significant to tourism.

SOCIO-CULTURAL BENEFITS

Tourism as a Force for Peace

Travelling brings people into contact with each other. As sustainable tourism has an educational element it can foster understanding between people and cultures and provide cultural exchange between guests and hosts . This increases the chances for people to develop mutual sympathy, tolerance and understanding and to reduce prejudices and promote the sense of global brotherhood.

Strengthening Communities

Sustainable Coastal Tourism can add to the vitality of communities in many ways. For *e.g.* events and festivals of the local communities where they have been the primary participants and spectators. Often these are refreshed, reincarnated and developed in response to tourists' interests.

The jobs created by tourism can act as a very important motivation to reduce emigration from rural areas. Local people can also increase their influence on tourism development, as well as improve their jobs and earnings prospects through tourism-related professional training and development of business and organizational skills.

Revitalization of Culture and Traditions

Sustainable Tourism can also improve the preservation and transmission of cultural and historical traditions. Contributing to the conservation and sustainable management of natural resources can bring usually the chance to protect local heritage or to revitalize native cultures, for instance by regenerating traditional arts and crafts.

Encouragement Social Involvement and Pride

In some situations, tourism also helps to raise local awareness concerning the financial value of natural and cultural sites. It can stimulate a feeling of pride in local and national heritage and interest in its conservation. More broadly, the involvement of local communities in sustainable tourism development and operation seems to be an important condition for the sustainable use and conservation of the biodiversity.

Benefits for the Tourists of Sustainable Tourism

The benefits of sustainable tourism for visitors are plenty: they can enjoy unspoiled nature and landscapes, environmental quality of goods or services(clean air and water), a healthy community with low crime rate, thriving and authentic local culture and traditions.

SUSTAINABLE TOURISM STRATEGY

Analysis of Status-quo

- Development of previous tourism management or related strategies for the specific area (What can be used? Has it been implemented? Which lessons are to be learnt?)
- A stakeholder analysis (Who has an interest in sustainable tourism development? Who are the main actors?)
- Facts and figures of the local educational system, economical and social structure

- Anecdotal and traditional knowledge

Methods for collecting this information:

- Interviews with stakeholders
- Questionnaires distributed and collected by e-mail, fax or personally in oder to compile standardised data and perform a statistical analysis
- Invitation to focus group meetings (*e.g.* meetings on environmental education, biodiversity management, good governance and fisheries)
- Literature search in the local library and the internet

Strategy Development

A Sustainable Tourism Strategy is based on the information collected . It defines the priority issues, the stakeholder community, the potential objectives and a set of methodologies to reach these objectives.

These include:

- Conservation of specific coastal landscapes or habitats that make the area attractive or are protected under nature conservation legislation
- Development of regionally specific sectors of the economy that can be interlinked with the tourism sector (*e.g.* production of food specialities and handicrafts)
- Maximising local revenues from tourism investments
- Enabling self-determined cultural development in the region, etc.

Action Plan

The Action Plan describes the steps needed to implement the strategy and addressing a number of practical questions such as: which organizations will take up which activities, over what time frame, by what means and with which resources? As the actions have to be considered on the basis of regional circumstances, there is no standard action plan for all. However, Action Plans usually include measures in the following fields:

- *Administration: e.g.* Promotion of co-operation between sectors and of cross-sectorial development models; involving local people in drafting tourism policy and decisions
- *Socio-economical sector: e.g.* Promoting local purchasing of food and building material; setting up networks of local producers for better marketing; development of new products to meet the needs of tourists, etc.
- *Environment: e.g.* Improving control and enforcement of environmental standards (noise, drinking water, bathing water, waste-water treatment, etc.); identification and protection of endangered habitats; creation of buffer zones around sensitive natural areas; prohibition of environmentally harmful sports in jeopardised regions; strict application of Environmental Impact Assessment (EIA) andStrategic

Environmental Assessment procedures on all tourism related projects and programmes

- *Knowledge:* Training people involved in coastal tourism about the value of historical heritage; environmental management; training protected area management staff in nature interpretation; raising environmental awareness among the local population; introducing a visitors information programme (including environmental information)

CONCLUSIONS

During the last century, beaches have completely reversed their role: they have become the driving force behind the economic welfare instead of just being an inhospitable place. However, the demographic pressure and the overuse of the territory related to those factors, in the hinterland (dams in the rivers, farming and tourism) as well as in the proper beach (sewage discharge, dry goods extraction and crops) have caused a general decrease in the contribution of sediments to the beaches with a continental or a marine origin. It is hard to find a unique solution for all those problems.

However, it should be absolutely essential to follow these points:

- First, an Integrated Coastal Zone Management
- Second, a better dissemination of the existing information should be achieved. For that purpose, a better coordination of the existing governmental bodies that deal with coastal management is necessary.
- Third, an improvement of the environmental education is essential for a sustainable development of the coast.

ENVIRONMENTALLY SUSTAINABLE CRUISE TOURISM: A REALITY CHECK

Since the early 1970s sustainable development has become a unifying concept for environmental planning. Politically, sustainability ideals have been given prominence at the UNCED Conference in 1987, the Earth Summit in 1992 and through implementation of Agenda 21. However, the delivery of sustainable development, translating theory into practice, has proved elusive. The concept makes important links between environmental conservation and socio-economics (*i.e.* quality of life) but contentious issues include the balance between hard and soft sustainability; how the environment is valued; and how to address the dominance of unsustainable vested interests.

These issues extend to the debate about the future of tourism . Tourism by its very nature is a resource dependent industry and some commentators argue that sustainable tourism is unachievable given the industry's ability to pollute and consume resources. This view has been summarised as follows: "Tourism contains the seed of its own destruction; tourism can kill tourism, destroying the very environmental attractions which visitors come to a location to experience". Alternatively, in theory, tourism can embrace sustainability principles by having regard for environmental carrying capacity, social responsibility and the integration of tourism with local peoples' wishes. In 1992 Tourism Concern and Worldwide Fund for Nature defined sustainable tourism as tourism and associated infrastructure that both now and in the future :

1. operates within natural capacities for the regeneration and future productivity of resources—natural, social and cultural;

- Recognises the contribution that people and communities, customs and lifestyles past and present, make to the tourism experience;
- Accepts that these people must have an equitable share in the economic benefits of tourism; and
- Is guided by the wishes of all stakeholders, especially local people and communities in host areas.

Much uncertainty concerning sustainable tourism has resulted from confusion with the related terms of ecotourism and responsible tourism. As a result sustainable tourism has proved difficult to define and, as a consequence, often difficult to implement and evaluate. Within the broad framework of sustainability the tourism industry has, nevertheless, made efforts to establish green credentials.

Green Globe 21, the World Travel and Tourism Council's environmental management programme for travel and tourism companies and destinations, has developed its own certificate, based on ISO 14001, in an attempt to highlight leading edge initiatives. The International Hotels Environment Initiative (IHEI), which seeks to reduce consumption and waste, is another example of a positive environmental change agent. However, on balance, it has been suggested that while action based on the wider use of techniques such as environmental auditing by tourist firms can bring incremental improvements in environmental performance, in terms of sustainable tourism, this is likely to be from one sub-optimal position to another .

To date relatively little work on sustainable marine tourism has been undertaken, although exceptional marine sites, such as the Great Barrier Reef, have developed comprehensive sustainable tourism strategies and management plans .

This is a sector which is growing fast and which will present significant future environmental management challenges. Orams , when defining marine tourism, emphasised the importance of access to the marine environment and our dependence on equipment to enjoy water-based leisure experiences. Ultimately, he argued, the supply of marine activities and destinations will be constrained by environmental quality.

The aim of this paper is therefore to review the environmental sustainability of cruise tourism, which represents a major activity within the marine tourism sector.

Cruise Tourism

Discussions of cruising in the context of its origin, change and development have been the subject of other studies, which explain that cruise tourism has developed in phases. At its inception, in the 1920s, cruising was the preferred mode of travel for the world's social elite. Post World War 2 cruising declined, losing trade to passenger aircraft. However, the latter part of the 20th century has witnessed a tremendous revival. Cruise companies have aggressively targeted different market segments, attracted younger passengers, offered fly cruise options, raised cruise capacities and changed cruise durations, prices and itineraries. Reviews of this global phenomenon have demonstrated an 8 per cent annual growth since 1980, and in 1997 cruise tourism catered for 8.5 million customers . A year later passenger numbers increased to an estimated 9.5 million carried by a worldwide fleet of 223 ships. Currently three major companies, Carnival Corporation, Royal Caribbean International and P and O Princess Cruises, dominate the business. A recent industry analysis cited the launch of Disney Cruise Line's first ship Disney Magic (indicating the influence of family cruising); industry orders for new cruise ships in excess of $ 9 million USD; and the dominance of the Caribbean, Mediterranean and Alaska as principal destinations to be key points which reflect the state of the modern cruise tourism business .

Crannell considered the development of more super-mega cruise ships as the main way the industry will develop into the 21st century.

These new generation of ships are:

- Reliant on economies of scale (*i.e.* the mass tourism market);
- At the cutting edge of design and technical innovation; and
- Offer a multifaceted recreational shipboard experience.

Not untypical is the Grand Princess which at a cost of US$ 450 million accommodates 3000 passengers and a crew of 1100. She boasts comprehensive amenities including luxury sports facilities and virtual reality simulation distractions for passengers' amusement . Even larger ships, such as Royal Caribbean's Voyager of the Seas and P and O's Oceana, with increased passenger capacity, aim to generate further economies of scale and higher profits. The industry predicts a phenomenal growth to 10 per cent of market share (13 million passengers) by 2005. This optimism is based on assumptions of latent demand and the development of new destination markets.

It has also been argued that cruise tourism destinations benefit from potentially dramatic economic benefits. This includes passenger and crew spending together with fees charged for dockage, fresh water and any head tax. Cruise ships also have to be provisioned with fuel and consumables. As a result US$ 10,000 average daily spend from a cruise ship visit is not unrealistic. Dwyer and Forsyth provided a framework to evaluate these economic factors and substantiated the benefits using an Australian case study.

Geographically the world can be mapped into cruise regions reflecting different densities of demand . One result of the boom in cruise tourism, however, is congestion at traditional destination venues. In 1998 the Caribbean received 50 per cent of total world capacity cruise tourism placement . Many established Caribbean destinations receive more cruises than stopover tourists. In response, cruise lines are considering multi-dimensional expansion to different cruise excursion destinations in future.

Carnival Cruise Lines business development plans, for example, include:

- Development of 'new geographical markets'—through Airtours and Costa Links;
- 'Migrating to better products'—through Holland America Line; and
- 'Attracting new lifestyles'—through Windstar cruises.

Some hitherto less popular traditional locations, such as the Asia-Pacific, are predicted to grow from a small base . Other destinations are completely new. For example, from 2002 P and O are offering cruises to South America with visits to Machu Picchu, the Patagonian Fjords and the beaches of Rio de Janeiro.

Against this background of growing popularity, increasing ship size and sophistication, high profits and changing geography, Dowling and Vasudavan cite 'embracing both natural and social environmental issues' as one of the major challenges facing the cruise industry in the new millennium. Some commentators have argued that cruise tourism, being a formally organised and spatially confined leisure activity, can be viewed as a sustainable and sociologically harmless option . Others contest this, highlighting problems associated with waste generation and disposal, together with pressures exerted on fragile environments and host communities . To date, however, no holistic sustainability assessment has been attempted.

Environmental Considerations

A fundamental difficulty with sustainability assessments is that of quantifying and costing environmental impacts in the same way that economic benefits can be presented. Furthermore, with marine activities it is particularly difficult to allocate impacts to specific sources. For example, air pollution from seagoing shipping in general, not just cruise ships, is thought to be responsible for a large percentage of the sulphur found in the atmosphere above the oceans. European research to quantify ship emissions more precisely, including in-port emissions, is on-going .

The environmental impact of cruise tourism however, can at least be categorised using a life-cycle analysis (LCA) approach. This is a methodology, more typically applied to a manufactured product, but was adapted by British Airways (BA)/UK CEED to study the impacts of tourism on the Seychelles . Impacts associated with each stage of the 'life-cycle' of a holiday product.

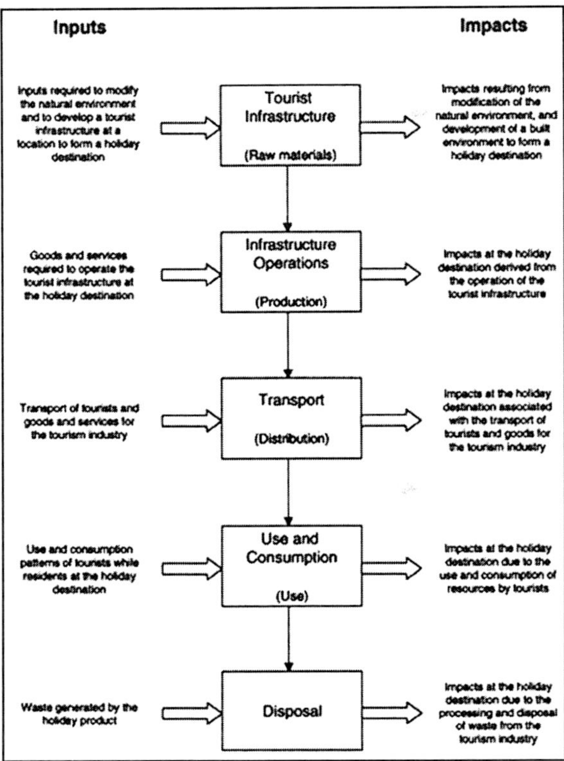

Fig. LCA of a Holiday Product.

Using the LCA methodology cruise tourism impacts include:

- Infrastructure impacts such as ship construction, the creation of cruise passenger terminal facilities and berthing access requirements. Modifications to the natural and built environment to enable destinations to serve as a cruise line destination involve loss of natural habitat, exploitation of local construction materials and changes to local coastal wave and sediment patterns.
- Operational impacts involving the use of energy, water and air quality pollution, and impacts on the environment such as antifouling and accidental or deliberate physical damage to marine ecosystems (*e.g.* anchor damage).
- Distribution impacts associated with tourists' travel and the logistics of supplying a cruise liner with provisions. Whilst this applies principally to air travel impacts associated with transferring people to and from departure and destination points, it also includes consideration of the environmental carrying capacity of destinations and the requirement for landside transport links.
- Use impacts which comprise the cultural impact of wealthy tourists and overcrowding created by large numbers of visitors at one

destination, together with pressures on cruise destination environments including, for example, water consumption, use of chemicals and detergents, the impacts of recreational activities on wildlife such as disturbance and littering, and pressures on endangered species through exploitation for gifts and curios.

- Waste impacts including those related to relevant categories regulated by the International Maritime Organisation (IMO). The International Convention for the Prevention of Pollution from Ships (MARPOL Protocol) currently contains six annexes, four of which pertain to wastes from ships. Oils, garbage, sewage, plastics and hazardous substances require adequate waste reception facilities, waste handling and disposal.

DISCUSSION

The projected increase in cruise tourism, combined with the environmental considerations, raises a number of key sustainability issues. These are considered below in terms of different strategies and management initiatives that both operators and destinations can employ to fulfil their sustainable development obligations. Whether these initiatives are being implemented, and thus their potential effectiveness, is then examined on the basis of evidence available from secondary sources. Clearly tourists themselves also have a duty to care for the environment but in many ways this too can be engendered or heightened by responsible operators and destinations.

Operators

A summary of environmental sustainability strategies and various management initiatives available to cruise tourism operators, adapted from Orams, is presented inTable 1.

Table. Environmental Sustainability Strategies and Management Initiatives for Cruise Operators.

Strategy	Management initiative
Physical	Vary itinerary
	Limit passenger numbers
	Destination rehabilitation/conservation projects
Regulatory	Corporate environmental policy
	Environmental management systems
	Promotion of environmental practices
Economic	Full environmental cost accounting
	Investment in 'clean' technologies
	'Rewards' for environmental awareness
	Positive use of tourist revenue
Educational	Liaison with destinations re: sustainability
	Corporate environmental reports
	Codes of practice
	Dissemination of good practice

Varying Itineraries to Avoid Exceeding Carrying Capacity

Generalised secondary evidence suggests that cruise lines are aware of the fact that their operations can have a profound impact on destinations. Chronic environmental degradation as a direct result of cruise tourism, particularly in popular destinations such as the Caribbean, suggests that cruise itineraries are yet to be determined by operators on the basis of sustainability issues.

Uebersax described a complex downside to the cruise industry in the Caribbean including:

- Pollution of sea floors, harbours and coastal areas;
- Degradation of scarce water resources;
- Destruction of coral reef habitat;
- Public health concerns ashore; and
- Pressures resulting from waste disposal problems for communities already unable to cope with their own domestic commercial municipal waste.

However, rather than reducing the number of visitors to the Caribbean, visitor numbers are rising rapidly elsewhere too. Princess Cruises, for example, now sail to six continents.

In addition to the Caribbean, according to their web site, destinations include Alaska, the Panama Canal, Europe, Mexican Riviera, South America, South Pacific, Hawaii/Tahiti, Asia, India, Africa, the Holy Land, Canada/New England, Bermuda and world voyages. In many places cruises are combined with land tours and associated infrastructure, such as riverside wilderness lodges in Alaska. In future itineraries are likely to include hitherto less popular destinations but this will be in addition to, rather than instead of, well established cruise venues.

Passenger Numbers

As explained previously cruise tourism is establishing different market segments. The new super-mega cruise ships are designed to take huge complements of passengers. Smaller, more traditional ships cater for niche markets.

Mass cruise tourism has been likened to all-inclusive resort experiences, with the cruise ship itself providing the holiday experience rather than any destinations to be visited .

It could be argued that environmentally sound cruises, perhaps for which tourists also pay some form of 'green levy', should be encouraged to cater for increasing numbers as a more sustainable option than despoiling fragile terrestrial destinations. As yet, however, there is no evidence that operators are prepared to charge an 'environmental premium'; indeed competition is resulting in reduced fares and special deals, and passenger target numbers envisage substantial increases.

Destination Rehabilitation/Conservation Projects

Although Royal Caribbean, for example, has set up an Ocean Fund to support marine conservation and oceanic environmental research, investment by cruise operators in destination rehabilitation projects is the exception rather than the rule. A specific example of a cruise line company, which has invested in an ecological restoration project, is the rehabilitation of Cayman coral reef ecosystem by Holland American Line. Following accidental damage to a major reef by the cruise ship Maasdam in 1996, Holland America Line undertook a successful restoration that involved salvaging damaged reef fragments, removing rubble, reattaching living corals and subsequent monitoring. Only some 25–30 per cent of the restored reef has survived but there is positive evidence of coral recruitment. This example is a high profile incident where the damage is clearly attributable to one operator but there is little evidence that cruise operators are tackling the effects of cumulative environmental impacts.

Environmental Management

The 'flag state' in which any cruise ship is registered is responsible for certifying compliance with international pollution prevention standards. To complement regulations the adoption of a corporate environmental policy, environmental management systems, environmental auditing, screening of suppliers and corporate environmental reporting are now standard in many resource dependant industries.

Whilst being very much compliance driven, much of this drive towards more environmentally sound operating standards depends on corporate commitment. The appointment of William Reilly, former US Environmental Protection Agency (EPA) Administrator, to oversee Royal Caribbean's environmental activities is an example of such commitment by a cruise operator. Published environmental policies, such as P and O's Health, Safety, Welfare and Environment Group Policy Statement, publicly affirm the importance now given to minimising any adverse environmental impacts.

Waste management planning is a key issue. Business generally is currently under pressure to adopt waste policies that move waste generation up the waste hierarchy by prioritising waste reduction and encouraging reuse and recycling rather than disposal options. Uebersax suggested that the average cruise ship produces 1 kg of burnable waste, 0.5 kg food waste and 1 kg glass and tin waste per person per day. The Bluewater Network Petition, initiated by a coalition of 53 US environmental non-governmental organisations, concluded that cruise ships represent 'point sources of enormous volumes of wastes which can have significant impacts on the marine environment and public health' [31 p.7]. Evidence submitted by the Network to the US EPA in 2000 stated that a typical cruise ship can generate an estimated 1,000,000 gallons of grey water on a 1-

week voyage, as well as significant amounts of hazardous chemical from on board printing, photo processing and dry cleaning operations.

More sustainable waste disposal options are being adopted by cruise operators including recycling targets; zero discharge of hazardous wastes and cleaning chemicals; installation of improved devices for separating oil from bilge water and wastewater prior to discharge; better treatment of 'grey' waste water; and the installation of on-board waste management systems and equipment. In 2001 the International Council of Cruise Lines (ICCL), an industry trade association that represents the interests of 17 passenger cruise lines in the North American cruise market and more than 60 cruise industry suppliers, adopted a new set of mandatory waste management practices and procedures on its members' behalf .

Positive moves include:

- Supply chain considerations—introducing more environmental-friendly and reusable products;
- Materials recovery—enabling separation and recycling of packaging, glass and plastics thus reducing the production of incinerator ash;
- Controlled disposal of toxic waste products such as silver from photo processing, chlorinated dry cleaning fluids and sludge contaminated filter materials;
- Pulp processor maceration of organic waste (mainly food waste); and
- Co-generation incinerators.

Safety Management System (SMS) Plans, which contain many of the elements of an environmental management system, have been implemented by some of the major cruise line companies. SMS Plans are certified in accordance with IMO's International Safety Management (ISM) Code.

In 1998 the P and O Group produced a second corporate environmental report (CER) containing environmental performance data at a corporate level. The latter comprised total group impact in terms of waste generated and the percentage recycled, oil consumption and carbon dioxide emissions contributing to global warming, ozone depletion, air pollution (sulphur oxides), marine pollution (oil spillage) and resource use (water) figures. This CER, which is available both in hard copy and on the web, is among the latest generation of such reports. It acknowledges impacts, sets out clear environmental policies and establishes specific annual targets for environmental improvement.

Examples of these targets for 1998/1999 included:

- Fuel use minimisation campaign to effect a 1 per cent overall reduction;
- Replacement of Halon fire fighting systems;
- 10 per cent per capita reduction in water consumption and studies into the feasibility of recycling laundry water and air conditioning condensation to reduce water consumption;

- Reduction of on-shore disposal of oily sludge by 10 per cent; and
- Phasing out of the most harmful volatile organic compounds (VOCs).

The impact of non-biodegradable anti-foulings, endocrine disrupting chemicals, which adversely effect the hormonal functioning of marine wildlife, is a specific problem for the shipping industry generally. Phasing out the use of tributyltin (TBT) anti-foulings on all ships by 2008 is under consideration by the IMO. Greenpeace recently undertook a direct action protest to highlight this issue, targeting the Cunard flagship Queen Elizabeth 2 (QE2). In future, possibly in response to the Greenpeace protest, the QE2 will receive TBT-free material .

Other examples of good practice, highlighted by Dowling and Vasudavan , include Royal Caribbean International's 'Save the Waves' policy; Holland America Line's 'Seagoing Environmental Awareness' on board programme; and the Cunard QE2's 'Garbage Management Plan'.

Technological Improvements to Reduce Operational Impacts

Evidence from other sectors of industry is that increasingly companies are investing in 'best available technology not exceeding excessive cost' (BATNEEC) to comply with environmental legislation or pre-empt such legislation.

Examples of this within the cruise industry are evident, particularly for newly commissioned vessels.

The introduction of new Azipod azimuthing electronic propulsion systems offers a high system redundancy, increased manoeuverability, fuel savings and improved handling in an emergency . Gas turbines, hitherto confined to the world's navies because of their inherent expense, are being fitted by Royal Caribbean in two new series of ships .

Gas turbines create less noise and can reduce exhaust emissions by up to 90 per cent. Other examples of technology investment include exhaust gas cleaning devices; a new generation of oil water separators; and homogenisers to reduce nitrogen oxides (NOx) emissions.

Newer vessels, incorporating technologies able to meet stricter pollution standards, are more likely to be able to comply with Lloyds Register's environmental class designation—Environmental Protection Rules for the Control of Operational Pollution or EP Rules—and benefit from any associated reductions in port dues .

Rewards for Environmental Awareness

Rewards for environmental awareness are unusual, but may become more common place in response to incentives to comply with legislation, as suggested by a US$ 250,000 reward to passengers who witnessed and video taped a trail of plastic waste sacks being dumped into the sea by Princess Cruises.

Educational Initiatives

There is some evidence that more conscientious and environmentally aware cruise operators, operating in specific regions, supply behavioural codes of practice to crew and customers, together with lectures and guides at landing sites. An analysis of tourism impacts in Antarctica, differentiated between smaller ships offering ecotourism and larger operations with an emphasis on sightseeing rather than education . However, the overriding emphasis within the main operators' literature is on conspicuous consumption with little or no mention of environmental stewardship.

Destinations

A summary of environmental sustainability strategies and various management initiatives available to cruise tourism destinations, also adapted from Orams.

Table. Environmental Sustainability Strategies and Management Initiatives for Cruise Destinations.

Strategy	Management initiative
Physical	Facility placement
	Facility design
	Sacrifice areas
Regulatory	Limit visitor numbers
	Close areas to activities/uses
Economic	Differential fees
	Damage bonds
	Fines
	Rewards
	Promotion of local produce
Educational	Printed material
	Signs
	Guided walks/talks
	Liaison with operators

How can Destinations Manage the Impacts of Cruise Tourism?

The 'port state' can conduct its own examinations to verify a visiting ship's compliance with international standards. Nevertheless, operational waste impacts on destinations are a major concern. In 2000, for example, the Central Council of the Tlingit and Haida Indian Tribes of Alaska passed a resolution citing the threat posed by cruise line discharges to subsistence foods . In tropical waters coral competes with sewage for oxygenated water. Traditionally, for subsistence economies in these areas, the ocean has been able to flush away sewage produced by relatively small populations. Mass marine tourism requires proper ship-generated waste-reception facilities. The Wider Caribbean, for example, is designated as a 'Special Area' under MARPOL 73/78 Annex V, and the IMO has initiated a regional programme to improve waste management systems and invest in MARPOL compliant bins and barges. A strong case can be made for restricting cruise landfalls to the urban coast, particularly for home ports and much visited destinations, with a properly certified mature waste industry with very limited stopovers at rural destinations in order to maintain their exclusivity and environmental integrity.

Some US States (*e.g.* Florida) are pursuing Memoranda of Understanding and agreeing Codes of Conduct with the cruise ship industry as a way to promote better environmental behaviour. Tourism management strategies and management plans are also perceived to be crucial to the effective stewardship of cruise tourism destinations. The Cayman Islands, for example, with a host population of 33,000, received approximately 600,000 days visits from cruise ship passengers in 1998. Of these an estimated 28 per cent participated in diving activities. The Cayman Islands rely on Marine Parks Regulations, enacted in 1986, to control recreational fishing, boat speeds, anchoring and in-water activities. Zoning plans restrict marine activities around each island and dive boats are licensed and their capacity is limited.

. Which Destinations are Environmentally Unsuitable?

The environmental carrying capacity of destinations is an important factor. To this end the authorities in Alaska have determined a finite number of allocated cruise ship slots to the region. The Cayman Islands Government is similarly considering the creation of permanent moorings for cruise ships. Currently, at this popular destination, all cruise liners are required to anchor in Hog Sty Bay off the Grand Cayman capital of George Town, and the number of cruise ship passengers who may visit Grand Cayman on any one day is limited to 6000 . Evidence suggests, however, that in other destinations carrying capacity is being ignored. For example, plans for a major new port complex, capable of taking 660 cruise liners and 1.6 million tourists a year, on the British Caribbean islands of Turks and Caicos have been reported by the media . If correct, the scale of these proposed infrastructure requirements and the need to import over 6000 workers from Haiti and Dominica imposes both threats to wildlife and attendant social problems. Schemes of this nature are clearly environmentally unsustainable.

Economic Measures

Some destinations are beginning to secure substantial fines for environmental damage. For example, in June 1998 Holland America Line were fined US$ 2 million for an illegal discharge of oily bilge water in Alaska's Inside Passage that occurred in 1994. Royal Caribbean Cruises were fined an unprecedented US$ 18 million on pleading guilty to 21 felony counts of violating federal water pollution laws in 1999. This involved deliberate dumping of waste oil and hazardous chemicals into US harbours and coastal areas. The State of Alaska has subsequently filed a civil lawsuit against Royal Caribbean Cruises who could face fines of US$ 100,000 plus penalties of US$ 10,000 per violation per day. The fact that all these examples relate to the US is significant. In 2000 the Bluewater Network Petition, put pressure on the US EPA to take a more active role in monitoring cruise ships, prompting new proposals and regulations for environmental enforcement. These include an EPA Cruise Ship White Paper and prospective Cruise Ship Discharges Assessment Report , the US Coast Guard's 'Operation Cruise Watch' and State governments' initiatives in Alaska, Florida and California. As yet, however, there are no indications that less developed countries are prepared to apply the same level of control. And even in North America, despite progress with respect to environmental compliance, the US General Accounting Office (GAO) has identified a continued need for improvement . Concern about over-capacity has prompted some destinations to introduce passenger head taxes. These vary considerably. Bermuda currently actively limits cruise ships and imposes the highest cruise passenger head tax set at US$ 63. The Bahamas have set tax at US$ 15. And voters in Alaska's capital city Juneau, which receives 600,000 cruise ship passenger visits per year, are expected to be in favour of a US$ 5-per-passenger head tax to offset environmental impacts. Whether these taxes are actually used for environmental amelioration is questionable and difficult to verify.

Another economic issue is associated with a perceived lack of cruise-ship related spending in local communities . The level of economic benefit accruing to the destination is contested. Flag State Control, whereby cruise operators do not pay national taxes, mitigates against intra-societal equity on the basis that cruise lines retain all the profits of the operation, benefiting from the oceans as a common resource and 'free good'. Figures quoted by the industry are often confined to a small group of stakeholders; in other words the self-contained nature of cruise ships can exacerbate 'leakage' of tourist revenue. A vivid illustration of this being taken to extremes is Disney Cruise Lines purchase of their own destination at Castaway Cay. On the other hand, an analysis in the Caribbean, which compared leakage from stopover visitors with cruise visitors, concluded that cruise passengers are more likely to spend on low-leakage activities such as sightseeing and handicraft shopping . This is an area where more detailed and destination specific research is currently limited , and where, for example, issues such as the risk of economic dependency on tourism should also be evaluated.

Can Educational Management Tools Help Destination use Impacts?

Low-impact messages which attempt to influence visitor behaviour are perceived as good practice . Marion and Rogers examined the use of different communication media as part of an integrated strategy directed at cruise visitors to the Virgin Islands National Park. The United Nations Environment Programme (UNEP), for example, has recently launched simple new communication tools to help protect coral reefs . In future interactive on-board television will provide destinations with an opportunity to incorporate subtle environmental messages aimed at educating and influencing shore excursions.

CONCLUSION

Sustainable tourism is a contentious subject, which has received considerable academic scrutiny.

In practice it can be concluded that:

- Tourist operators, perhaps through fear of increased regulation, are gradually introducing more environmental considerations.
- Some destinations are adopting strategies and management plans but this is still largely confined to examples of good practice and individual projects.
- Tourists as consumers have largely failed to exert the fundamental pressure necessary to ensure real environmental improvements.

The health of the oceans is critical to the future of the planet, and the 21st century will see rapid growth of tourism based on marine resources. Cruise tourism provides the means for large numbers of tourists to make use of the oceans and the impact of cruise activities and associated infrastructure will increasingly require management solutions. Furthermore, to be regarded as sustainable tourism, cruise tourism must also deliver enduring improvements in social welfare.

Whilst cruise tourism presents a potential market opportunity for destinations, mobile mass tourism challenges sustainable tourism ideals. *Evidence from this sector to date suggests:*

- The need to continue to take a long-term view fostering holistic integrated management planning involving international agencies, cruise line operators and host communities;
- The need for operators to continue to invest in and promote the Best Possible Environmental Option (BPEO);
- The need for political will to safeguard destinations, given the proven adverse impacts of poorly managed cruise tourism;
- The need for greater profit sharing between cruise line shareholders and destination communities; and
- The need for both operators and destinations to raise their customers' environmental awareness.

A particular concern is the current disparity between developed and less developed countries in terms of destinations' control of and interface with the cruise line industry. International regulatory mechanisms are in place but better universal implementation and enforcement is needed. Strict operational requirements supported by monitoring and surveillance in Alaskan waters, for example, contrast with much less visible environmental protection being demonstrated in the Caribbean. This is exacerbated by lack of infrastructure, such as the severe shortage of waste facilities in many less developed countries. Currently the major drive to achieve more comprehensive waste management practices is being led by the US. Sustainable development requires attention to environmental quality and equality. Sustainable cruise tourism requires the enforcement of an environmental protection 'level playing field' across the world's oceans and between the world's marine tourism destinations, in partnership with all the cruise line operators—big and small.

8

Community Economics of Cruise Tourism

Cruise tourism is of small, but increasing, importance in Central America and the Caribbean, is of substantial importance in particular port locations, and is being touted as a desirable local economic development opportunity within the region. Tourism, like all engines of economic development, has desirable and undesirable features.

Little objective research about cruise tourism economics and community economic development exists. The results that are available appear to be rather site specific, in part due to strong differences between terminal main (dis-)embarkation ports and semi-terminal (primarily for tourist visitation) ports (McKee and Mamoozadeh, 1994). Johnson (2002), citing conflicting reports on purchasing patterns among cruise tourists (Hall and Braithwaite, 1990; Henthorne, 2000), argues that the specifics of the community economic impact of cruise tourism constitute an important hole in the literature base on the industry. Most recently, the Barbados Minister of Tourism strongly affirmed the need for an independent environmental economic assessment of the industry on and in the Caribbean region (CTO, 2004) and no studies exist focusing on the cruise industry in Costa Rica.

A thorough understanding of the industry facilitates recognition of the potentials and pitfalls of a chosen driver of economic development. Economic issues surrounding the cruise ship industry include direct and potential impacts on the port authorities and port communities, hidden environmental impacts on marine and coastal ecosystems, development alternatives to cruise ships for port communities, distributional impacts and cultural implications of cruise tourism development and socio-economic impacts of disembarking crew members, in addition to the typically tracked tourist expenditures.

This paper illustrates an economic approach to understanding the cruise tourism industry as a driver of economic development through a preliminary analysis of the industry in Costa Rica. The objective of this approach is to describe the role and activities of the cruise ship industry in Costa Rica and identify sources of economic benefit and cost such that more informed local policy decisions about the cruise ship tourism might be made and a more comprehensive enquiry into this important question might be initiated in the near future. This approach should be applicable to communities wherever cruise tourism currently exists or is under consideration to be included in the portfolio of community economic activities.

APPROACH

Cruise tourism influences all four aspects of the tourism market: transportation, accommodation, tourism services and tour operations (McKee, 1988). The cruise industry can provide either complementary or competing goods and services to local providers. Four principal economic agents are of interest to this study: cruise tourists, cruise ship employees, port communities and countries, and the cruise company itself. A number of particular challenges in estimating the economic impact of cruise ships have been identified: 1) The crew is non-local, so they do not pay income tax in the locality, their jobs do not "count" towards local economic development, and there is significant leakage of their wage expenditures to other ports and their home countries; 2) The cruise liner ownership is non-local and corporate, so they do not typically pay host nation income taxes, nor are they required to adhere to local labour standards or a number of other laws, and are likely to invest their profits outside of the port region or country; And 3) for some tourist visits the cruise is a part, but not the sole purpose of the trip, making it challenging to establish which expenditures can be attributed to the cruise industry (Braun, et al., 2002).

A mix of primary and secondary data collection, including expert interviews and tourist surveys, descriptive and econometric analysis are appropriately applied to these challenges in order to illuminate socio-economic issues and information surrounding cruise tourism as an engine of economic development in Central America and the Caribbean. We illustrate general approaches to the community economic analysis of cruise tourism through preliminary work undertaken in Costa Rica.

Personal interviews and secondary data constitute the primary information sources for this first estimation of the effects of cruise tourism on Costa Rica. These sources of information are appropriately used in other regional locations as well. For various parts of the study, detailed below, artisans, travel agencies, port administrators, municipal officials, tourism agencies, university personnel and others were interviewed or otherwise consulted in the port communities of Limon, Puntarenas and Caldera. The Vice Minister of Public Security, tour operators who work directly with the ships, port agents and researchers at the university of Costa Rica were also interviewed for this research. In addition, cruise passenger data collected by the Costa Rican Institute of Tourism (ICT) were analyzed. The data for this study were collected from June through August 2004. More statistically rigourous approaches can be applied at each juncture in order to improve the confidence with which we can extrapolate results to broader populations and make policy recommendations. Recommended applications of appropriate economic valuation methods including travel costs method (TCM), the contingent valuation method (CVM) and export base analysis (EBA), providing complementary and supplementary information to our first estimates are detailed below.

CRUISE INDUSTRY GROWTH AND REGIONAL ECONOMIC DEVELOPMENT

We begin with a review of the information available describing the role and growth of the cruise ship industry within the broader context of the tourism industry in Central America and the Caribbean. We use published information and secondary data sources for this overview, supplemented by personal interviews with key informants within the industry.

In our subsequent analysis, cruise ship company personnel will be interviewed with regard to ship passenger capacity, total number of passengers on board, number of passengers disembarking at a particular location, and the number, type and value of tours and other port services sold on board. Similar information will be collected from ship personnel regarding ship employees. In addition, company personnel will be interviewed to reveal the nature and amount of local purchases undertaken by the ship itself as well as any payments made for port services, docking fees, or waste disposal.

PROFILE OF CRUISE TOURISTS

Next, we use data and information collected through surveys by the national tourism institute (ICT) of Costa Rica and other available secondary information, including promotional information provided by the industry on their web sites, to create a profile of the typical cruise trip involving Costa Rican ports of call.

In a more general approach, profiles of tourists and tourism of each country often can be collected from secondary data sources (*e.g.*, phone book, census, published and gray literature) and from interviews of national tourism authorities where necessary. Among the useful sorts of information to be collected include: the political economic history of cruise tourism and of tourism, national cruise tourism and tourism policy, the role of the cargo ship industry, and issues or concerns regarding (cruise) tourism as a driver of economic development that do not find themselves in the readily available secondary data (*e.g.*, drugs, crime, prostitution, unwelcome cultural change).

UNDERSTANDING CRUISE TOURIST EXPENDITURES

Third, we use ICT data to provide a preliminary description of cruise tourist expenditures in Costa Rica, creating a basis for a more detailed future study that would formally analyze tourist expenditures, their distribution locally, and their sensitivity to cost and service quality changes using the travel cost method (TCM).

The travel cost method (TCM) is a commonly employed analytical tool to facilitate understanding of the demand for tourism services. TCM employs surveys of tourists to obtain a profile of their actual trip expenditures and elicits sensitivity to an exogenous change in travel costs, demographic characteristics, and trip characteristics in order to derive a demand curve for tourism visitation. TCM would allow us to extrapolate survey results to broader populations, infer willingness to pay for tourism services, explore the effect of local, national, or industry policy changes on tourism behaviour and, therefore, economic impact.

In order to undertake a TCM of cruise tourism, we suggest a stratified random sample of cruise tourists should be interviewed upon their return to the ship after visiting the port of call. The 15-20 minute survey would ask tourists about their expenditures at that port of call, their (anticipated) expenditures on their entire trip, the sorts of activities they undertook at the port of call and on their trip, and some demographic information.

The information gleaned from the TCM would be combined with information collected from ship personnel and secondary information in order to estimate the total value of cruise tourism expenditures to the cruise ship industry and to the local economy. This information may be used to better understand the relative bargaining position, dependence or interdependence of these two principal stakeholder groups.

UNDERSTANDING CREW EXPENDITURES

TCM, when combined with interview and secondary information, is also appropriate to use to reveal cruise ship employees' purchasing behaviour while in port, preferences for goods and services, and sensitivity to changes in the quality or cost of those services. However, the survey instrument employed should be somewhat different and the demand curve derived will be distinct from that found for the cruise tourists, recognizing the potential for distinct preferences, demographics and budget constraints for employees relative to tourists.

ESTIMATING LOCAL ECONOMIC IMPACT

In addition to tourists and crew members, the ships themselves are a source of revenue and costs for port communities and demand for port community services. Port authority officials will be interviewed regarding port policies and cruise-liners. Information will be collected regarding services provided and fees charged. Infrastructural needs and demands of cruise ships relative to cargo ships and any local cargo ship policies affecting the cruise industry. Basic information regarding the frequency, size and seasonality of cruise-liners will also be collected.

Although a great deal of economic impact information can be derived from travel cost surveys, it is both important and useful to obtain an understanding of the economic contribution of cruise tourism from the perspective of local businesses for a number of reasons. The TCM survey will reveal expenditures in the port country, but not necessarily the port community. If the distribution of the costs and benefits of cruise tourism development between the port community and the country as a whole do not fall equitably, there may be a potential need or justification for corrective social, environmental or economic policy. Secondly, not all local expenditures remain in the local economy. The size of the local multiplier is dependent upon the amount of indirect and induced local purchases driven by the direct purchases of tourists. For example, 1983 Caribbean port expenditures by cruise ship passengers ranged from $16.50 in St. Christopher and Nevis to $35 in Antigua and Barbuda (McKee, 1988). The apparent differences in economic impact per visitor may be exacerbated or eliminated if the differences in purchasing behaviour are from products with substantial local content or are from imported luxury goods. The local multiplier for cruise ship expenditures can be understood through a survey of port area businesses.

Based on anecdotal evidence, we reason that the vast majority of tourists who choose to disembark, but who do not purchase a tour, will travel less than a mile from the ship. Moreover, services provided directly to the ships are likely to be located quite near the port. As such, we propose to produce a categorized compendium of businesses found within a mile of the port and to survey a representative sample of these businesses by type to reveal their relative dependence on tourism in general and cruise tourism in particular as well as the size and seasonality of this dependence. Local economic impact and multiplier estimates can be derived from this approach. Therefore, the likely economic impact of policy changes or exogenous changes in tourism behaviour can also be derived from these estimates.

ESTABLISHING AND ESTIMATING OTHER SOURCES OF BENEFITS AND COSTS DUE TO CRUISE TOURISM

The cruise industry poses a significant source of potential pollution and environmental risk. In addition, the industry may be responsible for socially unsavory impacts of tourism development that would provide valuable information to local decision-makers, whether or not the information is derived specifically from that locality.

For example, few ex ante approaches exist for estimating the potential cost of potential impacts of pollution due to cruise ships, cargo ships or other types of development. In all such cases, we are dependent upon case history, and a literature review to establish what has happened in the past, its probably impact and consequences, and to attempt to get a gauge of the likelihood of it happening in the future in a particular location. This is not an exact science by any means, but it is the best we have and valuable lessons and precautionary actions might be considered locally appropriate based upon those lessons learned. Such broad categories of considerations and concerns will be catalogued by this research. Where appropriate, the likelihood, extent and estimated impacts of these features will be derived from available information and used as a means to illustrate the issues.

ANALYSIS AND RESULTS

REGIONAL GROWTH OF THE CRUISE INDUSTRY

The long haul passenger jet destroyed the passenger shipping industry in the 1960s. Cruise ships made the jump from sea travel as transport to sea travel as leisure. Cruise tourism is now the fastest growing part of the tourism sector (Klein, 2002; TIES, 2004; McKee and Mamoozadeh, 1994). Cruise ships carried 500,000 passengers in 1970, some 8.5 million (6 million Americans) in 1997 (Economist, 1998) and about 9.8 million passengers in 2003 (BREA, 2004). The cruise industry accounts for 1.4 per cent of all international tourists, ranking 20th if the industry were a nation, and 2.7 per cent of global tourism receipts (8th) (Kester, 2002). In North America the number of people taking cruises doubled between 1990 and 2000 and Americans constitute some 72 per cent of the global cruise market, although cruising is becoming more popular with Europeans in recent years (Kester, 2002).

In 2002, the global cruise industry capacity was 183 vessels and about 213,000 berths growing at an annual rate of about 7 per cent (Kester, 2002). A more recent count of the global fleet of cruise ships is currently 220 ships, though the industry announced plans to increase that fleet by 25 per cent between 2000 and 2005. The cruise ship industry also plans 56-70 new terminals (docking points) in the US over the next 15 yrs (Blue Water News, 2004). Not only will there be more ships, but ship capacity is increasing as well. Older cruise liners typically had capacities of around 1,000 passengers. In 2002, the average cruise liner had 1,163 berths, weighed 43,000 tons, and was in service for about 15 yrs. The largest four cruise corporations have a generally younger (10 yrs) and larger (1,5000 berth average) fleet (Kester, 2002). A modern 70,000 tonne cruise liner can house 2,000 people, while a new 135,000 tonne ship can house 3,100.

Globally, eight companies dominated the industry in the late 1990s (Douglas and Douglas, 1999). Currently, it is controlled by two: Carnival Corporation and Royal Caribbean Cruise Lines. Carnival Corporation includes Carnival, Holland, Costa, Cunard, Windstar and Seaborn cruise companies. Royal Caribbean Cruise Lines includes RCI, Celebrity and Island cruise companies (Klein, 2003a). Carnival Corporation reported profits of $1.02 billion on revenues of $4.37 billion (30 per cent return on investment) in 2002, making it the most profitable leisure company in the world. Royal Caribbean reported $254 million in profits on $3.15 billion in revenues (9 per cent return), P and O Princess, $301 million on $2.45 billion (14 per cent), and Star Cruises, including Star, Norwegian and Orient cruise lines, reported $82.6 million in profits on $1.57 billion (6 per cent) in revenues (Klein, 2003a).

In 2003, P and O Princess became part of Carnival Corporation. Profits and total revenues for the top four cruise lines combined were $1.66 billion and $11.54 billion, respectively, or a 17 per cent industry level return on investment in 2002 (Klein, 2003a). Cruise ships typically enjoy 90-95 per cent occupancy rates, relative to the 70 per cent rates striven for in the hotel sector (Economist, 1998; Pattullo, 1996a). Despite, or perhaps resulting in, their profitability, both Carnival and Royal Caribbean are registered in "flag-of-convenience" nations, so they avoid many U.S. environmental and labour laws and don't pay U.S. corporate income tax (Klein, 2003a).

The cruise industry is heavily concentrated in the Caribbean, Alaska and the Mexican Riviera. Some 2/3 of the global cruise ship capacity is located in the Caribbean during the winter months (October-March) and about ¼ in the summer months (April-September). In 2002, Carnival Cruise Lines controlled 38 per cent of the market in the Caribbean and Mexican Riviera, Royal Caribbean commands 26 per cent, P and O Princess had 6 per cent and Star Cruises some 8 per cent of total passengers. With the merger between Carnival and P and O Princess in 2003, two carriers account for more than 2/3 of all cruises in the region. Between the winter and summer months, the global fleet shifts substantially towards Alaska (0-16 per cent), the Mediterranean (8 per cent-31 per cent), and Atlantic Europe (0-18 per cent)(Kester, 2002). The trend towards larger ships should increase rather than decrease this seasonality (McKee, 1988).

CRUISE TOURISM AS ECONOMIC DEVELOPMENT

McKee (1988), Fish and Gunther (1994) and others find a number of fairly unique concerns and opportunities with regard to the encouragement of cruise tourism as an engine of economic development. These concerns focus on local control and the distribution of local costs and benefits of cruise activities. We focus on the relationship between the industry and general economic development impacts on ports of call rather than on the specific issues covered in other sections.

First, communities and local businesses dependent upon cruise tourism must compete in an environment dominated by very few multi-national corporations. The local economy becomes dependent upon the economic conditions of international consumers and on the global economic opportunities available to the cruise ship industry, rather than local economic conditions. The dependence relationship between industry and locality is exacerbated by research findings indicating that there is a high degree of substitutability among sun and fun category tourism destinations (Caribbean Islands, southern Mexico, southern Europe) (Fish and Gunther, 1994). Such conditions reduce local volition, economic development alternatives and profit margins and increase potential local economic variability.

McKee (1988), McKee (1986) and McKee and Mamoozadeh (1994) argue that there may be some unique opportunities provided by cruise tourism as a driver of natural resource based economic development. For example, port calls create a brief taste of a location that may result in a longer visit in the future that may not have been otherwise considered. Gabe et al. (2003) find that the clientele served by cruise ships is at a substantial variance from the more typical Maine visitor. In addition, since cruise tourists bring their beds with them, environmentally and financially costly investment in local built infrastructure can be postponed or avoided entirely. Fewer local tourist services imply lower local dependence on tourist expenditures and, potentially, a more informed approach to further tourism development planning. However, it also implies lower local tourist expenditures, thus economic activity, and local multiplier effects.

Unfortunately, for many cruise destinations, though probably not Costa Rica, construction materials are largely imported and the better known resorts and hotels are foreign-owned. For example, Alaska, similar to many island economies, demonstrates high levels of leakage (wage, high cost of goods sold (low value added), and service), low levels of economic diversification and infrastructure development (McDowell Group Inc., 2000). The low degree of local value-added, or high degree of leakage out of the local economy, results in a relatively low amount of positive economic impact. Increasing the proportion of local content, or reducing the imported content, of tourism services, increases local multipliers.

Most items in "duty free" shops have very little local content. Wilkinson (1989) estimates that 40 per cent of money spent in Caribbean Island economies immediately leaks out to multinational hotel chains and airlines, resulting in abysmal income multiplier estimates of 0.58-1.195 (Fish and Gunther, 1994). These, and the few other published results that are not derived from consulting firms, have lead researchers to strongly question the accuracy of the 2.5 multiplier used by Price Waterhouse's FCCA contracted study in 1994 (Pattullo, 1996a) and beyond (*e.g.*, Price Waterhouse Cooper, 2004).

Local multipliers will be higher for terminal (home) ports for cruise ships than for ports that simply entertain day visitors from the ships. In addition, multipliers are higher as the population and complexity of the local economy increases. Braun et al. (2002) found that the total impact of the cruise industry increased almost two fold by expanding the scale of analysis from Brevard County to include all of Central Florida. Moreover, the share of economic impact shifted away from cruise liners (89 per cent vs 94 per cent)and towards passengers (7 per cent vrs 5 per cent) and crew (4 per cent vrs 2 per cent) as the scale of analysis became smaller. That is, passenger and crew spending is concentrated near the port, whereas cruise liner spending is more geographically dispersed.

Although the cruise industry initially touted exotic ports of call as a principal thrust of its tourism experience, increasingly marketing campaigns focus on the on board amenities available to cruisers. "Mass cruise tourism has been likened to all-inclusive resort experiences, with the cruise ship itself providing the holiday experience rather than any destinations to be visited" (Ubersax, 1996). This shift from floating hotels to floating resorts increases the incentives for the industry to maximize the time (and money) cruisers spend on board and minimize their time in port.

As such, cruise ship companies are in direct competition with local communities for the expenditures of cruise tourists (McKee, 1988; McKee and Mamoozadeh, 1994) and with land based resorts for the tourism market more generally (Kester, 2002; Pattullo, 1996a). In order to maximize their take, the industry sells land based tours to selected providers on board for a substantial markup (typically 50 per cent) and contracts with local retailers for "preferred" status in exchange for as much as 40 per cent of gross sales (Klein, 2003a). Some, including Disney Corporation, have gone so far as to purchase their own islands, cays, or beaches, generating the least possible positive local economic impact (Pattullo, 1996a). "With respect to the Caribbean region, it has been suggested that 'there is little interaction between the passengers and the economy and the population of the islands they visit' (Barry et al., 1984)"(McKee, 1988).

There is great variety and, therefore, site specificity in predicting the amount of ship board vs in port spending by cruise tourists. Although many costs of cruise vacations are included in their prices, Klein (2003) finds industry wide averages of $220-232 per day in ship board spending. This constitutes a sharp increase relative to CLIA's 1987 report of $22.50 per day (McKee and Mamoozadeh, 1994), even adjusting for inflation and, potentially, income differences over the period. Klein (2003) implies that the changes in ship board spending come at a cost to land based spending and are due to changes in the marketing of cruises as floating resorts rather than simply floating hotels. Since about 90 per cent of cruises are between two and 8 days in duration (Douglas and Douglas, 1999), and the average cruise is about 7 days (Kester, 2002; McKee and Mamoozadeh, 1994; Pattullo, 1996a), approximately $1,500 in tourist spending per trip in addition to the cost of the cruise itself can be estimated from Klein's numbers. Kester (2002) calculates an average of $1,341 in revenues per cruise across all cruise types.

Average land expenditures for cruise tourists in the Caribbean range from $15 to $270 in 2001 (CTO, 2003), differences driven largely by the purchases of imported luxury goods with little local content. Pattullo (1996) finds 45-67 per cent of onshore expenditures went to duty free shopping, 17 per cent to tours and attractions and 8 per cent on food. Gabe et al. (2003) finds an average land expenditure of $85.26 in Bar Harbour, Maine, an estimated $105.82 including tours purchased on board. Both means are somewhat skewed by jewelry purchases (Gabe et al., 2003). In the US Virgin Islands some 80 per cent of onshore purchases is for duty free shopping, while the similar figure for Martinique is 50 per cent (Pattullo, 1996a).

THE ROLE OF CRUISE TOURISM IN COSTA RICA

Tourism, particularly ecological and cultural tourism, is strongly encouraged as an engine of sustainable economic development in Costa Rica. More than 1 million visitors spend more than US$1 billion annually, drawn by its natural beauty, agreeable climate and reputation for political stability and safety (Tables 1 and 2). The quality of Costa Rica's protected areas, beaches and volcanoes continue to be the most highly rated features of the country by visitors (ICT, 2004). Although the vast majority of visitors to Costa Rica arrive via airplane, an increasing number of tourists gain access to the country's rich natural and cultural history via cruise ship.

Although cruise ship tourism has been an active and growing portion of the global tourism sector since the 1970s, cruise ships first arrived in Costa Rica in the early 1990s. Cruise ship visits to Costa Rica have increased from about 150 ships in 1993 to 215 in 2004, after peaking at over 250 ships in 1999. Cruise tourists, however, have increased over the period from just over 100,000 in 1993 to about 320,000 in 2004, due to increasing ship capacities (ICT, 2004). Cruise tourism, therefore, constitutes an increasing share of all tourism visits to the country, from approximately 1 in 7 tourist arrivals in 1993 to nearly 1 in 4 in 2003, although cruise ship visits are approximately one-seventh the length of stay of the average tourist visit to Costa Rica.

Initially, cruise ships docked at the Pacific ports of Puntarenas, Calderas and Golfito. By the end of the 1990s ships were also docking at the Atlantic/Caribbean port of Puerto Limon. Currently, visits to Puntarenas appear to be on the decline while visits to Puerto Limon seem to be on an upward trajectory, accounting for approximately 2/3 of cruise ships and tourists to Costa Rica (ICT, 2004). The cruise ship tourism season strongly coincides with the high season (December-March) for tourism in the rest of Costa Rica, exacerbating potential congestion and other development challenges of strong seasonality. Cruise tourists represent as many as one in three visitors visits during the high season.

A typical 10 day vacation cruise, including Costa Rican ports of call, costs as little as $1,200 to as much as $4,500 and includes some 7 or 8 port destinations. A typical $1,200 itinerary for cruises that land in Costa Rica on Carnival/Royal Caribbean cruise lines is Miami, Aruba, Panama Canal Transit,

Puntarenas, Acapulco, Mazatlan, Cabo San Lucas, and Los Angeles. A $2,000 cruise itinerary including Costa Rican ports of call on Princess Cruises/Holland America is: Los Angeles, Cabo San Lucas, Acapulco, Puntarenas, Cartagena, Ocho Rios (Jamaica), Aruba, and Miami. A luxury cruise of $4,500 on Crystal/ Silversea Cruises includes an itinerary of Fort Lauderdale, Florida, Aruba, Puntarenas, Acapulco, Puerto Vallarta, Cabo San Lucas, and Los Angeles.

Three cruise lines comprise an increasingly large market share of the Costa Rican cruise tourism industry, accounting for ½ of all ships in 1999 increasing to some 2/3 of all arrivals in 2003. Royal Caribbean's ships now provides ¼ of all cruise ship visits to Costa Rica, while Carnival's various carriers account for another 1/3 of the Costa Rica cruise ship tourism market. Thus, Carnival and Royal Caribbean currently comprise well more than ½ of the Costa Rican cruise tourism industry, a degree of market power that could provide particular negotiation challenges to current and potential port communities.

COSTA RICA'S CRUISE TOURISTS

While a bit more than ½ of tourists to Costa Rica are North Americans, more than 80 per cent of cruise ship passengers, or 800 people on average, whose voyage passes through Costa Rican ports, are from North America. About 17 per cent of all tourists and cruise tourists to Costa Rica are European (ICT, 2003). US residents show a preference for the Caribbean Coast, comprising some 2/3 of all passengers to Puerto Limon, but only about ½ of cruise tourists to Puntarenas. About 70 per cent of cruise passengers are married and a parallel number travel with a partner or family. Cruisers to Puerto Limon have substantially more educational attainment and, as might be expected, reported annual income than visitors to Puntarenas. However, the general tourist population is substantially more educated and younger than are Costa Rica's cruise tourists. Some 70-80 per cent of cruise tourists to Costa Rica are 45 yrs old or greater, while the average visitor to the country is about 40 yrs old. Similarly, Gabe et al. (2003) report an average respondent of 60 yrs old with less than 5 per cent of respondents younger than 40 yrs old in their study of Maine cruise tourism.

Cruise ships are in Costa Rican ports for an average of 12 hrs per visit. Similarly, Gabe et al. (2003) report ships spend an average of 9 hrs in port (7-12 range) in Maine, while the average respondent spent about 5 hrs off the ship. Since their visit is so brief, cruise tourist expenditures in Costa Rica come from tours, local transportation, food and beverage, souvenirs and incidental purchases. Some 90 per cent of passengers disembark at Costa Rican ports of call, while 10 per cent remain on board. Approximately 45-65 per cent (400-600 people) of those who choose to disembark prepurchase local tours while on board, about 15 per cent (135 people) purchase tours upon arrival at the port and the remaining 20 per cent (180 people) do not purchase tours. The average passenger purchases 4-5 tours on his 10-day vacation and no more than one at any given port.

According to Kester (2002) over 80 per cent of cruise tourists worldwide participate in panoramic visits, shopping and sightseeing, 50-80 per cent participate in excursions, cultural visits, beach activities and gastronomy, and about 10 per cent engage in golf and tennis. For Costa Rica, the most popular tours for passengers who disembark in Limon are Tortuguero turtle sanctuary (27 per cent), a forest canopy aerial tram ride through Braulio Carrillo National Park (17 per cent), a scenic train trip (16 per cent), and a banana plantation tour (12 per cent). The most popular tours for passengers who disembark in Puntarenas are the city of San Jose (23 per cent), a small boat tour in a mangrove estuary (22 per cent), traditional arts and crafts in Sarchi (19 per cent), an aerial tram ride through Braulio Carrillo (8 per cent) and a coffee plantation tour (Café Britt)(8 per cent). Generally speaking, of those who purchase tours, approximately ½ are oriented towards the natural environment of Costa Rica, whereas closer to 20-25 per cent could be considered culturally oriented. In addition, respondents mention several other factors making Costa Rica an attractive port of call including: nice people, banana and coffee plantations.

The ICT (2003) estimates that cruise tourists spend just under $100 each during their stay in Costa Rica. Recent surveys indicate that expenditures by visitors to Puntarenas are in line with these expectations, while estimated expenditures by visitors to Puerto Limon are somewhat higher. Expenditures per visitor have varied little in nominal terms over the past decade, but total expenditures have increased from about $15 million in 1996 to more than $26 million in 2003 (ICT, 2003). However, Klein (2002) finds that in general spending from cruise passengers in port communities has dropped by half since 1994 due to changes in demographics and on-board spending.

LOCAL ECONOMIC IMPACT OF TOURIST EXPENDITURES

Tourism expenditures are considered exports because new money comes from outside of the region in order to purchase goods and services from inside the region. Export industries, also called base industries, are essential to regional growth and development because they increase the amount of regional economic activity, whereas nonbase industries simply increase the rate of circulation of goods and services within a region and do not create any new wealth. Export base analysis (EBA) tracks the flow (or multiplication) of new outside money through the local economy. Local multipliers increase with the complexity of the local economy and with the proportion of local goods and services purchased to create the good or service ultimately purchased by the tourist. Although a formal TCM/EBA analysis would be the most rigourous approach to address this issue, available secondary information combined with expert interviews can provide a reasonably accurate perspective to inform any such subsequent analysis. ICT surveys indicate that only about $28-36 of cruise tourist expenditure pass directly from tourist to local goods and service providers. For example, through surveys we estimate approximately 80 artisans sell about $74 worth their wares each at each port and for each ship (Guiliano et al., 2004). If at most 800 (400) tourists per ship are exposed to the artisans, the average expenditure on arts and crafts would be about $7-8 ($14-16) per person.

Approximately 35 per cent of tours purchased are ½ day in duration, allowing participants to return to the ship for their prepaid meals. The cruise operator also compensates local tour companies for the tours purchased on board. The cruise line typically captures as much as 50 per cent of the fees charged the tourists for these local tours (Klein, 2002), so we might calculate an average of about $70-75 per cruise tourist, or 70-75 per cent of total local tourist expenditures, finds itself in the local economy.

The economic impact of that $70 increases (multiplies) with the proportion of locally produced goods purchased (*e.g.*, locally grown and processed agricultural products, locally grown and produced arts and crafts) and decreases with the proportion of imported goods (*e.g.*, canned and bottled beverages, film, sunscreen, pharmaceuticals). Braun et al. (2002) estimate cruise passenger spending mutipliers of 1.43 in employment effects, 1.62 for wages and 1.88 in value added creation for an economically complex and highly populated terminal port in Central Florida. INCAE (2004) estimates that about $0.40 of each tourist dollar spent in Costa Rica remains in the local economy, potentially implying a local multiplier or 1.4 and a total local impact of about $98 per cruise tourist to Costa Rica.

CRUISE SHIP EMPLOYEES AND LOCAL ECONOMIC IMPACT

It would be most appropriate to undertake a TCM of ship employee behaviour while in local ports, informed by interviews with ship personnel, port personnel and secondary data. Until that time which such analysis can be undertaken, we provide estimates based upon the latter two categories of information.

The ratio of employees to passengers on most cruise ships is approximately 1:2 or 1:3 (McKee and Mamoozadeh, 1994), increasing to four employees for every five passengers on luxury liners (Klein, 2003a). Thus, each cruise ship that comes to a Costa Rican port carries 500 to 1000 employees (*e.g.*, musicians, maids, cooks, etc.). Based on anecdotal evidence, approximately 40 per cent of ship employees tend to disembark at each port of call. Costa Rican ports of call are thought to be popular with ship employees in part due to the country's reputation for value in dental and health care. More detailed surveys would reveal whether this hypothesis is viable. In 2000, 16 per cent of cruise ship workers earned less than $500 per month, 38 per cent earned $500-999, 19 per cent earned $1,000-1,400, 17 per cent earned $1,500-1,900, and 12 per cent earned more than $2,000 per month (Klein, 2003a). Crews are decidedly less American relative to the passengers (Douglas and Douglas, 1999) and clearly earn less income than passengers, making it likely that they would have distinct in port consumer preferences as well.

Ship employees are not typically served by the tour operators selling tours on the ship and tend not to mix with the passengers while in port. Due to their duties, ship employees tend to have an average of only 6 hrs to explore each port of call and have substantially lower incomes than a typical cruiser. One operator in Limon who markets to ship employees relates that he captures approximately 20 per cent of the ship employees with shorter duration tours and activities including rafting, canopy tours, national park visits, beach parties at an average of about $60 per person. This generates about $3,840 in gross revenues and $1,920 in profits per cruise ship to the tour operator. McDowell Group Inc. (2000) found off ship expenditures of crew members of between $5 and $20 per visit to an Alaskan port, or about 5-10 per cent of tourist expenditures per visitor to the same location.

It is also appropriate to employ export base techniques to ship employee expenditures since they are not local people. Braun et al. (2002) finds multipliers for crew spending of 1.66 employment impact, 1.59 wage effect and 1.66 in value added creation for Central Florida. If the local multiplier for cruise ship employee purchases in Costa Rica is more like 1.4 (due to lower population and less economic complexity), and at this point there is insufficient evidence to suggest otherwise, the total local economic impact per visiting ship employee purchasing a tour is about $84 or about $5,380 in local economic impact per ship, excluding local expenditures of employees who left the ship but did not purchase tours.

CRUISE SHIPS, PORT AUTHORITIES AND LOCAL BUSINESS

Individual ships compensate ports for services provided to them. Cruise ships are charged per passenger and per meter for a stay of up to 12 hrs, for services related to passenger disembarkation. Expert interview and the review of official documents is the only manner in which to reveal this information. The results of such an approach and analysis are provided here.

On average, ports charge per passenger port fees in the neighborhood of $5.00 per passenger (Klein, 2003a), representing more than $1,375,000 in fees potentially captured by Costa Rica in 2003. However, there is a great deal of variation in per passenger charges. In 1993, St Maarten had no per tourist charge, Dominica charged $2 and the Bahamas charged $15 per cruise tourist (Pattullo, 1996a). Bermuda charges a regional high of $63 per day tripper from the cruise ships, while Juneau, Alaska charges only $5 per head (Johnson, 2002). Within the Caribbean Basin this variation is said to be driven by competition among potential port nations and quality of facilities on offer. The Caribbean Community (Caricom) and the Organization of Eastern Caribbean States have made efforts to standardize the per tourist charges across their member countries. However, it has not been successful (Pattullo, 1996a) and a "race to the bottom" to capture cruise business is largely observed (Uebersax, 1996).

Puntarenas charges only $2.50 per passenger, generating a potential loss of $687,500 relative to industry standard if applied across the Costa Rica. However, since November 3, 2003, cruise ships have been charged $2.09 per passenger in Puerto Limon. This charge has been reduced over time from $3.50 prior to September 11, 2001, to $2.75 per head from September 2001 to November 2003. For a representative thousand-passenger ship, this 40 per cent fee reduction from recently charged fees represents a loss of $1,410 per ship to the Limon port authority in nominal terms. This amounts to about $268,000 in lost fees 2003 alone relative to Costa Rica's relatively low port charge and about $800,000 lost locally in 2003 relative to modest industry norms.

Puerto Limon receives about 7 to 11 times as many cargo ships as it does cruise ships during the high tourist season. In Puntarenas, the number of cruise ship visits is steadily declining, while the number of cargo ships is steadily increasing. From the perspective of the port authority, when the port is working at or near its capacity any cruise ship docked represents a (fraction of or multiple of) cargo ship that could not be attended. As a result, typical revenues (and costs) of cargo ships should be weighed against that of cruise ships in the port authority's accounting framework. It is considered a nearly universal practice to give docking priority to cruise ships over cargo ships, to the considerable detriment to the latter. Wood (1982) contends that it is the nature of the cruise ship industry not to wait in line; but rather to move along to another port when faced with even slight delays, which contributes to the universality of this port priority policy. Wood (1982) finds that this priority policy for cruise ships is generally unjustified economically.

The port of Limon charges cruise ships $0.48 per meter per hour and each cruise ship is charged a flat rate of $5,864 to dock the ship for passengers to disembark. Puntarenas charges $0.35 per m-hr and a flat rate of $4,800 for a ship of typical cruiseline size. In Puerto Limon, cargo ships pay a flat rate by registered weight, a rate per meter-hr that is almost three times the cruise ship rate ($1.27/m-hr), a port use fee of $0.87 per tonne, tugboat charges of $0.19 per registered tonne, and a within port navigation fee of $33.47 per trip. The analogous payments in Puntarenas are substantially higher. The side-by-side comparison of the relative contribution of similar cruise ships versus cargo ships to the local port authority in Puerto Limon and Puntarenas. It shows that cargo ships in Puerto Limon pay almost twice as much to the port than cruise ships under the current fee structure, while cargo ships pay about seven times the fees paid by cruise ships in Puntarenas. Even if the per passenger fees reflected industry norms, cargo ship payments would exceed cruise ship payments by some $3,000 per ship in Puerto Limon. Since 1999, the city of Puntarenas has charged $1.50 tax per cruise ship passenger (but not ship employee) and a flat fee of $50 for each ship flying under any flag other than Costa Rica to cover the additional costs of maintaining an appropriate human environment for tourists. To date, Limon has no such taxes, but is taking the idea under consideration. The ship may purchase supplies while in port, may add or exchange employees, or may require special services for employees. Since Costa Rica is known for the quality of its dental care, there is some, if not a huge amount of, activity in the local provision of these services to cruise ship employees. Similarly, the ships may or may not purchase water locally at a rate of $10 per tonne in Limon or $2.58 per tonne in Puntarenas (200-400 tonnes per ship). Ships tend not to purchase fruits and vegetables locally, since Costa Rica is not among the cheapest locations for such items in the region.

Job quantity versus job quality is a consistent challenge of economic development. This can particularly be the case with nonconsumptive natural resource based industial development like tourism, where many of the jobs created are in the service and retail trade sectors. In an analysis of the contribution of cruise ships to the Alaskan economy, McDowell (2000) found that the local jobs created to serve the cruise industry were 77-94 per cent of the average private sector wages in host communities. The jobs created were primarily in the transportation, retail and service sectors.

CRUISE SHIPS AND THE ENVIRONMENT

Although it has been argued that cruise tourism offers a unique opportunity for sustainability due to its spatial confinement and predisposition to precise management, problems associated with waste generation and disposal, other pressures on fragile and unique natural environments, and social and economic impacts on host communities continue to be vetted (Johnson, 2002). Cruise tourism pollutes sea floors, harbours and coastal areas, degrades scarce water sources, destroys coral reef habitat, creates public health concerns ashore, and generates pressure on land based waste disposal sites (Uebersax, 1996 in Johnson, 2002). Negri and Hayward (2000) and Negri et al. (2002) find that cruise ships constitute significant sources of water pollution and reef damage due to improper oil, fuel, and waste disposal and the use of toxic paints. Uebersax (1996) indicates that the average cruise ship produces 1 kg of burnable waste, 0.5 kg of food waste and 1 kg of glass and tin waste per person per day.

Three of the four largest cruise lines have been convicted of breaking US environmental laws since 1998. P and O Princess was also convicted, but earlier in the 1990s (Klein, 2003a). In 1998, P and O Group released a corporate environmental report that acknowledged the impact of cruise liners in terms of waste generated and the percentage recycled, oil consumption and carbond dioxide emissions, ozone depletion, sulphur dioxide emissions, oil spillage, and water use (Johnson, 2002). In 2000 the Bluewater Network petitioned the US Congress to consider cruise ships as point sources of water pollution (Johnson, 2002). Cruise lines have paid more than $60 million in fines over the past 5 yrs and $90 million over the past decade for illegal dumping or concealing it (Klein, 2003a). With a few notable exceptions (one case each in Egypt, Mexico and Brazil), the enforcement of these environmental regulations has been by the United States (Klein, 2003a). In 1998 Holland America was fined $2 million for illegal discharges of oily bilge in Alaska in 1994. Royal Caribbean was fined $18 million for 21 felony counts of violating US water pollution laws, dumping oil and hazardous chemicals, in 1999. A $250,000 reward was awarded to passengers of the P and O Princess cruise who bore witness to intentional dumping of plastics and other waste by the cruiseliner (Johnson, 2002).

Klein (2002) among others argues that "the cruise industry has the resources to build cleaner ships, stop dumping in coastal waters and contribute to coastal environmental protection and clean-up, but prefers to forward unenforceable voluntary agreements less likely to impact the bottom line if violated. They are getting a free ride..." Holland American Line has been involved in attempting to restore accidental reef damage, although there appears to be rather limited success. Unlike this case where the blame is clearly traceable to a single operator, there is little evidence of the industry addressing the more general cumulative effects of cruise tourism on the worlds' marine and terrestrial ecosystems (Johnson, 2002).

Although there are no studies directly relating cruise ships, waste and natural resource use in Costa Rica, cruise ships do not have a particularly good reputation when it comes to the preservation of the natural environment from which they profit. The cruise ships that dock in Costa Rican ports do not practice recycling. Garbage disposal is currently and temporarily prohibited in Puerto Limon. In Puntarenas, and in Puerto Limon when it is permitted, only dry solid waste is accepted. The ships pay private local vendors for these services. The industry currently pays nothing for environmental protection from the risk of accidental spills/dumping, monitoring or cleanup. To the extent that cruise tourists exploit private businesses when they are in Costa Rica, disposal of their waste should be considered accounted for. However, when they travel to public areas and use public facilities, the degree of compensation for waste generation and resource use is less clear, but should probably not vary considerably from other types of tourists on average.

TOURISM IN THE POLAR REGIONS: FACTS, TRENDS AND IMPACTS

Evaluating tourism impacts, both beneficial and otherwise, requires knowledge of total numbers as well as where, when, and how tourists cause impacts. For example, the many thousand cruise-ship passengers who passively view the Arctic from offshore, and occasionally disembark to visit land based souvenir shops, affect the region in ways that differ from the smaller numbers actively engaged in ecotourism or wilderness recreations activities such as river rafting, mountaineering, and sport fishing. By accurately identifying the full array of tourist activities and their behavioural patterns, then placing that information within the context of their natural and human resource settings, we can begin to understand key relationships.

NEARLY TWO CENTURIES OF ARCTIC TOURISM

The Arctic has attracted tourists since the early 1800's. The earliest Arctic tourists were individual anglers, hunters, mountaineers, and adventurers attracted to abundant fisheries, exotic wildlife species, and remote regions. Many articles describing their recreational pursuits appeared in the growing genre of recreation, mountaineering, hunting, and fishing periodicals that emerged in the mid-1800's (Conway, 1897; Williams, 1859; Suydam, 1899). During the same era, several pioneering travelers to the Arctic published journals that became popular guide books for future Arctic tourists (Lainige, 1807; Scidmore, 1885, 1896).

Mass tourism in the Arctic has thrived since the mid-1800's when steamships and railroads aggressively expanded their transportation networks providing access to numerous destinations throughout the Arctic. Tourism entrepreneurs, such as Thomas Cook, formed partnerships with railroad and steamship companies and thereby pioneered the popular tourism industry (Brendon, 1991). By the 1880's, the "Land of the Midnight Sun" in the Scandinavian Arctic, Alaska, and the popular excitement of the Klondike Gold Rushes firmly established the Arctic's mass tourism market (Dufferin, 1873; duChaillou, 1881, Pacific Steamship Company, 1885).

During the past two centuries numerous advances in transport technologies have contributed to the steady growth of Arctic tourism. At the present time, advanced ship technologies together with improved marine charts and navigational aids have allowed cruise ship travel to increase exponentially. Diesel locomotives, four wheel drive and tracked vehicles further opened access to vast regions of the Arctic (Rand McNally, 1922). And, most importantly, air transport in all of its forms, provides immediate travel to the Arctic. Collectively, these improved transport technologies not only added numbers of tourists, but also expanded the seasonal and geographical reach of Arctic tourism.

ANTARCTIC TOURISM

Antarctic tourism began in 1957-59 with four visits by Argentinean and Chilean naval transports, which accommodated tourists whose fares helped to pay costs of servicing the national expeditions (Reich, 1980). Antarctica received extensive international publicity from the explorations led by Richard Byrd, Vivian Fuchs and Edmund Hillary. Entrepreneurial tour operators recognized the commercial value of feasible access and positive international publicity. In 1966 Lars Eric Lindblad began expedition cruising to the Antarctic and initiated the use of zodiacs to land passengers at diverse sites. As a result of the success of the Lindblad model, government affiliated voyages were quickly superseded by dedicated cruises in small 'expedition' ships carrying 50-120 passengers. For many years this type of travel dominated the trade. Increasing numbers of expedition ships are transporting larger numbers of passengers, and making more landings at several hundred sites. The first larger cruise ship to enter the field, Ocean Princess in 1990-93, had a capacity of 480 passengers, but carried only 250-400 on its annual Antarctic voyages. The most recent development has been the advent from 2000 of liners carrying between 800 and 3,700 passengers, including crew members.

Over the last decades, tourism activities have expanded tremendously with the number of ship-borne tourists increasing by 430 per cent in 14 years and land-based tourists by 757 per cent in 10 years (IAATO 2007). The tremendous increase of ship-borne tourism and its impacts on the Antarctic environment resulted in the members of the Antarctic Treaty adopting a resolution (May 2007) which recommends the Parties of the Treaty to:

1. Discourage or decline to authorize tour operators that use vessels carrying more than 500 passengers from making any landings in Antarctica; and
2. Encourage or require tour operators to:
    a. Coordinate with each other such that not more than one tourist vessel is at a landing site at any one time;
    b. Restrict the number of passengers on shore at any one time to 100 or fewer, unless otherwise specified in applicable ATCM Measures or Resolutions; and
    c. Maintain a minimum 1:20 guide-to-passenger ratio while ashore, unless otherwise specified in applicable ATCM Measures or Resolutions.

Commercial air transport of tourists to the Antarctic includes both small groups traveling to the continent and larger numbers viewing from overflights. Adventure Network International (ANI) has been providing flight services to Patriot Hills in the Heritage Range since 1985 and other charter air companies have provided tourist transport between South Africa and Dronning Maud Land, and between Punta Arenas, Chile and King George Island (Swithinbank, 2000).

POLAR TOURISM TODAY – DIVERSE AND GROWING

Polar tourism is now a mature industry providing diverse experiences in both Polar Regions. The polar tourism industry is enticing an increasing clientele with expanding numbers of attractions, recreational activities, international destinations, and visitor accommodations. And now that regularly scheduled excursion travel is provided to both the Arctic and Antarctic, year-round polar tourism has become a reality.Polar Tourism's Diverse Markets

Polar tourism is not a single, monolithic industry, but rather a collection of diverse specialty markets that appeal to an equally diverse clientele. Each of these distinct markets is growing and expanding for an obvious reason – they appeal to tourists who are willing to pay for the unique experiences they offer. The five highly specialized market segments currently dominating the polar tourism economy are best defined in terms of their primary attractions and the ways in which those attractions are experienced. This approach to classifying tourist markets explicitly acknowledges tourist expectations, the service delivery methods used to realize those expectations, and the distinct impacts resulting from those activities.

The five markets are:

1. The mass market, comprised of tourists primarily attracted to sightseeing within the pleasurable surroundings of comfortable transport and accommodations.
2. The sport fishing and hunting market, with participants who pursue unique fish and game species within a wilderness setting.
3. The ecotourism market, consisting of tourists who seek to observe wildlife species in their natural habitats, and experience the beauty and solitude of natural areas. These tourists are also concerned with conserving the environment and improving the well-being of local people.
4. The adventure tourism market, providing a sense of personal achievement and exhilaration from meeting challenges and potential perils of outdoor sport activities.
5. The culture and heritage tourism market, a very distinct market comprised of tourists who either want to experience personal interaction with the lives and traditions of native people, learn more about a historical topic that interests them, or personally experience historic places and artifacts.

Each market has distinct visitor experiences and economic dimensions, involving different tourists' motivations, expectations, on-site behaviour, and resource uses. Market segmentation provides a useful framework for understanding polar tourism in terms of the use of natural and cultural resources, economic activity, and visitor behaviour. But obviously, tourists themselves are not constrained by this classification: they participate freely in many types of activities (Snyder and Stonehouse, 2007).

The enormous geographic scope of the five markets deserves emphasis. All eight Arctic nations, and their seas and oceans host all five markets, while

Antarctica hosts most of them with the exception of the sport fishing and hunting and the culture and heritage markets. Most of that geography consists of land masses that are true wilderness and oceans with the world's most severe maritime conditions. The challenge of managing tourism across those vast lands and seas is well known to the Arctic nations and to those concerned about Antarctic tourism.

ENVIRONMENTAL, ECONOMIC, SOCIAL AND CULTURAL IMPACTS OF POLAR TOURISM

ENVIRONMENTAL IMPACTS

There are serious concerns that tourism is promoting environmental degradation in the Polar Regions (especially in the Arctic) by putting extra pressures on land, wildlife, water and other basic necessities, and on transportation facilities (GEO 2002 and GEO 2006). According to the Arctic Council Working Group on the Conservation of Arctic Flora and Fauna (CAFF), the main environmental impacts of tourism in the Arctic are the following (CAFF 1997, 1998, 2001):

- The transport of tourists to the Arctic, in itself, increases the volume of ship and airplane traffic. In addition to the impacts on climate by long distance air and water traffic, increased ship traffic in these waters could lead to increased risks of groundings and other accidents, the results of which can include oil spills and other environmental consequences.
- Many visitors want to see areas of great beauty or richness, such as bird colonies, marine mammal haul-outs, and caribou aggregations. Because there are relatively few places where such sights are accessible and reliable, tourist traffic is often concentrated. Arctic vegetation is typically unable to withstand repeated trampling, and paths of bare ground have appeared in some heavily visited spots.
- Helicopters, used sometimes for recreational purposes, are noisy and produce a variety of sounds that are disturbing to seabirds. Helicopters cause panic flights and can lead to egg loss particularly in birds.
- In the forest-tundra areas of the Arctic, tourism, including sport hunting and fishing, attracts moderate though increasing numbers of visitors. This places additional pressure on the region's resources, sometimes leading to conflicts between local and visiting hunters. The forest-tundra in general has a low tolerance for trampling. Even the temporary presence of humans often leaves a lasting impact.
- Visits to Arctic seabird colonies by tourists are rapidly growing. Currently cruise ships visit or sail by colonies in the low and high Arctic of Canada, west Greenland, Iceland, Norwegian coast and

Svalbard, eastern Russia, and the US (Alaska). Colonies chosen for visitation tend to be large and spectacular and usually are home to species such as murres, puffins, kittiwakes, and fulmars. During a colony visit, passengers typically board smaller boats from the larger ships, and cruise by colonies observing the seabirds and taking pictures. Occasionally passengers make landings at suitable colonies and view the seabirds from above or below the cliffs.

- Recreational activities, such as boating and fishing, cause local disturbance at bird colonies in several Arctic countries. In the Russian far-east, coastal and lowland species such as ducks, gulls, terns and Spectacled Guillemots are frequently disturbed by visitors.
- Garbage, waste, and pollution are significant problems for many tourism operations, especially as decomposition is slow and waste remains visible atop the permafrost in many Arctic areas.

In the Antarctic the most important impact of tourism concerns the disturbance of cetaceans. Certain studies have lent increasing strength to concerns that human activities may be influencing the fitness of these animals. Tourism activities in Antarctica present also a risk to the marine environment (pollution resulting from operations or maritime accident (*e.g.* grounding)) as well as to terrestrial ecosystems as over 80 per cent of the tourists land one or more times during their journey (introduction of alien species; disturbance of birds colonies; damage to the vegetative cover (*e.g.* lichen). In addition, high-risk unsupported (adventure) tourism can potentially impact on national research programmes in terms of search and rescue operations.

The main positive impact of polar tourism, if well done, is its educational value. Arctic and Antarctic visitors are fascinated by the sheer beauty, wilderness and natural phenomena of the polar environment. This can be used to make them not only to ambassadors for the protection of the visited regions, but also supporters of conservation activities and organizations worldwide.

Bibliography

A.K. Bhatia.: *International Tourism Management* : Sterling Publications, Delhi, 2001.

A.K. Sarkar.: *Indian Tourism, Management, Motivation and Mobility*, Rajat Publications, Delhi, 2003

Aaradhana Salpekar.: *Indian Tourism, Wildlife Tourism and Ecotourism,* Jnanada Prakashan,Delhi,2009.

Amrita Bhagnani.: *Handbook of Tourism*, Abhijeet Publications, Delhi, 2012.

Annamalai Murugan.: *Hospitality and Tourism Laws With Conventions*, Abhijeet Publications, Delhi, 2012,

Ashim Gupta.: *Hotel Tourism and Catering Management*,Centrum Press, Delhi, 2011.

B S Badan and Harish Bhatt.: *Hospitality and Tourism,* Commonwealth Publications, Delhi, 2007.

Babu P George and Alexandru Nedela.:*International Tourism : World Geography and Developmental Perspectives,* Abhijeet Publications, Delhi, 2007.

David Carr.: *Implication for Tourism Planning and Destination Management,* Discovery Publications, Delhi 2011.

A.K. Sarkar.: *Action Plan and Priorities in Tourism Development*, Kanishka Publications, Delhi, 2010.

Alexandru Nedelea and Babu P. George.: *Comparative Tourism Marketing : Case Studies*, Abhijeet Publications, Delhi, 2010.

Arvind Gautam.: *Critical Analysis of Hospitality and Tourism Industry*, Axis Publications, Delhi, 2010.

B.S.Badan and Harish Bhatt.: *Culture and Tourism*, Commonwealth Publications, Delhi, 2007.

Babu P. George and Sampad Kumar Swain.: *Advancements in Tourism Theory and Practice : Perspectives from India*, Abhijeet Publication, Delhi, 2005.

David Carr.: *Community Tourism and Natural Resource Conservation*, Discovery Publications, Delhi, 2011.

Dileep Makan.: *Conceptualization of Tourism*, Adhyayan Publications, Delhi, 2006.

Dilip Das.: *Critical Issues in Tourism*, Murari Lal and Sons, Delhi, 2011.

Gagandeep Singh.: *Civil Aviation and Tourism Administration*, Aadi Publications, Jaipur, 2011.

Geetanjali.: *Career in Tourism*, Centrum Press, Delhi, 2010.

Gulshan Soni.: *Consumer Protection in Hospitality Travel and Tourism*, Aman Publications, Delhi, 2011.

Jack Randall.: *Agriculture Tourism*, Discovery Publishing House, Delhi, 2011.

Jitendra K. Sharma.: *Contemporary Tourism and Hospitality Management*, Kanishka Publications, Delhi, 2006.

K. S. Gulia.: *Discovering Himalaya : Tourism of Himalayan Region (2 Vols-Set) Coimbatore*, Isha Book, Publications, Delhi, 2007.

Krishan K. Kamra and Mohinder Chand.: *Basics of Tourism: Theory, Operation and Practice*, Kanishka Publications, Delhi, 2002.

Mahadev Kertwal.: *Advertising in Leisure and Tourism*, Cyber Tech, New Delhi, 2012.

N. Jayapalan.: *An Introduction to Tourism*, Atlantic Publications, New Delhi, 2001.

Neeta Mehta.: *Dynamics of Tourism,* Random Publications, Delhi, 2012.

P.K. Bal.: *A Text Book of Hospitality Tourism and Aviation*, Cyber Tech Publication, New Delhi, 2011.

Prateek A. Aggarwal.: *Aspects of Crosscultural Interaction and Tourism*, Mohit Publications, Delhi, 2005.

Prem Nath Dhar.: *Cultural and Heritage Tourism: An Overview,* Kanishka Publications, Delhi, 2008.

R.M. Ahuja.: *A Hand Book of Adventure Tourism*, Sumit Enterprises, Delhi, 2011.

Rattandeep Singh.: *Commonwealth Games and Sports Tourism : Global and National Perspectives*, Kanishka Publishers, Delhi, 2010.

Ravee Chauhan.: *Advanced Book on Marketing of Tourism*, Vista International Publishing House, Delhi, 2011.

Romila Chawla.: *Accommodation Management and Tourism*, Sonali Publications, Delhi, 2006.

Romila Chawla.: *Agri-Tourism*, Sonali Publication, Delhi, 2006.

Index